Public Finance and the Quest for Efficiency

Les finances publiques et l'exigence de l'efficience

PUBLIC FINANCE AND THE QUEST FOR EFFICIENCY

LES FINANCES PUBLIQUES ET L'EXIGENCE DE L'EFFICIENCE

Proceedings of the 38th Congress
of the International Institute of Public Finance
Copenhagen, 1982

Edited by Horst Hanusch

Wayne State University Press, Detroit, 1984

Library of Congress Cataloging in Publication Data

International Institute of Public Finance. Congress
    (38th : 1982 : Copenhagen, Denmark)
    Public finance and the quest for efficiency = Les
finances publiques et l'exigence de l'efficience.

    1. Finance, Public—Congresses.   I. Hanusch, Horst.
HJ113.I73   1982   350.72   84-7561
ISBN 0-8143-1776-6
ISBN 0-8143-1777-4 (pbk.)

Printed in the United States of America.

International Institute of Public Finance

A Brief Survey of Historical and Current Matters

The International Institute of Public Finance was founded in Paris in 1937. It held two conferences before the Second World War, and members have since met at least once a year from 1947 until the present. The Institute now has over 800 members from some 50 countries, and annual conferences are normally attended also by some non-members with a special interest in the particular topic.

The aims of the Institute are scientific. Its objectives include in particular: the study of Public Finance and Public Economics, the research and publications in both of these areas, the establishment of scientific contacts and exchange of knowledge and experience between persons of all nationalities. The Institute is exclusively and directly concerned with the furthering of public interest. The activities of the Institute have been recognized on an international level by the Economic and Social Council of the United Nations, which conferred upon it the Statut Consultatif B.

The Institute provides a forum for those concerned with problems of public economics, broadly defined. It has over the years aspired to sustain high academic standards. In the selection of topics and their investigation, it has directed itself towards matters of practical importance and towards issues of implementation, as well as of principle. The membership embraces both academic economists whose prime interests are in teaching and research, and public officials who face the problems "on ground": the unifying characteristic is acceptance of a proper standard of intellectual rigor.

Membership is essentially individual though corporate subscriptions are welcome. The Institute is proud of the involvement in its activities of members from countries of all kinds of political persuasion and all levels of economic development.

The Institute is governed by a Board of Management whose decisions require approval by the general assembly of members, with a President and Vice-Presidents elected for a period of three years. The Institute is administered by an Executive Committee (present membership, Professor Jean-Claude Dischamps, President, Paris; Professor Karl W. Roskamp, President elect, Detroit; Professor André van Buggenhout, Brussels; Professor Victor Halberstadt, Leyden; Professor Helga Pollak, Göttingen).

All questions concerning the Institute should be directed to:

Mrs. B. Schneider, Executive Secretary
International Institute of Public Finance
University of Saarland
D-6600 Saarbrücken 11
West Germany

Institut International de Finances Publiques

Un aperçu de son passé et de ses activités actuelles

L'Institut International de Finances Publiques fut fondé à Paris, en 1937. Il tint deux congrès avant la dernière guerre mondiale. En 1947, il put réunir à nouveau ses membres et, depuis, ceux-ci se sont rencontrés au moins une fois par an aux quatre coins du globe. L'Institut compte, aujourd'hui, plus que 800 membres appartenant à 50 pays et ses congrès annuels sont régulièrement suivis non seulement par ceux-ci mais également par des nonmembres intéressés par tel ou tel sujet.

Les buts poursuivis par l'Institut sont purement scientifiques. Ses objectifs incluent en particulier: l'étude des finances publiques et de l'économie publique, la mise en oeuvre de recherches et la publication de travaux dans ces domaines ainsi que l'établissement de contacts scientifiques et l'échange de connaissances et d'expériences entre des personnes de toute nationalité. L'Institut est guidé exclusivement et directement par le souci de l'intérêt général. L'Institut a vu sa mission reconnue, sur le plan international, par le Conseil économique et social des Nations-Unies, qui lui a conféré le statut consultatif B.

L'Institut offre un terrain de rencontre pour les spécialistes intéressés par les problèmes d'économie publique, au sens large du terme. Le maintien d'un niveau scientifique très élevé est pour ses responsables une préoccupation permanente. Dans le choix des sujets et la manière de les traiter, il s'attache aussi bien aux problèmes théoriques qu'aux problèmes pratiques et à leurs solutions. Ses membres sont des spécialistes universitaires et de la recherche scientifique, et des hauts fonctionnaires qui assument d'importantes responsabilités. Tous sont d'un niveau intellectuel notoirement reconnu.

L'Institut est composé essentiellement de membres individuels et il réunit dans ses activités des personnalités de pays relevant de tous les systèmes d'organisation politique et de tous les niveaux de développement économique.

La direction de l'Institut est assurée par un Comité de Direction conformément aux orientations définies par l'Assemblée Générale des membres. Son administration incombe à un Comité Exécutif actuellement composé de:

Président, le Professeur Jean-Claude Dischamps, Paris.
Futur Président, le Professeur Karl W. Roskamp, Détroit.
Vice-Présidents, les Professeurs André van Buggenhout, Bruxelles,
Victor Halberstadt, Leyden, et Helga Pollak, Göttingen.

Toute question relative à l'Institut est à adresser à:

Madame B. Schneider, Secrétaire Administrative,
Institut International de Finances Publiques
Université de la Sarre
D-6600 Saarbrücken 11
(R.F.A.)

Contributors

Andic, Suphan, Professor at the University of Puerto Rico, Rio Piedras, P.R., USA.

Badelt, Christoph, Dr., Wirtschaftsuniversität Wien, Vienna, Austria.

Bohm, Peter, Professor at the University of Stockholm, Stockholm, Sweden.

Buchanan, James M., Professor at the George-Mason-University, Fairfax, Va., USA.

Cao-García, Ramón J., Professor at the University of Puerto Rico, Rio Piedras, P.R., USA.

Culyer, Anthony J., Professor at the University of York, Heslington, UK.

Fisk, Donald M., Professor, US-Department of Labor, Washington, D.C., USA.

Frey, Bruno S., Professor at the University of Zurich, Zurich, Switzerland.

Gilbert, Guy, Assistant Professor at the University of Paris X-Nanterre, France.

Goudswaard, Kees P., Assistant Professor at the University of Leyden, Leyden, The Netherlands.

Halberstadt, Victor, Professor at the University of Leyden, Leyden, The Netherlands.

Hanusch, Horst, Professor at the University of Augsburg, Augsburg, FRG.

Haveman, Robert H., Professor at the University of Wisconsin, Madison, Wis., USA.

Herber, Bernhard P., Professor at the University of Arizona, Tucson, Ariz., USA.

Hirsch, Werner Z., Professor at the University of California, Los Angeles, Ca., USA.

Holland, Daniel M., Professor at the Massachusetts Institute of Technology, Cambridge, Mass., USA.

Kirsch, Guy, Professor at the University of Fribourg, Fribourg, Switzerland.

Ladha, Krishna, Carnegie-Mellon-University, Pittsburgh, Pa., USA.

Länger, Wolfgang, University of Augsburg, Augsburg, FRG.

Lee, Dwight R., Associate Professor at the George-Mason-University, Fairfax, Va., USA.

Leibenstein, Harvey, Professor at Harvard University, Cambridge, Mass., USA.

ix

Mueller, Dennis C., Professor at the University of Maryland, College Park, Md., USA.

Münch, Klaus-Norbert, Dr., University of Augsburg, Augsburg, FRG.

Pommerehne, Werner W., Dr., University of Zurich, Zurich, Switzerland.

Rauscher, Gerhard, University of Augsburg, Augsburg, FRG.

Recktenwald, Horst Claus, Professor at the University of Erlangen-Nuremberg, Nuremberg, FRG.

Romer, Thomas, Professor at the Carnegie-Mellon-University, Pittsburgh, Pa., USA.

Rosenthal, Howard, Professor at Carnegie-Mellon-University, Pittsburgh, Pa., USA.

Schneider, Friedrich, Dr., University of Zurich, Zurich, Switzerland.

Seldon, Arthur, The Institute of Economic Affairs, Westminster, UK.

Shibata, Hirofumi, Professor at the University of Osaka, Osaka, Japan.

Sichev, Nikolai, Professor, Rector of the All-Union Extramural Financial and Economic Research Institute, Moscow, USSR.

Sitaryan, Stepan, Professor at the University of Moscow, Moscow, USSR.

Weck, Hannelore, Dr., University of Zurich, Zurich, Switzerland.

Wolf, Charles, Jr., Professor, The Rand Corporation, Santa Monica, Ca., USA.

Wolfe, Barbara L., Professor at the University of Wisconsin, Madison, Wis., USA.

Preface

The topic of the 38th Congress of the International Institute of Public Finance was "Public Finance and the Quest for Efficiency". There was a good reason for choosing this subject.

With the advent of considerable economic difficulties in many parts of the world, during the 1970's and early 1980's, a genuine quest for greater efficiency in public sectors arose. This concern determined the scientific work of the 38th Congress. It decided the selection of the main themes which were discussed. On all of this I elaborate at length in my introductory article. I can therefore be brief in this place and confine myself to the pleasant task of thanking all those who contributed to make the Copenhagen Congress a success and rewarding experience.

To begin with, I want to thank our Danish hosts. Under the chairmanship of Professor Dr. B. Rold Andersen, supported by Professor Dr. Jørgen Lotz and Dr. Rolf Norstrand, the Local Organisation Committee created an atmosphere that made the days in Copenhagen a great event for all participants in the Congress. The financial aid of The Municipal Fund of V.A.T. and the Danish Social Science Council considerably helped the good efforts of the Organisation Committee and was much appreciated.

To edit a Proceedings Volume in English and French may turn out to be a risky enterprise for someone who has a different native language. Without the capable and sacrificing assistance of Wolfgang F. Stolper, I would not have been able to tackle the problem. His often critical but always sympathetic remarks made it a pleasure to screen, together with him, all contributions. I am especially indebted to him.

In addition, I owe many thanks to the members of the Scientific Committee. In particular, I like to mention Karl W. Roskamp. While preparing the Congress I could always rely on his vast experience as an Executive Vice President and on his advice. During the Congress itself, many participants helped to assure success. I want to express my thanks especially to the authors and discussants as well as to the chairmen.

Furthermore, I want to thank Madame Bernadette Dischamps for her care in translating the summaries into French and Mrs. Birgit Schneider, Secretary of the International Institute of Public Finance, who lent me a helping hand before and during the Congress. The arduous task of organizing the Congress and the numerous efforts required in the editing of the papers led to a heavy burden on some of my assistants at the University of Augsburg. I am especially indebted to Peter Biene, Brunhilde Doll, Lothar Thürmer and Karl-Heinz Weiss for their devoted and competent assistance and to Brigitte Ploner for typing most of the manuscript. Last but not least, my thanks are due to Mrs. Barbara Bendert, Mrs. Margot Demarais, and Miss Alice Nigoghosian, all of Wayne State University, who put the manuscript into final shape for publication.

Horst Hanusch
University of Augsburg, F.R.G.

President of the International Institute of Public Finance—responsible for the 38th Congress: Professor Jean-Claude Dischamps, France

Members of the Scientific Committee for the 38th Congress were:

   Horst Hanusch, Chairman, Federal Republic of Germany
   Karl W. Roskamp, Executive Vice-President, United States of America
   B. Rold Andersen, Denmark
   Nikolai Sichev, Union of Socialist Soviet Republics
   André Vlérick, Belgium

Contents

Public Finance and the Quest for Efficiency

Horst Hanusch

1.

Efficiency in the public sector has challenged economists for a long time. The problem had to be dealt with since optimal use of resources to achieve specific ends became their prime concern. Economists realized early that efficiency considerations are of great importance if a framework for actions and decisions is to be established. To get the public sector efficiency problem into proper perspective it is therefore useful to briefly consider some historical developments.

In the mercantilist era the "state", in the person of the sovereign, was the focus of considerations which concerned the riches of the monarch and, through them, the welfare of his subjects.

Later, in the work of Adam Smith one finds that inverse relationship between the interests of the state and its citizens which has prevailed for the economic system of the Western world to our days: the focus being now the individual and his self-interest. In Smith's conceptual framework the riches of the nation and the whole community are intimately connected with the individuals' welfare. Indeed the dictum was: let all individuals maximize their advantages and the well-being of the nation approaches its zenith.

In such a world, an "economic theory of the state" remains, quite understandably, of subsidiary interest: the aims of the community have to take into consideration the necessities of the market and of competition. Based on this liberal heritage, the modern state in Western countries finds its task primarily there where the market *fails*, and fails to such an extent, that its power of self-correction ceases and only public intervention can avoid welfare losses to the individual and the community.

Today, however, the great Adam Smith would be surprised at the large proportion of the productive powers of a country used by the public

Public Finance and the Quest for Efficiency. Proceedings of the 38th Congress of the International Institute of Public Finance. Copenhagen, 1982, pp. 1–9. Copyright © 1984 by Wayne State University Press, Detroit, Michigan, 48202.

sector, squeezing through the small door his conception had left open for collective needs.

The theory of economic policy, based on the macro-economic insights of John Maynard Keynes, and the theory of public goods, based on the micro-economic ideas of welfare economics, have developed the theory of market failures to such a subtle and occasionally cunning instrument of market criticism that the state and the multiplicity of its economic activities have become more and more important. On the other hand, this approach has *not* required a consideration of the efficiency of the public sector because "market failure" alone is deemed to be sufficient to explain and justify the activity of the state.

Thus, we find ourselves in the Western world in the paradoxical situation that in almost all developed economies half of the social product goes through the hands of the state and is spent in a manner that has hardly changed since the days of the absolute prince.

It has gradually been realized—and not in economics alone—that the modern state has hardly less economic influence than it had in mercantilist days, and that only the term "efficiency" has acquired a very different meaning. In contrast to Adam Smith, today questions arise once again whether the welfare of the community is still indissolubly identified with the market induced welfare of the individuals. In fact, individual welfare may rather depend on the prosperity of the state. It becomes necessary—so it is claimed—to develop a theory which does not restrict itself to an examination of the efficiency of the market, but which extends, in principle, the analysis of economic failures to the public sector as well. The theory of market failures must be complemented by a theory of government failures.

2.

At first, every scientist engaged in questions of public sector efficiency has to form a clear idea about the nature of the state and its economy. It will crucially influence the questions asked, the methods and approaches applied and the paradigm and set of definitions used.

Two polar concepts of the state may be distinguished. First, the state may be regarded as a paternalistic subject ranking above individuals. This concept is basically underlying the analysis of Stepan Sitaryan and Nikolai Sichev. Their considerations center on questions relating to the volume of resources required and to the improvement of financial instruments in order to come up with the economic and social plans of a socialist state.

On the other hand, one may conceive the state as an institution legitimatized only by fulfilling those wishes of individuals which cannot efficiently be satisfied by a market economy. Horst Claus Recktenwald's courageous attempt to formulate a comprehensive theory of welfare losses in the public sector is based on this concept of the state. If one accepts in the liberal tradition of Adam Smith such an idea of the state, one will be inclined to transfer basic principles of the market to the public sector economy. These principles are essentially supply and demand, and their interaction in an adequate system of allocation and financing.

3.

The division of the program of the Congress into problems of demand, supply, and financing obviously reveals my preference for a theory of the state centering on the citizen and his need for collective goods and services. The public sector is thus considered as an institution whose main function is to satisfy individual needs.

The allocative mechanism co-ordinating the demand and the supply of public activities is expressed in democratic elections coupled with a system of tax financing on the basis of either the benefit or the ability-to-pay principle.

4.

From this point of view, "efficiency" may, of course, have different dimensions and meanings. On the one hand, it can refer to a general model of the public economy which brings together all three elements, i.e. demand, supply and financing in a consistent manner and determines an optimal decision calculus for the public sector. On the other hand, it may be related to only one of the three elements, thus considering efficiency as a specific problem of demand, or of supply, or of financing.

5.

The general models of the public economy normally refer to efficiency as applying to the optimal allocation of resources both in the state and between the state and the market economy. Those models which transfer the price mechanism paradigmatically to a public sector providing pure collective goods even succeed in demonstrating the conditions for an opti-

mum-optimorum-concept of efficiency within a welfare economic framework. The best-known model of this kind has been developed by Paul
Samuelson. Less ambitious models, based on a democracy with majority
rule and the compulsory element of tax financing, restrict their efficiency
considerations to an allocation of resources which the majority of voters
wants. The median-voter model, as elaborated by Howard Bowen, is the
most famous example for this kind of research.

6.

In all these models, inefficient allocations are necessarily defined as
deviations from the theoretically determined optimum. Depending on the
particular model, the quest for more efficiency as well as the political
possibilities for its improvement have quite specific meanings.

This approach to public sector efficiency has not been the guideline for
the program of this congress. I did not primarily intend to draw the attention to still unsolved problems of general equilibrium theory or an analytically consistent and all embracing framework. My main objective was
rather to design a program which would shed some light on the whole range
of efficiency research in public finance. I therefore decided to focus on the
fields of demand, supply, and finance and on the problems and deficiencies
related to each of them in the public sector.

My selection of topics within these fields aimed at a discussion of
subjects which in my opinion have gained a prominent position in the
recent efficiency debate and which probably will occupy our discipline also
in the future. These issues have been discussed, and have led to the following results.

7.

In public finance, efficiency problems of *demand* are generally treated in
an individualistic approach of direct or indirect democracy. The methodology used ultimately follows the tradition of general equilibrium models for
the public sector. Allocative efficiency is therefore still of primary interest.

Two topics characterize the present discussion. On the one hand,
problems of efficient decision making in a democracy are considered on the
assumption that citizens and voters dominate the political process. On the
other hand, problems of information which may arise because of the specific properties of public goods are intensively discussed. The structure of

the program in the working group "demand" tries to reflect these two main issues.

Dennis C. Mueller in particular has treated a fundamental question of democracy. In contrast to the usually applied model of majority voting, he analyses a different voting mechanism: voting by veto. His procedure is susceptible to coalition formations but it allows unique solutions even in situations in which majority voting leads to cyclical majorities. This is especially true when voters have no information about the preference orderings of the other voters, a property that is of particular interest when a decision has to be made in which distributive elements are involved.

Considerations of a positive rather than a normative nature about the decision process and its efficiency in representative democracies have been investigated by Guy Kirsch, Hirofumi Shibata and Charles Wolf. Kirsch calls attention to the role of political parties in generating public needs. Party competition, however, cannot prevent voters from being imperfectly informed about their needs and the political alternatives of supply. Shibata and Wolf consider two additional causes for biased decisions in representative democracies. Whereas Shibata in particular identifies the decision mechanism of majority voting as a cause for potential exploitation of majorities by minorities, Wolf concentrates, above all, on the separation between financing and consuming public goods. He fundamentally differs from Shibata in so far as he claims, that a majority would tend to exploit minorities in the political process.

Arthur Seldon in his stimulating contribution considers cost-benefit analysis as an instrument of deciding whether and to what extent a public good is to be provided. His critical discussion leads to the result that decisions should be shifted from the supply to the demand side of the budgetary process. To do so requires other tools than cost-benefit analysis, particularly micro-economic ones. In a British example, Seldon points out the relevance of financing public budgets by charges instead of taxes in order to increase the efficiency of providing public goods.

Bernhard Herber analyses the extent to which the production process in the public and private sectors is determined by government decisions. His innovative approach, using the Delphi method, leads to the result that the influence of the government on the whole economy of a country can hardly be overestimated.

Peter Bohm deals with instrumental possibilities to reduce information problems relating to the demand for public goods. His main point leads to applicability. The interval-method he proposes can be used to force local authorities to reveal their preferences in terms of their willingness-to-pay.

Werner Pommerehne and Friedrich Schneider consider a different instrument to force individuals to reveal their true preferences: the referendum. They examine to what extent the referendum can be used as an instrument to relate the provision of public goods more closely to the wishes of the voters. Their analysis empirically proves that voting processes in a direct democracy are, in specific situations, significantly superior to those in a representative democracy.

But even the superior alternative is not free of defects, as Thomas Romer, Howard Rosenthal and Krishna Ladha convincingly demonstrate. Even direct voting processes in the form of referenda permit potential suppliers to influence in their own interest the proposals. And by influencing the voting alternatives, they can also alter the results of the voting process.

8.

As far as the *supply* of public goods is concerned, the literature has dealt with questions of efficiency regarding two institutional levels. On the one hand, the process of political decision-making is examined: do politicians in their decisions really respect the wishes of the citizens and voters? Or, do they follow only their own, probably ideologically motivated interests?

On the other hand, the behavior of public administrators or bureaucrats is extensively explored: do appointed officials really execute the politics of government? Or, do they more or less pursue their own strategic interests?

In the first case, difficulties of and barriers to adjusting public supply to collective demand are disclosed. Therefore, allocative efficiency is the main concern. In the second case, the internal processes of producing and providing public goods and services are analysed, mainly from the viewpoint of production- or X-efficiency.

Such studies of bureaucracy have become increasingly important, with the empirical analyses clearly dominating. Normative aspects of optimal organisation, efficient management, and adequate decision and evaluation techniques in the public sector, however, are losing their former preeminence. One reason for this development might be the result of bad experiences of many countries with the implementation of management techniques like the planning-programming-budgeting-system. The former atmosphere of euphoric expectation has changed into one of pessimism and resignation. Moreover, since these normative issues are sufficiently treated in numerous publications, I have not stressed them in the program of the Congress.

Based on the insight that political decision makers do not always act according to the preferences of the demanders, Christoph Badelt proposes to use elements of a voluntary sector as an effective means to increase the allocative efficiency in the supply of certain goods and services thus far provided by the public sector. Although the welfare effects connected with the voluntary sector cannot ultimately be evaluated, Badelt makes some interesting and plausible suggestions, indicating that a cooperation between the public and the voluntary sector would enormously increase the efficiency in the provision of public goods particularly in the area of social services.

Such questions of institutional choice play nowadays an important role, especially in Germany, where the necessity for reforming our "social market system" is extensively discussed. Regrettably, the time available makes it impossible to deal comprehensively with all interesting ideas. After long reflection I decided to focus the working group *supply* on the issue of X-inefficiency on public production and provision.

The contributions of Donald Fisk as well as of Klaus-Norbert Münch, Wolfgang Länger and Gerhard Rauscher, analyse public sector productivity and report about the state of art of analyses in their countries. I believe that the existing empirical studies already allow the conclusion that, all conceptual and empirical difficulties notwithstanding, X-inefficiencies in public production are the rule rather than the exception but that nevertheless productivity in the provision of some local services increased at least within the last decade.

Of the numerous approaches in the theory of bureaucracy, which try to explain these facts, it seems to me that the socio-economic interpretation of Harvey Leibenstein is one of the most interesting. Surprisingly, he concludes that even significant external pressures or shocks do not necessarily lead to an automatic decrease of bureaucratic inefficiencies.

Another group of authors has dealt with an issue which is already relevant in modern public finance and which will probably gain even more importance in the future: what are the effects of government activities on the market system, and how are these effects to be evaluated from the point of view of macro-economic goals?

In this context, Suphan Andic and Ramón Cao-García inquire into the allocative inefficiencies in the market economy which result from regulatory interventions.

Reflecting critically on the composition and the content of the program, I have to confess that the question of regulatory inefficiency is one of the topics which had unfortunately to be neglected.

Victor Halberstadt, together with Robert Haveman, Barbara Wolfe and Kees Goudswaard examine the influence of public transfer expenditures on the growth of GNP. Although they can, of course, not determine unequivocally the extent of this influence, their paper suggests that the disincentives of transfers are much overestimated in the current literature.

9.

The classic question of the effects of public sector activities on the market has become increasingly the subject of an efficiency research, which centers on the *revenue side* of the budget. In the process of answering this old question, the relevance of approaches, which evaluate the efficiency effects of tax financing within welfare economic analyses (for instance optimal tax theory), seems gradually to decrease. If my interpretation of recent developments in public finance is right, many economists nowadays are extensively concerned with a systematic integration of public economics into macroeconomics and phenomena like inflation, unemployment, declining productivity and decreasing GNP gain priority in research.

The state is no longer regarded as an isolated economic subject, or merely as an actor of financial policy, influencing the market exogeneously. Instead, it has to be integrated as an endogenous part in micro- and in macroeconomic models based upon individual decisions in commodity and/ or in factor markets. The effects on and the variations of market decisions resulting from the existence of the state and, more importantly, from its budgetary growth, are the basis for efficiency considerations related to objectives like satisfactory growth, full employment and price stability. In such a context, the *incentive research* has apparently received renewed priority. The relevant approaches include even the hidden sectors of a shadow economy.

From the viewpoint of the state, this kind of efficiency seems to be quite unsophisticated. The state ultimately is confronted with an old and well-known problem: can the required financial resources for its various activities be secured or not? Macro-economic analysis is thus reduced to the financial aspects of a balanced budget, or, conversely, questions of financing the public sector become the prime consideration of macro-economic analysis. The economic reactions of market actors to government activities are reflected in a tax revenue function, the so-called Laffer-curve, that may serve as an intellectual basis for a general concept of economic policy.

In the past few days, a number of contributions has dealt with the incentive effects of tax financing on labor and commodity markets. All papers use directly or indirectly the analytics of the Laffer-curve. The contribution of James Buchanan and Dwight Lee as well as that of Guy Gilbert mainly restrict their analysis to tax effects on certain markets. The paper presented by Hannelore Weck and Bruno Frey takes account in addition of possible migration effects into a shadow economy.

Gilbert enriches the production theoretic specifications of the Laffer-curve by introducing a dynamic approach. Buchanan and Lee develop a new analytic framework for the Laffer-curve by presenting a demand-side specification. They arrive at the interesting conclusion that a rational government, maximizing tax revenues in the short-run will in the long-run lie on the declining slope of the Laffer-curve. Thus rationality in the long-run implies the readiness to forego short-term maximization strategies.

The empirical investigation of Daniel Holland shows, however, that incentive effects of tax financing need not be restricted solely to such voluntary substitution processes as assumed by the Laffer-curve. In addition, each type of tax financing risks that individuals will try, if possible, to escape from their fiscal obligations by veiling the amount of the tax base legally or illegally. For the USA, Holland investigates in detail this evasion through understating the tax base for several taxes and time periods and proposes measures to combat effectively such defraudation. Different opinions, however, are possible about his advice.

Finally, Werner Z. Hirsch derives conclusions from experiences with the California tax limitation act. He argues that bureaucratic efficiency has increased in California since the proposition 13 was enacted in 1978.

10.

Let me now end my survey by posing a last and rather subjective question: did the results of the congress justify all our efforts? I definitely believe that this is the case and I emphatically answer Anthony Culyer's question whether there is a place for economists seeking to enhance efficiency in the affirmative. I would like to thank all those warmly who have made the congress an outstanding success.

The Public Waste Syndrome:
A Comprehensive Theory of Government Failures*

Horst Claus Recktenwald

I. Frame and Aim—A Vademecum for Analysis

Since men are forced to behave efficiently, they are faced with the question whether to provide goods and services individually or collectively. Historically they have done both simultaneously. And since men collectively supply and finance scarce means for particular basic needs (like security at home and defense abroad, road construction, and water provision) they are forced to argue about the just distribution of benefits and burdens. They also complain about the inefficient administration of collective property. This eternal problem is as familiar to nomadic tribes as to the Greek Polis and the modern state.

Using much time and ingenuity, economists have built up a sophisticated theory of market failures. It served as a justification for state intervention in the market, or for its substitution by the state, yet without knowing the answer to the crucial question: does the state utilize the limited resources more economically than the market? Indeed, we know relatively little about the efficient and just provision of public services and the removal of market failures [Buchanan (1968); Recktenwald (1980)].

When the government may provide, though it does not necessarily produce, half of the national product, the importance and urgency of such research is obvious. In centrally planned socialist countries without a free market in which a comprehensive bureaucracy rather than private initiative decides on *all* aspects of the provision of goods this topic is obviously even more important.[1]

*Professor of Economics, Friedrich-Alexander-University Erlangen-Nürnberg. I would like to thank Karl-Dieter Grüske and Astrid Rosenschon for very helpful suggestions and J.M. Buchanan, H. Hanusch, R.A. Musgrave, W.A. Niskanen and A.T. Peacock for critical advice.

Public Finance and the Quest for Efficiency. Proceedings of the 38th Congress of the International Institute of Public Finance. Copenhagen, 1982, pp. 11–26. Copyright © 1984 by Wayne State University Press, Detroit, Michigan, 48202.

This is the background for my discussion. I attempt to explain only the *nature* and *causes* of potential (not actual) waste in the public sector. I shall try to develop a framework to list these reasons in a theoretically meaningful and interrelated way. Potential welfare losses caused by (a) the state as a monopolistic supplier with a bureaucratic apparatus and (b) the wasteful use by consumers are the focal points. Neither optima nor minima will be determined, nor will particular propositions be empirically examined.

My procedure is simple: First, I shall deal with those causes of inefficiency which derive either from man's nature or are system induced. The interactions of these two sets of causes lead to a new analytic concept to describe welfare losses in the state itself and in the market caused by public activity. Second, both groups of causes are investigated from three points of view: (a) self-interest vs. public interest, (b) the monopolistic and badly controlled supply of public goods, and (c) the inefficient use of excessive demand. Third, on the basis of these discussions I formulate two new concepts of potential welfare losses (Q- and R-Inefficiency). Finally I offer some suggestions for reforms.

II. Causes of Inefficiency Stemming from Man's Nature—Pattern of Behavior with Axiomatic Character

Philosophy and science have by observation, experience, experiments, and reason discovered inefficiencies when limited resources are utilized collectively. These inefficiencies may stem from (a) man's nature, or (b) from the political and bureaucratic organization of the supply and the administration of public goods and of their use and financing. Mankind's fundamental experiences form the first group of causes that are valid at any time and at any place. They have an axiomatic character, and are neither fictitious nor constructed[2] for analytical purposes. They can be experienced and observed by everybody at any time. This archetypical pattern of behavior is located between reason and instinct and may be related more to (i) the individual or (ii) the collective.

ad (i): (1) Self-interest (not egoism or disinterest) is man's crucial incentive and drive in his "universal, continual and uninterrupted effort to better his own condition" [A. Smith, quoted in Recktenwald (1978, 72)] e.g., to secure his existence, to increase his welfare, and also his "place" in the community. This motive of self-interest is of course universally valid.

(2) Man stands up for himself more than for others, especially more than for an abstract *bonum commune*.

(3) If he does not know his or other's foregone choices he will be unable to value a good according to its scarcity. A political substitute generally

does not know either. Asking for his preference or willingness to pay, without actually forcing him to pay, means that we neglect this fundamental experience. Utopian claims for *absolute* security, health, justice, or freedom in a world of scarcity are the consequence.

ad (ii): (1) Man alone perceives needs. Needs are never collective but the *means* of efficiently and justly meeting them may be. This does not deny that the needs of different individuals mutually influence each other.[3] (Veblen effect, Sax's mutualism, etc.)

(2) Goods actually or supposedly supplied free of charge are generally used wastefully, i.e., not with *diligentia quam in suis*.

(3) Goods collectively provided free of charge (meritoriously) will be consumed even if they should be consumed only when the individual sees an advantage for himself.

(4) Man alone has the propensity to prefer fiction to fact. This may result in false evaluation, in a free-rider mentality, and in making excessive demands. It may prevent a political reform of a collective system.

(5) The propensity for perfection, such as regulating all possible cases, (Max Weber's limitless casuistic) results without financial constraints in a flood of rules and laws. Nobody knows the costs or is personally responsible for this activity. Besides this, two further basic experiences of mankind favor the welfare losses in a collective [Aristotle (1971), Aquinas (1951)]:

(6) Man takes better care of his own things than of those of others.

(7) Order in a community is kept more easily and less costly if property rights are clearly determined, thus avoiding quarrels about utilizing collective property and distributing the burden of financing, maintenance, and repair.

In the short run, these fundamentals of human behavior might be counteracted under special conditions yet in the long run no one can eliminate them by force without serious welfare losses.

Theories that exclude or severely restrict these basic experiences in their assumptions or behavioral equations are false, or they at least distort reality. Their modeling of reality is therefore dubious. Hence, Schumpeter's sarcastic judgement of Ricardo's profit theory may be relevant for them: "It is an excellent theory that can never be disproved and which lacks nothing but sense." [Schumpeter 1951, 161]

III. Causes of Potential Welfare Losses Inherent in the Political and Bureaucratic System

Experience and insight have revealed at least five groups of causes of potential inefficiency in the public system.

(1) The (Disproportional) Political and Administrative Apparatus

A variety of determinants affect the production and provision of, and "demand" for, public goods. Thus, a realistic supply function S_{pg} may include the following variables of behavior or aims of public agents:

$$S_{pg} = S (W, P_a, R, P, V, K, B, G, M)$$

Where the symbols have the following meaning:

S_{pg} = supply of public goods
W   = electorate
P_a = political parties
R   = government
P   = parliament
V   = administration
K   = audit
B   = citizen initiative
G   = lobby
M   = media

Evidently, a most complex political and administrative apparatus influences directly or indirectly the quantity and composition of the supply of public goods and its financing. [Baumol and Quandt (1964)] Two-dimensional models (like the bureaucracy theories) oversimplify, therefore, reality. Rising costs of the information and the losses due to friction (e.g., competence conflicts) are obvious. Thus, the inflexibility of bureaucratic administration paralyzing all initiative and caught in the network of prolific legal regulations requires much energy in the fight for hierarchical competences. We know little about the true costs of individual administrative acts or policy decisions, such as preparation, execution, and consequences of individual laws and regulations. The general assertion that just laws and a just administration are expensive is meaningless without proof and verification. [Lohmar (1978)] What "more justice" means and what it costs, remains totally ambiguous. Nobody ever asks.

An area of potential welfare losses is evidently that the information monopoly of bureaucracy weakens Montesquieu's control mechanisms of the separation of powers and political competition. Seen analytically the main reason for this failure is that there is also a division of labor in the public sector, without, however, the efficient coordination of the market. Division of labor without a continuous evaluation of the services by exchange loses its very meaning.

(2) The Dissolution of the Principle of Political and Economic Integration—Fatal Separation of Giving, Taking, Supplying, and Deciding

On the market, decision, service, and payment are linked by exchange and price and because the persons concerned are directly and visibly involved with each other. With the provision of public goods, on the contrary, the payer, user, decision-maker, and supplier (whether producer or provider) are as a rule separated. Consequently, allocative efficiency is never ensured. Figure 1a illustrates the complete separation of suppliers (A), decision makers (E), users (N) and payers (Z) of public goods with the result that free rider mentality may become all pervasive. Figure 1b illustrates several possible degrees of interdependence of A, E, N, and Z with the effect that free rider behavior F diminishes, and in the case of total integration (the dashed area) disappears. (Fig. 1) On the market, with its millions of spontaneous individual decisions, efficiency is continually enforced. The separation of benefits, costs (usually unknown) and decision in the state implies the danger of wasting limited means. This lack of visible connection is often legally sanctioned by the non-affectation principle that governs nearly 90 percent of public revenues. It is, indeed, one of the most important causes of welfare losses because the behavior of all persons concerned is fundamentally changed.

The decoupling of demand from the need to pay quite naturally overburdens and "corrupts" man. It encourages the egoistic behavior of individuals and groups and it lessens the communal spirit. The inevitable consequences are both a claim mentality and a free-rider conduct of the individual, the group, region, or generation, when they use, pay for, decide upon, or provide public goods. This separation of parameters that are integrated in man's natural behavior, evaluation, and decision making in a world of scarcity must spoil his sense of fair conduct.

(3) The Constitutional Structure of Government as a Source of Inefficiency

An important cause of inefficiency may be the political and regional organization of the state when the principle of economic and political integration is modified. This principle is not to be confused with the principle of *fiscal* equivalence which is too narrow. [Recktenwald (1980, 83)] If payer, user, decision-maker, and supplier in a state are not organized and involved according to the distribution of spatial benefits, the provision of public services may be suboptimal and the horizontal and vertical compensation mech-

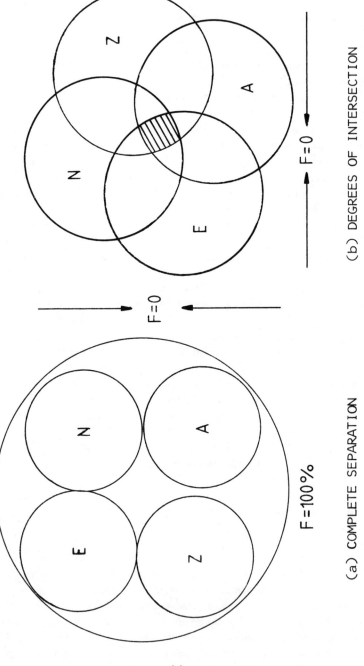

Figure 1: *Degrees of Separation of Giving, Taking, Supplying and Deciding*

F=100%

(a) COMPLETE SEPARATION

F=0

F=0

(b) DEGREES OF INTERSECTION

16

anisms may also work inefficiently. Only where proven economies of scale exist, considerable overlapping of benefits and burdens occurs, and regional help is politically unavoidable, can we test whether a centralized or one of many decentralized solutions is to be preferred. Historically, however, efficient alternative mechanisms of decentralized co-operation were scarcely applied and tested. It ensures, of course, that financing of and deciding upon the supply of a public good are made simultaneously and according to use. I have explained this type of loss elsewhere. [Recktenwald (1983b)]

(4) Missing Incentives and Sanctions

The public system lacks sufficient incentives and effective sanctions against uneconomic behavior of *all* persons and institutions involved. "Material" and non-pecuniary interest in personal productivity is unknown. Virtually automatic and guaranteed annual wage increases with a powerful trade union tend to reduce personal incentives. Long-life employment without risk of dismissal or job, as well as political patronage in many posts have similar effects. Furthermore, there is no *technological* pressure to shift labor from less to more productive employment. Where the professional ethos (or sociologically speaking, the sense of common welfare) is as yet poorly developed to motivate performance, this collective organization must work most inefficiently. The public system of sanctions has the same effect. Personal and institutional recourse for poor planning, incorrect forecasts, misjudgement, wrong decisions, failure, and non-performance is excluded because success is not measured and expert knowledge and formal administrative competence are separated.

(5) The Antiquated Budget and Accounting System

Comfortable ignorance is not a monopoly of politicians, bureaucrats, or economists. But from the point of view of rational decision making and efficient performance, there is hardly any other field of human activity that has such an out-of-date accounting system as the public sector. This antiquated cameralistic approach is certainly insufficient for the political guidance and management of a community that uses half its national income to provide public services. If the modern budgetary system is to reflect the government's program, is to be the base of political decisions, and to reveal success and failure, a system of accounting based on the following will hardly suffice: a pattern in which (a) budgetary, financing, and property accounting are largely separated; (b) no figure indicates the outputs (not to mention the benefit-cost ratios); and, (c) little information is given about how justly benefits and costs are distributed among individuals, regions, and generations.

Many reasons help to explain this backwardness. Its roots are in the cameralists and the English classics.[4] The state's main aim was to meet its financial need or to cover costs as a non-profit institution. Thus the collective entity never endeavored to maximize the *net* social benefit or at least to minimize costs in a world of scarcity. [Recktenwald (1978) (1980)].

IV. Public Activity which leads to Welfare Losses

(1) Follow-up (Corollary) Costs for the Budgets, Private Households, and Enterprises

As long as we have no accounting of who bears the cost and where the costs arise in the public sector, it is impossible to develop realistic production and cost functions which allow for all costs. Even the efficiency of collecting taxes remains unknown. Moreover, cameralistic accounting does not register the follow-up costs of a project, which may be a large area of inefficiency. These financial and non-pecuniary corollary costs extend to the own budget, other departments, other districts or generations, and the private sector. The compliance costs that private households and enterprises assume as the result of public law are largely unknown. Thus the private sector provides free services to the state in addition to taxes. It is a sort of bureaucratic cost shifting as a hidden part of the state's share of the national product.

(2) Inefficient Regulation—Wrong Economic and Financial Policies

Another and largely unexplored complex of causes for inefficiencies are government regulations, prohibitions, and prescriptions. It includes regulations which ought to have been but were not enacted and extends to the stabilization of the market economy, and to external effects. We are dealing here mainly with inefficient means and not aims.

Recently a start has been made in the analysis of welfare losses which occur when the tax system either reduces private activity or leads to tax evasion (shadow economy, illicit work).[5] The Laffer curve attempts to explain these effects. And finally there are excess burdens of a tax which play a central role in optimal taxation theory. [Recktenwald (1983a)]

V. The Interaction of Causes

(1) Political and Bureaucratic Self-Interest and Public Welfare

Unfortunately, we lack a comprehensive theory that systematically applies the principle of self interest to political and bureaucratic behavior and public welfare. [Recktenwald (1980) (1983b)] Adam Smith did, however, clearly recognize this problem. He gave interesting examples, such as the payment of judges, schoolmasters, or clergymen or the inevitable alienation of an institution's aim from its original purpose (and therefore from the actual users and payers), thus becoming a goal in itself and often self-perpetuating. But he and we have failed to develop a model for the state comparable to the most refined one for the market.[6]

Observation and some empirical analyses suggest that bureaucrats' attempts to achieve pecuniary and non-pecuniary advantages (e.g., better pay, less effort, more power, advancement, preference, and prestige) normally increase costs and thus public expenditures, but hardly ever productivity. (But see Fisk, this volume) An example is the expenditure glut at the end of the fiscal year because the bureaucrats expect that unexpended funds will lead to a cut in next year's budget. Usually, neither the average nor marginal costs nor the output nor the benefits of their activity are known to the controlling politicians themselves. The correlation of the politicians' self-interest and the common welfare is similarly negative.

(2) Public Monopolist with Power of Coercion

As a rule the community provides public goods as an absolute monopolist. Therefore one is inclined to apply the static (Cournot) monopoly theory in order to explain and measure welfare losses. [e.g., Bergson (1973, 853), Harberger (1954, 77–82), Lutz (1956, 28ff), Peacock and Rawley (1972), Recktenwald (1951), and Rosenschon (1980)]. Indeed, this concept provides a better insight into the nature of public monopolies with durable power than into the mechanism of the dynamic market. The reasons are obvious: The public differs from the private monopolist.

(a) His market control is *absolute* which means that there exists neither potential competition nor effective monopoly control by the state. Entry is prohibited even for other public suppliers. This means welfare losses in an uncontestable market à la Baumol (1982) and Stigler (1976). In addition, in case of a competence conflict administrative costs must rise.

(b) Even competition by substitution is virtually impossible and often prohibited by law.

(c) Incentives or compulsion to technological innovation and to better management and organization are lacking, unlike, e.g., on oligopolistic markets where they may be decisive to increase productivity.

(d) There is no pressure to reduce costs corresponding to the pressure emanating from the owners of private capital for net returns.

(e) The public monopolist's "demand" curve is relatively inelastic since public goods are usually necessities of life or even must be consumed as merit goods.

(f) As a rule risk is zero because financial losses are covered by the budget.

(g) The self-interest of politicians and bureaucrats is positively correlated with an expansion of expenditures instead of an increase in productivity.

All these reasons support the argument that a public monopolist works less efficiently than a private one if we apply a static model. The public provision will become worse when we look at behavior and competition in a dynamic context, namely in the context of the functioning of contestable markets that continuously force structural and technological changes.

VI. Two New Concepts for Potential Welfare Losses in the State (R- and Q-Inefficiencies)

I have outlined a framework based on my anatomy of potential welfare losses in a community. It is a framework into which the numerous cases known from experience and analytical insight can be set. The curves in the following figures are *hypothetical* and variable. Since there are many causes for inefficiency, I have grouped them under headings:[7] the supply side (figure 2), and the demand side (figure 3).

(1) Losses in the Provision by Public Monopolies (R-Inefficiency)

The amount OP of public goods supplied (figure 2) is assumed to be the result of the political process. On the ordinate OE measures the marginal (= average) costs at the best possible technique. They are assumed to be constant. The cost block EFZW pictures the R-Inefficiency. It indicates the excess average and marginal costs due to an uneconomic administration and political process. Thus, the true costs of a public measure (*and hence the cost-benefit ratio*) cannot be controlled by the politicians because the account-

Figure 2: *R-Inefficiency*

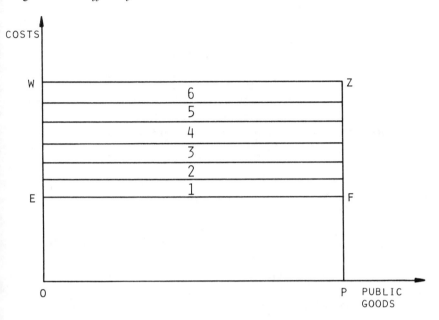

ing system does not disclose them. Yet the main reason lies in the negative correlation between the bureaucrats' self-interest and the productivity within a warranted budget.

I have chosen only six criteria in order to explain R-Inefficiency with some examples. In figure 2, total losses are assumed to be additive, though this need not be the case.

(a) Area 1 represents the excessive costs involved when the state itself produces services (in Western Germany approximately 16% of public expenditures). In section II and III I have enumerated detailed reasons for the specific excess costs. They are closely associated with the lack of incentives and penalties, the static monopoly and an out-dated accounting system. The excess labor costs could even be considered a special reason if they exceed labor productivity.

(b) When the state buys goods on the market, a hidden R-Inefficiency may occur (area 2) when the least expensive offer has qualitative flaws. This may lead to subsequent costs in the budget.

(c) Area 3 represents the cost of inefficient administration of collective property. (the uneconomic treatment of the "people's" property by individuals will be dealt with under Q-Inefficiency.)

(d) Further welfare losses may occur when the revenue is collected, administered, and spent uneconomically (area 4). Smith's fourth tax canon refers to this sort of inefficiency. A classic example are the petty taxes whose collection costs more than they yield.

(e) Excessive follow-up cost of a public activity settled in the own or in other authorities' budgets are pictured in area 5. The shifting of cost onto private households and enterprises (e.g., compliance costs) is another important field.

(f) Finally, the regional distribution of expenditure and revenue competencies may be inefficient when the integration principle is disregarded (Wust (1981)). As a consequence we need costly horizontal and vertical mechanisms which have to adjust the burden and benefits between regional and local institutions (area 6).

(2) Welfare Losses on the Demand Side (Q-Inefficiency)

The citizen can also contribute to inefficiency as a voter and user. His claims on the collective are inevitably excessive when the user and payer are separated. (See figure 1). The citizen does not consider his true opportunity cost when he demands public goods since in general he believes that others bear the burden. In addition to these excessive claims by the voter there is also a demand for public services which is artificially produced by politicians or bureaucrats. Guided by their self-interest and often supported by a lobby, they may try to increase demand by asking for citizens' "preferences" while suggesting a preference to them or simply assuming one. Realized, it results in a supply that is greater than the amount based on the user's true willingness to pay. We may call it "political demand" evaluated as an assumed "benefit". It differs, of course, from Musgrave's merit wants.

The extent of this Q-Inefficiency in any given case depends essentially on how and by whom public services are evaluated and to what extent the costs are actually internalized. Another cause of Q-Inefficiency lies in the excessive use of existing public services and property when they are provided free of charge.

Figure 3 pictures these interrelations. The evaluated use of resource costs appear on the ordinate, the amount of public goods on the abscissa. The average and marginal costs are assumed to be *minimal* and constant. No account is taken of any R-Inefficiency.

Let OP be the marginal (=average) costs of the public good. If one starts with the beneficiaries' willingness to pay (A'A), as is usually assumed in the literature, the demand increases

(i) if it is believed that in fact the user will not be required to pay. In this case, welfare losses arise up to the amount of NALM;

(ii) if the willingness to pay will be overstated by the individuals (C'C),

Figure 3: *Q-Inefficiency*

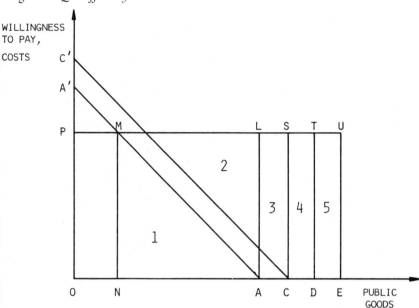

for example to ensure the provision of a certain kind of public good. Then, an additional welfare loss of ACSL (area 3) occurs.

(iii) Besides these losses which are caused by the citizen's overstatement or his failure to take his opportunity cost into account, an artificially produced supply may lead to the following waste: politicians and/or administrators guided by self-interest and supported by interested parties (lobbies) can suggest or, what is more convenient, assume an excessive demand. Their self-interest may be manifested in personal, institutional, or regional prestige, or in re-election. Such a behavior is made easier when the payers of tax-financed projects are unknown e.g., when the activity is completely or partially financed by general taxes (universities, sport facilities, theatres, streets). Area 4 indicates the excessive political supply (closed down sanatoriums or swimming pools), area 5 the overcapacities that bureaucrats have initiated.

VII. Political Implications and Fundamental Reforms

The starting points for a fundamental reform are the administrative apparatus, the accounting system and supplementary concepts (besides the transparent financing by applying the integration principle). Here are some examples (Recktenwald (1972), (1980)):

(a) "rules of service" really related to performance (which join decision-making and factual competence).

(b) the obligation for every authority to identify the direct and over-head costs of a measure (such as tax collection or laws) including all direct and indirect costs. Benefit-cost analysis may help at least to think in alternatives and to disclose the cost-effectiveness and (where possible) the net result. By this means, R-Inefficiency can be penalized and economy can be rewarded and political control of the performance of the bureaucratic monopoly becomes more effective. Thus, it will be easier for the politician to allocate the financial means to the budgets more reasonably.

(c) Further, supplementary ideas are the program budget (which discloses the success of a government's political program) and the concept of budget incidence that indicates the distribution of benefits and burdens. In doing so illusions can be eliminated by disclosing the result of the *re*distribution according to persons, generations, and regions and by disclosing actual "free-riding".

(d) Finally, the control apparatus should work according to economic and political efficiency criteria and not only according to legal formalities.

To expect that politicians and administrators could achieve the insight and gather the energy in order to heal themselves from this proliferation syndrome of waste is unfortunately wishful thinking. The reason has been well known to observers in history: this fundamental reform will never be in their self-interest.

Notes

1. "Our active work sinks into a dead sea of paper. A bureaucratic morass sucks up all of us." This is W.I. Lenin's complaint two generations ago. In our days the individual is exposed to an extreme degree to a strong alienation pressure by collective power hiding behind anonymous and formal regulations.

2. In the sense of Newton's "Hypotheses non fingo". Newton (1714).

3. Providing *collectively* the means naturally means that we need the state or any "Zwangskollektiv" without having to revert to the fiction of an organ *sui generis* or a "Höheres Wesen" or a wise dictator (à la Samuelson). This pattern of behavior does not result in a shallow utilitarianism.

4. German economists, e.g., F. List, L. v. Stein, H. Dietzel, have dealt with the state's productive performance, but have insufficiently analyzed it.

5. See papers by Frey, Buchanan and Lee, Gilbert in this volume.

6. I present this classical paradigm of economic order as the result of my analysis of A. Smith's, John Locke's and other classical works. See Recktenwald (1978), 56–83, (1980), 25–

29. There I have integrated Smith's three main works: *The Wealth of Nations*, *The Theory of Moral Sentiments*, and *The Essays on Philosophical Subjects*, analyzed from the point of view of economic order.

7. Q- and R-Inefficiencies have nothing to do either with Leibenstein's X-Inefficiency and his arguments and empirical testing or with Parish's and Ng's modification of his model. The three authors explain the discretionary costs by means of market control and of the insufficient pressure on costs by the private capital owners on the managers. Apart from the fact that the reasoning seems to be less realistic in a world of dynamic competition, their argument is different from both my dual system of integrated causes and my comprehensive analysis of the public sector. H. Leibenstein (1978, 329), R. Parish and Y.K. Ng (1972, 301–308). More critical arguments in A. Rosenschon (1980).

References

Aquin, Thomas von (1952–55) *Summa Theologica*, Kerle Verlag, Heidelberg-München, 6 vols.
Aristotles (1971) *Politik*, translated by O. Gigon, 2nd. ed., Artemis Verlag, Zurich-Stuttgart.
Baumol, W.J. and Quandt, R.E. (1964) "Rules of Thumb and Optimality, Imperfect Decisions", *American Economic Review*, vol. 54.
Baumol, W.J. (1982) "Contestable Markets", *American Economic Review*, vol. 72, no. 1.
Bergson, A. (1973) "On Monopoly Welfare Losses", *American Economic Review*, vol. 63.
Buchanan, J.M. (1968) *The Demand and Supply for Public Goods*, Rand McNally, Chicago, Illinois.
Harberger, A.C. (1954) "Monopoly and Resource Allocation", *American Economic Review*, vol. 44.
Leibenstein, H. (1978) "On the Basic Proposition of X-Efficiency Theory", *American Economic Review*, vol. 68.
Lohmar, U. (1978) *Staatsbürokratie*, Goldman Verlag, Munich.
Lutz, F.A. (1956) "Bemerkungen zum Monopolproblem", *Ordo Jahrbuch*, vol. 8.
Newton. I. (1714) *Philosophiae Naturalis Principia Mathematica*, Amsterdam.
Niskanen, W.A. (1971) *Bureaucracy and Representative Government*, Chicago.
Parish, R. and Ng, Y.N. (1972) "Monopoly, X-Efficiency and the Measurement of Welfare Loss", *Economica*, vol. 39.
Peacock, A.T. and Rawley, C.K. (1972) "Welfare Economics and the Public Regulation of Natural Monopoly", *Journal of Political Economy*, vol. 80.
Recktenwald, H.C. (1951) "Zur Lehre von den Marketformen", *Weltw. Archiv*, vol. 80.
Recktenwald, H.C. (1971) *Tax Incidence and Income Redistribution*, Wayne State University Press, Detroit.
Recktenwald, H.C. (1972) "Mehr Rationalität im Prozess staatlicher Entscheidung?", IIPF (ed.), *New Methods of Making Budgetary Choices*, Budapest, Paris, Saarbrücken, p. 254–261.
Recktenwald, H.C. (1978) "An Adam Smith Renaissance Anno 1976?", *Journal of Economic Literature*, vol. 16.
Recktenwald, H.C. (1980) *Markt und Staat*, Göttingen, Vandenhoeck und Ruprecht, Göttingen.
Recktenwald, H.C. (1983a) *Staatswirtschaft und Geldwirtschaft*, Beck Verlag, Munich.
Recktenwald, H.C. (1984) "Das Selbstinteresse—zentrales Axiom in der ökonomischen Wissenschaft", forthcoming.
Rosenschon, A. (1980) *Verschwendung in Staat und Markt. Eine vergleichende Analyse*, Vandenhoeck und Ruprecht, Göttingen.
Schumpeter, J.A. (1951) "The Review of the Troops", *Quarterly Journal of Economics*, vol. 65.
Stigler, G.J. (1973) "Free Riders and Collective Action", *Bell Journal of Economics and Management Science*, vol. 2.
Wust, H.F. (1981) *Föderalismus, Grundlagen für Effizienz in der Staatswirtschaft*, Vandenhoeck und Ruprecht, Göttingen.

Résumé

Cet article souligne l'importance de l'inefficience dans les économies de marché comme dans les économies centralisées, et essaie d'expliquer par une approche globale la nature et les causes des gaspillages au moins potentiels dans le secteur public. La démarche est simple: on décrit d'abord, en détail, les facteurs d'inefficience inhérents à la nature humaine ou propres au système. Les deux sont étroitement liés. Les interactions de ces deux ensembles de causes sont à la base d'un concept analytique qui explique les pertes sociales engendrées par l'activité publique dans l'Etat lui même et sur les marchés. On étudie ensuite ces deux groupes de causes interpendantes de trois points de vue:

(a) l'intérêt personnel par rapport à l'intérêt public
(b) l'offre monopolistique et mal contrôlée des biens publics
(c) l'usage inefficace et la demande excessive.

Enfin, sur la base de ces résultats, on formule de nouveaux concepts en termes de pertes potentielles de bien-être et l'on propose quelques éléments de réforme.

Strengthening the Role of Finances in a Planned Economy

Stepan Sitaryan and Nickolai Sichev

The problem of finances under socialism and of their role in the development of a planned economy is complex and multidimensional. It is related to economic policy, planning and management, organization of production, scientific and technological progress, economic incentives and price formation. The problem is closely linked to a correct understanding of the nature of commodity-money relations in a socialist economy, and of their place within the system of the planned management of a national economy.

I. The Planned Development of Socialist Production

The point of departure and the determining aspect in an overall appraisal of the entire set of the financial issues is the planned nature of the socialist economy. This is the basis which determines the new type of financial management, with its inherent principles, organizational methods, and structure.

The socialist economy adopted from the very beginning planning as a purposeful activity to assure the balanced development of the whole economy. Vladimir I. Lenin said that national economic activity required a long-term plan and that a giant task of the socialist revolution was to transform the whole of the state-economic mechanism into a single economic mechanism which allowed hundreds of millions of people to be guided by a single plan.

The planning system of the USSR has been constantly developing to meet new conditions and tasks confronting the economy. Substantial changes have been introduced into the economic planning system of the USSR during the past years. These changes contributed to:

Public Finance and the Quest for Efficiency. Proceedings of the 38th Congress of the International Institute of Public Finance. Copenhagen, 1982, pp. 27–37. Copyright © 1984 by Wayne State University Press, Detroit, Michigan, 48202.

— enhancing the role of the state-plans elaborated on the basis of scientifically substained technical and economic norms governing the use of material, labor, and financial resources;
— comprehensive solutions of economic and social problems, concentration of forces and resources for implementing major nationwide programs, formation of material and financial reserves needed for a proportionate and balanced development of the national economy;
— raising the effectiveness of production, improving work quality, achieving high final national-economic results, and speeding up the development of the intensive factors of economic growth and scientific and technological progress;
— a closer harmonization of current and long-term problems of the sectoral and territorial development of the country.

The present stage in the development of the Soviet economy is characterized by an enhanced role of finances in planned economic guidance. This has basically been due to the following causes:

— first, the significant increase in the size of the financial resources and the need to implement large-scale socio-economic and scientific and technological programs calling for large individual financial inputs;
— second, the growing role of finances in balanced economic development, in a closer and more flexible coordination in the mobility of the material and cost proportions of society's production;
— third, a further development of cost-accounting relations in enterprises and associations, whose activities cannot be enhanced without an increased effectiveness of financial levers and instruments.

II. Dynamics and Structure of Financial Resources

How many financial resources are necessary to develop social production has been and remains one of the main issues of economic policy. The volume of the resources needed depends on the size of the gross social product and the national income, and on how effectively the material, labor, and financial resources are used. It follows that with the increasing gross social product, national income and greater effectiveness of social production, the country's financial resources must also increase.

It is natural that the large scale of the socialist economy should determine the significant size of the financial resources. Suffice it to say that, to carry out the measures mapped out for the eleventh five-year period (1981–1985), the plan provides for over 2,500 billion roubles, which is 20% more than in the previous five-year period.

A characteristic feature of the dynamics of financial resources is that their growth rates are higher than those of national income. This trend, observed over several of the past years, will also apply to growth rates of net income and the depreciation payments fund.

Of significant interest in characterising the final resources of the USSR national economy is the analysis of their structure and the changes that are now at work in the dynamics of the different financial sources. We turn now to this.

The financial resources come from the profits of state enterprises and organizations; the net income of collective farms; the capital turnover tax; depreciation payments; payments to the social security fund; receipts from property and personal state insurances; taxes and collections from the population; incomes and receipts from foreign economic operations; etc. All these incomes arise in the process of the distribution and redistribution of the social product and the national income of the country. Changes in the structure of the financial resources reflect the general process of the intensification of the economy, a constant increase in its size, and the changing sectoral proportions of social production.

A leading place in the financial resources of the national economy of the USSR belongs to profit which in the present five-year period will amount to 720 billion roubles, a 40% increase over comparable preceding figures. The growth in profit is to be assured principally through an increased volume and reduced costs of production. The capital turnover tax, another major resource of the state, is also to increase by 40% in the eleventh five-year period.

Changes will occur in the structure of tax receipts from incomes by individual industries, with the share of tax receipts from associations and enterprises of heavy industry increasing and that of the light and food industries decreasing.

The size and share of the depreciation payments fund, another major source, will undergo a notable change. In the present five-year period, the national economy's depreciation fund is planned at 439 billion roubles, and its share in the financial resources in 1985 will reach 17.4% compared to 15.5% in 1980.

The centralized fund composed of payments to the state-run property and personal insurance intended to carry out measures to prevent natural disasters and accidents, to make good damages and losses sustained by economic or other entities, as well as to repay insurance premiums under contracts concluded by citizens under various insurance schemes will, between 1981 and 1985, amount to 65 billion roubles, 17.3 billion roubles, or 36.2% more than during the previous five years.

The financial resources of the state come also from social security payments of associations, enterprises and organizations. The role of receipts from taxes on individuals is limited: in 1985, receipts of personal income taxes will amount to only 5.5% of the total volume of the financial resources, and their share will decrease compared to 1980.

The financial resources are created both in a centralized and decentralized manner. Thus, the financial resources of the state, the fund of budget means, of the state social security, of property and personal insurance, etc., are formed in a centralized manner. The financial resources of the associations, enterprises and organizations, which include part of the profit kept by the economic entities, the depreciation fund used as a source for financing overhauls and complete restoration of capital goods, the economic incentives funds and others are basically formed in a decentralized manner.

The size of the centralized and the decentralized financial resources and their optimum ratio are determined on the basis of the plans for the country's economic and social development. The bulk of the financial means is concentrated in the hands of the state. Thus, between 1976 and 1980, 65.9% of all the financial resources was accumulated in the state budget of the USSR. The remainder was used directly by enterprises, associations, and organizations for the development of production and economic incentives.

III. Participation of Finances in Expanded Reproduction

The process of expanded socialist reproduction in the USSR proceeds with the active participation of finances whose utilization makes it possible to assure increases in the country's economic might, a proportionate development of economic sectors, continuous and high, stable rates of economic growth, as well as changes in the structure of society's production.

Both the finances of associations, enterprises and economic sectors, and the overall national finances principally representing the means of the state budget exert an impact on the processes of production, distribution and utilization of the social product and the national income.

In the present five-year period, the finances to assure expanded reproduction will increase. Over 1,600 billions roubles from all sources are allocated to develop the national economy. This includes 870 billion for the development of industry as against 690 billion during the preceding five years. The means will be used to expand and improve the material and technological base of production, and to increase output.

A significant part of the financial resources is channelled into the development of heavy industry which is the foundation of the socialist economy. Investments in heavy industry will increase by 30% over the tenth five-year period. Large financial resources are being directed into implementing the long-term, purpose-oriented fuel and energy program.

During the eleventh five-year period, increased financial resources are provided for developing the progressive sectors of production to assure speedier scientific and technological growth, to bring about the saving of labor and to intensify production. Between 1981 and 1985, over 720 billion roubles will be channelled into creating and developing the agro-industrial complex in connection with the elaboration of the food program of the USSR and other goals.

In the present five-year period, the budget will have an increased role in assuring expanded reproduction through a more rational distribution, redistribution, and utilization of the financial resources among economic sectors, economic regions and Republics for the development of the country's productive forces. The budget's participation will increase in coordinating the financial plans of the individual sectors of the national economy, the credit and lending plans, as well as in identifying internal economic resources and strengthening the financial control over the economic performance of associations, enterprises, and ministries.

IV. The Influence of Finances in Enhancing the Effectiveness of Society's Production

The important role of finances in raising the effectiveness of society's production is reflected in the growth of national and net income in the form of profits and capital turnover taxes. Between 1970 and 1980, the USSR's national income increased by 55%.

The growth of national and net income will be assured by the intensification of production, the acceleration of scientific and technological growth, the growth in labor productivity, the reduction of production and turnover costs, improvements in product quality, utilization of the capital goods and operating capital, etc. Net income will increase to 1,280 billion roubles during the five years, more than 23% over the past five years.

Finances will facilitate a more effective utilization of the production and technological potential of the country to increase national income on the basis of comprehensive programs designed to resolve major scientific and technological, economic and social problems within the framework of a single national plan.

Above all, the financial resources are directed into improvement of the technical equipment of labor, the accelerated mechanization and automation of production processes, the development and introduction of radically new machines and progressive technologies, which will increase the output of machines and lead to the creation of efficient large-scale assemblies of highly-economical equipment, etc. All these will make it possible to reequip all sectors of the national economy with highly-efficient machinery, to increase the energy-to-man ratio by 34% in industry and 45% in agriculture. The scientific and technological progress calls for significant spending on the pursuit of fundamental and applied research. Under the present five-year plan, a total of over 120 billion roubles is to be spent on research.

An increased impact of finances on the acceleration of technological progress will come with the transition of the research, designing scientific production associations and others to a cost accounting system in organizing their research and development work of creating and commissioning new machinery on the basis of contracts. In the five-year plans, the volume of work in research and development (with a yearly phasing) is mostly planned as percentage of the net output. These norms are differentiated by industrial ministries.

A single fund for the development of science and technology has been set up in all ministries in order to utilize more efficiently the financial means for research and development activities and in order to link more closely the amount of financial resources allocated for new machinery. The resources for this fund come mainly from planned profits of the scientific production, of industrial associations, and of research organizations.

Finances have been increasingly used to raise the effectiveness of production through a comprehensive system of measures for saving material, labor, and financial resources. Implementation of these measures will make it possible to save during the present five years 205 million tons of fuel equivalent, 8.5 million tons of ferrous rolled metal, and other material resources.

Improvement of product quality is one of the main sources of saving labor and assuring growth of its productivity, saving material resources and capital investments and enhancing the effectiveness of production. The impact of finances on raising product quality will be increased through a broader application of "encouragement" additions to the wholesale price of new highly effective products of industrial and technological destination corresponding to the best national and foreign standards, and through discounts in the wholesale prices of second-category products down to half of the profits from their marketing.

In raising the efficiency of socialist production, the role of the material and moral incentives is increased. The new five-year plan provides for a better procedure in the formation and utilization of the material incentives fund, and of the funds for socio-cultural activities and housing construction. The principal indicators for the formation of the material incentives fund are: the growth of labor productivity, output of top-quality products, and implementation of the plan for the supply of products to customers in line with the agreements or contracts concluded. The resources of the material incentives fund, earned for fulfilling the main directives of the work of the associations and enterprises, come from profits according to norms established.

The increased effectiveness of society's production in the eleventh five-year period will be assisted by a restructuring of the economic mechanism to accomodate the goals set by the 26th CPSU Congress for the national economy of the USSR. This calls for a better scientific substantiation of the current and long-term plans, balancing them, and gearing the system of indicators to the final national economic performances and the interests of the consumers; a more intelligent utilization of the financial levers, cost-accounting, system of labor remuneration, prices and economic incentives, introduction of stable (five-year) norms governing payments for funds, of a normative method for profit distribution, formation of the wages fund and material incentives funds; and, finally, improving the organizational structure of management in all the sectors of the national economy. In keeping with, and on the basis of, these measures, the financial mechanism will be improved.

It is clear that the upgrading of the role of finances in a socialist economy is not only concerned with the steady growth of the amount of financial resources—though the fact in itself is of importance—but also with the strengthening of the impact of the financial mechanism in developing the socialist economy and raising its effectiveness. The degree and the effectiveness of this impact are largely determined by the degree of the development of the financial mechanism, the quality of the financial planning and by the effectiveness of the financial instruments and levers. The financial mechanism of the socialist economy is constantly developing and improving, as it adjusts to the new conditions and tasks of the development of the socialist economy. Speaking about the present stage, one can point out that the principal direction in improving the financial mechanism lies in strengthening its impact in terms of intensification of the economy. The process proceeds along several lines. To mention the most important of them:

— first, the very process of financial planning is improving;
— second, the system of the relationships of the state enterprises with the budget in the field of distribution and centralization of incomes is undergoing a transformation;
— third, the impact of the financial levers on a better utilization of the material labor and financial resources is increasing.

The improvement of financial planning is reflected in the upgrading of long-term financial planning. At present, financial plans at all levels are worked out for five-year periods with an annual phasing. This is a qualitatively new stage in financial planning, since previously its planning was confined, as a rule, to an annual-plan framework.

Significant changes are being introduced into the system of relationships between the enterprises and the state budget. The main thing here is that these relations are arranged on the principle of the so-called normative distribution of profit.

Using this method, ministries and enterprises are assigned in advance, in the plan, a share which goes towards financing their own needs: the development of production, science and technology, and the establishment of the necessary incentive funds. The remainder goes into the budget. In addition, in order to enhance the responsibility of the ministries and enterprises toward the budget, they are obligated to guarantee the amount of their contribution to the budget.

Such a method creates on the one hand conditions for broadening the independence of ministries and enterprises in the use of financial resources, and on the other increases their responsibility vis-a-vis the state to honor their financial commitments.

Finally, the third trend lies in the fact that such financial instruments and levers undergo broader development which directly induce a better utilization of production, labor, material and financial resources available to the enterprise. This is reflected in the fact that enterpries make purpose-oriented payments into the budget whose size depends on their resources. Such payments include: payments for production funds and those for water. These payments are arranged so as to stimulate a better utilization of the production and water resources and thus to assure their rational utilization.

V. The Role of Finances in Resolving the Social Program

Finances actively contribute to implement the social program of the development of society, and to raise the well-being of the Soviet people.

The main source of meeting the material and cultural needs of the members of the socialist society is the national income. The share of the consumption fund in the national income will increase from 75.3% in 1980 to 78% in 1985.

Finances are instrumental in forming and utilizing the funds for the remuneration of labor, material incentives and public consumption.

The decisions of the 26th CPSU Congress set the task to assure in the coming five-year period a further growth in the well-being of the Soviet people on the basis of a stable and steady development of the national economy and its increased effectiveness. The average annual wages of factory and office workers will go up 14.5% during the five years, while remuneration of collective farmers for work on the collective farm by 20%.

In the eleventh five-year period, the material incentives funds will increase, and their formation will depend more on improved quality indicators. Their growth will also be influenced by increasing the fund for factory and office workers' wages.

The role of the public consumption funds in carrying out the social program of the Soviet people is being upgraded. The fringe benefits accruing from those funds will, during the five years, amount to 664 billion roubles, 137 billion more than in the previous five years. Ninety percent of payments and fringe benefits will come directly from the budget. The public consumption funds are to be used to finance activities in health, education, culture, and social security. Thus, during the five years, spending on health-care and recreation for the Soviet people will amount to 193 billion roubles, and on education 199 billion.

The well-being of the Soviet people is being improved by the implementation of the housing program. 530 million sq.m. of housing area are being commissioned. From all the sources, including the budget, over 93 billion roubles will be channelled into housing construction.

The improved material position of the working people is also shown by the growing volume of individual saving-deposits. Between 1970 and 1980, the total amount of deposits increased from 46.6 billion to 156.5 billion roubles, or almost 3.4 times. The average size of the deposit has almost doubled. In the eleventh five-year period a further growth of individual deposits is expected.

Implementation of the social program charted will permit a substantial improvement in the well-being of the Soviet people, and finances will play an increasing role in tackling this noble task.

VI. Summary

The determining aspect in an overall appraisal of all financial issues is the planned nature of the socialist economy. The planning system of the USSR has constantly developed, and continues to develop, as conditions and tasks of the economy change.

The present stage of development of the Soviet economy is characterized by an enhanced role of finances in planned economic management. This is basically the consequence of the substantial increase of the financial resources and the need to implement large-scale socio-economic and scientific and technological programs calling for large individual financial inputs.

It is also due to the growing role of finances in the realization of expanded socialist reproduction. The role of finances in raising the effectiveness of social production and strengthening the process of its intensification is increasing, as is their role in the balanced economic development and in solving the evolution of social programs of socialist society.

This paper presents some new figures which characterize the volume of financial resources of the USSR necessary for the development of industry, agriculture, and other sectors of the national economy, and to meet the material and cultural needs of members of the socialist society.

The main consideration of this paper is devoted to the question of improvement of the financial levers and instruments in the system of economic mechanisms. The most important trends in that improvement are: ameliorating the process of financial planning; transforming the system of the relationships of the state enterprises with the budget in the field of distribution and centralization of incomes; increasing the impact of the financial levers to better utilize the material, labor, and financial resources.

Résumé

La planification est l'élément déterminant de toute appréciation globale de tous les problèmes financiers d'une économie socialiste.

Le système planifié de l'U.R.S.S. s'est constamment développé et continue à se développer alors que les conditions et les tâches de l'économie changent.

Le stade de développement actuel de l'économie soviétique se caractérise par un rôle accru des finances dans une gestion économique planifiée. Celà résulte principalement d'une augmentation substantielle des ressources financières et de programmes sociaux-économiques, scientifiques et technologiques de grande envergure qui nécessitent de larges ressources financières. Cela est dû assi au rôle croissant des finances dans la mise en oeuvre des investissements nécessaires à une économie socialiste en croissance. On assiste à l'accroissement du rôle des finances pour augmenter l'efficacité de la production sociale et renforcer le processus de son intensification, ainsi que pour assurer un développement économique équilibré et résoudre l'évolution de programmes sociaux dans une société socialiste.

Cet article présente de nouvelles statistiques qui montrent le volume des ressources financières de l'U.R.S.S. nécessaires au développement de l'industrie, de l'agriculture et d'autres secteurs de l'économie nationale, et aux besions matériels et culturels des membres de la société socialiste.

L'étude principale de cet article est consacrée à la question de l'amélioration des leviers et instruments financiers dans le système des mécanismes économiques. Les moyens les plus importants pour cette amélioration sont: améliorer le processus de planification financière; transformer le système des relations des entreprises publiques avec le budget dans le domaine de la distribution et de la centralisation des revenus; accroître de façon plus efficace les leviers financiers dans l'utilisation du matériel, de la main-d'oeuvre et des ressources financières.

The Quest for Efficiency in the Public Sector: Economists Versus Dr. Pangloss

(or why conservative economists are not nearly conservative enough)

Anthony J. Culyer

The end of a Congress is not the place for heavy arguments and it is no part of my intention today to overload you with weighty reflections on what has passed during the last few days, nor indeed to burden your already taxed intellects with new theories or new facts about anything at all. The end of a congress may, however, be an appropriate place to amuse, titillate or irritate. I shall try to irritate you—possibly I shall raise a wry smile or two but basically I want to annoy. I shall try to do so by putting a set of dilemmas to you, each of which will, I hope, make you thoroughly uncomfortable.

As economists, we all—or nearly all—subscribe to the fundamental postulate of human action that individuals are expected utility maximisers. This, coupled with the assumption that individual tastes vary and the further assumption that compensated demand curves have negative price elasticities, leads to nearly all the important propositions that economists have to make about the real world—whether they are being normative or positive (or simply fudging the difference between the two). For example, the positive theory of exchange uses the assumptions I have just mentioned to predict that there will be only one price for each economic good. Any variance in prices will be explained by the presence of transaction, transport, etc costs. Since these are real social costs, we do not consider such a situation as a market failure. On the contrary, the market is doing just the job it should. How does this happen? It happens because prior decisions have also been taken about the market institutions that enable trade to take place: the definition and enforcement of private property entitlements, the law of contract, conventional ideas of decent behavior, and so on. These institutional arrangements can similarly be seen as the product of individual

Public Finance and the Quest for Efficiency. Proceedings of the 38th Congress of the International Institute of Public Finance. Copenhagen, 1982, pp. 39–48. Copyright © 1984 by Wayne State University Press, Detroit, Michigan, 48202.

maximisation and bargaining: private property rights, for example, will not be established when the expectation is that enforcement costs, etc. will exceed the gains from trade and the orderly conduct of affairs. Put less strongly, individuals will not choose to change existing arrangements unless those seeing a benefit therefrom can also compensate those who anticipate a loss. It is, therefore, not just our theory of processes *within* markets that depends on utility maximising subject to constraints; it is our theories of political action, family behaviour, public or private bureaucracy, and our theories of the choice of allocative institution (market or state) that also depend on the same behaviour-generating postulate.

Economic efficiency or, as it is sometimes called, Pareto-efficiency (the two terms are synonymous), is defined as an arrangement from which no change can be made that does not impose uncompensated harms on someone. This is indeed our only concept of full efficiency. It does not incidentally imply *consumer* sovereignty, but the sovereignty of *all* individuals. It therefore follows, I suggest, that, since at any moment in time our positive theory of exchange tells us that all genuine gains from trade will have been exhausted, then at every moment of time there will be an *efficient* allocation of resources. This will be true of gains from deals done *within* a constitutional and institutional context and it is also true of the chosen (or existing) constitutional and institutional context itself. It is true of so-called market activities. It is true also of nonmarket activities. It is also true of public sector activities. For were it not so, and unexploited net social gains existed, then it cannot be the case that individuals are expected utility maximisers. They may, of course, regret consequences they did not foresee. But, at the time, what *was*, was *efficient*. They may also, of course, regard the constitutional context as unfair, unfree or unjust, so that, for example, the powerless and poor have no means to bribe the powerful and rich. But that is a question of distribution, not efficiency. To be logically consistent, then, we must, I suggest, accept that at any moment in time all is for the best (efficiency wise) otherwise it would have paid someone to incur costs persuading others to agree to change it, to incur costs identifying and compensating those who lose, to incur costs of enforcing any contracts thus made. Turning specifically to the topic of our congress, it follows therefore, that the public sector too is always efficient. And so it appears that the quest for efficiency in the public sector is an *empty* quest—not because the public sector can *never*, *inherently*, be efficient (as some of us seem to have argued here), but because it is *always* efficient. Economists must therefore be Panglossians. The size, scope and composition of the public sector in all countries must represent an economically efficient allocation. And that has to be as true of the USSR as it must be of HongKong.

I am not, of course, suggesting that all—or even most—institutional changes that do take place are Pareto-efficient moves. They nearly always involve uncompensated harms and may even result in a less efficient resultant state of affairs. But it does not follow that putting the change into reverse will necessarily improve things, for the reverse change is itself costly (it may even be more costly than the original change) and meanwhile society may well have changed in important ways not previously accounted for. So there is an assymetry here: absence of change, according to Dr. Pangloss, implies that all is for the best; the presence of change *may* but only "may" imply that things are going to be for the better.

Recall the words that Voltaire put into Dr. Pangloss' mouth:

"Il est démontré, disait-il, que les choses ne peuvent être autrement; car tout étant fait pour une fin, tout est nécessairement pour la meilleure fin. Remarquez bien que les nez ont été faits pour porter des lunettes; aussi avons-nous des lunettes. Les jambes sont visiblement instituées pour être chaussées, et nous avons des chausses. . . . par conséquent, ceux qui ont avancé que tout est bien ont dit une sottise; il fallait dire que tout est au mieux."

Also sprach Dr. Pangloss; and while few economists subscribe to so all-pervading an optimism about the current state of any society, many—especially good price theorists—are indeed prone to the view that the theory of exchange implies—at least as far as *efficiency* is concerned—that things actually are for the best and that the private sector (or for that matter, though few price theorists would ever say as much, the public sector) is at all times and in all places Pareto-efficient. After all, were it not, it would have been changed: gainers would have bribed losers from any change in the composition, scale or organisation of the public (or private) sector, or in the balance between public and private, and Pareto-efficient moves to Pareto-efficient states would be made. If they are not, so the argument will go, then all must be for the best (really one should, of course, say *a* best), for the costs of making the change, of overcoming inertias, bribing bureaucrats, or meeting whatever other transaction costs might exist, must—as evidenced by behavior—be too large or too uncertain relative to benefits (which may themselves also of course be too uncertain).

You might object that the means available to a society for effecting change are needlessly cumbersome, costly and imperfect and that they lead to extremely poor revelations of people's preferences. But, as I have argued, the same Panglossian argument applies here too: even constitutional and institutional changes are costly; and to ignore such costs is to advocate Pareto-inefficient constitutions and institutions. Absence of constitutional or institutional change, or of any change in the procedures by which decisions are reached, is behavioral evidence for their efficiency whether the society in question is best characterised as feudal, capitalist, socialist, or anything else. Optimal institutional structures and optimal preference revelation are not going to be *perfect*, for an efficient constitutional and institutional arrangement will normally entail the presence of residual costs of decision making, bargaining and transacting in the everyday world. These are genuine opportunity costs like any other opportunity cost. Most conservative economists are therefore far too radical: their presumption that merely the market is efficient is not enough. The public sector is efficient too. The political system is efficient. *Everything* is efficient. Everything is wonderful!

Economists are naturally unhappy with Dr. Pangloss' conservatism and nonscientific tautology, whether on social or methodological grounds, or both. Candide too had his doubts. Yet it does have one signal virtue of a methodological type: in trying to account for the social phenomena we observe it compels us to ask the question "why does something happen or why does a particular arrangement exist—it has to be efficient for *something* or *someone?*": a question that has led to remarkable developments in the positive economics of politics, bureaucracy, the family and a host of untraditional spheres for the application of economic analysis. Moreover, to cast the Panglossian view aside does seem to require one to ignore (that is treat as zero) *some* social costs (in particular, transaction costs) and hence involve one in the fallacy of the free lunch—again an anathema to all good price theorists. How then can we escape? For it looks as though we economists are all—and always have been—redundant as moralists, welfarists and experts in the means of enhancing efficiency.

Escaping Dr. Pangloss' Clutches—Conservative Radical Style

One time-honoured manner of escape from the enchantments of Dr. Pangloss is to retain (conservatively) the individualistic postulates as both the underpinnings of behavioural models and the ideological basis for identifying "welfare" and changes in it, and to seek to promote change (perhaps radically) through *persuasion*. This view is founded on the proposition that economists know some things better than others know them; in particular, that economists have a comparative advantage in identifying Pareto-efficient states and Pareto-efficient moves. The possibility is thereby opened up that absence of change is not itself evident of the efficiency of the current state of things; it is merely the result of failure of gainers (and losers) to perceive the net advantages of change and also to devise appropriate means of ensuring the acceptability of any change. How many cost-benefit analyses of public sector activity, for example, press beyond the computation of net benefits to the detailed identification of losers from the change, the size of their losses, and means by which they may be compensated sufficiently to accept the change? (It must be said that all too frequently even economists fail to address themselves to this second type of question which accounts, I conjecture, for the failure of so many results of cost-benefit analysis to have been acted upon).

Into this category of persuasion falls an immense range of economic policy advice: marginal cost pricing for nationalised industry; vouchers for education; redistribution in cash rather than kind; removal of price controls; reliance on markets for resource allocation. Intellectual activity here consists in the invention, reinvention, or resurrection of policy means that are alleged to lead to improved efficiency in the public (or private) sector, where the means proposed may be rules, mechanisms or behavioural constraints. Yet, while economists may succeed in persuading one another of the value of such things (or at least suceed in persuading fellow-members of a particular school of economics) they often fail dismally to persuade anyone else.

One set of reasons for this may, of course, be that efficiency is but one of the moral objectives that societies should seek and that it may conflict with others. But, even in the quest for efficiency itself, it may be that economists are giving unpersuasive advice. Efficient pricing rules, for example, are not only subject to the problems of second best, there are a set of even more fundamental issues relating, as our former president Jack Wiseman has so often told us, to the very notion of opportunity cost: in particular its evanescent and subjective nature as the perception of the most highly valued alternative course of action at the moment of decision in a highly uncertain world.

Or consider the application of a fundamental theorem of welfare economics that, provided certain conditions were met, a market will not only produce a Pareto-efficient allocation but, provided the government can determine an appropriate distribution of purchasing power in the community, it can even produce a Pareto-efficient allocation that the government may prefer on distributional grounds. This argument is not, of course, based on any Panglossian considerations.

We know that the circumstances required for this fundamental theorem to hold are extremely demanding and are not in practice met. Nonetheless, entire armies of economists devote their attention to trying to persuade the community that efficiency would be enhanced by returning substantial areas of the public sector to the market place. This sometimes involves going to quite extraordinary lengths. For example, I can think of no society that even *approximates* the formal theoretical conditions for Pareto-efficiency in its health service markets, yet this has not inhibited many economists on the one hand from attributing all the apparent ills of our health services to the interference of the state nor, on the other, from confidently predicting substantial welfare improvements from effecting such a shift. The truth is that in health, as in many other areas, we do not know enough to advocate sweeping reforms based on general theories asserted to be true under only highly restrictive circumstances. At least Dr. Pangloss was *modest* in his policy recommendations (indeed one could scarcely be more modest!) whereas our reformers, whether of the left or the right, typically erect more policy edifices than theory or evidence can usually support.

Or take, alternatively, the widespread arguments one hears about the *behavioural* response of managers, bureaucrats, producers and consumers to changes in the constraints they confront. Much of this literature asserts that public sector management and bureaucracy will be less efficient than management and bureaucracy in the private sector. At their naivest, those who recommend policy based upon such theorising fall into the trap of assuming that the *only* efficiency-generating source of behaviour is the pursuit of wealth, which must surely be one of the naivest—not to say amateur—psychological theories around. Even at their more sophisticated the new theories of managerial, bureaucratic and political behaviour are still too infant and too little exposed to systematic empirical test for us to assert their logical implications as empirically well-founded and for us really to be able to assert their beneficence as confidently as some do.

As it happens I *do* believe that economists have a comparative advantage in the invention, reinvention and resurrection of policy instruments that may identify newly perceived opportunities for increased efficiency. But I would conjecture that we are most valid when we are empirically most specific and most persuasive when we are most modest in the extent of change proposed. The bold claims from right or left for the efficiency of markets or collectivism are simply not persuasively sustainable.

Escaping Dr. Pangloss' Clutches—Radical Radical Style

The other time-honoured manner of escape for those still wanting to be normative is to be radical both about the basic postulates as well as about the promotion of social change. For example, one may reject the essentially static concept of Pareto-efficiency. Instead one may advocate competition as an agent of efficiency via the process of discovery and invention. This particularly German/Austrian way of looking at things emphasises process (and progress) so that efficiency is, as it were, a *process of becoming* rather than a *state* that can be usefully described in terms of the familiar marginal conditions (even if they include uncertainty, externality and intertemporal trading).

It is not clear to me, however, that "competition" is so easily measured that one can say that it is "more" here and "less" there (is a race between 500 more competitive than one between two?), nor is it clear to me that the types of competition observed in the public sector are systematically more or less conducive to dynamic efficiency than those observed in, say, the tomato market. Moreover, although I am ignorant of any applications of this sort of analysis to specific problems in the public sector (they doubtless exist), I am quite confident that such applications are neither so numerous nor their empirical results so widely accepted in the economics fraternity that they can escape the difficulty noted above with the static theories of managerial, bureaucratic and political behaviour. They may be promising beginnings, but they are scarcely an adequate basis for persuasive and specific policy advice. Indeed, all the arguments with which I am familiar in this genre are entirely *a priori* and disturbingly general. They may be the intellectual stuff of which revolutions get made but they offer little assistance in the quest for efficiency in the public sector (or any other). Revolutions, of course, are omelettes made by breaking eggs and have nothing to do with economic efficiency.

An alternative escape route is to question the maximand. The traditional individualistic framework provides both the basis for the utility maximising analysis of behaviour (whether in groups or individually) and also the basis for the social welfare function: the rockets of both positive and normative economics are fired from the same launching pad. It is, therefore, unsurprising that Dr. Pangloss poses a problem mainly for economists who use neoclassical individualism as their *modus operandi*. But for those who adopt more proximate maximands, say, a target for steel output, or who view the business of health services as increasing the health of populations, or the business of schools as keeping teachers in employment, the problem disappears. Similarly, those enamoured of a "merit want" approach to many of the activities in the public sector (particularly, perhaps, those in the social services—including health, education and housing) cut the Panglossian knot with a single bold sweep of a sword. It is not surprising, of course, that economists who adopt this strategy attract the contempt of the methodological individualists. But they do (at least) have the virtue of using a methodology that gets them decisively out of Dr. Pangloss' clutches and that, moreover, enables them to relate much more easily to policy customers unencumbered with one awkward—and hard to communicate— part of the utilitarian baggage of neoclassicism.

Should We Take Dr. Pangloss Seriously?

I think we should. It is common to label *prima facie* departures from Pareto-efficiency in the market as "market failures". Setting aside adverse distributional affects (which may be important, but are not directly relevant to efficiency questions) the usual sources of failure that are adduced include phenomena like monopoly (natural or otherwise), externalities, and failure to establish and enforce exchangeable property rights. Source of "government failure" can be similarly categorised. The standard microeconomic approach to such issues is to identify potential efficiency gains. We do not assert that the optimal degree of pollution is necessarily zero, but that it is determined by an equality between the marginal benefit of reduced pollution and the marginal cost of effecting a reduction. We do not assert that all monopoly must be prohibited, but contrast, say, the loss of scale economies that may be incurred by breaking monopolies with the net gains in consumer and producer surplusses that may result. We do not assert that all entitlements and contracts should be clearly defined in law, be legally binding and coercively enforced, but balance expected gains against prospective costs of enforcement, etc.

An economic Dr. Pangloss does therefore have a point. For if all individuals are utility maximisers, and if we believe in the theory of exchange, and if Pareto-efficiency is defined as an allocation from which no move can be made without imposing an uncompensated reduction in utility somewhere in the community, then all costs and benefits will have been considered. Trades not made; monopolies not broken; institutions not invented and used; voting systems not used; collective or individual arrangements not adopted; points not attained on contract curves; and so on, must all have not been engaged in or attained because they were judged too costly. Market, or government, failure, according to Dr. Pangloss, is *apparent* not real: it is the product of imperfectly specified optimality conditions, in particular, conditions that omit some relevant marginal (or total) social costs.

It is surprising that economists have not taken Dr. Pangloss more seriously. I detect—though it would be invidious to name names—that economists using methodological individualism who come from market economies tend *implicitly* to adopt a Panglossian view of the *market*. But scarcely anyone takes this view of the public sector. Instead, there is an assymetry: market allocations are presumptively efficient and public sector allocations presumptively inefficient. This leads to an assymetry in the locations of burdens of proof: economists advocating, for example, a transfer of activity from the private to the public sector are required to demonstrate the *a priori* and empirical reasons for so doing (there being no general presumption that such a transfer of activity will yield a Pareto-improvement). By contrast, economists advocating a transfer of activity from the public sector to the private are rarely required by their fellow professionals to do other than rehearse some general *a priori* arguments (for in this case there is a shared presumption about the Pareto-efficiency of such a transfer of activity). Of course, outside the economics fraternity no such presumptions may exist.

What I should like to suggest is that we should take Dr. Pangloss more seriously and argue that the burden of proof lies on him who advocates *any* change; that the general presumption is that *whatever* is, is Pareto-efficient; at its weakest, that the quest for efficiency in the public sector is neither more nor less problematic than the quest for efficiency in the private sector.

For those who are uncomfortable with the Darwinian and conservative implications of Panglossian methodology, there seem to be four tenable escape routes, of which two have been described. The first is to argue that the economist's role in the quest for efficiency is entrepreneurial: the invention, reinvention or resurrection of allocative mechanisms; and the provision of information about the incidence of the costs of change and how such losses may be compensated—at least for those with sufficient political power to sabotage any reform. The test of their success in identifying potential Pareto improvements is whether their entrepreneurial inventions get adopted. And they have no business to complain when their inventions are rejected, for when they *are* rejected, the inventions were plainly failures. Since economic advice is nearly always rejected, this is an unpromising escape route. The second escape route is to reject the individualistic basis of the concept of Pareto-efficiency in favour of more limited and specific objectives possibly linked with a specific recognition that one is seeking least cost methods of meeting particular levels of merit wants. Since nearly everyone disapproves of the merit good approach, this too is an unpromising escape route. I leave it to each of you to select your own route from these two unpromising prospects.

There are, however, the other two escape routes—though I doubt whether any of you will find them even as appealing as the previous two (which is why I have given them no attention hitherto):

One is to argue that most of what economists deplore in the public sector is the result of mistakes: collective policies were originally adopted in high expectation of success and were even, perhaps, Pareto-efficient in terms of expected utility. But the hopes are dashed and economists pursuing the quest for public sector efficiency are there to document the failure, explain why it occurred and show how to avoid it in the future. The trouble with this view is that the so-called mistakes seem to persist beyond any reasonable learning period. For example, what public regulatory policy has been more consistently decried by economists for at least 50 years than rent controls. There are dozens of articles allegedly demonstrating their inefficiency. They are a classic case study in nearly every textbook. Moreover they have also been demonstrated to have regressive distributive consequences. I cannot think of a single economic voice in their support. Yet rent controls persist and they persist in nearly every developed country in the world. Yet if they were *really* inefficient, their removal would have enabled a net gain to accrue to everyone, landlords and tenants. Ergo, they are either efficient or individuals are not utility maximisers. So, while mistakes may happen from time to time there is something in the Panglossian view that they do not happen very often. There seems little mileage in this way out.

The final escape route is simply to *ignore* the basic problem of inconsistency to which Pangloss is really drawing our attention. After all, we have got along for many years with the inconsistencies between, say, macroeconomics and microeconomics. One could simply sweep the problem under the carpet. However, I don't think this is a route many of you would choose, for even if an ultimately completely consistent economic theory of human action can never be attained, we are surely bound to seek it. Whether we are going to be Panglossian or anti-Panglossian we should at least seek consistency, for Dr. Pangloss is surely right in drawing our attention to the inconsistencies in much current practice: whether it be the inconsistency of accounting for some opportunity costs but not all; or the inconsistency of assuming that individuals simultaneously realise all achievable mutual gains from trade while leaving some unexploited; or the inconsistency of assuming that individuals choose rationally *within* institutional contexts but choose their institutions irrationally; or the inconsistency of having differential presumptions about the degree of efficiency in the public sector relative to the private. Inconsistency is a great enemy. As Voltaire would have said (though not, I think, of inconsistency) *Ecr. l'inf!*

Resumé

Le Docteur PANGLOSS soutient que, puisque tous les individus maximisent toujours l'utilité attendue, tous les gains que l'on attend du commerce sont réalisés ex-ante, sous réserve de toutes les contraintes de caractère réel. De plus il soutient que toutes les institutions mises en place par les collectivités pour des transactions d'affaires connaîtront le maximum d'efficacité souhaitée étant entendu aussi qu'elles sont soumises aux contraintes inhérentes aux ressources naturelles et qu'elles savent que les individus maximiseront l'utilité qu'ils en attendent quel que soit le système de réglementation et d'institutions que l'on adopte. En conséquence, tout est toujours pour le mieux, ex-ante, et il n'y a pas de place pour des économistes réformateurs qui chercheraient par exemple à changer l'équilibre entre secteurs publics et privés pour des raisons d'efficacité. Mais ont-ils vraiment une place après tout? Nous suggérons quatre possibilités restreintes qui semblent être consistantes avec la logique à la fois constante et pénible du Docteur Pangloss.

THE DEMAND OF
GOVERNMENT ACTIVITIES

Economics of Representative Democracy: A Model of Skewed Representation*

Hirofumi Shibata

Introduction

For many minds, including those of some of the most esteemed scholars of our age, a democracy operates on the basis of majority control of public decisions, and, therefore, it works, they speculate, to benefit the majority of voters. Anthony Downs, in his justly famous *An Economic Theory of Democracy* (1957) noted that in a democracy the poor are able to use their large number of votes to obtain a transfer of wealth from the rest of society (pp. 198–201). Also well-known is the so-called Director's law, which states that the power of the median-income voter in a democracy causes a redistribution of wealth from both extremes of the income distribution toward the median (Stigler, 1970; Tullock, 1971). These authors differ in their identification of the majority, but both take for granted the ability of the majority to exploit the political machine for their benefit.

Nevertheless, observed phenomena do not seem to bear out the assumed ability of a majority. A case in point is the 1978 passage of Proposition 13 in California, in which a group of citizens supporting the tax limitation movement successfully imposed, through a referendum, limits on local taxes and expenditures. If public-sector decisions in the legislature represent the preference of the majority, one would not expect a proposal to restrict taxation and expenditures to receive majority support from voters. The California outcome turned out not to be an isolated anomaly. Tax limitation movements spread quickly though the United States; limits

* I wish to acknowledge the most helpful comments given on earlier drafts of this paper by the members of the public economics workshop of National Institute of Public Finance, Tokyo, Japan, Professors Harvey Leibenstein of Harvard, Cambridge, U.S.A, Jürgen Müller of Deutsches Institut für Wirtschaftsforschung, Berlin, F.R.G., Gilberto Muraro of University of Venice, Italy, and Horst Hanusch of University of Augsburg, F.R.G.

Public Finance and the Quest for Efficiency. Proceedings of the 38th Congress of the International Institute of Public Finance. Copenhagen, 1982, pp. 51–67. Copyright © 1984 by Wayne State University Press, Detroit, Michigan, 48202.

were imposed on local taxes and expenditures in localities of nearly half of the states, and state expenditures and revenues were restricted in nine states.[1] The movement even crossed the Pacific Ocean to Japan, where tax revolt is now evident. Many Japanese wage earners feel discriminated against as compared with a relatively small group of independent entrepreneurs such as merchants and farmers and are demanding redress of their tax status.

Some observers express the nagging suspicion that governmental machines are in fact controlled by minorities. For example, Brennan and Buchanan (1977) assume that a few people who benefit from big spending by government control the government, and Mackay and Weaver (1978) argue that bureaucrats who formulate political agenda carefully can in fact make government work in their interest.

Democracy is, in practice, representative democracy. Yet only a few economists have paid serious attention to implications of the obvious fact that what is critical in public decision making in a representative system is the share of seats in the assembly of representatives rather than the share of popular votes. Also ignored by some is the fact that arrangements in a representative democracy for translating votes into legislative seats are often not proportional.[2] Usually, territorially defined electoral districts translate voting returns into a distribution of legislative seats. Even when the number of voters per legislative seat is identical among all electoral districts, if only a few representatives represent a large number of voters, a function that maps the share of voting returns of a particular group onto the share of legislative seats representing their interest will not be single valued. The size of possible bias between the share of legislative seats representing a particular interest group and the share of votes controlled by that group increases as the number of seats allotted per district declines. Such bias creates particularly acute problems in the English and U.S. electoral system of "single-member districts," the system in which each electoral district is represented by a single representative in a parliament. The party winning a majority of the popular vote could fail to take a majority of legislative seats, while the party representing only a minority could succeed in capturing the majority of seats. In New Jersey state elections, Tufte (1973, p. 543) noted, although on the average only 39 percent of all voters voted Republican between 1926 and 1947, that party was able to control a majority of seats in the legislature during that period.

This paper analyzes first some relationships between a political group's share of votes and its share of legislative seats in a single-member district system. It will be shown that a special interest group controlling as little as one-quarter of all votes can capture a majority of the seats in the legislature. Also it will be demonstrated that the leverage a minority can exert in increasing its share of the seats in legislature is a function of the number of electoral districts.

The paper then analyzes the consequences of voters' utility maximization in a representative democracy. Any governmental program contains an income redistribution aspect, some of which can be postulated as a zero-sum game between those who benefit from and those who are hurt by enactment of a program. In a zero-sum game, the larger the number of people belonging to the losing side, the greater the benefits accruing to the winning group. This implies that the smaller the number of members in the group supporting a program which is enacted, the larger the payoffs to each member of that group. This feature of zero-sum games gives utility-maximizing voters a strong incentive to form a political coalition of the minimum size that can win an election with the help of a minority's leverage as found in a representative system. Political groups often have to take electoral law as given and are prevented from practicing gerrymandering (reapportioning electoral districts for their own benefit). The paper, however, suggests that by choosing campaign issues wisely a group can create a specific distribution of voters among different districts so as to yield maximum leverage and that the group which is most successful in this art (and therefore can promise the largest payoffs to its members) will win the election.

These considerations yield a number of testable hypotheses. Some of them are that (1) the winner of an election will invariably represent a minority group, because a minority can promise a larger payoff per member than a majority; (2) election platforms of competing political parties tend to become identical, for the minimum winning groups tend to be limited; and (3) there is a built-in bias toward the growth of government, for political parties can serve the interests of minorities better under a larger government than under a smaller.

Throughout this paper, I shall assume the following. (1) Voters wish to maximize their payoffs from tax-public-expenditure decisions, and hence they vote for the representatives who will most efficiently help them to do so. (2) A political party formulates its election platform in such a way that the policies proposed maximize the expected benefits accruing to specific groups of voters and hence mobilize special interest groups in support of the party's candidates.[3] (3) The number of voters in the community is fixed, and the voters do not migrate between electoral districts. (4) The payoff to the political party, such as the campaign contributions that it receives, is a fixed proportion of the payoffs that will accrue to the voters supporting the party's candidates if the party wins the election and succeeds in enacting the proposed policies.[4] (5) Political parties attempt to maximize their payoffs.[5] (6) The role of a representative is that of an agent acting according to the preferences of the majority of voters of the district from which he is elected.[6]

Sizes of the Minimum Winning Minorities

Two questions must be dealt with first: (1) what is the minimum ratio of minority voters to all voters that is necessary for the minority to capture, under the most favorable circumstances, the majority of the seats in the assembly of representatives, and (2) is the minimum number of votes necessary to win a group decision always smaller under an indirect than a direct democracy?

The answers to these questions are given in Propositions 1 and 2.

Proposition 1: A minority of voters can capture a majority of legislative seats in a representative system of democracy in which multiple electoral districts partition the voters into equally sized, mutually exclusive groups, each of which elects a single representative;[7] and the proportion of the votes of the minimum winning minority will approach ¼ of the total votes as the number of electoral districts and that of voters in each district increase in the absence of abstentions.[8]

Proof: Let α (≥ 1) be the smallest possible number of electoral districts in which voters in support of an issue must win in order to see the representatives supporting the issue hold a majority of legislative seats, and β (≥ 1) be the minimum number of votes required to win in a district. The total votes necessary from supporters is thus $\alpha\beta$. The maximum number of voters in the opposing group must be $\alpha(\beta - 1)$ in districts in which the group supporting the issue wins plus $(\alpha - 1)(2\beta - 1)$ in districts in which it loses. Accordingly, the minimum proportion of the winning minority's votes to all votes (m) is

$$m = \frac{\alpha\beta}{\alpha\beta + \alpha(\beta - 1) + (\alpha - 1)(2\beta - 1)} \tag{1}$$

$$= \frac{1}{1 + \dfrac{\beta - 1}{\beta} + \dfrac{\alpha - 1}{\alpha} + (\dfrac{\alpha - 1}{\alpha})(\dfrac{\beta - 1}{\beta})}$$

But because $\lim\limits_{\alpha \to \infty} (\dfrac{\alpha - 1}{\alpha}) = 1$ and $\lim\limits_{\beta \to \infty} (\dfrac{\beta - 1}{\beta}) = 1$,

$$\lim\limits_{\substack{\alpha \to \infty \\ \beta \to \infty}} m = \frac{1}{4}. \tag{Q.E.D.}$$

If a political system is based on two layers of representation, as is the case in which the electorate chooses provincial representatives who in turn elect members of the national committee whose majority vote determines the outcome of a public issue decision, the minimum number of minority voters that can capture a majority of the national committee could decline to as few as $(\frac{1}{2})^3$ or 12.5 percent of all voters.

Proposition 2: The minimum number of votes necessary to win a majority of the seats in a parliament is always smaller than the minimum number of votes necessary to win a majority of the votes under the direct democracy, assuming no abstentions and an equal number of voters in each electoral district.

Proof: We prove this proposition for the case where the number of districts and that of voters in each district are odd integers. Let R (≥ 1) and N(≥ 1) represent the number of districts each of which elects a single member of the assembly (and hence the number of representatives) and the number of electors in that political unit (a community), respectively. Obviously $N \geq R \geq 1$. We assume one man one vote and that a representative must win a majority of votes in his district to be elected.

The minimum necessary number of votes to win the majority in each district (n) is

$$n = \frac{N}{2R} + \frac{1}{2} \tag{2}$$

The minimum necessary number of votes for a minority group to win a majority of seats, denoted by M, is

$$M = (\frac{N}{2R} + \frac{1}{2})(\frac{R}{2} + \frac{1}{2})$$

or

$$M = \frac{1}{4}(N + 1) + \frac{1}{4}(R + \frac{N}{R}). \tag{3}$$

Since the first term of the left-hand side of (3) is constant, we only have to examine the value of the term in the parenthese in the second term, (R + N/R). But f(R) = R + N/R is a strictly convex function and has a value equal to (N+1) at R = 1 and R = N. Therefore, for any values of R greater than 1 and smaller than N,

$$R + \frac{N}{R} < N + 1 . \tag{4}$$

But because in a representative democracy, R is an odd integer between 1 and N,

$$M = \frac{1}{4}(N + 1 + R + \frac{N}{R}) < \frac{1}{4}(N + 1 + N + 1) = \frac{1}{2}N + \frac{1}{2} \tag{5}$$

where the value $(N/2 + 1/2)$ is the minimum number of votes necessary to win in a direct democracy, of course.[9]   (Q.E.D.)

Party Competition and the Minimum Winning Coalitions of Voters

Having shown that a representative system of democracy is liable to be exploited by a minority, I shall now argue that given utility-maximizing electors, inter-party competition for votes will force political parties to exploit this feature of the representative system.

Utility-maximizing electors are expected to cast their ballots for candidates of the party whose proposed set of policies (that is, platform) promises the largest payoffs to their votes. But the largest payoffs tend to accrue to a coalition of voters that can win the election with the smallest possible members. Hence, political parties compete for votes by attempting to organize a coalition of the smallest possible number of voters whose support is critical in capturing a majority of seats in the parliament. Of course, in most cases, geographical boundaries of electoral districts are historically determined and unalterable each election time and so-called gerrymandering is not possible. But a political party can define its campaign platform in such a way that under an existing districting, the voters expected to benefit from the party's platform constitute an overall minority but are distributed among the electoral districts in a pattern that enables them to capture the majority of legislative seats. In other words, a political party, by choosing its party platform wisely, can create a minority coalition of a size sufficient to win a majority of seats among the given electoral districts.

To show starkly the redistributive nature of a governmental tax and expenditure program and to analyze the political processes in the framework of an N-person, zero-sum game, let us assume that a governmental program works, in effect, in such a way that a given amount of tax monies collected equally from all the voters is distributed among a specific group of voters.[10] A free school lunch program financed by a poll tax is an example. Let us also assume that with respect to each single bill (or a set of bills) an election is held and in each electoral district a representative for the majroty is elected; each representative casts his vote according to the preference of the majority of voters in his electoral district; a majority of representatives of the assembly then renders the decision on each bill.

In this situation, proposal of a bill specifying the expenditure pattern and finance thereof will partition the electorate of a community into two mutually exclusive and complementary sets: one of electors benefiting from the enactment of the bill and the other of the remainder of the electors. The group of electors supporting the bill may be regarded as a coalition in support of the bill, and the remaining electors, whether bound in an alliance or not, may be regarded a single opposing coalition.

To be precise, let the community consist of a set of electors (players),

$$I = \{1, 2, 3, \ldots, N\}. \tag{6}$$

Proposal of a specific bill partitions I into two complementary subsets S and −S such that $S \cap -S = \varnothing$ and $S \cup -S = I$. Because the total number of voters, N, is finite, although the number of possible proposals is infinite, S must be one of 2^N possible patterns of coalitions, including one that consists of all the voters, I, and another that includes no voter, the null set, $\varnothing$.

Let v(S) be the payoff that S can get from passage of a bill and v( ) be a real-valued set function whose domain is the subsets of N and be referred to, following von Neumann and Morgenstern (1944), as the characteristic function. The characteristic function of a zero sum game has the following properties:

(i) $v(\varnothing) = 0$
(ii) $v(S) = -v(-S)$
(iii) $v(I) = 0$
(iv) $v(S \cup T) \geqslant v(S) + v(T)$ where $S \cap T = \varnothing$.

Let all one-person coalitions have the same characteristic value equal to −t:

$$v(\{i\}) = -t \qquad (i = 1, 2, \ldots, N). \tag{7}$$

Equation (7) is the minimum payoff that one voter would sustain under the worst condition, that is, when he is playing for himself against a coalition of all others. It may be viewed as the tax which a player must pay while receiving no benefits from the public program(s) enacted. Therefore, the maximum that any coalition of p people, S_p, where $2 < p \leqslant -2$, can lose is pt. Because of property (ii) of the zero-sum game, the maximum gain for S_p, the complement of $S_{(N-p)}$, is $t(N - p)$. Hence for $2 \leqslant p \leqslant (N - 2)$, the range of v(S) is $-pt \leqslant v(S_p) \leqslant (N - p)t$.

A tax-expenditure program that essentially redistributes evenly among the members of a coalition the tax monies collected equally from the rest corresponds to one of those which von Neumann and Morgenstern have referred to as symmetric games. The feature of a symmetric game is that all coalitions receive multiples of t, or

$$v(S_p) = \begin{cases} (N - p)t & \text{if} \quad S_p \in W \\ -pt & \text{if} \quad S_p \in L \\ 0 & \text{if} \quad S_p \in B \end{cases}, \tag{8}$$

Where W, L, and B are sets of winning, losing, and blocking coalitions, respectively. The sets W, L, and B are defined respectively as

$$W = \{S \mid v(S) > 0\}$$
$$L = \{S \mid v(S) < 0\} \tag{9}$$
$$B = \{S \mid v(S) = 0\}$$

Where $W \cap L = \varnothing$, $W \cap B = \varnothing$, $L \cap B = \varnothing$ and $W \cup L \cup B = I$. Further, if $S \in W$, $-S \in L$, and if $S \in B$, $-S \in B$. As the limiting cases, we define that $I \in W$ and $\varnothing \in L$, although $v(I)$ and $v(\varnothing)$ are zero.

Let us introduce the idea of the pro-rata gain, that is, a player's share in the value of the coalition to which he belongs, assuming that the payoff accruing to a coalition is equally divided among its members. The pro-rata gain of a coalition with p people is $v(S_p)/p$. From (8) for $S_p \in W$, we find

$$\frac{d}{dp}\left[\frac{v(S_p)}{p}\right] = \frac{d}{dp}\left[\frac{(N-p)}{p}t\right] < 0. \tag{10}$$

Hence the smaller the number of members in a coalition, the greater the pro-rata gain from the viewpoint of the members of that coalition.[11] We define

$$a = \underset{p}{\text{Max}} \, [v(S_p)/p],$$

the largest pro-rata gain which can be achieved by any coalition. If $v(S_p)/p$ = a for several values of p, one of them must be the smallest. Accordingly, we define

$$p^* = \text{Min} \, [p \mid v(S_p)/p = a]. \tag{11}$$

Obviously, however, not all positive coalitions are realizable, that is, not all of them can win the election. Let us define as the winning coalitions (W) all subsets of I with at least $N/2R + 1/2 (\equiv n)$ members in at least $R/2 + 1/2 (\equiv r)$ electoral districts, and as the minimum winning coalitions (W^m) all subsets of I with exactly n members in exactly r districts. Because rn = p^*, the set W^m constitutes our solution set, for a coalition in W^m can award the maximum payoffs to its members.

The elements of sets W and W^m are identified as follows. In each district, winning an election is a simple game.[12] A simple game is completely defined when the players and the set of winning coalitions have been specified. Thus the game in the jth district can be specified by a pair

$$G_j = (N_j, W_j), \tag{12}$$

where N_j and W_j are the players and the set of winning coalitions, respectively, in the jth district. Let W_j^m be the set of minimum winning coalitions in that district.

In our decision rule, there is a "supergame" playable by the players each of whom represents the winners of district game G_j. Because I consists of R districts, let players in the supergame be

$$J = [1, 2, \ldots, j, \ldots, R] \tag{13}$$

The supergame designated by G^+ itself is a simple majority game and can be identified by

$$G^+ = (J, W^+), \tag{14}$$

where W^+ is the set of all winning coalitions of the supergame in the subsets of J. Let W_h^+ (h = 1, 2, . . . , q, q + 1, . . . , H) be the hth winning coalition in W^+, and W_h^{+m} (h = 1, 2, . . . q) be the hth minimum winning coalition in which $W_h^+ = W_h^{+m}$ for h = 1, 2, . . . , q; q = $\binom{R}{r}$ and H = $\binom{R}{r}$ + $\binom{R}{r+1}$ + . . . + $\binom{R}{R}$.

The game of the community as a whole, designated by (I, W), is then given as

$$(I, W) = \sum_{h=1}^{H} \prod_{j \in W_h^+} (N_j, W_j), (h = 1, 2, \ldots, H), \tag{15}$$

where $I = N_1 \cup N_2 \cup \ldots \cup N_R$, and $N_1 \cap N_2 \cap \ldots \cap N_R = \varnothing$,[13] The set of minimum winning coalitions is specified as

$$W^m = \sum_{h=1}^{q} \prod_{j \in W_h^{+m}} W_j^m, (h = 1, 2, \ldots, q). \tag{16}$$

Obviously, $W^m \subset W$. The number of coalitions in W^m is

$$| W^m | = [_{N/R}C_n]^r {}_R C_r. \tag{17}$$

Note that (I, W) is no longer a majority game; consequently, the number of players in a coalition alone does not determine whether it is winning, losing, or minimum winning.

Formation and Stability of Coalitions

We have identified our solution set W^m, but little has been said in this formulation of how a specific coalition comes into being and whether, once the solution coalition has been formed, the imputation vector, $\vec{x} = (x_1, x_2, x_3, \ldots, x_N)$, is acceptable to the players so partitioned. Let us examine, through an example, the process of the formation and the stability of the coalition. We define a coalition as stable when no subset of players in that coalition can do better by leaving the current coalition and forming or joining another.

Consider a community with nine voters,

$$I = \{1, 2, 3, 4, 5, 6, 7, 8, 9\}, \tag{18}$$

partitioned into three single-member electoral districts, $\{1, 2, 3\}$, $\{4, 5, 6\}$, and $\{7, 8, 9\}$. In this case there are $27 = [\binom{3}{2}]^2\binom{3}{2}$ possible minimum winning coalitions because the minimum number of voters required to win the majority of seats is four, two of whom belong to any one district and the remaining two of whom belong to one of the remaining two districts.

In a symmetric game, in which all players' bargaining powers are the same, the game has a finite symmetric solution consisting of vectors of imputations. In our example, $\vec{x}$ equals $[5/4, 5/4, -1; 5/4, 5/4, -1; -1, -1, -1]$, as well as 27 other vectors obtainable by permuting payoffs in $\vec{x}$ in such a way that in each vector only two of the three districts contain two players receiving imputations equal to $5/4$, where $5/4 = \text{Max}\ [v(S)/p]$; $S \in W^m$. This solution states that four of the players in the winning coalition will divide the value accruing to a four-person winning coalition equally among them, while the remaining five lose.

Among the set of minimum winning coalitions, which one in particular would actually win an election cannot be answered in this framework. Game theory establishes only the solution set elements, of which there is usually more than one. Innumerable factors that shape the real world determine the final outcome. For example, the publicness of most government expenditure programs imposes additional constraints on choices of voters in a coalition and reduces the number of feasible coalitions in W^m. A political party may foster the formation of a particular coalition among the set of minimum winning coalitions by promoing a program which benefits a specific type of people—the rich, the poor, or whomsoever—more than others in order to identify itself as a party of the group of people thus favored.

Let us consider a free school lunch program in order to highlight the roles of the institutional and political factors. Assume that the most economical and administratively feasible way of classifying the students bene-

Table 1

Various Free School Lunch Programs and Supporting Coalitions

Program and the Party Sponsoring the Program	Schools Covered by the Program	Subset of Voters forming Coalition	Characteristic Value of the Coalition	Pro-rata Gain
No. 1	K,E,J,H	{1,2,3,4,5,6,7,8,9}	0	0
2	E,J,H	{2,3,4,5,6,7,8,9}	1	1/8
3	K,E,H	{1,2,3,4,6,7,8,9}	1	1/8
4	K,J,H	{1,5,6,7,8,9}	3	3/5
5	K,E,J	{1,2,3,4,5}	4	4/5
6	E,H	{2,3,4,6,7,8,9}	2	2/7
7	J,H	{5,6,7,8,9}	4	4/5
8	E,J	{2,3,4,5}	5	5/4
9	K,H	{1,6,7,8,9}	−5	−1
10	K,E	{1,2,3,4}	−4	−1
11	K,J	{1,5}	−2	−1
12	H	{6,7,8,9}	−4	−1
13	E	{2,3,4}	−3	−1
14	J	{5}	−1	−1
15	K	{1}	−1	−1
16	–	{∅}	0	0

fiting from the program is by the types of schools which they attend. Classfying them by ages, for example, turns out to be too expensive, for it requires services facilities in schools which only a few eligible students attend.

Assume further that each one of the nine voters has a child currently in a school: voter 1 in K (kindergarten), voters 2, 3, and 4 in E (elementary school), voter 5 in J (junior high school), and voters 6, 7, 8, and 9 in H (high school). This program is to be financed by a tax (-1) currently imposed equally on each voter. An election is called to determine which categories of schools (including the empty set) should be included in the program in the current year. A program covering all schools, for example, would yield pro-rata gains equal to zero and would be at least not rejected, if not supported enthusiastically, by voters if it were the only proposal. But there will be competing proposals, as listed in Table I.

All programs from 1 to 8 are winning if each of them is put to a vote in isolation, and Programs 9 to 16 are losing. However, if all programs are competitively proposed by, say, 16 political parties sponsoring each, only Program 8 (and hence the 8th party) can win because voters 2, 3, 4, and 5 find Program 8 awarding them the largest pro-rata gains and will form a coalition supporting it. Moreover, they can win without any additional votes. If Program 8 is absent initially, the same voters would have supported another program, say Program 5. But in the competitive political environment any party wishing to win the election would surely discover such a superior platform as Program 8 and defeat Program 5 along with the party supporting it. Being unable to win over at least one voter from the coalition {2, 3, 4, 5}, no other programs (parties), all of which require some defector(s) from that coalition to win, can possibly win. Nor can the coalition of those excluded, {1, 6, 7, 8, 9}, defeat Program 8, for it can elect only one representative. All rational parties' programs then will converge on the tenets of Program 8, and the election may turn out to be a non-issue contest as far as policies are concerned, and each party may woo voters of the same minimum winning coalition, {2, 3, 4, 5}.

In the above discussion, the relative sizes of the pro-rata gains determined which minimum winning coalition dominated the other coalitions. However, one may ask whether inner disagreement over the distribution of the joint payoff among the members destabilizes the minimum winning coalition. To answer this question, let I be partitioned into four subsets, $K = \{1\}$, $E = \{2, 3, 4\}$, $J = \{5\}$, and $H = \{6, 7, 8, 9\}$ and assume that each subset behaves as a single player. Because with respect to the alternative policies discussed so far the roles of all players in each of the above four subsets are completely symmetric, there will be no reason why payoffs should be different among the players within each subset. Only the distribution of payoffs between the subsets becomes an issue. The coalitions {E ∪ J}, {J ∪ H} and {E ∪ H} now replace coalitions {2, 3, 4, 5}, {5, 6, 7, 8, 9}, and {2, 3, 4, 6, 7, 8, 9}, respectively, and $v(\{E, J\}) = 5$, $v(\{J, H\}) = 4$, and $v(\{E, H\}) = 2$. It appears now that J, by threatening to leave E for H, can extract a larger share of the joint payoff of 5 than E can get. Of course, if J presses too hard, E can, in turn, counter-threaten J to desert J for H. These two would then have to vie with one another for H's partnership. Negotiations based on these threats, counter-threats, and competition yield the equilibrium payoffs that must satisfy the following conditions:

$$w_E + w_J = v(\{E, J\}) = 5$$
$$w_J + w_H = v(\{J, H\}) = 4 \qquad\qquad (19)$$
$$w_E + w_H = v(\{E, H\}) = 2$$

where w_H, w_J, and w_E are equilibrium payoffs of H, J, and E, respectively. Solving the above simultaneous equations, we obtain $w_H = 0.5$, $w_J = 3.5$, and $w_E = 1.5$ and the equilibrium payoff configurations such that

$$(-1, 1.5, 3.5, -4; K, \overline{EJ}, H),$$
$$(-1, 3.5, 0.5, -3; K, \overline{JH}, E), \quad \text{and}$$
$$(-1, 1.5, 0.5, -1; K, \overline{EH}, J).$$

Note that voter J (or E or H) can always get 3.5 (or 1.5 or 0.5), irrespective of whom he (or she) forms a coalition with as long as he can find a partner. K ends up receiving -1 in any situation, for this voter has no bargaining power: K is a dummy, not needed to win an election. All three coalitions are in set W, but the imputations in them dominate each other and accordingly do not reveal which coalition will become the solution. Then, it appears, this result is at loggerheads with our contention that minimal winning coalitions tend to form. But we must take the payoffs to political parties into account.

One of the points stressed in this paper is the role of political parties in organizing voter coalitions. It is assumed that a party receives as the payoff for its role as the successful organizer of the winning coalition a fixed proportion of the sum of the payoffs accruing to the members of that winning coalition. Consequently, parties promote formation of a coalition with the largest characteristic value. In our above example, although voter E (J or H) is indifferent as to who is his partner as long as he can form a coalition with him, a political party can not be indifferent. It will receive the largest payoff by fostering formation of the coalition, $\{E \cup J\}$, for its characteristic value, $v(\{E, J\}) = 5$, is the largest among those of the three possible winning coalitions. Thus the presence of competing political parties and their quest for a larger payoff tend to result in the formation of the minimum winning coalition, provided that such a coalition is institutionally and economically feasible under the existing conditions, and also to induce all parties to propose the same platform.

Conclusions

The analysis of this paper yields a number of interesting hypotheses which are testable, at least in principle. The following represents some of them.

(1) When an election is fought on a set of economic issues in a representative democracy of the single-member-district system, the majority of representatives or the winning party will always represent the interests of a minority of voters. Hence if the same set of proposals that the legislators would approve were to be put to a referendum of all voters, the proposals would be defeated. California's Proposition 13 may be viewed as a partial but affirmative test of this hypothesis.

(2) Platforms of competing political parties tend to become identical regardless of the number of parties involved in the election, par-

ticularly when the number of institutional constraints is large. Note
that, unlike that hypothesis derived from the Downsian model or a
modified Hotelling spatial model (1929), applicability of this hypothesis is not limited to a two-party case, for it does not need to
have the voters systematically arrangeable along a single line in the
order of intensity of their support for the two parties' platforms.

(3) There is a built-in-bias toward the growth of government in a
representative democracy. Because the larger the government, the
greater the payoffs accruing to political parties as well as to minority groups, all parties direct their efforts to propose platforms
which increase the size of government, and there will be no countervailing political moves. For the same reason, income redistributive expenditures tend to grow faster than the expenditures providing pure public goods.

(4) No inference can be made as to which income groups will be
favored under a representative democracy. All income groups, the
rich, the poor, and the middle income, have opportunities to form
politically potent minority coalitions and redistribute income on
their behalf. Success or failure in this attempt depends upon the
group's political skill, and there seems to be no direct relationship
between income levels and political skills.

(5) People in the majority group tend to abstain from voting while
those in the minority do not. The voters in a minority group will
be keenly aware of the effect of their votes upon the fate of the bill
that a party is proposing on behalf of the minority, for the number
of beneficiaries of the bill will be trimmed to the necessary minimum, while the members of the majority opposing the bill will
sense the fact that many of their votes will be wasted owing to the
distribution pattern of their votes among electoral districts.

Finally, this paper assumes that the political parties possess the necessary information on the voters' preferences. When this assumption is relaxed, the propositions stated above have to be moderated somewhat, but, I
believe, they remain fundamentally unchanged.

Notes

1. For articles written specifically on the tax limitation movements, see a number of
articles appearing in *National Tax Journal, Supplement* (1979) and also in *Tax and Expenditure
Limitations*, Helen F. Ladd and T. Nicholas Tideman, eds. (1981).

2. Exceptions include James M. Buchanan and Gordon Tullock (1965) and Albert Breton (1974). For a review of public choice theories, see Dennis C. Mueller (1976, 1979).

3. I follow here A. Down's (1957, p. 28) fundamental hypothesis: "parties formulate policies in order to win elections rather than win elections in order to formulate policies."

4. Incidentally, many professional politicians and legislators are lawyers by trade, and this method of charging clients fees for their services finds cognate practices in the legal profession.

5. Here I depart from the Downsian approach in which political parties are assumed to maximize votes. As will become clear later, the behavior of maximizing votes conflicts with the voters' utility maximization and will repel voters from the party.

6. As to the role of representatives, there is a long history of debate over the question of whether a representative behaves (or should behave) as the agent or trustee of his constituents. See Burke (1860), and Eulan et al. (1959).

7. "Single-member districts" and "mutually exclusive electoral districts" are common in English and U.S. political systems, while "multi-member district" and "two tiers of electoral districts" are found in continental European countries. See Rae (1967).

8. Buchanan and Tullock (1965, p. 221) and Breton (1974, p. 45) conjectured similarly but gave no rigorous proof. Breton was partially incorrect in stating that "As R (the number of constituencies) and/or N (the number of citizens) increase without bound . . ." when he should have stated "As both R and N increase without bound . . ." See a formal proof given in the text.

9. A shift from a direct to an indirect democracy thus entails a trade of a more accurate expression of the group's preference for some other advantages, one of which may be a saving in the administrative cost of the group decision.

10. Alternatively, we may consider a case in which a public good that yields equal benefits to all is financed by the revenue from discriminatorily imposed taxes such as a progressive income tax, property taxes, excise taxes, etc., or of course a situation in which a public expenditure yielding discriminatory benefits is financed by the revenue raised through discriminatory taxes.

11. William Riker (1962) was the first to argue that rational politicians do not attempt to maximize votes (or plurality) but seek to form a minimum winning coalition. He termed this "the size principle." But he proceeded to analyze election systems in which a winning coalition must obtain more than one-half of the total votes (1962, p. 256), in which the maximization of plurality and formation of a minimum winning coalition are not significantly different strategies, as argued by Hinich and Ordeshook (1970, p. 772). When, however, one combines it with the possibilities of a genuine minority's winning an election, as I have done in this paper, Riker's size principle does become significant.

12. A simple game is a game in which the range of characteristic function takes exactly two values, say 1 and 0; all coalitions which get more than $\frac{1}{2}$ of the district's votes are defined as winning and get 1, and the rest, as losing and get 0.

13. In equation (15)

$$W_{j \times g} \equiv \{S \mid S \cap N_j \in W_j \text{ and } S \cap N_g \in W_g\},$$

and

$$W_{j+g} \equiv \{S \mid S \cap N_j \in W_j \text{ or } S \cap N_g \in W_g\}$$

$(j, g \in J; j \neq g)$.

References:

Brennan, G. and J. Buchanan. "Towards a Tax Constitution for Leviathan," *Journal of Public Economics*, 8, 1977, pp. 255–273.

Breton, A. *The Economic Theory of Representative Government.* Chicago: Aldine-Atherton, 1974.

Buchanan, J.M. and G. Tullock, *The Calculus of Concent*. Ann Arbor: The University of Michigan Press, 1965.
Burke, E. *The Works of Edmund Burke, with a Memoire*. New York: Harper and Brothers, 1860.
Downs, A. *An Economic Theory of Democracy*. New York: Harper and Row, 1957.
Eulan, H. et al. "The Role of the Representative: Some Empirical Observations on the Theory of Edmund Burke", *American Political Science Review*, 53, 1959.
Hinich, M. and P.C. Ordeshook. "Plurality Maximization vs. Vote Maximization: A Spatial Analysis with Variable Participation," *American Political Science Review*, 64, 1970, pp. 772–791.
Hotelling, H., "Stability in Competition," *Economic Journal*, 39, 1929, pp. 41–57.
Ladd, H.F. and T.N. Tideman (eds.), *Tax and Expenditure Limitations*. Washington, D.C.: The Urban Institute, 1981.
Mackay, R. and C. Weaver. "Monopoly Bureaus and Fiscal Outcomes: Deductive Models and Implications for Reform," *Policy Analysis and Deductive Reasoning*, G. Tullock and R. Wagner (eds.), Lexington, Mass.: D.C. Heath, 1978.
Mueller, D.C. "Public Choice: A Survey", *Journal of Economic Literature*, 14, 1976, pp. 395–433.
Mueller, D.C. *Public Choice*. Cambridge: Cambridge University Press, 1979.
von Neumann, J. and O. Morgenstern. *Theory of Games and Economic Behavior*. Princeton: Princeton University Press, 1944.
Niemi, R.G. and Deegon, J., Jr. "A Theory of Political Districting". *American Political Science Review*, 72, 1978, pp. 1301–1323.
Rae, D.W. *The Political Consequence of Electoral Laws*. New Haven & London: Yale University Press, 1967.
Riker, W.H. *The Theory of Political Coalition*. New Haven & London: Yale University Press, 1962.
Stigler, G. "Director's Law and Public Income Redistribution". *Journal of Law and Economics*, 13, 1970, pp. 1–10.
Tufte, E.R. "The Relationship between Seats and Votes in Two-Party Systems". *American Political Science Review*, 67, 1973, pp. 540–554.
Tullock, G. "Problems of Majority Voting", *Journal of Political Economy*, 67, 1959, pp. 571–579.
Tullock, G. "The Charity of the Uncharitable". *Western Economic Journal*. 9, Dec. 1971, pp. 349–392.

Résumé

Cet article essaie de construire une théorie de démocratie représentative en utilisant une démarche analytique courante en économie.

Il suppose, à côté d'électeurs faisant leurs choix en fonction d'une utilité maximum, des partis politiques qui rivalisent pour obtenir des voix en fournissant à un groupe d'électeurs des services d'organisation qui aident le groupe dans sa tentative de redistribuer les revenus en leur faveur par l'utilisation de l'appareil étatique contre une contribution monétaire calculée comme une fonction du revenu net revenant aux membres du groupe qui reçoit cet avantage. On utilise ensuite la théorie des jeux à N. personnes pour analyser la formation de coalitions politiques dans un système représentatif composé de districts électoraux à un seul représentant, dont l'une des caractéristiques est la possibilité pour un groupe minoritaire de gagner la majorité des sièges au Parlement. Cet article propose un certain nombre d'hypothèses intéressantes et vérifiables. Parmi ces dernières on trouve: (1), le groupe majoritaire au Parlement représente les intérêts d'une minorité de votants, (2) les programmes électoraux de partis politiques rivaux tendent à devenir identiques même si plus de deux partis principaux existent, et (3), les partis politiques souhaitent vivement accroître l'importance du gouvernement.

Voting by Veto and Majority Rule

*Dennis C. Mueller**

Majority rule is, without question, the most commonly used voting procedure. If one asks students, untrained in public choice, why this might be so, they typically respond that it is fair, egalitarian, or mention some other similar quality. These properties were formally demonstrated some 30 years ago by Kenneth May (1952), who showed that majority rule treats both the individuals and issues impartially, properties that have come to be known as anonymity and neutrality. For those who value these impartiality properties[1], May's theorem would appear to make a most compelling case for majority rule, were it not that the rule is only decisive in a choice between two issues. When three or more issues are involved, one needs to impose the transitivity axiom, but majority rule generally does not satisfy transitivity. Given that most committees do choose from more than two alternatives, the attractive properties May associates with majority rule seem to vanish into the same abyss into which Arrow assigned all other voting rules.

In this paper, I described a voting procedure that possesses a form of anonymity and neutrality properties, resembles majority rule in other important ways, and yet is readily applicable to situations with more than two alternatives. We first describe the process and illustrate some of its properties with simple examples (Sec. 1). In Sec. 2 we establish some important properties of the procedure in the n voter case. In Sec. 3 we contrast its axiomatic properties with those of majority rule. Summary and conclusions follow in Section 4.

* An early draft of this paper was presented at the seventh Bosphorus Workshop on Industrial Democracy in Istanbul, June 1982. I would like to thank all of the participants in this meeting as well as those of the IIPF-congress who commented on my paper, and especially my two discussants Semih Koray and Jozef M. Ritzen.

Public Finance and the Quest for Efficiency. Proceedings of the 38th Congress of the International Institute of Public Finance. Copenhagen, 1982, pp. 69–86. Copyright © 1984 by Wayne State University Press, Detroit, Michigan, 48202.

70   DENNIS C. MUELLER

1. How the Process Works

1.1. The Mechanics

Voting by veto (hereafter VV) has two steps. In the first, each of *n* committee members makes one proposal, e.g. the quantity of a public good and a tax formula to finance it. A *status quo* outcome, *s*, is assumed to exist; *s* could be no action, what was done last year, or anything else. An issue set consisting of *n* proposals by the committee members and the *status quo* now exists.

In step 2, an order of veto voting is first determined by some random device. In the order thus determined, each individual eliminates one issue from the set of *n + 1*. The issue left after all *n* individuals have veto voted is the winner.

1.2. An Example

Three voters, *A*, *B*, and *C*, propose issues *a*, *b*, and *c* which together with *s* form the issue set. Let the individual preference orderings be as in Table 1, ignoring the two entries in parentheses.

Assume each individual knows the other voters' preference orderings. Suppose the randomly determined order of veto voting is *A* then *B* then *C*. *A* can make his proposal a winner by vetoing *b*. If B then vetoes either *a* or *s*, *C* will veto the other issue in this pair (*s* or *a*), and *c* wins. Since *B* prefers *a* to *c*, *B*'s best strategy is to veto *c*, leaving *C* to veto *s* making *a* the winner.

Now suppose the randomly determined voting order to be *A C B*. *A* no longer can get his proposal to win. If *A* vetoes *c*, *C* vetoes *a* or *s*, and *b* wins. If *A* vetoes *b*, *C* vetoes *a* and *c* wins. Since *A* prefers *c* to *b*, he will veto *b* leaving *c* to become the winner. The winners for the 6 possible permutations of voting sequences are as follows:

ABC → a   BCA → b

ACB → c   CAB → c

BAC → a   CBA → b

Each issue proposed by a committee member has a one in three chance of winning.

The preferences in Table 1 produce a cycle over *a*, *b* and *c* in pairwise

Table 1

Voting by Veto: Example 1

	Voters		
Issues	A	B	C
a	1	2	3(2)
b	3	1	2(3)
c	2	3	1
s	4	4	4

voting under majority rule. Thus, in this opening example, the parallel between majority rule and VV seems close. Where the former produces a cycle over 3 issues, VV selects a winner at random with equal probability.

Now replace the two entries in Table 1 for *C*, by those in parantheses, i.e. assume *C* now prefers *a* to *b*, all other rankings remaining the same. With this one change, the probability of *a*'s winning jumps to 5/6. The only order of veto voting that selects a different issue is *CAB*, which leads to *c*'s victory.

This example illustrates an important incentive property of VV. *A* increases the probability of his/her proposal winning by advancing it in the preference ordering of another voter. Thus, the procedure establishes incentives to make proposals that, although perhaps favoring oneself, stand relatively high in the other voters' preferences. Of course, the same incentive exists for all voters, and a competition to make the proposal standing relatively highest in all voters' preferences can ensue.

2. Voting by Veto with n Persons

2.1. Selecting a Winner from the Set of n *+ 1 Proposals*

Let us start our examination of the *n*-person case at the point where both the *n+1* proposal set, and the order of voting have been determined. We maintain until Section 2.5 the assumption that each voter knows the orderings over all *n+1* issues for all voters.

The last to vote in the sequence rejects one of the two remaining proposals. His/her best strategy is to reject the proposal ranked lowest of the two, making the other the winner. The last voter's strategy choice is *straightforward* as defined by Farquharson (1969, p. 30).

The second last voter (V_{n-1}) receives three proposals, call these i, j, k, and rejects one. Suppose k is ranked lowest of the three by V_n, the last voter. V_{n-1} by rejecting k, allows V_n to choose between i and j. V_n may pick the issue V_{n-1} prefers, or may not. But V_{n-1} can guarantee that the issue he/she prefers in this pair wins by simply vetoing the other member of the pair, thereby forcing V_n to reject k. Thus, vetoing k can never make V_{n-1} better off, and may leave him/her worse off. Rejecting k is not an admissable strategy for V_{n-1}, in the sense of Farquharson (1969, pp. 28–9). Remove k and V_{n-1} is left to choose between i and j. The proposal not rejected will win. The choice is again straightforward. V_{n-1} eliminates the least preferred of the pair (i, j).

Similar reasoning applies to the $(n-2)$th voter. V_{n-2} receives 4 issues, vetoes one and passes on 3. Vetoing two of these, the one ranked last by V_n, and the one ranked last of the remaining 3 by V_{n-1}, are inadmissable strategies. V_{n-2} is left with a straightforward choice between the two remaining issues.

Continuing on up to the first voter, V_1 chooses from the full set of $n+1$ proposals. Vetoing $n-1$ of them are inadmissable strategies, since each of these can be associated with one other voter in the sequence who will reject it, if V_1 does not. V_1 has the straightforward strategy of rejecting the lower ranked of the two remaining proposals.

Thus, when each voter in the sequence removes from the issue set he/she receives all of those proposals whose rejection is an inadmissable strategy, each voter has but one, straightforward, binary choice between the two remaining issues. Farquharson's (1969, pp. 38–49) fundamental theorem applies directly and we have the following result:

Proposition 1. Voting by veto produces a unique winning issue from any set of $n+1$ proposals, and a given order of veto voting by the n voters.

2.2. Characteristics of Losing Issues

While Proposition 1 establishes that VV always selects a unique winning issue, given an order of veto voting, it does not tell us anything about the characteristics of the winning issue. Is there something we can say about the winning issue just by looking at the preferences of voters over the $n+1$ issues before an order of veto voting has been determined? The answer is yes.

First of all, it is obvious that no issue ranked last by any voter can win. This voter will remove it from the set if no subsequent voter does. Thus, all issues ranked last by one or more voters can be set aside as sure losers.

Suppose several voters rank the same issue k last, however, so that more than one issue is left as a possible winner after removing all issues ranked last by one or more voters from consideration. If, now, two or more voters who rank k last also rank the same issue j second last, then j cannot win. For then there must be one voter in the sequence who is free to veto j, even though he/she ranks k lower, knowing that there is at least one voter to follow, who also ranks k last.

By analogous reasoning, no issue ranked third from last by at least 3 voters, who rank the same 2 issues below it, can win. But we can say more. Suppose there are 3 voters who assign possibly different ranks to an issue i, but agree that only two issues j and k, but not necessarily both, are worse than i. Then i cannot win. An example is illustrated in Table 2. Voters U and V both rank i 3rd from last $(n-1)$, and rank j and k lower (but note not in the same order). W ranks i second last, and only k lower. Regardless of which voter comes first under veto voting, eliminating j or k is an inadmissible strategy, and that voter is free to veto i. We can generalize.

Proposition 2. Let N_r^i be the maximum number of voters, who rank in common at most $r-1$ different issues below i. Then neither i nor any of the $r-1$ issues ranked in common below it can win under any order of veto voting, if and only if there exist $r-1$ issues, such that $N_r^i \geq r$.

Proof of sufficiency. Proof is by induction. For the case where $r = 1$, the proposition is obvious. Any voter ranking i last (i.e. there are 0 issues ranked in common below it) vetoes i, if he foresees that no one following him in the sequence will veto it, since he must rank any other possible winning issue above i.

Now assume the proposition holds for a given proposal j and the $m-1$ proposals ranked below it, i.e. $r = m$, $1 < m < n$. Let E^m be the set of m proposals that cannot win. Now assume that for each of the m voters whose preferences determine E^m there exists an issue $i \epsilon E^m$, such that $(iPk) \rightarrow k \epsilon E^m$, where P stands for "strictly preferred". Further, let us assume that this holds for some $m+1$th voter V_i. We now have $m+1$ voters who rank in common only members of E^m below i. Now let an order of veto voting be determined leaving out both voter V_i and issue i. Since all m voters whose preferences determine E^m rank i above the elements of E^m, this does not alter the possibility of any of these issues winning. They are all zero. Let V_k be the voter who would reject a given issue R_k, $R_k \epsilon E^m$. Each V_k voter need not be one of m whose preferences define E^m, but let us assume they are. (If they are not additional voters are freed to reject i.) Let us order these m voters according to the order they come up in the sequence V_1, V_2, etc. associating with each R_1, R_2 . . . Now let us insert voter V_i anywhere in the sequence and add issue i, that is assume V_i follows the first g members of the m voter subset, and precedes the last $m-q$, $0 \leq q \leq m$. Two possibilities exist: (1) none of the q proposals R_1, R_2 . . . R_q are ranked by V_i below i, in which case V_i ranks at most $m-q$ proposals below i, all of

Table 2

Voting by Veto: Example 2

			Voters		
Issues	1	2. . . .	U	V	W. . . .
1					
2					
.					
.					
.					
i			n−1	n−1	n
j			n	n+1	
k			n+1	n	n+1
.					
.					
.					

which will be vetoed by the $m-q$ voters from the set of m, who have yet to vote. The rejection of any of these is an inadmissible strategy for V_i, and he will reject i unless some other voter will. (2) At least one of the proposals R_1, R_2 . . . R_q is ranked by V_i below i. For at least one of the voters preceding V_i, the rejection of the proposal he would have vetoed must now become an inadmissable strategy. He leaves this proposal for V_i to reject. This other voter now rejects the next highest proposal, which is either a member of E^m or i. If a member of E^m some third voter is freed to reject i, and so on. Since all of q voters preceding i rank only members of E^m below i, V_i's rejection of one of the issues R_1-R_q must free one of these q voters to reject i. Either way i cannot win.

To prove necessity, we must be able to construct a sequence that makes i a winner whenever $N_r^i < r$ for all r. We do so simply by ordering all voters from those ranking i highest to those ranking it lowest—ties among voters can be placed in any order. To see that this works, start from the end of the veto voting sequence and work back. There cannot be any voters ranking i $n+1$st among the $n+1$ issues, since $N_1^i < 1$. Let there be z_n voters $(0 \leq z_n \leq n)$, who rank i nth. They each rank but one issue lower than i. Since $N_2^i < 2$, no 2 voters ranking i nth can rank the same issue last. Thus, these z_n voters eliminate z_n issues other than i as possible winners. Next come the z_{n-1} voters ranking i $n-1$th, $(0 \leq z_{n-1} \leq n-z_n)$. For each of these z_{n-1} voters there must be one issue not among the the z_n already eliminated he/she ranks below i; otherwise we would have 3 voters ranking but 2 issues below i, violating $N_3^i < 3$. Similarly there cannot be 3 voters ranking i $n-1$th and having together only 2 issues, not among the z_n already eliminated is a possible winner ranked below i. Thus, for each of the

Table 3

Distribution of Preferences for Divide-the-Cake Game

Issues	Voters								
	V_1	V_2	V_3	V_4	$\ldots$ V_k $\ldots$		V_{n-2}	V_{n-1}	V_n
1	1	2	2	2	2		2	2	2
2	2	1	3	3	3		3	3	3
3	3	3	1	4	4		4	4	4
.									
k					1				
.									
n−1	n−1	n−1	n−1		n−1		n−1	1	n
n	n	n	n		n		n	n	1
n+1	n+1	n+1	n+1		n+1		n+1	n+1	n+1

z_{n-1} voters ranking i n−1th, there must be one issue ranked below i that has not already been eliminated as a possible winner. As we continue backwards through higher ranks, the same must be true. Each time we encounter another voter, Proposition 2 guarantees that this voter ranks at least one issue, not previously eliminated, below i, and it is this issue the new voter will remove in the veto voting sequence. Eventually we reach the first voter in the sequence who again removes an issue other than i, leaving i to go on and be the winner.

2.3. Some n-Person Examples

In Table 3 a distribution of preferences is presented in which all voters rank the same issue last (say the *status* quo), a different issue first (e.g. their own proposals), and all order the other $n-1$ proposals in the same way. This distribution of preferences might arise in an n-person "divide-the-cake game". Let B be the value of the benefits to be divided, each person receiving nothing under the *status quo*. Each individual K proposes an equal division of B with some extra e_k for K, i.e. $B/n + e_k$ for K and $B/n - e_k/(n-1)$ for everyone else.[3] Each K ranks his/her proposal first, the others from smallest e_k to largest, the *status quo* last. Only issues 1 and 2, the first and second most egalitarian issues, can possibly win. Issue 3 cannot win by Proposition 2 because $n-1$ voters rank it lowest, save for the n−2 issues (4 through n+1). But the n−1 voters ranking issue 2 second or third rank in

Table 4

Distribution of "Single-Peaked" Preferences

				Voters						
Issues	V_1	V_2	V_3	...	$V_{n/3}$	$V_{n/3+1}$	$V_{n/3+2}$	...	V_{n-2}	V_{n-1}	V_n
1	1	2	4		2n/3−2	2n/3	2n/3+2		n+1	n+1	n+1
2	2	1	2		2n/3−4	2n/3−2	2n/3			n	n
.											
.											
.											
n/3	n/3	n/3	n/3		1	2	4				
.											
.											
2n/3+1	2n/3+1	2n/3+1			2n/3+1	2n/3+1	2n/3−1				
2n/3+2	2n/3+2	2n/3+2			2n/3+2	2n/3+2	2n/3+1				
.											
.											
.											
n	n	n	n		n				5	3	1
n+1	n+1	n+1	n+1		n+1	n+1	n+1		7	5	3

common a total of n−1 issues lower than 2. By Proposition 2 issue 2 wins if V_2 comes first, V_1 second, and the other voters follow in any order, or in fact under any sequence of veto voting, where V_2 is first and is not followed by V_3. Since these sequences occur with probability $1/n - (1/n)(1/(n-1))$, the probability that issue 1, the most egalitarian, wins, approaches one as n grows large.

In Table 4 a distribution of "single-peaked" preferences is illustrated. Although the preferences of Table 4 can be easily related to the usual single-peaked, single dimension figure used to demonstrate the median voter theorem, it is not necessary that issues take on any spatial characteristics to be able to eliminate issues as possible winners using Proposition 2. What is needed to eliminate issues as possible winners is some commonality among voters in their rankings of the different issues. Such commonality is present in Table 4 but much less so than in Table 3. Applying Proposition 2 to the preferences in Table 4, we find that one third of the issues on each end of the distribution can be eliminated as possible winners under all sequences of veto voting. This result is VV's analogue to the median voter theorem.

Finally, we could construct an n-person analogue to the first example presented in Section 1. All voters rank the same issue last, but every other issue is ranked first by one voter only, second by one voter, etc. Each issue would then have an equal (1/n) probability of winning under VV.

2.4. The Voter's Decision at the Proposal Stage

Proposition 1 tells something about the VV procedure once the order of voting is determined, Proposition 2 tells something about the procedure given the set of proposals. We now wish to examine the voter's proposal decision, given what he/she knows about the VV process from Propositions 1 and 2.

The voter's decision calculus is analysed most easily in spatial terms. Let X and Y be characteristics of the collective good to be decided by a committee. Each member K has a utility function defined over $X \times Y$, $U^k(x,y)$, reaching a maximum in the positive orthant.

Given Propositions 1 and 2 each voter K expects the probability of a given other voter J rejecting k, to be greater the lower it stands in J's ranking of the $n+$ proposals. K can reasonably expect his proposal (x_k, y_k) to stand lower in J's ranking, the further (x_k, y_k) is from J's most preferred point (x_j, y_j). Assuming K knows where (x_j, y_j) is, K's subjective probability that J and only J rejects K can reasonably be written as $\pi_j^k(x_k, y_k)$, which reaches a minimum at (x_j, y_j).

To win a proposal must escape rejection by all other voters. Call π^k the probability that any of the other $n-1$ voters reject k, then[4]

$$\pi^k = \sum_{J \neq K} \pi_j^k$$

Although π_j^k is discontinuous, it is reasonable to assume that π^k approaches a continuous function with a minimum at Z, the center of the distribution of peak utilities of the n voters, as n, the number of voters, becomes infinitely large. If K takes the proposals of the other voters as given, he will form some expectation of the level of utility he will experience if his proposal does not win. Call this $\overline{U}^K$. K's task is then to propose a pair of characteristics (x_k, y_k) so as to maximize expected utility $E(U^K)$

$$E(U^K) = (1 - \pi^k)U^K + \pi^k \overline{U}^K \tag{1}$$

Maximizing (1) with respect to x_k and setting equal to zero

$$U_x^K - U_x^K \pi^k - U^K \pi_x^k + \pi_x^k \overline{U}^K = 0 \text{ or}$$

$$U_x^K (1 - \pi^k) = \pi_x^k (U^K - \overline{U}^K) \tag{2}$$

and analogously for y_k

$$U_y^K (1 - \pi^k) = \pi_y^k (U^K - \overline{U}^K) \tag{3}$$

Dividing (2) by (3) we have

$$U_x^K / U_y^K = \pi_x^k / \pi_y^k \qquad (4)$$

π_x^k is the sum of the marginal changes in the probabilities that the other voters reject proposal k. In making a proposal other than (x_k, y_k), K obviously moves in a direction that lowers the probability of k's rejection, moves in a direction in which the negative π_{jx}^ks outweigh the positive.[5] K must thus move toward that part of the $X \times Y$ orthant where the preponderance of peak preferences are, toward the center of the distribution of peak preferences.

In moving away from (x_k, y_k), K chooses a path balancing the loss in utility from a change in x_k or y_k against the marginal reduction in the probability that k is rejected, caused by these changes. Eq. (4) defines this path. If a center of the distribution of peak preferences of all voters is envisaged in the $X \times Y$ orthant, then π_x^k / π_y^k can be bought of as iso-probability loci around this center.[6] Each contour further from the center represents a higher probability of rejection. Eq. (4) defines a pseudo-contract curve running from K's peak preference to the center of the distribution of voter peak preferences, along which K's marginal rate of substitution of x for y is equated to the ratio of the marginal probabilities of k's rejection from changes in x and y.

Eqs. (2) and (3) define the distance along this pseudo-contract curve K chooses for his proposal. The marginal reduction in utility from a change in x away from x_k times the probability the proposal wins, must equal the increase in the probability k wins times the extra utility k promises over what individual K expects to obtain should his/her proposal not win.

2.5. Voting by Veto with Prudent Voting

So far we have assumed that, at the veto voting stage, each individual knows the rankings of all of the other voters over the proposal set, and each follows a sophisticated voting strategy. The information requirements of this assumption are strong, particularly with large numbers of voters. The most obvious alternative assumption is that each voter is ignorant of the preferences of other voters, and follows the prudent strategy of removing the lowest ranked of those proposals that are left in the issue set when he/she votes.

There are two plausible strategies one might assume voters to follow in the presence of such uncertainty. One is the risk averse strategy of maximizing the utility enjoyed under the worst possible of all outcomes. This strategy requires that each voter remove the lowest ranked proposal from those left in the issue set when he/she votes.

The other plausible strategy choice is to apply the principle of insufficient reason, assign each of the proposals an equal chance of winning if left in the issue set and maximize expected utility. For the *m*th voter in the veto voting sequence this requires rejecting that proposal which maximizes

$$E(U^M) = (\frac{1}{n-m+1} U_1^M + \ldots) = \frac{1}{n-m+1} \sum_{i=1}^{n-m+1} U_i^M$$

where U_i^M is M's utility should proposal i win. There are $(n-m+2)$ possible ΣU_i^Ms, each one consisting of the sum of utilities over all of the issues M receives less the utility of one issue M might veto. Obviously this sum will be highest by leaving out the lowest ranked issue of the $n-m+2$ received. Both maximin risk aversion and expected utility maximization under the principle of insufficient reason lead to the prudent strategy of removing the lowest ranked issue from the set a voter receives.

Fortunately, if each individual follows this prudent strategy at each step of the veto voting sequence, both Propositions 1 and 2 still hold (Moulin (1981a)). Under sophisticated voting, the issue that is ranked last from the full issue set by the last voter cannot win. If this individual were to come first in the sequence, and vote prudently, he/she would eliminate the same issue. Under sophisticated voting, the issue, that is ranked last by the second last voter from the set remaining after the last voter's lowest ranked issue has been removed, cannot win. If this voter comes second and the last voter first, the same two issues are removed under prudent voting. The outcome under one sequence of veto voting, when all vote prudently, is identical to the outcome under sophisticated voting for the reverse voting sequence, and both Propositions 1 and 2 follow immediately.

3. An Axiomatic Comparison of Voting by Veto and Majority Rule

The purpose of any collective choice rule is to pick a winner or set of winners out of a set, S, of possible outcomes. Following Sen (1970, p. 10), we define the set of best elements as the choice set.

Definition, Choice Set. An element x in S is a best element of S with respect to the binary relation R if and only if $\forall$ y: $(y \in S \rightarrow xRy)$. The set of best elements in S is called its choice set, $C(S,R)$.

Voting rules can be thought of as procedures for determining choice sets, what Sen (1970, p. 14) calls choice functions. Much of the collective choice literature can be viewed as attempting to establish the normative properties of various choice functions, i.e. in what sense the elements in the choice set, given voting rules, are determined best, or alternatively as stating some normative conditions, which a set of best choices should satisfy and then seeing which, if any, collective choice functions belong to this set.

The axioms of most interest when comparing VV with majority rule are:

Anonymity (A). A social choice function is anonymous if it only depends on the numbers of voters having a given preference ordering.

Neutrality (N). Any permutation σ of the alternative set induces a natural permutation σ on the utility profiles. We say that the social choice function f is neutral if $f(\sigma(w)) = \sigma f(w)$ for any such permutation σ and every profile w.

Positive Responsiveness (S). A change in any individual K's preferences from $xI_K y$ to $xP_K y$ or from $yP_K x$ to $xR_K y$, all other individuals' preferences unchanged, must change a social choice function's ranking from xIy to xPy, where I_K and P_K represent the indifference and strict preference relationships for individual K. I, P, and R represent the analogue preference relationships in the social ordering.

Nonnegative Responsiveness (R). A change in any individual K's preferences from $xI_K y$ to $xP_K y$ or from $yP_K x$ to $xR_K y$, all other individuals' preferences unchanged, must not change a social choice function's ranking from xPy to xIy or from xIy to yPx.

A fifth axiom often invoked is *Unlimited Domain (U).* The domain of the social choice function must include all logically possible combinations of individual orderings.[7]

May's (1952) theorem states that majority rule is the only decisive collective choice rule that is consistent with axioms A, N and S, and Sen (1970, pp. 72–74) proves a similar theorem for axioms U, A, N, and S.[8] However, May's theorem is only applicable where there is a choice between two alternatives. Majority rule then picks one of them as best, or declares them equally good. Once the issue set is expanded to 3 or more issues, majority rule is not capable of defining a choice set, as is well known from the Arrow theorem and cycling literature (Sen (1970, pp. 71–74)).

VV can pick a winner from any set of $n+1$ elements, and we wish now to examine its relationship to the axioms that are associated with majority rule.

The first important point to be made about VV is that strictly speaking, it does not determine a choice set. When its application is viewed prior to the determination of an order of veto voting, it can be seen to translate the proposal set into another set, in which each proposal has a probability of being chosen *the* best. Let us call this set a probabilistic choice set.

Definition, Probabilistic Choice Set. Let S be an $n+1$ element set $x_i \in S$, i = 1, $n+1$. Let $C(S,\pi)$ be the set S with each x_i assigned a probability $\pi_i, 0 \le \pi_i \le 1$, $\sum_{i=1}^{n+1} \pi_i = 1$, of being chosen the best element in S. Then $C(S,\pi)$ is a probabilistic choice set.

By analogy, a probabilistic collective choice function can be defined as a function mapping S into $C(S,\pi)$. Similarly, to relate VV to the axioms of social choice, each axiom must be given a probabilistic interpretation. Where axiom A states that the social preference relation R does not change if any two individuals' preferences are interchanged, we would need, when discussing VV, an axiom A_π, probabilistic anonymity, stating that the probability of any issue being chosen as the best is not changed, when the preferences of any two individuals are interchanged.

Redefining axioms A, N, S and R in this way, it is easy to see that VV is consistent with A_π, N_π and R_π, as well as U, as originally stated. Let us start with U. At the proposal stage, no problems arise by allowing any possible individual orderings over the set of feasible alternatives. Once a set of proposals has been made VV operates only over this set, but any individual preference orderings over it can be allowed.

VV's selection of a winning issue from S depends on two things: the set of individual orderings over S, and the position of each person in the veto voting sequence. Prior to the random draw, each individual has an equal chance of being assigned any position in the voting sequence. Interchanging individuals prior to the random draw does not affect these probabilities, and therefore does not affect the probability of any proposal winning. Thus, VV's assignment of probabilities to issues is independent of the identities of the individuals, prior to the random draw, A_π.

N_π holds prior to the selection of an order of voting, N holds after the selection. Once the order of voting has been determined, Proposition 1 asserts that there is a unique winning proposal for any set of individual preference rankings. Suppose this is w for a given set of rankings and order of veto voting. Relabel w z and z w and z will now win. Relabel these proposals prior to the random draw and π_w will become π_z and π_z will become π_w.

But VV does not satisfy a probabilistic version of positive responsiveness. An issue ranked last by any one voter has a zero probability of winning, even if it were to rise in the preference rankings of all other voters. But an improvement in an issue's ranking by any voter cannot lower a proposal's probability of winning, and could raise it. Thus, VV is consistent with a probabilistic version of R but not S.

How serious a normative handicap is it to satisfy R_π instead of S_π? As a practical matter, ties between issues are unlikely under majority rule with large numbers of voters, and impossible under VV whatever the circumstances, since VV always selects a single issue as the best. But VV may assign two issues the same probability of winning, prior to the random draw. Should one issue's rise in a voter's preference order, relative to one or more other issues, always increase its chance of winning relative to these other issues, or is it enough that the rise does not lower its chance of winning? Convincing normative arguments in favor of S or S_π over R or R_π are not obvious. An important feature of VV is that any one voter can veto a proposal he ranks last. This feature makes it possible to defeat a Condorcet winner under VV, and makes VV inconsistent with S_π. But tyrannies of the majority are possible when Condorcet winners are present, and so the protection VV gives the individual against a discriminatory proposal might be regarded as worth the cost of satisfying only R_π rather than S_π.

Sen (1970, pp. 68–74) has shown that while A, N and S imply majority rule as the collective choice rule, A, N and R lead to the Pareto-extension rule, i.e. all pairs which are Pareto incomparable are regarded as socially indifferent. This result bears some weight in our discussion of VV, since all proposals will fall within the Pareto set. But we have seen that the procedure sets up incentives for voters to make proposals that are not only Pareto optimal, but cluster toward the center of the distribution of peak preferences, and in execution, the procedure tends to eliminate proposals ranked relatively lower than other proposals. Thus, within the Pareto set, VV typically assigns quite different probabilities to the different proposals winning, and is less vague than the Pareto extension rule, thereby blunting some of the stigma of satisfying R_π rather than S_π.

4. Summary and Conclusions

The properties of fairness and egalitarianism associated with majority rule stem from its consistency with the anonymity and neutrality axioms. Voting by veto is consistent with probablistic variants of these two axioms. It is not, however, consistent with a version of the neutrality axiom that implies independence of irrelevant alternatives.

From the Arrow theorem, we know that one of the 5 axioms used in the theorem must be relaxed if we are to achieve a social welfare function consistent with the others, and a good argument can be made for choosing the independence axiom to be relaxed (Mueller (1979), Bergson (1954), Hansson (1973)). Roughly speaking none of the $n+1$ alternatives in the issue set is irrelevant under voting by veto. These consist of the *status quo* and the n proposals by the individual members to improve the *status quo*. It is how an issue ranks for each individual against *all* other proposals that counts in determining whether an issue is chosen as *the* best issue. VV partly avoids the "Arrow problem" by relying on a richer information base than Arrow allowed by invoking the independence axiom.

VV also partly avoids the "Arrow problem" by not demanding that the collective choice rule define a social ordering. Instead, VV simply assigns probabilities to the various proposal once they are made, and then, via the execution of the procedure, picks a winner. Having a probabilistic choice set may be one of the prices to be paid for not having a choice set that is either embarrassingly small or vacuously large.

Whether a probabilistic choice set is desirable or not must depend on the criteria used in assigning probabilities to different issues. VV bases these probabilities on the individual preference orderings and is consistent with both the Pareto and nonnegative responsiveness axioms. Moreover, the more consensus that exists in a community regarding the ordering of issues, the higher up in the ranking of the voters an issue will have to be to win under VV. In the extreme case of complete disagreement (orthogonality) of preferences, VV simply assigns equal probabilities to each of the alternatives and produces a fair resolution of what would be an indeterminant outcome under majority rule. With single-peaked preferences of the type that produces a median voter outcome under majority rule, VV assigns the median proposal the highest probability of winning, declining probabilities the further an issue is from the middle, zero probabilities to the one third of issues located at each tail of the distribution.

VV can also yield desirable outcomes in situations where majority rule may not. A game of "divide the benefits among *n* voters" is the type of game that can lead to hopeless cycles under majority rule. But under VV, voters have an incentive to propose an equal sharing among all *other* voters, less any one discriminated against veto the proposal, and the procedure picks the most or at worst second most egalitarian of the proposals made.[9] Thus, where VV produces a probabilistic generalization of the median voter theorem when preferences are single-peaked, it produces an n-person generalization of the normal solution to the cake-cutting game.

The cake-cutting example illustrates the importance of the proposal stage to VV. The preferences presented in Table 3 reflect a set of proposals for dividing the cake that would not ordinarily arise under majority rule, if each committee member were charged with making one proposal. The bulk of the social choice literature analyses the operation of a voting rule over an exogenously and arbitrarily defined issue set, or over an unlimited range of options. Such a wide open spectrum of possible outcomes must raise the chance for conflict and/or irresolution. VV not only includes the formulation of proposals in the procedure, but provides incentives to compromise, to offer proposals that fall somewhere between what one prefers oneself, and the outcomes preferred by others.

VV is inherently individualistic. It is likely to work best when each individual acts independently, maximizing his/her own utility but taking account of the preferences of others. The veto each receives protects against a discriminatory proposal, but only one. Coalitions of one group can succeed against any smaller group. VV should function best, where even small coalitions are difficult.[10]

The normative properties of virtually all voting procedures from majority rule ("the tyranny of the majority") to the demand revealing and point voting processes are vulnerable to coalitions. How serious this vulnerability would be in practice is not apparent. VV, as well as the demand revealing and point voting procedures, have been viewed as processes for revealing preferences for public goods, not for resolving distributional questions, where "natural" coalitions may exist. With a pure public good, all individuals can potentially be made better off, a coalition of the whole is in principle feasible, the unanimity rule is the logical voting rule. The usual arguments against the unanimity rule are that it takes too long, and/or is subject to strategic behavior, which is to say that the transaction costs of forming a grand coalition are prohibitive. VV and the other new voting processes may be viewed as alternatives to the unanimity rule, and can be used when coalitions are difficult to form. When coalition formation is easy, the optimal voting rule for public goods is unanimity, or Wickell's near-unanimity rule. In either case, the problem of revealing preferences for public goods in an ethically appealing way seems potentially more solvable today than it appeared to be a decade ago.

Notes

1. But not all do. For a critique see Plott (1976).
2. This rule was first presented in Mueller (1978), where an alternative proof of proposition 1 appears.
3. It is shown in Mueller (1978) that an equal division of $B/n - e_k$ among the other $n-1$ voters minimizes the probability of k's rejection.
4. Of course, once the proposal set exists and an order of voting established, the probability of one voter rejecting k will not be independent of another. But prior to the proposal set's formation, the probabilities can be reasonably assumed to be independent and summed.
5. The second order conditions guarantee this.
6. Of course with small numbers of voters these contours may not be smooth, but the direction of movement is still toward the center.
7. The statements of S, R and U follow Sen (1970), A and N follow Young (1974).
8. Sen's statement of the neutrality axiom differs from ours in such a way as to imply Arrow's Independence of Irrelevant Alternatives, where the above N does not. The above N seems to be a reasonable generalization of May's definition of neutrality to more than 2 issues. The independence axiom is often invoked to reduce the scope for strategic manipulation of the procedure. The two-step nature of VV makes it less vulnerable to strategizing than other procedures dependent on the complete preference ordering of each voter, like the Borda count. For example, we have seen that each voter's strategy set reduces to a single, straightforward strategy when voters are completely informed about all other voters' preferences, the situation in which other procedures are usually most vulnerable. But VV's relationship to the independence axiom cannot be pursued here.
9. In a previous paper I demonstrated that a risk averse voter will propose an equal division of the benefits, so that the existence of two risk averse voters in the committee suffices to produce the egalitarian outcome (Mueller, 1978).
10. For an analysis of the properties of VV when coalitions are present see Moulin (1981b).

References

Bergson, A. (1954). On the Concept of Social Welfare. *Quarterly Journal of Economics*, 68, pp. 233–53.

Farquharson, R. (1969). *Theory of Voting*. New Haven: Yale University Press.

Hansson, B. (1973). The Independence Condition in the Theory of Social Choice. *Theory and Decision*, 4, pp. 25–49.

May, K.O. (1952). A Set of Independent, Necessary and Sufficient Conditions for Simple Majority Decision. *Econometrica*, 20, pp. 680–4.

Moulin, H. (1981a). Prudence Versus Sophistication in Voting Strategy. *Journal of Economic Theory*, 24, pp. 398–412.

Moulin, H. (1981b). The Proportional Veto Principle. *Review of Economic Studies*, 48, pp. 407–16.

Mueller, D.C. (1978), "Voting by Veto", *Journal of Public Economics* 10, pp. 57–75.

Mueller, D.C. (1979). *Public Choice*, Cambridge: Cambridge University Press.

Plott, C.R. (1976). Axiomatic Social Choice Theory: An Overview and Interpretation. *American Journal of Political Science*, 20, pp. 511–96.

Sen, A.K. (1970). *Collective Choice and Social Welfare*. San Francisco: Holden-Day.

Young, H.P. (1974). An Axiomatization of Borda's Rule. *Journal of Economic Theory*, 9, pp. 43–52.

Résumé

Cet article décrit le procédé de vote avec veto, en définit quelques propriétés et l'oppose à la règle du vote majoritaire. On montre que voter avec veto satisfait les deux propriétés les plus importantes de la règle majoritaire, l'anonymat et la neutralité, lorsqu'on définit ces axiomes selon les lois de la probabilité. La nature probabiliste de cette procédure implique d'utiliser un ensemble de choix probabiliste plutôt que l'ensemble de choix déterministe employé par la plupart des théories de choix social, c'est-à-dire que l'on peut considérer que voter avec veto revient à désigner un vainqueur dans un ensemble de propositions en utilisant un procédé de classement qui attribue des probabilités à chaque question en fonction des préférences des électeurs. Alors que la nature probabiliste des questions soumises à un vote avec veto est quelque peu désavantageuse, on montre que ce désavantage est contrebalancé par les avantages que ce procédé présente sur la règle majoritaire car on peut l'appliquer à n'importe quel ensemble de questions et il en sort toujours un gagnant.

En votant avec veto, on incorpore le stade de la proposition en question dans le processus. Voter avec veto a l'avantage supplémentaire de pouvoir faire inciter des propositions qui se situent relativement haut dans l'ordre des préférences des autres électeurs. Ainsi, si l'on définit les questions pour un ensemble spatial, les électeurs auront tendance à faire des propositions se situant vers le centre de la distribution des propositions et le vote avec veto désigne un gagnant dans le second tiers de ces propositions. Quand cet ensemble offre la possibilité de diviser un prix fixé entre les membres d'un comité, voter avec veto conduit à proposer des divisions relativement égalitaires du prix parmi les différents membres et désigne ensuite l'une des deux propositions les plus égalitaires comme gagnante. Ces propriétés et d'autres aussi intéressantes du vote avec veto en font, parmi l'ensemble des procédures qui définissent un choix probabiliste, l'une de celles qui méritent de plus amples recherches.

If at First You Don't Succeed: Budgeting by a Sequence of Referenda*

Thomas Romer, Howard Rosenthal and Krishna Ladha

I. Introduction

The institutional structure of political decision-making can have important influence on the allocation of resources by the public sector. Recent
theoretical work has focused on the way the rules governing the formulation
of proposals in expenditure referenda affect the results of such elections.
This research places particular emphasis on the importance of *agenda control*
by those in charge of public goods provision.[1] In the context of expenditure
referenda, agenda control means restricted access to the power to make
proposals that will be placed on the ballot. Acknowledging the existence of
such power is in contrast to those models in which access to the agenda is
unlimited.[2] In agenda control models, the preferences and actions of the
group that makes proposals—the agenda *setter*—together with the institutional "rules of the game" become fundamentally important determinants of
the outcomes.

The Agenda Control Model

Romer and Rosenthal (1979a) provided a theoretical model that deals
explicitly with agenda control and its effects on the determination of collective expenditures by referendum. They consider a process in which the setter
is the supplier of a collectively financed good. The setter is assumed to have
preferences strictly increasing in the level of spending. Budgets (and, effec-

*Financial support for this research was provided by National Science Foundation Grant SOC
79 - 17576.

Public Finance and the Quest for Efficiency. Proceedings of the 38th Congress of the International
Institute of Public Finance. Copenhagen, 1982, pp. 87–108. Copyright © 1984 by Wayne
State University Press, Detroit, Michigan, 48202.

tively, tax rates) are determined by simple majority vote in referenda that confront voters with a "forced choice" between the setter's proposal and an exogenous, prespecified *reversion* expenditure level. If the setter's proposal fails, the reversion is enacted. The reversion plays a crucial role in the process, since a sufficiently low reversion can be used as part of a threat strategy by the setter in order to extract higher spending from voters. The model identifies a relationship between reversions and proposals as an important potential test for the presence of agenda control by budget-maximizing setters.

In some contexts, the setter may be allowed more than one attempt to pass a budget. Typically, there is a legislated limit on the number of elections that can be used to determine a given period's budget. The sequence of referenda terminates whenever a budget is approved or the limit is reached or the setter chooses to stop making proposals—whichever comes first. How the setter formulates his proposals over a sequence of referenda depends not only on the reversion but also on such factors as the setter's uncertainty about citizen preferences and voter turnout, the length of the sequence and the possibilities the setter has for learning about the electorate from one referendum to the next. In Romer and Rosenthal (1979a), the sequence and the uncertainty facing the setter are modeled in a fairly simple way. Voters do not behave strategically. In deciding how to vote, a citizen does not take into consideration the possibility that the setter may try again if his proposal loses. Uncertainty is present due to random turnout. Citizens are assumed to vote with an exogenous and known (to the setter) probability that is independent of the proposal on the ballot and is constant over the sequence. The reversion is also fixed during the sequence of elections used to determine a given period's spending. Under these conditions, a (risk neutral) setter wishing to maximize the expected budget would plan a sequence made up of proposals that decline from one referendum to the next.

The Empirical Context

The empirical investigation of propositions emerging from this framework has focused on public school budget referenda in Oregon school districts. The institutional structure of these elections conforms quite closely to the process analyzed by Romer and Rosenthal. Local school budgets are determined by a referendum process in which the proposals emerge from the school bureaucracy. Reversions are defined by the state constitution and are, from the point of view of a given year's budget, predetermined. In many districts, the reversion is too low to operate the schools without additional funds. Spending in excess of a district's reversion must be approved by the voters. There are provisions for holding more than one referendum in a year, but at most eight elections (depending on state law in a given year) may be called.[3] In some districts, failure to pass a referendum has resulted in the schools' being closed for several months. As the setter model would predict, this outcome is very infrequent. That it occurs at all, however, demonstrates that the setter's threat is a very real one.

Spending: The Impact of Reversions and Information

The initial emphasis of the empirical work was on the impact of reversions on expenditures. Romer and Rosenthal (1982b) and Filimon et al. (1982) showed that taking reversion effects into account yields a significant improvement over the standard "median-voter" specification of a log-linear spending equation: agenda control does matter. The setter's ability to use the reversion as a threat was found to be particularly strong when the reversion is at or below the "threshold level", defined as the spending necessary to keep schools open.

While pointing to the importance of reversions, these estimates also indicated that it is not tenable to assume that either the setter or the voters act as if they have full information. On the setter's side, the results were inconsistent with the predictions of the certainty model and suggested that setter errors due to turnout fluctuations or imperfect knowledge of voters' preferences may be important. At the same time, voters appear to be quite ignorant of resources available to the district from outside grants (i.e., state aid), and setters are able to exploit that ignorance. The lack of voter awareness of outside grants aids the setter directly (increased spending due to the grant) and through the reversion effect. (The voters perceive the reversion, which includes state aid, to be lower than it actually is.)[4]

Voting

But expenditures are only one side of the story. In studying the interaction of economic and political forces, it seems natural to consider both political as well as economic outcomes. Specifically, in a budget referendum, these correspond, respectively, to the result of the election (measured, for example, by the fraction of those voting who approved of the proposal) and the expenditure proposed to the voters. Of course, these are jointly determined. A two-equation model of voting and spending was introduced in Romer and Rosenthal (1982a). Since the present paper builds on this two-equation framework, it is useful to review it briefly.

If a budget-maximizing setter had full information about voter turnout and preferences, he would choose an expenditure proposal that made the decisive voter just indifferent between voting for the proposal and choosing the reversion. The proposal would correspond to the largest expenditure acceptable to at least half the voters. This would imply that referenda would just barely pass—the Yes vote would be very close to 50%. When the setter faces uncertainty, however, the expected voting outcome could be different than this. A risk-neutral setter expecting random turnout may make a proposal whose expected Yes vote is not 50%; that is, the setter may "aim" for a different result. (In fact, when the setter can potentially make a sequence of proposals, he may initially even make proposals that he expects to lose. We return to this later.) If the setter makes errors in formulating his expenditure proposal, then there may be additional deviations from a 50% yes vote.

The possibility that the setter makes errors creates a link between a spending proposal and the corresponding vote result. Suppose that, based on his information about voter turnout and preferences, the setter makes a proposal that he expects to yield $a\%$ yes vote. Because his information is imperfect, however, suppose that his proposal is "too high". This positive error in setting his proposal will result in a lower than expected yes vote. Similarly, a negative error in setting the proposal will tend to raise the yes vote above $a\%$. The two-equation model captures this dependence by including the setter's expenditure proposal error as a variable in the voting equation. Although the coefficient on this variable could not be directly estimated, the prediction that its sign is negative could be tested by estimating the covariance of the residuals from the two equations. This estimate was in fact consistent with the predicted sign, lending further support to the agenda control model.

Planning and Learning in a Sequence of Elections

Neither the single-equation expenditure models nor the two-equation model deal with considerations that arise when there is the possibility of holding more than one election to determine a given year's budget. (The expenditure equation models use data from the winning election, while the two-equation model uses data from the year's first election.) The availability of the sequence is empirically important. In our sample of 111 Oregon school districts that held budget elections in 1971 (for the 1971–72 school year), only 69 passed proposals on the first try. Of the remaining 42 districts, 25 passed on the second try and 13 on the third, while four districts passed proposals only on the fourth attempt.

We have already pointed to one element of the setters' strategy in a sequence: plan on a series of proposals, each somewhat smaller than the one before it. In this way, the risk of losing is traded off against the opportunity to gain from a favorable turnout from high-demand voters. In the framework that led to this result, the setter's uncertainty was due entirely to random turnout fluctuations. The results of a losing election in a sequence provided no new information to be used in determining the next proposal. There is no link, therefore, between the vote outcome in one election and the proposal in the next election.

Suppose, however, that the setter had some uncertainty about voter preferences, as well as turnout. Then the observation of the vote on a first election loss may provide the setter with some information about his "expenditure error". (As in the two-equation model, there would be a negative relationship between this error and the voter outcome.) He may then use this information to adjust his proposal for the second equation, relative to what it would have been otherwise. This updating would create a link between the vote in the first election and the spending proposal in the second election. The updating would continue after each failed proposal.

In the next section of this paper we develop an econometric specification of a setter model of referenda with a sequence of elections. The model has six equations—an expenditure equation and a vote equation for each of the first three elections—that are linked through the model's error structure. The expenditure equations incorporate the reversion effects as well as imperfect information by setter and voters. The voting equations include parameters that reflect the setter's errors in making proposals. We stopped at the third election because there are too few four election observations (4) for estimation of a four election model. Section 3 presents the results of our estimates of this model.

2. Spending and Voting in a Sequence

The Spending Equation

The core of our model is the expenditure equation developed in Filimon et al. (1982). This equation incorporates an estimate of voter preferences, the effect of reversions, and the possibility of voter ignorance of state aid. We modify this specification to capture errors made by the setter and to take into account the sequence of proposals.

The basis of the setter's proposals is the distribution of the largest expenditure acceptable to voters in his district, given the district's reversion, together with an estimate of turnout probabilities. If there were only one election, this information would generate an expenditure proposal, which we assume is adequately approximated by:

$$\ln \overline{E}_p = \ln \overline{E}_d + \theta_1 \overline{H} + \theta_2 \ln \overline{Z} + u + e' \tag{1}$$

In this specification, the variables with overbars represent *perceived*, rather than actual quantities, to reflect the voter's possible lack of information about outside grants. Thus, $\overline{E}_p$ is the perceived budget proposal, measured in dollars per student. $\overline{E}_d$ is the underlying demand for perceived expenditures (per student) of a "representative" voter, in the absence of reversion considerations. The variables $\overline{H}$ and $\overline{Z}$ depend on the reversion as perceived by this voter. The error terms u and e' reflect errors by the setter and by the modeler, respectively.

Demand

We characterize the "representative" demand for perceived expenditures by using a log-linear specification that is standard in the literature:

$$\ln \overline{E}_d = \beta_0 + \beta_1 \ln \overline{Y} + \beta_2 \ln P + \beta_3 \ln S + e'' \tag{2}$$

where

$\overline{Y}$ is perceived household income
P is tax price faced by the household
S is number of students in household
e'' is an error term

Agenda Control Effects

The reversion variables are defined as follows:

$$\overline{H} = \begin{cases} 1 & \text{if } \overline{Q} \leq \mu \\ 0 & \text{if } \overline{Q} > \mu \end{cases}$$

$$\overline{Z} = \begin{cases} \mu & \text{if } \overline{Q} \leq \mu \\ \overline{Q} & \text{if } \overline{Q} > \mu \end{cases}$$

$\overline{Q}$ is the perceived reversion per student. The parameter μ, which is to be estimated, is a nonnegative constant corresponding to the "threat threshold". If the reversion is below this threshold, the reversion is insufficient to operate the schools. Consequently, for reversions at or below μ, the setter's threat position vis-à-vis the voters is stronger than for higher reversions. Moreover, this threat is equally strong for any reversion perceived by the voters to be below the threshold. Equation (1) characterizes this relationship by positing that, *ceteris paribus*, proposed spending is constant for $\overline{Q} < \mu$. When the perceived reversion is above the threshold, proposed spending is taken to be a loglinear function of the reversion. The threshold effect implies $\theta_1 > 0$. With uncertain voter turnout, Romer and Rosenthal (1979a) suggest that the sign of θ_2 is ambiguous.

Voter Perception and State Aid

Actual and perceived quantities may differ because of misperception by voters of state aid available to the local school district.[5] This aid is in the form of lump-sum per-student grants. If A is the amount of the grant per student, we let $(1-\rho)A$ be the amount perceived per student, where ρ is a parameter to be estimated and is assumed equal across school districts. The perceived quantities are then defined as:

$$\overline{E}_p = E_l + (1-\rho)A \tag{3}$$

$$\overline{Y} = Y + (1-\rho)rA \tag{4}$$

$$\overline{Q} = Q_l + (1-\rho)A \tag{5}$$

E_l is the proposed expenditure to be financed out of local taxes. Y is the "representative" household's income and r is this household's tax share. Q_l is the local portion of the reversion. In Oregon, it is composed of a lump-sum intermediate district payment and an amount specified by the state constitution. If the local expenditure proposal passes, total spending per student is:

$$E = E_l + A$$

State aid affects local spending through three channels:

— *Individual incomes:* Perceived state aid affects perceived income, through (4), and hence demand for local spending. This is the income effect typically captured in standard models of public spending (with $\rho=0$).

— *"Flypaper"*: State aid can be added on to spending from local sources. If the aid is not fully perceived by voters, perceived total spending can differ from actual; if $\rho > 0$, then $\overline{E}_p < E$. This is a "flypaper" type of effect: the greater ρ, the stickier the "flypaper".

— *Reversion and threshold:* State aid forms part of the district's reversion. Even if state aid is correctly perceived by voters ($\rho = 0$), this reversion effect would cause the impact of aid on spending to differ from the impact of the income effect alone (Romer and Rosenthal (1980)). For relatively low reversions, the setter benefits from imperfect perception of state aid. If $\rho > 0$, the perceived reversion is less than the actual reversion, increasing the setter's threat position vis-à-vis the voters (relative to $\rho = 0$). This effect is enhanced for districts whose actual reversion $(Q_I + A)$ is above the shut-down threshold μ, but whose perceived reversion $\overline{Q}$ is below the threshold.

On the whole, the "flypaper" and "reversion" effects are likely to outweigh the income effect, so that the setter will typically benefit from higher values of ρ (see Filimon et al. (1982)).

Expenditures with a Single Election

Substituting (2) into (1) gives the specification for a single-election expenditure equation:

$$\ln \overline{E}_p = \beta_0 + \beta_1 \ln \overline{Y} + \beta_2 \ln P + \beta_3 \ln S + \theta_1 \overline{H} + \theta_2 \ln \overline{Z} + u + e$$

The errors e' and e'' are errors in specifying the reversion effect and the underlying demand, respectively. We assume that across observations they each have i.i.d. normal distributions with zero mean. They cannot be separately identified, so we write them as $e = e' + e''$. The *setter's error* u is due to the setter's lack of information about turnout and voter preferences. Since the setter does not make the errors captured by e, we will call e the *econometrician's error* (even though this is a mild misnomer, in that the econometrician also makes the error u).

Spending Proposals in a Sequence

To place the process in the context of a sequence, we redefine variables slightly, to distinguish between various elections. We let $\overline{E}_1$ be the perceived proposal on the first, $\overline{E}_2$ the perceived proposal on the second, and $\overline{E}_3$ the perceived proposal on the third election. Then

$$\ln \overline{E}_1 = \beta_{01} + X\beta + \theta_1\overline{H} + \theta_2\ln \overline{Z} + u_1 + e_1 \tag{6}$$

$$\ln \overline{E}_2 = \beta_{02} + X\beta + \theta_1\overline{H} + \theta_2\ln \overline{Z} + u_1 + e_1$$
$$+ \text{(learning update)} + e_2 \tag{7}$$

$$\ln \overline{E}_3 = \beta_{03} + X\beta + \theta_1\overline{H} + \theta_2\ln \overline{Z} + u_1 + e_1 + e_2$$
$$+ \text{(second learning update)} + e_3 \tag{8}$$

The expression $X\beta$ is shorthand for the RHS of (2), minus the intercept and error term e''.

Equations (7) and (8) differ from (6) only through the error structure and the constant term. To motivate the latter difference, we first note that, by law, the reversion in a district is the same for each election in a sequence. Furthermore, we assume that voters are randomly drawn from the same population in each election and that voters do not behave strategically. Then the model presented in Romer and Rosenthal (1979a) leads, in the absence of learning by the setter, to the hypothesis of a sequence of declining proposals. Given our relatively small sample of districts with multiple elections, we allowed only the constant to change across elections, and predicted $\beta_{01} > \beta_{02} > \beta_{03}$.

As to the error structure, the econometrician makes additional errors e_2 and e_3 in the second and third elections. These errors pertain to specification of the learning update. The setter's error in (7) and (8) consists of his error on the first proposal, u_1, modified by whatever adjustment he makes by learning. If the outcome of the first election yields information that the setter uses to update what would otherwise have been his second proposal, then the second expenditure equation should incorporate this updating. Similar considerations apply on the third attempt. In order to discuss the specification of setter learning, we must deal with the voting equations.

The Voting Equations

The voting variable we will be concerned with is the *vote logit* V, defined as

$$V = \ln\left[\frac{\text{Number of Yes Votes}}{\text{Number of No Votes}}\right]$$

A fundamental simplifying assumption concerning voter turnout (i.e., the fraction of the electorate that votes) is that it is unrelated to the reversion or the setter's proposal. A risk-neutral setter maximizing the expected budget under perfect knowledge of voter preferences and turnout probabilities would generally choose a sequence of proposals such that the corresponding expected vote logit would differ from zero (i.e., the expected yes vote is other than 50%). Let the expected vote logit for such a setter on the tth election be α_t ($t=1,2,3$). The analysis of sequences in Romer and Rosenthal (1979a) suggests that $\alpha_3 > \alpha_2 > \alpha_1$. Of course, actual logit values would differ according to turnout fluctuations.

If the setter makes errors due to his misperceptions of voter preferences or turnout probabilities, the vote outcome should reflect this error. As we discussed in the Introduction, there should be a negative relationship between the setter's error in his proposal and the vote logit. A proposal that is too large (relative to a zero-error proposal) will lead to an expected logit less than α_t, while a proposal that is too small will drive the expected logit above α_t.

In combining these effects, we have the voting equations

$$V_t = \alpha_t + \delta u_t + v_t, \quad t=1,2,3 \tag{9}$$

The subscripts refer to election numbers. The errors v_t reflect specification errors or other factors independent of the expenditure equations. (We will assume that v_1, v_2, and v_3 are uncorrelated and have identical normal distribution with zero mean.) The parameter δ, whose sign is predicted to be *negative*, is a straightforward (and admittedly crude) characterization of the way setter errors are translated into vote outcomes. We assume that this relationship is the same in all elections. Less defensibly, we also assume that the parameters α_t and δ are constant across school districts.[6]

Learning: A Heuristic Representation

Using equation (9), we can develop a heuristic approximation to represent learning by the setter. A given proposal $\overline{E}_t$, with no setter error, is expected to lead to a logit of α_t. How the setter responds to a particular vote outcome V_t will depend on his assessment of the relative importance of the error term v_t. We assume that the setter knows both δ and the variance of every error. Since v_t has zero mean, if its variance is also known to be very close to zero, then the deviation $V_t - \alpha_t$ must be due nearly entirely to the setter's error. In this case, it seems reasonable for the setter to adjust his next proposal by $-(V_t - \alpha_t)/\delta$, relative to what would otherwise have been his optimal proposal on that election. (In other words, if $V_1 < \alpha_1$, this means cutting back the second proposal—recall that $\delta < 0$.)

When the variance of v_t is large, relative to the variance of the setter's error, then the deviation $V_t - \alpha_t$ does not provide very much information. In this case, the adjustment of the next proposal should be at best a fraction of $-(V_t - \alpha_t)/\delta$. For example, if the variance of v_1 is positive while that of u_1 is very close to zero, then nearly the entire deviation $V_1 - \alpha_1$ must be due to factors other than setter's error. Consequently, little or no adjustment of the second proposal is called for on the basis of information obtained from the first election outcome.

A simple way to incorporate this kind of updating into the second and third expenditure equations is to include a term $-s(V_t - \alpha_t)/\delta$, where the parameter s ($0 \leq s \leq 1$) represents the adjustment factor. We will assume that this parameter is the same across all jurisdictions.

Including this "learning update" term in (7) and (8), we can rewrite the second and third expenditure equations as:

$$\ln \overline{E}_2 = \beta_{02} + X\beta + \theta_1 \overline{H} + \theta_2 \ln \overline{Z} - s(V_1 - \alpha_1)/\delta + u_1 + e_1 + e_2 \quad (10)$$

$$\ln \overline{E}_3 = \beta_{03} + X\beta + \theta_1 \overline{H} + \theta_2 \ln \overline{Z}$$
$$- s(V_2 - \alpha_2)/\delta + u_2 + e_1 + e_2 + e_3 \quad (10')$$

Since

$$(V_t - \alpha_t)/\delta = u_t + v_t/\delta,$$

the setter's errors in (10) and (10') become

$$u_2 = (1-s)u_1 - sv_1/\delta$$
$$u_3 = (1-s)u_2 - sv_2/\delta = (1-s)^2 u_1 - s(1-s)v_1/\delta - sv_2/\delta$$

The whole system can then be rewritten as:

$$\ln \overline{E}_1 = \beta_{01} + X\beta + \theta_1 \overline{H} + \theta_2 \ln \overline{Z} + u_1 + e_1 \quad (11a)$$

$$V_1 = \alpha_1 + \delta u_1 + v_1 \quad (12a)$$

$$\ln \overline{E}_2 = \beta_{02} + X\beta + \theta_1 \overline{H} + \theta_2 \ln \overline{Z} + (1-s)u_1 - sv_1/\delta + e_1 + e_2 \quad (11b)$$

$$V_2 = \alpha_2 + \delta(1-s)u_1 - sv_1 + v_2 \quad (12b)$$

$$\ln \overline{E}_3 = \beta_{03} + X\beta + \theta_1 \overline{H} + \theta_2 \ln \overline{Z} + (1-s)^2 u_1$$
$$- s(1-s)v_1/\delta - sv_2/\delta + e_1 + e_2 + e_3 \quad (11c)$$

$$V_3 = \alpha_3 + \delta(1-s)^2 u_1 - s(1-s)v_1 - sv_2 + v_3 \quad (12c)$$

The errors u_1, e_t, and v_t are assumed to have the following structure. A given error is assumed to be uncorrelated across school districts and have, in each district, the same normal distribution with zero mean. The error variances are:

$$\text{Var}(u_1) = \sigma_u^2 \quad \text{Var}(v_1) = \text{Var}(v_2) = \text{Var}(V_3) = \sigma_v^2$$

$$\text{Var}(e_1) = \tau_1^2 \quad \text{Var}(e_2) = \tau_2^2 \qquad \text{Var}(e_3) = \tau_3^2$$

Furthermore, the econometrician's errors e_t are uncorrelated with each other or with any other disturbance term. Because turnout is independent of the setter's proposal, the setter's error u_1 is uncorrelated with the voting equation errors v_t. We assume that turnout does not depend on the outcome of elections, so that the v_t are also uncorrelated.

In specifying the model, we had to trade off generality against the estimation problems posed by the small number of observations with second or third elections. We decided to allow proposals to change only through the intercepts and the learning update. We did not allow for temporal variation in σ_v^2. We have three econometrician's error variances, τ_t^2. The model is not identified unless we assume the econometrician errs in modelling the updates as well as in modelling the initial proposal.

3. Estimation and Results

The income, tax-price, and students per household variables that appear in the expenditure equation were computed as follows. Income, Y, is median family income adjusted for school bond and other prior school tax commitments. Tax price, P, per dollar of per student spending was measured as tax share multiplied by enrollment in the school district. In turn, we computed tax share as a ratio of median housing value to total assessed valuation. As a measure of the number of students in the voter's household, S, we used the ratio of total school enrollment to the number of families.[7] Data on basic variables appear in Table 1.

The threshold effect associated with the reversion variables creates a discontinuity in equations (11) when the perceived reversion equals the threshold parameter μ. In order to make the likelihood function and its partial derivatives continuous, we used a technique developed by Tishler and Zang (1979). This involves approximating the discontinuous variable $\overline{H}$ and the variable $\overline{Z}$ (whose first derivative is discontinuous) by twice continuously differentiable polynomials whenever the perceived reversion falls in an interval within $\pm\gamma$ of the threshold; γ is a prespecified positive

Table 1

Description of Variables

		Mean	Standard Deviation
E_1:	proposed total expenditure per student, first election, 1971–72 (dollars),		
	all districts	957.09	180.36
	districts failing first election	984.60	188.80
E_2:	proposed total expenditure per student, second election, 1971–72	972.51	194.05
	districts failing second election	935.10	116.65
E_3:	proposed total expenditure per student, third election, 1971–72	912.76	105.93
Y:	median family income, adjusted for local school bond taxes and intermediate education district taxes and receipts (dollars)	9341.93	1320.18
R:	true cash value of all taxable real estate in district (dollars)	100,337,000	139,489,000
K:	median housing value (dollars)	13,411.20	3291.61
D:	total students, measured by average daily membership	2591.52	3602.58
P:	tax price = DK/R (dollars)	0.378	0.151
A:	(lump sum) state aid per student from the Basic School Support Fund (dollars)	228.54	57.40
Q_1:	local reversion per student (dollars)	258.01	150.60
S:	Students per family	0.973	0.203
V_1:	vote logit, first election*	0.140	0.369
V_2:	vote logit, second election*	0.073	0.300
V_3:	vote logit, third election*	0.199	0.315

*Antilogit of mean V_1 = 53.49%. Antilogits of ± one standard deviation: 44.29% and 62.46%.

Antilogit of mean V_2 = 51.81%. Antilogits of ± one standard deviation: 44.33% and 59.22%.

Antilogit of mean V_3 = 54.95% Antilogits of ± one standard deviation: 47.10% and 62.57%.

[The antilogit of V is given by $1/1(1+e^{-V})$.]

Number of observations in sample: 111. [42 districts had two elections, 17 districts had three.]

constant.[8] In the estimates that we report here, we have set $\gamma=2.0$, less than 1% of the estimated threshold.

The error structure of the system (11)–(12) is also used in the estimation. We let σ_{11} be the error variance of the first expenditure equation, σ_{22} that of the first voting equation, σ_{33} of the second expenditure equation, and σ_{44} of the second voting equation, etc. Similarly, σ_{12} is the covariance between the first expenditure equation and the first voting equation, etc. The variances and covariances of the error structure in equations (11)-(12) can then be expressed in terms of the individual error variances and the structural parameters s and δ.

$$\sigma_{11} = \sigma_u^2 + \tau_1^2 \tag{13}$$

$$\sigma_{22} = \delta^2\sigma_u^2 + \sigma_v^2 \tag{14}$$

$$\sigma_{33} = (1-s)^2\sigma_u^2 + \tau_1^2 + \tau_2^2 + (s^2/\delta^2)\sigma_v^2 \tag{15}$$

$$\sigma_{44} = \delta^2(1-s)^2\,\sigma_u^2 + (1+s^2)\sigma_v^2 \tag{16}$$

$$\sigma_{55} = \tau_1^2 + \tau_2^2 + \tau_3^2 + (1-s)^4\,\sigma_u^2 + [(1-s)^2+1](s^2/\delta^2)\sigma_v^2 \tag{17}$$

$$\sigma_{66} = \delta^2(1-s)^4\,\sigma_u^2 + [s^2(1-s)^2+1]\sigma_v^2 \tag{18}$$

$$\sigma_{12} = \delta\sigma_u^2 \tag{19}$$

$$\sigma_{13} = \tau_1^2 + (1-s)\sigma_u^2 \tag{20}$$

$$\sigma_{14} = \delta(1-s)\sigma_u^2 \tag{21}$$

$$\sigma_{15} = \tau_1^2 + (1-s)^2\sigma_u^2 \tag{22}$$

$$\sigma_{16} = \delta(1-s)^2\sigma_u^2 \tag{23}$$

$$\sigma_{23} = \delta(1-s)\sigma_u^2 - (s/\delta)\sigma_v^2 \tag{24}$$

$$\sigma_{24} = \delta^2(1-s)\delta_u^2 - s\sigma_v^2 \tag{25}$$

$$\sigma_{25} = \delta(1-s)^2\sigma_u^2 - (s/\delta)(1-s)\sigma_v^2 \tag{26}$$

$$\sigma_{26} = \delta^2(1-s)^2\sigma_u^2 - s(1-s)\sigma_v^2 \tag{27}$$

$$\sigma_{34} = \delta(1-s)^2\sigma_u^2 + (s^2/\delta)\sigma_v^2 \tag{28}$$

$$\sigma_{35} = \tau_1^2 + \tau_2^2 + (1-s)^3\,\sigma_u^2 + (s^2/\delta^2)(1-s)\sigma_v^2 \tag{29}$$

$$\sigma_{36} = \delta(1-s)^3\sigma_u^2 + (s^2/\delta)(1-s)\sigma_v^2 \tag{30}$$

$$\sigma_{45} = \delta(1-s)^3\sigma_u^2 + (s/\delta)[s(1-s)-1]\sigma_v^2 \tag{31}$$

$$\sigma_{46} = \delta^2(1-s)^3\sigma_u^2 + s[s(1-s)-1]\sigma_v^2 \tag{32}$$

$$\sigma_{56} = \delta(1-s)^4\sigma_u^2 + (s^2/\delta)[(1-s)^2 + 1]\sigma_v^2 \tag{33}$$

These twenty-one equations in the seven parameters s, δ, τ_1^2, τ_2^2, τ_3^2, σ_u^2, and σ_v^2 yield an overidentified system. In estimating (11)-(12) by full information maximum likelihood methods, however, we can incorporate the overidentifying restrictions (13)-(33). In this way, the estimated parameters will be the set that minimizes the variance-covariance matrix of the estimated standard errors of these parameters. The maximum likelihood procedure recognizes that some observations have no second or third elections. (Details about the derivation of the likelihood function are available from the authors.)

Results of the maximum likelihood estimation are presented in Table 2. To indicate the stability of most parameters, we present estimates for the case where just the first election data are used, then the first two elections, and finally the first three elections. In all three cases, the coefficients on income (β_1), tax price (β_2), and number of students in the household (β_3), and their estimated standard errors are very close to the estimates from the single-equation expenditure model of Filimon et al. (1982). The same is true of the reversion coefficients θ_1 and θ_2, the threshold μ, and the perception parameter ρ. The impact of reversions and of voter misperception of outside grants is undiminished in the fuller system.

Perception and State Aid

The estimated perception parameter ρ is 0.97. While we readily reject the null hypothesis of complete information ($\rho=0.0$), we fail to reject the hypothesis that voters act as if there were no state aid ($\rho=1.0$). Thus, a dollar of state grant leads to a dollar of additional expenditure, with no reduction in local taxes. Using $\rho=1$, the direct proportional effect of aid on per student spending is $A/(E-A)$. From Table 1, for first elections, at the sample means this is $A/(E-A) = 228.54/(957.09 - 228.54) = 0.31$. For districts that have at least two elections, the mean value of A is 225.02. For these districts, at the sample means, $A/(E-A) = 225.02/(972.51 - 225.02) = 0.30$. The presence of state aid increased proposed expenditures by roughly 30 percent.

Proposed expenditures are raised another $100(e^{\theta_1}-1) = 14.3\%$ for those districts with reversions just below the threshold of \$211 relative to those districts just above the threshold. Full perception of state aid, whose mean of \$228.54 exceeds the threshold, would put nearly all observations above the threshold. Thus, voters' failure to perceive state aid may not only increase proposals by 30% due to direct perception effects, but, in a substantial number of districts, also by another 14.3% due to reversion effects.

We would also expect these effects to work in reverse, at least at the

Table 2

Maximum Likelihood Estimates

Structural Parameters	One Election Estimates		Two Election Estimates		Three Election Estimates	
	Estimate	Estimated Standard Error	Estimate	Estimated Standard Error	Estimate	Estimated Standard Error
β_{01}	-2.105	1.683	-1.947	1.720	-1.900	1.767
β_{02}			-1.961	1.723	-1.905	1.770
β_{03}					-1.918	1.772
β_1	0.775	0.180	0.768	0.185	0.762	0.189
β_2	-0.362	0.054	-0.364	0.054	-0.367	0.052
β_3	-0.242	0.078	-0.240	0.080	-0.242	0.082
θ_1	0.136	0.047	0.135	0.047	0.134	0.47
θ_2	0.186	0.085	0.185	0.085	0.186	0.087
ρ	0.972	0.196	0.974	0.202	0.975	0.202
μ	211.80	37.36	211.51	38.50	211.34	38.53
α_1	0.140	0.040	0.140	0.043	0.140	0.044
α_2			0.297	0.090	0.224	0.098
α_3					0.396	0.174
δ			-7.207	3.431	-5.378	2.001
s			0.092	0.193	0.222	0.223
Error Variances*						
τ_1^2			0.026	0.0055	0.025	0.0055
τ_2^2			0.0012	0.00026	0.0012	0.00028
τ_3^2					0.00065	0.00053
σ_u^2			0.0020	0.0020	0.0032	0.0024
σ_v^2			0.036	0.010	0.047	0.013
Ln of likelihood function	-731.12		-929.212		-1006.638	

*The parameters δ, τ_1^2, σ_u^2, and σ_v^2 are not identified in single election estimates. The reduced form estimates (and estimated standard errors) are: σ_{11}, 0.0273 (0.0057); σ_{22}, 0.136 (0.018); σ_{12}, -0.0125 (0.0060).

margin. The magnitudes of our estimates suggest that a *cutback* in state aid would not be offset, even partially, by local spending on public education.

Learning and Adjustment

The expenditure intercept terms β_{01}, β_{02}, and β_{03} have almost identical estimates, with large standard errors. This suggests that the underlying pattern of a sequence of decreasing proposals of the type suggested by Romer and Rosenthal (1979a) is not important.

The "learning update" parameter s is estimated at 0.222, with a standard error equal to this estimate. As might be expected, s is the parameter whose estimate is most affected by using the data from all three, as against only the first two, elections. The estimate is in the theoretically predicted range of [0,1] both times. In both cases, it is small relative to its standard error, but with the additional data the estimate equals its standard error whereas it is only one-half the standard error in the two-election case. This suggests that our failure to find substantial updating may relate to the small effective sample size with multiple elections.

Even with more data, however, we would be unlikely to discover an effect of appreciable importance. Setters do not appear to adjust proposals in light of election outcomes in the heuristic manner that we postulated.[9] Based on the expenditure equation estimates, it seems that the first spending proposal is also an excellent prediction of the second proposal in those districts where the first election fails. The data appear to bear this out. Of the 42 districts in which there was a second election, 16 first-election proposals were not changed and three were increased (by less than 3%). Of the remaining 23 districts where the first proposal was defeated, only 10 saw cuts by more than 2% between the first election and the second.

In contrast to the absence of significant updating, the setter's error influences vote outcomes as we expected. The sign of δ is negative: a proposal that is "too large" drives the vote logit below the "error-free" expected value. To get a feel for the effect of the setter's error on voting, we computed the impact that a $50 per student "error" would have in an "average" district. From Table 1, using statewide mean values and our estimate of $\rho=0.975$, an "average" first election perceived expenditure is $957.09 - 0.975 \times 228.54 = 734.26$. For a $50 error in perceived spending per student, u_1 is given by:

$$u_1 = \ln(784.26) - \ln(734.26) = 0.066$$

If $v_1 = 0$, the effect of a setter's error of this magnitude on the first election outcome is:

$$V_1 = \alpha_1 + \delta u_1 = -0.215,$$

which corresponds to a 44.6% Yes vote, as contrasted with the 53.5% Yes vote (implied by $\alpha_1 = 0.140$) that would be expected with $u_1 = 0$. On the second election, the effect of the error, adjusted by our point estimate of the learning update, can be calculated by setting v_2 also equal to zero, so that

$$V_2 = \alpha_2 + \delta(1-s)u_1 = -0.051,$$

which corresponds to a 48.7% Yes vote, rather than the 55.6% Yes vote (corresponding to $\alpha_2 = 0.224$) that would be implied by complete updating ($s=1$).

For the third election, a similar calculation shows

$$V_3 = \alpha_3 + \delta(1-s)^2 u_1 = 0.182,$$

which corresponds to a 54.6% Yes vote, rather than the 59.8% vote (corresponding to $\alpha_3 = 0.396$) implied by complete updating. Comparing the estimates of the voting equation intercepts, α_t, suggests that the expected vote logit on each later election is greater than that on the preceding election. This would be consistent with the kind of sequence derived in Romer and Rosenthal (1979a). Yet, as we have seen, the expenditure equation estimates do not reveal a strong sequence effect. Given the data at our disposal, we cannot be definite about the net effect of the underlying sequence structure.

Some reconciliation of the results may be suggested by comparing the effect of the setter's error in the voting and the expenditure equations. In the second election voting equation, the total error variance is equal to $\delta^2 \sigma_u^2 = 0.0926$ plus $\sigma_v^2 = 0.0469$. Thus, because of the substantial magnitude of δ, errors by the setter are estimated to have twice the effect of the random turnout component on voting behavior. In contrast, most of the variance of the first expenditure equation is ascribed to the econometrician's inability to capture the purely static feature of demand, since $\tau_1^2 = 0.025$ is nearly eight times the estimated setter error variance, $\sigma_u^2 = 0.0032$. The "noise" in the static model may make it difficult to discuss the sequence effects. In any event, we estimate that setters do not make substantial errors[10] (at the mean first election proposal of $957.09, setter errors of $\pm\sigma_u = .0566$ would result in proposals of $917 and $1000), a result in line with our basic premise that setters actively pursue a goal of budget-maximization.

Another clue to these results may lie in the findings of Rubinfeld (1977), who used survey data on individuals to analyze voting in a Michigan school district. There were two elections to pass a budget. The first one lost, but the second proposal—identical to the first—passed, with increased voter turnout. The critical difference in the second election appears to have been greater participation by women with school-age children who tended to vote for the proposals. A plausible interpretation is that the first election loss influenced the turnout on the second election, particularly by those who were particularly threatened by a possible shutdown of the schools.

Carrying this over to our results suggests that setters are aware that turnout is likely to increase on later elections. (Indeed, Romer and Rosenthal (1983) have shown, for a much larger sample, that turnout is systematically larger on the passing election than on the first election.) Moreover, setters may be expecting relatively higher turnout by groups favoring the proposal. And voters may even change positions on the proposal. Our sample contains observations where the absolute number of No votes falls even when turnout increases substantially, hinting that some voters who initially vote No may change their votes as the closing of the schools becomes a more imminent possibility. These factors counteract the considerations for cutting the proposal, but are still consistent with expecting a higher Yes vote on a later election even if the proposal is unchanged. The parameters α_2 and α_3 may be capturing this expectation. At the same time, the setter's failure to correct his initial error may be working against the full realization of a Yes vote consistent with α_2 or α_3. If $u_1 > 0$ in districts with a first election loss, then this effect is negative, particularly if s is close to zero. Consequently, second and third election outcomes (whose sample means are 51.8% and 54.9%, respectively) may be much closer than the Yes vote implied by α_2 (approximately 56%) or α_3 (60%).

Conclusion

This research has largely confirmed the agenda setter model's ability to account for the *static* properties of cross-sectional spending and voting in Oregon. Estimates of the demand parameters (β), reversion parameters (θ and μ), and perception parameter (ρ) are unaffected by sequence effects. The number of elections needed for passage and voting in a given election both appear largely determined by the interaction of the setter's error (σ_u^2) and "random" effects on voting (σ_v^2). If we group the districts by whether one, two, or more than two elections were required to pass, we find that group means of both the exogenous and endogenous variables vary little in comparison to the within-group standard deviations. Earlier research

(Romer and Rosenthal, 1982a) showed that the exogenous variables have no direct ability to explain the vote logits. The only systematic effect on voting is the setter's behavior. The parameter δ is negative as predicted, and the estimate is 2.7 times its standard error.

We have not dealt successfully with the *dynamics*. The insignificant variation in the β_{0t} and the insignificant value of s leave us with no evidence for either a pre-planned decreasing sequence of proposals (Romer and Rosenthal, 1979a) or heuristic learning.

Most work in the political economy of public finance, including ours, assumes constant indirect preferences for spending and either constant or random turnout. Our results make these assumptions less attractive. Finding the α_t consistent with the model even in the absence of significant β_{0t} or s suggests that turnout and preferences may vary systematically in a dynamic context.

Notes

1. In addition to the works cited in the text, agenda control in the context of public expenditures has been explored by Denzau and Mackay (1980) and Mackay and Weaver (1978).
2. The most frequently invoked (by economists) such model is the "median voter" framework. Although usually not explicitly specified, implicit in this model is the assumption of open or competitive agendas, with no restrictions on access to the agenda.
3. These remarks apply to the Oregon institutional structure prior to 1979. The actual number of elections allowed was subject to change by state legislation. The limit has never been more than eight elections. For the period covered by the data we used in this paper, the limit was six.
4. These findings are consistent with the oft-cited "flypaper effect" of intergovernmental aid (see, e.g., Gramlich, 1977; Whitman and Cline, 1978). The tendency for spending to increase by roughly the amount of such aid is consonant with and reinforced by the setter's behavior.
5. Courant et al. (1979) and Oates (1979) have also offered arguments for "flypaper" due to perception effects. For a brief critique of these arguments, see Filimon et al. (1982).
6. In general, the voting effect of the setter's error will depend on the entire distribution of voters' preferences. Consequently, δ may vary from one district to another. Constraining δ to be constant is a strong assumption.
7. Our use of medians in the empirical specification should not be taken to mean that we regard a "median" voter as pivotal. The "multiple" and "fractile" identification problems discussed in Romer and Rosenthal (1979b) imply that one cannot conclude from a loglinear model that a "median" voter is decisive (in the case of a median voter model) or pivotal (in the case of a setter model). Moreover, even if preferences are single-peaked and there is full turnout, we cannot expect the voter with median demand to be at the median on every independent variable, except under very restrictive conditions. Consequently, we do not view the equation for the proposal of the setter to be a vehicle for identifying whether a voter with specific characteristics is decisive or pivotal.
8. For more details on the use of this approximation, see Filimon et al. (1982).
9. We experimented with a modified version of the "learning update" by hypothesizing that adjustments occur only if the first election loses by more than a given percentage of votes; thus,

$$\text{"Learning Update"} = \begin{cases} 0 & \text{if } V_1 \geqslant \bar{\alpha} \\ -s(V_1 - \alpha_1)/\delta & \text{if } V_1 < \bar{\alpha} \end{cases}$$

Here $\bar{\alpha} < 0$ is a prespecified parameter. We estimated the system on two-election data for several values of $\bar{\alpha}$, corresponding to a range of first election vote outcomes from 30% Yes to 49% Yes. The likelihood function was maximized for $\bar{\alpha}$ corresponding to an approximately 47% Yes vote. The estimated parameters were essentially identical to our original estimates. Allowing for a "zone of indifference" did not alter our finding that the update parameter s is not significantly different from zero.

10. We computed $\ln(E_1 - \rho A) \pm \sigma_u$ at the sample means of E_1, A and $\rho = 0.975$. $917 and $1000 correspond to the values of E_1 implied by this computation.

References

P.N. Courant, E.M. Gramlich, and D.L. Rubinfeld, "The Stimulative Effects of Intergovernmental Grants: Or Why Money Sticks Where It Hits," in P. Mieszkowski and W. Oakland (eds.), *Fiscal Federalism and Grants-in-Aid*, The Urban Institute; Washington, D. C., 1979.

A.T. Denzau and R.J. Mackay, "A Model of Benefit and Tax Share Discrimination by a Monopoly Bureau," *Journal of Public Economics*, June 1980.

R. Filimon, T. Romer, and H. Rosenthal, "Asymmetric Information and Agenda Control: The Bases of Monopoly Power in Public Spending," *Journal of Public Economics*, February 1982.

F.M. Gramlich, "Intergovernmental Grants: A Review of the Empirical Literature," in W.E. Oates (ed.), *The Political Economy of Fiscal Federalism*, D.C. Heath, Lexington, Mass., 1977.

R.J. Mackay and C. Weaver, "Monopoly Bureaus and Fiscal Outcomes," in G. Tullock and R. Wagner (eds.), *Policy Analysis and Deductive Reasoning*, D.C.Heath, Lexington, Mass., 1978.

W. Oates, "Lump-Sum Intergovernmental Grants Have Price Effects," in P. Mieszkowski and W. Oakland (eds.), *Fiscal Federalism and Grants-in-Aid*, The Urban Institute: Washington, D.C., 1979.

T. Romer and H. Rosenthal, "Bureaucrats vs. Voters: On the Political Economy of Resource Allocation by Direct Democracy," *Quarterly Journal of Economics*, November 1979a.

T. Romer and H. Rosenthal, "The Elusive Median Voter" *Journal of Public Economics*, October 1979b.

T. Romer and H. Rosenthal, "An Institutional Theory of the Effect of Intergovernmental Grants," *National Tax Journal*, December 1980.

T. Romer and H. Rosenthal, "An Exploration in the Politics and Economics of Local Public Services," *Zeitschrift für Nationalökonomie/Journal of Economics*, Supplement 2, 1982a.

T. Romer and H. Rosenthal, "Median Voters or Budget Maximizers: Evidence from School Expenditure Referenda," *Economic Inquiry*, October 1982b.

T. Romer and H. Rosenthal, "Voting and Spending: Some Empirical Relationships in the Political Economy of Local Public Finance," in G. Zodrow (ed.), *The Tiebout Model After Twenty-Five Years*, Academic Press, New York, 1983.

D.L. Rubinfeld, "Voting in a Local School Election: A Micro Analysis," *Review of Economics and Statistics*, February 1977.

A. Tishler and I. Zang, "A Switching Regression Method Using Inequality Conditions," *Journal of Econometrics*, 1979.

R. Whitman and R.J. Cline, *Fiscal Impact of Revenue Sharing in Comparison with Other Federal Aid: An Evaluation of Recent Empirical Findings*, Urban Institute, Washington, 1978.

Résumé

Nous utilisons un modèle économétrique, basé sur le modèle de
Romer-Rosenthal du contrôle de l'ordre du jour par des bureaucraties tendant à maximiser les budgets, pour analyser les résultats de referenda
budgétaires dans un échantillon de districts scolaires de l'Orégon.

En plus d'une estimation des effets du contrôle de l'ordre du jour, le
modèle permet d'estimer l'incapacité des électeurs à apprécier correctement
la disponibilité des subventions forfaitaires intergouvernementales dans leur
évaluation de la meilleure dépense. Les budgets sont établis par voie
référendaire. Dans le cas d'un référendum négatif, un nombre limité de
scrutins supplémentaires peut avoir lieu pour une année donnée. Ce modèle
nous permet d'évaluer dans quel degré celui qui établit l'ordre du jour (par
exemple, le directeur des écoles du district scolaire) apprend quelque chose
sur les préférences des électeurs à partir des résultats des référenda négatifs.

Les variables endogènes du modèle sont les propositions de budget et
les rèsultats de vote de chaque référendum pour une séquence de référenda
tenus dans chaque district scolaire. Les effets des propositions sur les com-
portements des électeurs et les effets d'apprentissage qui en résultent apparaissent à travers des paramètres structurels dans la structure des erreurs.
Ce modèle est apprécié en terme d'estimateur du maximum de vraisem-
blance non-linéaire. Les résultats (1) confirment le modèle théorique de
contrôle de l'ordre du jour et ses estimations sur les effets des propositions
du décideur de l'ordre du jour sur le comportement des électeurs; (2) montrent que la mauvaise perception des allocations publiques par les électeurs
conduit à des augmentations significatives des dépenses; (3) ne réussissent
pas à montrer si le décideur en tire quelques leçons.

Identification of Individual Preferences for Government Activity from Voting Behavior

Werner W. Pommerehne and Friedrich Schneider*

I. Introduction

The difficulty of measuring individual preferences for government activity, especially in the case of a public good, is a well-known major problem of resource allocation. The problem arises because there are no markets, no sales and no products in the public sector. At the same time, it is important for decisionmakers in the public sector to have some idea of taxpayers'/citizens' preferences for the various governmental services. As the knowledge of these preferences could be of considerable help in the day-to-day policy of allocating the public budget[1], a number of approaches have been developed in the last decade in order to reveal individual preferences for government activities. Among them is the analysis of referenda outcomes which will be applied here.

The referendum in its role as a political institution provides one possibility for revealing voters' preferences. Such information may be useful for decisionmakers in government in order to arrange a referendum proposal (or revise a defeated one) in such a way that it meets the wishes of a majority. In the following we investigate how information on individual preferences for government activity can be derived from referenda outcomes[2]. In part II, this is demonstrated by using a partial approach for analyzing the outcome of a referendum on the increase of public theater subsidy in the Swiss Canton of Basle-City. In part III, the approach is extended and a more complex referendum on the expansion of the so far national airport of Basle-City to an international one is considered. Part IV contains an evalua-

*We would like to thank our formal discussants, André Boyer and especially J.J. Ritzen for stimulating comments. We are also indebted to the Swiss National Science Foundation for supporting our research through grant NF-1821-078

Public Finance and the Quest for Efficiency. Proceedings of the 38th Congress of the International Institute of Public Finance. Copenhagen, 1982, pp. 109–126. Copyright © 1984 by Wayne State University Press, Detroit, Michigan, 48202.

tion of the results, and part V a comparison to some alternative approaches for revealing individual preferences for government activity. The final part VI presents a summary.

II. A Partial Approach: The Theater Subsidy Referendum

The example to be analyzed in the following is a referendum on an increase of public subsidies to the municipal theater (repertory theater and comedy) of the Swiss Canton of Basle-City in 1973. It proposed a rise of the annual public subsidy (for current expenditures) by 3 million Swissfrancs (SFrs.), from 10 to 13 million SFrs. It was defeated by 57% No-votes. In this case, a simple partial approach can be used because we may assume that an increase of the public subsidy by 3 million SFrs. will have no significant impact on prices of other goods and factors, on the economic development of the Basle-City region and, therefore, on the economic situation of the individual voter. The framework used here is based on Rubinfeld (1977).[3]

Let S_0 be the current level of annual public subsidy to the theater. The increase of the subsidy is ΔS. Thus, if the proposal were passed, the annual public subsidy would be at the level $S_0 + \Delta S$. The level of public subsidy most preferred by individual i, S_i^*, can be described by a function of his/her socioeconomic characteristics,

$$S_i^* = S^*(X) + u_i,$$

where X is a vector of characteristics and u_i is a random variable (accounting for the fact that vector X does not include all relevant characteristics and/or that the characteristics included are not wholly adequate proxies). If $S_i^* \leqslant S_0$, the taxpayer/voter is expected to vote No; similarly, if $S_i^* \geqslant S_0 + \Delta S$, a Yes-vote is expected. If S_i^* falls between S_0 and $S_0 + \Delta S$, voting behavior is not at all clear. In order to elucidate the voting decision, it is assumed that the level S_i' ($S_0 < S_i' \leqslant S_0 + \Delta S$), where individuals i's Yes-vote switches to a No-vote, can be described as

$$S_i' = S_0 + a\Delta S + v_i, \tag{1}$$

where $0<a<1$. Equation (1) shows that S_i' is equal to a linear combination of the levels S_0 and $S_0 + \Delta S$ plus a random variable v. As the theater subsidy proposal leaves some unspecified details of how the improvement of the performance quality is affected by the subsidy increment, the random variable v may be partly interpreted as capturing the variation in the individual perceptions of the effective impact of the proposal.

The voting rule thus reads:

$$\text{Vote Yes if } S_i^* \geq S_i' \tag{2}$$

$$\text{Vote No if } S_i^* < S_i'.$$

The probability of an individual voting Yes, P(Yes), is:

$$P(\text{Yes}) = P(S_i^* \geq S_i') \tag{3}$$
$$= P(v_i - u_i \leq S^*(X) - (S_0 + a\Delta S)).$$

Following Rubinfeld we assume that the cumulative distribution function for $v - u$ follows a standardized logistic distribution. Therefore, equation (3) can be rewritten as

$$P(\text{Yes}) = \frac{1}{1 + e^{-c(S^*(X) - S_0 - a\Delta S)}} \tag{4}$$

where c is a proportionality constant determined by the unknown variances of v and u. Assuming that $S^*(X)$ is a linear function of voter's attributes, X, equation (4) can be transformed into the estimation equation

$$\ln\left[\frac{P(\text{Yes})}{(1 - P(\text{Yes}))}\right] = -(cS_0 + ca\Delta S) + \beta X, \tag{5}$$

where β is the vector of coefficients to be estimated. As in most empirical analyses of referenda outcomes, no micro (individual) data are available in our case. We thus rely on aggregate data for the 21 cantonal districts. Furthermore, we assume that equation (5) can be aggregated over all voters in each district. This leads to the following specification

$$\ln\left[\frac{F(\text{Yes})_j}{(1 - F(\text{Yes})_j)}\right] = \alpha + \beta \overline{X}_j + B, \tag{6}$$

where $F(\text{Yes})_j$ is the fraction of those voters in district j who said Yes, $\overline{X}_j$ is the vector of means of the characteristics of X, α is the constant term[4] and B is the error term[5]. Equation (6) will be used to estimate the coefficients of the variables which, as we hypothesize, will influence voting behavior. The main hypothesis on the theoretical variables and the expected sign of the regression coefficients are, subject to the usual ceteris paribus assumption, as follows:

HYP 1: The higher the mean income in a district, the higher the expected approval rate on the theater subsidy referendum.

This is a standard hypothesis and reflects the assumption that a theater visit is a normal (and not an inferior) good.

> *HYP 2:* The higher the expected tax increase due to the subsidy, the lower the expected degree of approval.
> *HYP 3:* The higher the average transportation cost for reaching the theatre, the less likely the proposal is to be accepted.

The last two hypotheses reflect the monetary costs. Whereas transportation costs operate like price differentiation by districts, the prices of all other goods are the same for all individuals and hence have not to be considered here.

> *HYP 4:* The higher the average educational level in a district, the higher will be the expected approval rate.

This last hypothesis deals with a non-monetary cost aspect. It consists of the ability and efficiency to inform oneself about the specific content of a theatre performance, and it is also related to the ability to understand the performances and, thereby, to enrich one's mind. In other words: The shadow price of using cultural institutions is lower, the higher the educational level.

The estimation results of the already mentioned defeated theater referendum are given in table 1.[6]

In equation (1) the $\bar{R}^2$ with over 90 percent of explained variance indicates that the major influences are captured. All estimated coefficients have the expected sign and are—with the exception of the educational variable—statistically significant. The strongest marginal impact (measured by elasticity) has income, followed by expected tax increase and travel cost. The education variable has a fairly significant impact, indicating that well-educated voters may have a low shadow price when using cultural institutions.[7]

In equation (2), an interaction variable "weighted income" (product of income and educational level) is introduced. The reason for doing so is to avoid problems of multicollinearity.[8] The estimation results are slightly better than those for equation (1). The good overall result also becomes evident considering the simulation results for the 21 districts. Only in one district is the actual approval rate higher than 50% (52.6%); the simulations also indicate that only in this district the proposal would have been accepted by a majority (of 51.6%). The absolute average mean deviation of the predicted overall approval rate is 1.4 percentage points of the actual overall approval rate of 43.3 percent.

These quite satisfactory results demonstrate that the major determi-

Table 1

Estimation Results of Voters' Behavior: Referendum on Public Theater Subsidy in the Canton of Basle-City, Sept. 23, 1973; Weighted Logit Regression[a]

Equation:	Income (mean taxable income, in 1000 SFr.)	Weighted income	Expected Tax Increase (average marginal tax burden, in % of taxable income)	Transportation cost (average transportation cost: center of distr. to theatre, using public utilities, in SFr.)	Education (share of voter with high school or university degree, in % of those entitled to vote)	Constant term	$\overline{R}^2$
[1]	0.017** (4.65)	—	−0.011** (−2.94)	−0.004* (−2.21)	0.007 (1.66)	0.058	0.910
[2]	—	0.112** (3.78)	−0.011** (−3.27)	−0.003** (−2.77)	—	0.063	0.912

[a]Numbers in parentheses are the $\hat{t}$-values for the corresponding regression coefficients; coefficients with one asterisk (two asterisks) are statistically significant at the 95%– (99%–) level (two tailed test); $\overline{R}^2$ is the coefficient of determination (adjusted for the degrees of freedom).

nants of private demand for publicly provided goods are well captured. This can be additionally shown by using our model (equation [2] of table 1) making a forecast of the outcome of the revised subsidy proposal (June 23, 1974), which included a cut from three to two additional million SFrs. The forecasts and the actual results are shown in figure 1.

The figure shows that the forecasts come very close to the actual results, with an absolute average mean deviation of only 1.7 percentage points. For 18 of the 21 districts an approval by more than 50% is predicted, which actually happened. For the three remaining districts a defeat is predicted which again is correct. The actual overall approval rate is 59.9 percent, the predicted one 60.0%.

III. An Extended Approach: The Airport Referendum

Referenda quite often contain more complex proposals than those in the case discussed above. If approved, they will have a major impact on the economic and the environmental development. An example for such a referendum is the 1971 proposal to expand the (at that time) national airport of Basle-City to an international one. The referendum proposal suggested a public investment of 26 million SFrs., of which 9 million were a federal government grant and 17 million had to be financed by the Basle-City voters/taxpayers. It was defeated by 54% No-votes. An extended model is used to analyze this more complex referendum in order to examine whether this approach provides helpful information for the policy decision maker.

The voting behavior vis à vis a more complex referendum proposal cannot be modelled in the framework of a partial approach (e.g., as private demand for a single public good). Instead, it is appropriate to interpret the individual decision as the result of a comparison of utility levels, as for example done by McFadden (1976). The following presentation follows the more extensive treatment in Deacon and Shapiro (1975).

The voter/taxpayer is assumed to select the highest level of utility to be gained from the proposed alternatives. The arguments of the utility function which are influenced by the proposed alternative are e_k, environment of the canton; p_k, prices of other goods x; and $Y_k - T_k$, disposable income, where T_k stands for income tax as the by far most important tax. The subscript k indicates that these variables may be affected by the ensuing change in case of a majority approval of the referendum. The indirect utility maximum is then

$$\max U(x, e_k) = V(e_k, p_k, Y_k - T_k). \tag{7}$$

Figure 1: *Yes-Votes as a Share of Total Votes: Second Referendum on Public Theater Subsidy in the Canton of Basle-City, June 23, 1974.*

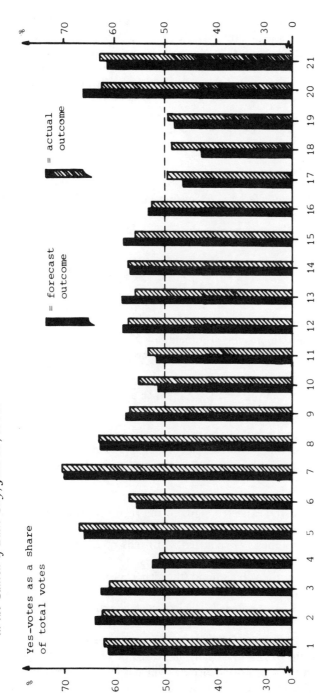

Let V_0 be the status quo and let V_1 point to a situation in which the runway and the passenger and freight facilities are drastically expanded—and thus the projected number of take-offs and landings is more than doubled. Voter's choice is determined by whether $V_1 - V_0$ is positive or not; if it is positive, a Yes-vote is called for. The difference in utility maxima is described by

$$V_1 - V_0 = \Delta V(e_0, p_0, Y_0 - T_0, \Delta e, \Delta p, \Delta Y - \Delta T) \qquad (8)$$

$$= \Delta V(z),$$

where z is the vector of arguments in ΔV. The subscript 0 indicates initial conditions and the Δ refers to changes resulting from the airport expansion. For the econometric specification, we choose a response favoring the airport referendum by a Yes-vote so that the probability of observing a Yes-vote is a rising function of ΔV

$$P(Yes \mid z) = \int\limits_0^\infty g(\Delta V \mid z) \, d(\Delta V). \qquad (9)$$

Assuming that the density function g is a logistic one and that there exists a linear relationship among the arguments of ΔV, equation (9) can be transformed into the following estimation equation

$$\ln \left[\frac{F(Yes)_j}{(1 - F(Yes)_j)} \right] = \gamma + \epsilon \cdot \overline{Z}_j + R \qquad (10)$$

where ϵ are the coefficients to be estimated, γ is the constant term and R is the transformed errors term. As with the theatre subsidy referendum, individual data are not available and thus we once again use aggregate data for the 21 districts.

The main hypothesis about the theoretical variables, the empirical proxies used, and the expected signs of the regression coefficients are presented in table 2.

The first hypothesis is standard and needs no further comment. Hypothesis 2 reflects that the expected increase of the noise level is a major point of concern in the voter's mind (the airport is only 2.7 miles away from the City center). Hypothesis 3 on the positive economic impact of the airport expansion can be tested using proxies like the expected decrease of unemployment. Unfortunately, no data were available; lacking are even data on the level of unemployment by districts at this time. Hypotheses 4 and 5 both relate to the drastically increased possibility of taking a plane from Basle instead from Zurich airport (which is 60 miles away from Basle), if the referendum is accepted. This fact can be described by a decrease of

Table 2

Hypotheses about Voters' Behavior: Airport Referendum in the
Canton of Basle-City, Sept. 25, 1971; Weighted Logit Regression

Hypotheses: *Theoretical variables*	*Empirical proxies used*	*Theoretically expected sign* *of the regression coefficients*
HYP 1: Expected tax increase	Average marginal tax burden (in % of taxable income)	negative
HYP 2: Expected environmental deterioriation	Forecasted mean noise level (NNI) if airport is expanded	negative
HYP 3: Expected improvement of cantonal economy	Expected decrease of unemployment (average percentage of those entitled to vote)	positive
HYP 4 HYP 5 } Expected decrease of travelling costs	{ *Business activities*: share of self-employed voters, weighted by the expected increase in the number of flights per day (average percentage of those entitled to vote) *Tourist activities*: share of voters with high school or university degree, weighted by mean taxable income (average percentage of those entitled to vote)	positive positive

117

travelling costs. Hypothesis 4 captures business activities, approximated by the weighted share of self-employed; hypothesis 5 relates to tourist activities, proxied by the mobility-variable of the weighted share of well-educated voters. As it is assumed that all other price changes are the same for each district, they will show up in the constant term.

The estimation result for the weighted logit regression is:

$$\ln \left[\frac{F(Yes)}{(1 - F(Yes))} \right] = - \underset{(-2.06)}{0.074^*} \quad \text{Expected tax increase}$$

$$- \underset{(-3.28)}{0.012^{**}} \quad \text{Forecast noise level}$$

$$\underset{(2.07)}{0.146^*} \quad \text{Weighted share of self-employed}$$

$$\underset{(2.04)}{0.292^*} \quad \text{Weighted share of well-educated}$$

$$0.044 \quad \text{Constant term}$$

$$\overline{R}^2 = 0.917; \text{ d.f.} = 16.$$

Again, the high $\overline{R}^2$ indicates that the major influences are captured by the model. All estimated coefficients have the expected sign and are statistically significant. The estimation results indicate that this approach is quite useful, even in the case of a more complex referendum proposal, with a variety of economic and environmental effects. This becomes evident when the simulation result for each district is compared with the actual result. Only in one district is the forecast error greater than three percentage points (two standard deviations of the mean of the residual). The absolute average mean deviation has a value of 1.4 percentage points of an overall actual approval rate of 45.5%.

In order to put the model to a more severe test, a forecast of the revised airport referendum five years later, in 1976, was made. The revised proposal differed from the defeated one with respect to the following features: (1) due to an increase of anti-noise investments, the projected mean noise level has decreased by 28 percent; (2) at the same time, the projected number of flights per day has risen by 20 percent; (3) from the proposed total investment of now 40 million SFrs. 17 million (42%) will be financed from the outside (in the case of the first referendum, it was only 34%) so that 23 million SFrs. will have to be financed by the Basle-City voters/taxpayers. This amount is higher than the one in the first airport referendum. The expected (average) marginal tax burden has slightly decreased by 9 percent due to an increase of 56 percent in mean taxable income 1971–76. The forecast and the actual results are shown in figure 2.

Figure 2: *Yes-Votes as a Share of Total Votes: Second Airport Referendum in the Canton of Basle City, Nov. 6, 1976.*

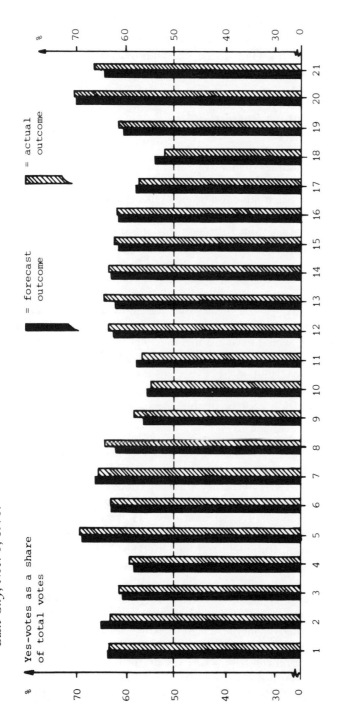

Figure 2 indicates that the differences between the predicted and actual outcome are again very small, with an absolute average mean deviation of 1.9 percentage points. The actual total approval rate is 62.7 percent, the forecasted one 62.6 percent.

IV. Evaluation of the Results

The two examples demonstrate that the major determinants of private demand for government activity can be captured by analyzing referenda outcomes.[9] This also holds for a proposal like the airport referendum which has multiple effects on the environment and the regional economy.

The information gained through this approach can be used for policy advice. For instance, if after the defeat in the first theater referendum, the decisionmakers in government had intended to revise the proposal so that it would have met the wishes of a majority of voters/taxpayers, the information could have been used to simulate the trade-off between an increase of the public subsidy for the theater and the approval rate. Simulating this trade-off (using equation [2]), a proposal for an increase of the subsidy by 2.6 million SFrs. would have just met the 50 percent approval rate, whereas the actually proposed increase by 3 million SFrs. (first referendum proposal) failed, and 2 million SFrs. (second referendum proposal) led to the predicted approval rate of 60 percent.

The information content of this approach may nevertheless be questioned for several reasons:

(1) It may be argued that the use of aggregated data does not necessarily indicate the individual preferences for government activities (Shively 1969). Whether this objection holds ultimately can be checked only by using both individual as well as aggregate data. In our case no individual data exist. However, in studies in which both kinds of data are used (Peterson (1975), Rubinfeld (1977), Bergstrom, Rubinfeld and Shapiro (1982)) quite similar results emerged. Another though weaker examination consists in making forecasts—which were satisfactory in our case.

(2) Another objection could be that only the behavior of the participating voters is analyzed, and therefore the results obtained are not representative for the whole citizenry. However, in our view, this deficiency is not so important as only those voters are relevant for the government who actually state their preferences in the voting process. And if the government can expect that their composition does not change drastically from one referendum to the next, the

information gained will help in arriving at a future proposal which will meet a majority of voters' preferences.

(3) A further objection could be that this approach provides useful information only when the issues proposed deal with a specific topic and are well-defined. The application to proposals with a general topic in which no concrete measures are specified—such as, for example, in the case of a general tax-expenditure-limitation referendum—may not provide much insight (see the studies by Mariotti (1978), Maggadino, Toma and Toma (1980), Courant, Gramlich and Rubinfeld (1980) and Freiman (1981)). It may fail. Generally, the results of such referenda are difficult to interpret—which is not wholly unexpected due to the vagueness of the implications of the respective proposals. Nevertheless, there still remains a wide range of government activities for which the analysis of referenda outcomes produces helpful information on individual preferences[10].

(4) Another objection could be that differences in tastes have to be explicitly taken into account, especially in such a case as the theater subsidy referendum. However, in most cases, taste differences cannot be captured, separate and independent, from observed behavior. Moreover, they may relate to very different aspects of the government activity in question. In the case of the theater subsidy referendum, it may be that there are different preferences due to variations in (a) tastes regarding the expected consumption good, (b) individual evaluation of the theater as an option good, (c) individually attributing a positive bequest value to the theater, and (d) individually deriving a positive prestige value from the existence of the theater. It is hard to see how all these possible differences in tastes can be measured independently and usefully applied for improving the explanatory power of the approach[11].

V. Comparison with Other Approaches

In spite of these possible objections, the analysis of referenda outcome seems to be a useful way to provide information on individual preferences for government activities. Thus, given the institution of referendum, it seems possible to derive information which can be used for concrete policy recommendations, such as, for example, how to mould a referendum proposal so that it meets a majority of voters' preferences. Of course, this does not mean that the analysis of voting behavior is the only way of revealing individual preferences for government activity. Therefore a short comparison to the major alternative approaches is presented[12].

A first alternative is to undertake a *survey*—an approach which is especially used for revealing citizens' preferences for cultural activities (see, for example Nielsen, McQueen and Nielsen 1976)—or to carry out a *controlled experiment*[13]. However, if carefully prepared, this approach needs much time and is rather expensive. Moreover, due to the quite often hypothetical situation and the absence of a real cost concept in people's minds, the problem arises that individuals may have only a weak incentive to make a serious decision and reveal their true preferences. Also, surveys may in particular be misused by those questioned to manipulate the results, since there is often little incentive to prevent them from vastly exaggerating their public likes and dislikes. One way to overcome this problem is to refine the survey questions in order to weaken people's incentives for concealing their true preferences. However, the problem then arises whether these "demand revealing mechanisms"[14] are well understood, a precondition for a reliable interpretation of the answers given. Compared to this approach the analysis of referenda outcome has some advantages: due to a given tax system there usually is no reason to suspect that voters would not state their true preferences for strategic reasons. Morever no hypothetical situation is created, and the voters are informed on both sides of the issue to a fair degree. A further advantage is the realism of the data; they reveal preferences from actual voting decisions under constraints.

A second alternative is to analyze revealed behavior, i.e., to look at reality and to assume that it can be expressed as the private demand for public services. This leads to a comparison of public expenditures in different jurisdictions, and to an analysis of the relation between expenditures and community characteristics in a *median voter* framework[15]. However, the theoretical as well as the empirical assumptions which must be made in order to use this approach are quite strong. Moreover, the question remains open whether the median voter approach provides sufficient information for public decisionmakers in a single jurisdiction and for their specific situation. The approach used in this paper provides exactly such detailed information on individual preferences for government activities in the single jurisdiction considered.

A third approach consists in measuring the demand for a *private good* which is (weakly) *complementary to* the government activity considered. Thus, the preferences, for example, for a publicly provided recreation area are measured by the (additional) travel and other private cost incurred in order to utilize the public good[16]. One problem with this approach is that people may derive a positive utility from the public good considered without participating in the consumption. For instance, in the case of the theater subsidy, it might be misleading to consider only the preferences of those who attend theater performances. Analyzing the outcome of a theater subsidy referendum has also the great advantage of capturing the preferences of those who attribute to the theater a positive option, bequest and/or existence value.

VI. Summary

The paper shows that—given the institution of the referendum—information on individual preferences for government activities can be gained from the analysis of referenda outcome. This is demonstrated by two examples of defeated referenda in the Swiss Canton Basle-City. The potential usefulness of this information for decisionmakers in government in their day-to-day policy is shown by the successful use of this instrument in predicting the outcome of the two revised referenda proposals: The forecasts come very close to the actual outcomes, indicating that this approach provides a simple information instrument to allow governmental policymakers to direct their activities along voter's preferences[17]. Its attractiveness is also due to the simplicity and plausibility of the basic assumptions.

Notes

1. Given the decision at the contractarian level about which institutional frame, and which rules of the political process, should be applied. For a discussion of the distinction between day-to-day policy and decisions at the contractarian level see Buchanan (1975) and Frey (1981).

2. The question whether the institution of referendum (under a given tax system) leads to a Pareto-efficient solution, to a Bowen-, or even to a Lindahl-equilibrium will not be discussed in our paper [see Noam (1980) and Pommerehne (1974) for an empirical investigation of these questions]. We are also not dealing with the question of how a given tax system has to be changed and/or the referendum system has to be modified for such solutions to come about [see in this context Holcombe (1977) and Holcombe and Taylor (1980)].

3. Similar models for analyzing referenda outcomes are developed in Peterson (1975), Barkume (1976, 1977), and Schroeder and Sjoquist (1978).

4. When estimating equation (6) the constant term includes the effect of $cS' = c \cdot S_0 + c \cdot a \cdot \Delta S$, while the variance linked with the logistic specification will be incorporated in the estimates of β.

5. Where $B = \ln[F(Yes)_j / (1 - F(Yes)_j)] - \ln[P(Yes)_j / (1 - P(Yes)_j)]$. As Theil (1971, p. 195) already showed, the error term B has a mean of zero (assuming a binomial distribution), but no finite variance. The approximation of B is done by using the expression $1/V_j[F(Yes)_j \cdot (1 - F(Yes)_j)]$, where V_j is the number of citizen in district j who actually voted. As this approximation also holds for small values of V_j, a weighted logit estimation procedure is chosen, where the weights are $(V_j \cdot F(Yes)_j \cdot (1 - F(Yes)_j))^{1/2}$.

6. A short description of the data and their sources are given in the appendix.

7. In addition, in a more detailed analysis of this referendum (Pommerehne 1982) various other non-monetary costs, especially the impact of opportunity cost of time are investigated—with no great success, however.

8. The partial correlation coefficient between income and education is .76. "Weighted

income" states that the educational level has somewhat different effects at different income levels.

9. This can also be shown if the results are compared to those arrived at with other compatible (though more laborious) approaches; see Pommerehne (1985).

10. This conclusion has lately been confirmed by Noam (1981, 1982) who uses a somewhat different methodology for analyzing the outcome of referenda—even on such issues as civil liberties, political participation rights, social policy and labor rights.

11. Indeed, if the number of subscribers to theater performances (as a share of those entitled to vote) is used as a proxy for that part of voters with very intensive consumption preferences, the results show no significant impact of this variable on the referendum outcome [also if the variable for the nonmonetary cost (education) is dropped]. A technical reason may be multi-collinearity among the independent variables income and the share of theater subscribers ($r = .89$). If we take out the income variable and re-run the regression, the proxy for differences in consumption preferences has a significant influence, but the overall explanatory power falls by 15 percentage points and the simulations as well as the predictions are worse compared to those in part II.

12. A more extended presentation and a critical evaluation of the various approaches is given in Pommerehne (1985).

13. See as a recent example Schneider and Pommerehne (1981).

14. For an excellent survey on these refined methods see McMillan (1979).

15. See, for example, Pommerehne (1978), Whithers (1979) and Schneider and Pommerehne (1983) for some recent applications of this approach.

16. For a presentation of this method see Pearce (1978, Chap. 4).

17. Moreover, the empirical results indicate that individuals when leaving the market and entering the political sphere do *not* alter their basic behavior from selfishness to altruism (as stated e.g. by Wilson and Banfield 1965). To the extend that the impact of the revised referendum proposals is realized beforehand by voters/taxpayers, observed voting behavior is consistent with self-interest.

Appendix

The data on voting returns are taken from official statistics (Amtsblatt des Kantons Basel-Stadt, various years). However, as they are only available for 25 precincts, they had to be recalculated for the 21 districts. This re-calculation was done using information at the smallest statistical unit, the 60 so-called statistical areas. The mean taxable income of the 21 districts for 1971 and 1976 were computed by Andreas Heussler (University of Basle). The mean taxable incomes for 1973 and 1974 were computed using the official income tax statistics and information on the change in the socio-economic composition of each district. The data or the expected tax increase are calculated from the same sources as the income data and using official tax rates (taken from the Steuertafel des Kantons Basel-Stadt). The data on the projected noise level and the expected increase in the number of flights per day (if the airport referendum would be accepted by the majority) which also were publicly discussed are provided by the EMPA (Eidgenössische Materialprüfanstalt), Zurich. All socio-demographic data (on education level, self-employed, etc.) are taken from the statistical yearbook of the Canton Basle-City (various years).

References

Barkume, Anthony J., Identification of Preferences for Election Outcomes from Aggregate Voting Data, *Public Choice*, 27 (1976), 41–58.

Barkume, Anthony J., Tax-Prices and Voting Behavior: The Case of Local Educational Financing, *Economic Inquiry*, 15 (1977), 574–586.

Bergstrom, Theodore C., Rubinfeld, Daniel L. and Shapiro, Perry, Microbased Estimates of Demand Functions for Local School Expenditures, Econometrica, 50 (1982), 1183–1205.

Buchanan, James M., *The Limits of Liberty: Between Anarchy and Leviathan*. Chicago and London: University of Chicago Press, 1975.

Courant, Paul N., Gramlich, Edward M. and Rubinfeld, Daniel L., Why Voters Support Tax Limitation Amendments: The Michigan Case, *National Tax Journal*, 33 (1980), 91–97.

Deacon, Robert T. and Shapiro, Perry, Private Preferences for Collective Goods Revealed through Voting on Referenda, *American Economic Review*, 65 (1975), 943–955.

Freiman, Marc P., Tax Limitation in Michigan, 1976–1978: What Changed? Mimeo, Wayne State University, 1981.

Frey, Bruno S., *Theorie demokratischer Wirtschaftspolitik*. Munich: Vahlen, 1981.

Holcombe, Randall G., The Florida System: A Bowen Equilibrium Referendum Process, *National Tax Journal*, 30 (1977), 77–84.

Holcombe, Randall G. and Taylor, Paul C., Tax Referenda and the Voluntary Exchange Model of Taxation: A Suggested Implementation, *Public Finance Quarterly*, 8 (1980), 107–114.

Maggadino, J. P.; Toma, Eugenia F. and Toma, Mark, Proposition 13: A Public Choice Appraisal, *Public Finance Quarterly*, 8 (1980), 223–235.

Mariotti, Steve, An Economic Analysis of the Voting on Michigan's Tax and Expenditure Limitation Amendments, *Public Choice*, 33 (1978), 16–26.

McFadden, Daniel L., Quantal Choice Analysis: A Survey, *Annals of Economic and Social Measurement*, 5 (1976), 363–390.

McMillan, J., The Free-Rider Problem: A Survey, *Economic Record*, 77 (1979), 210–235.

Nielsen, Richard P., McQueen, Charles and Nielsen, Angela B., Public Policy and Attitudes on Tax Support for Live Artistic Communications Media, *American Journal of Economics and Sociology*, 35 (1976), 149–160.

Noam, Eli M., The Efficiency of Direct Democracy, *Journal of Political Economy*, 88 (1980), 803–810.

Noam, Eli M., The Valutation of Legal Rights, *Quarterly Journal of Economics*, 96 (1981), 465–476.

Noam, Eli M., Demand Functions and the Valutation of Public Goods, *Public Choice*, 38 (1982), 271–280.

Pearce, D. W., ed., *The Valuation of Social Cost*. London: Allen and Unwin, 1978.

Peterson, George E., Voter Demand for Public School Expenditure, in: Jackson, John E., ed., *Public Needs and Private Behavior in Metropolitan Areas*. Cambridge, Mass.: Ballinger, 1975, 99–115.

Pommerehne, Werner W., Determinanten öffentlicher Ausgaben: Ein einfaches politisch-ökonomisches Modell, *Schweizerische Zeitschrift für Volkswirtschaft und Statistik*, 110 (1974), 454–491.

Pommerehne, Werner W., Institutional Approaches to Public Expenditure: Empirical Evidence from Swiss Municipalities, *Journal of Public Economics*, 9 (1978), 255–280.

Pommerehne, Werner W., Steuern, Staatsausgaben und Stimmbürgerverhalten: Eine empirische Untersuchung am Beispiel der öffentlichen Subventionierung des Theaters, *Jahrbücher für Nationalökonomie und Statistik*, 197 (1982), 437–462.

Pommerehne, Werner W., *Mikroökonomische Ansätze zur empirischen Erfassung der Präferenzen für öffentliche Güter*. Tübingen: Mohr, 1985.

Rubinfeld, Daniel L., Voting in a Local School Election: A Micro Analysis, *Review of Economics and Statistics*, 59 (1977), 30–42.

Schneider, Friedrich and Pommerehne, Werner W., Free Riding and Collective Action: An

Experiment in Public Microeconomics, *Quarterly Journal of Economics*, 96 (1981), 689–704.

Schneider, Friedrich and Pommerehne, Werner W., Macroeconomia della crescita in disequilibrio e settore pubblico in espansione: il peso delle differenze istituzionali, *Rivista Internazionale di Scienze Economiche e Commerciali*, 30 (1983), 306–320.

Schroeder, Larry D. and Sjoquist, David L., The Rational Voter: An Analysis of Two Atlanta Referenda on Rapid Transit, *Public Choice*, 33 (1978), 27–44.

Shively, W. Phillips, 'Ecological' Inference: The Use of Aggregate Data for Study Individuals, *American Political Science Review*, 63 (1969), 1183–1196.

Theil, Henri, *Principles of Econometrics*. Amsterdam: North-Holland, 1971.

Wilson, James Q. and Banfield, Edward C., Voting Behavior on Municipal Public Expenditures: A Case Study in Rationality and Self-Interest, in: Margolis, Julius, ed., *The Public Economy of Urban Communities*. Baltimore: John Hopkins University Press, 1965, 74–91.

Withers, Glenn A., Private Demand for Public Subsidies: An Econometric Study of Cultural Support in Australia, *Journal of Cultural Economics*, 3 (1979), 53–61.

Résumé

Cet article déduit par des modèles micro-économiques sur le comportement des électeurs des informations sur les préférences individuelles concernant les services publics. Dans le premier cas, on analyse un référendum sur l'augmentation des subventions publiques pour le théâtre de la ville de Bâle, qui était refusé par la majorité. L'instrument de l'analyse est un modèle partiel. Dans le second cas considéré, on analyse une proposition sur l'agrandissement de l'aéroport de Bâle, qui était aussi refusé par la majorité. Ici un modèle plus étendu est appliqué pour tenir compte (en cas de réalisation du projet) des effets probablement considérables sur les prix des marchandises et des facteurs et finalement aussi à la propre situation à l'avenir. Dans les deux cas, les résultats des simulations correspondent aux hypothèses déduites sur le comportement des électeurs informant les décideurs politiques par ce moyen sur les préférences individuelles concernant les services publics. Au-delà, l'utilité du modèle peut être rendu claire par des prévisions. On prédit le résultat d'un nouveau référendum après la révision des projets. Les résultats de la prévision sont, dans les deux cas, assez conformes aux résultats actuels.

Are There Practicable Demand-Revealing Mechanisms?

Peter Bohm

Has the current interest in demand revelation mechanisms for public goods produced instruments that can actually be used for decision-making in the public sector? So far, it does not seem so. Technical sophistication at the expense of practicability seems to characterize most of the theoretical research. The empirical research has either used hypothetical approaches or laboratory settings; hence, there is hardly enough evidence to convince politicians that they should turn over important public good issues to be determined by completely new methods for public decision-making.

In this paper, we present two nonhypothetical, nonlaboratory applications of what seems to be a practicable mechanism for revealing the demand for public goods. Both refer to real public goods, the production and financing of which are determined by the demand-revealing process.

1. The Applicability of Existing Methods

The theoretical and practical problems of estimating willingness to pay (WTP) for public goods have attracted a great deal of attention for quite some time now. The reasons for this development seem to include the following three points: First, recall the conventional wisdom until the beginning of the 1970s: (1) any individual who has a chance to be a free rider will be one and (2) there is no feasible institutional way to avoid misrepresentation of preferences. These views eventually became recognized as assumptions rather than facts and prompted an interest in developing alternative hypotheses. Second, the growing public sector in many countries made it imperative to intensify the search for alternatives to tax financing. Third, and perhaps most important, the fact that decisions about public goods

Public Finance and the Quest for Efficiency. Proceedings of the 38th Congress of the International Institute of Public Finance. Copenhagen, 1982, pp. 127–139. Copyright © 1984 by Wayne State University Press, Detroit, Michigan, 48202.

often have to be made without reliable information about consumer preferences has posed a considerable problem from the point of view of a well-
functioning democracy. There seems to be a need for instruments or institutions that are more appropriate or efficient than those of a representative
democracy, where the "representatives" often do not know what to represent on an individual issue.

While it is easy to understand why this field has lately received so
much attention, it is more difficult to comprehend the form in which it
appears in much of the economic literature. The main issues dealt with
seem to be:

(1) Is there a shrewd, foolproof mechanism that would make—in some
    sense—rational people reveal their preferences for public goods?
    The general idea here seems to be that, if the answer is yes, we
    should simply go ahead and use it for public decision-making. (See,
    e.g., Clarke (1971), Groves-Ledyard (1977), Tideman-Tullock
    (1976) and Green-Laffont (1979)).

(2) To what extent do people actually try to be free riders when there
    are incentives to do so? The idea here seems to be that, if people do
    not seem to react strongly to such incentives, we should not worry
    too much and simply use the WTP responses people give—to hy-
    pothetical questions for example—as an approximation to their true
    WTP (see, e.g., Marwell-Ames (1980), Bishop-Heberlein (1979)
    and Brookshire et al. (1982)).

It should be stressed that significant progress has been made in both
areas and that this may prove to be important in the long run. But from the
point of view of more immediate application, the emphasis on these two
issues appear misplaced. This for at least two reasons (see also Johansen
(1977) and Johansen (1981)):

First, where are the politicians who would let decisions be made by,
say, a Groves-Ledyard/Clarke mechanism, a mechanism that even students
in economics need considerable time to grasp and that is in several respects
subject to criticism, (see, e.g. Ng (1979))?

Second, if free-rider behavior is insignificant in several experimental
studies how can we rely on this being consistently so in actual public
decision-making? More important, would those who decide if and when the
suggested approaches should be used in practice, i.e. the politicians, be
convinced that these approaches would continue to work and work better
than their own wise deliberations?

Thus, it can be argued that neither issue (1) nor (2) observes the
implementation aspects and that, in fact, there is an undersupply of ideas
addressed to the more immediate needs of policy-making and of present-day

government institutions. In particular, research in this area should take into account what is feasible in a political context. As has been pointed out in Bohm (1979), this seems to require meeting at least an "intelligibility" as well as a "verifiability" condition, i.e.

(1) the proposed decision mechanism must be *simple and easily understood* by ordinary people; otherwise it will not work and is unlikely to be adopted by hesitant or even hostile politicians;

(2) if a mechanism cannot be *guaranteed* to elicit truthful WTP statements, it must be possible to *check* the actual extent of misrepresentation.

The background of the "verifiability" condition (2) should perhaps be explained a little further. First, it should be noted that the demand-revealing property of most methods is vulnerable to the formation of coalitions—and guarantees that coalitions cannot be formed can rarely be given. Second, each new practical application of a given method may run into problems of political controversy and may therefore be difficult to evaluate without any instrument for ascertaining the extent of truthful reporting. More specifically, those who do not like the outcome may try to disqualify it by making unsubstantiated, yet irrefutable, references to an allegedly extensive misrepresentation of preferences. Given such risks, politicians are not likely to accept the use of a demand-revealing method for decision-making on important issues unless its possible failure to reveal preferences can be observed. In other words, it is not enough to have shown that—in a strict, but limited, sense—*rational* people will truthfully report their WTP.

Few, if any, of the methods proposed in the literature meet the "intelligibility" and "verifiability" conditions (see Bohm (1979) and Johansen (1981)). An obvious reason for this insufficiency is of course that the two requirements are far from easy to fulfill or that they may be even impossible to fulfill without making important sacrifices in other respects. There is, however, one approach which seems capable of meeting the two conditions without sacrificing too much. This is the "interval method" discussed in Bohm (1979) and described in more detail below. Its general characteristics are as follows.

Instead of using one possibly demand-revealing method for eliciting WTP responses from potential consumers of a discrete public good under consideration, two simple, straightforward methods are employed *simultaneously*. A random sample of, say, 50% of the respondents is placed in a position that would give (preferably weak) incentives to *under*report individual WTP and the remaining respondents are subjected to a situation that would give (preferably weak) incentives to *over*report individual WTP. Doubling the aggregate responses from each group and allowing for a sampling-error correction, we get a lower and an upper bound on the true aggregate WTP (a lower bound from the first group which is subjected to incentives to underreport, but not to overreport, etc.). Given the criterion that the good is to be produced if true aggregate WTP exceeds production costs, the good will be produced if the interval which contains the true aggregate WTP as a whole exceeds the cost figure. Similarly, the good will not be produced if the interval falls short of the costs. Moreover, if the interval is small *and* the cost figure ends up inside the interval, the natural (or agreed upon) interpretation is that benefits approximately equal cost and that production is a matter of indifference.

If any of these situations occurs, the information base will be no worse than if an exact, true WTP figure could be arrived at. If the interval turns out to be very wide, that is, when an extensive misrepresentation of WTP is *revealed* to have taken place, we have a problem if the cost figure ends up well inside the interval. Now we cannot know if the true WTP exceeds or falls short of costs. However, when this is the outcome in actual practice, the rule could be to return the issue to the politicians, to be determined in the same way as would otherwise have been the case. Thus, no disadvantage (aside from "referendum" costs) would result from using the interval method, while it is possible that a clear-cut answer would be obtained, as suggested above. In addition, the method does not contain any complicated "tricks" for making demand revelation a dominant strategy. Thus, it may possibly meet the intelligibility condition (for details, see Sections 2–3 below). And it does not have to rely on respondents "behaving as they should", as significant misrepresentation would be revealed by this approach, hence meeting the verifiability condition.

The interesting question, of course, is how wide the interval is likely to be in real applications. If the design of the method and the incentives are such that a narrow interval is likely to emerge, the method would be more useful than if the interval is likely to be wide. In a laboratory—but nonhypothetical—experiment in 1969, no significant differences in average stated WTP emerged from randomly selected groups, some of which were subjected to clear incentives for underreporting and others to clear incentives for overreporting (see Bohm (1972)). The question then arises whether these results also hold when a real-world good is involved. Such a nonhypothetical and nonlaboratory test—formalized as an application of the interval method—required cooperation with a government.

In 1980–82, two chances for real-world tests appeared. Both cases concerned public goods in the form of *access* to a future market for a service, where access was nonrival but excludable. One case referred to a new kind of statistics and the other to a new bus line. The two cases will be discussed briefly in turn. (A detailed account of the tests will be published elsewhere.)

2. The Statistics Project—The Successful Test

2.1 The Background

In the general atmosphere of trying to reduce government expenditures the Swedish government appointed a committee to find ways of cutting down on the "extensive" production of statistics. One of the committee's tasks was to find instruments for evaluating costs and benefits of statistics produced by the government and to investigate new ways of financing the production of statistics otherwise made available at no cost to users.

The committee, which includes members of the Parliament from left to right (Social Democrats to Conservatives), agreed to let the fate of a project proposal from the Central Bureau of Statistics be determined by using the interval method. The project involved detailed statistics of housing in Sweden, which was assumed to be of interest to local governments (for their housing policy, evaluation of master plans, energy-saving measures, etc.). The basis for the statistics was a nationwide census which contained, among other things, a specification of certain characteristics of all dwelling units. If the project was to be carried out, the Bureau would arrange a system for data processing and data presentation, the overhead costs of which were estimated at $40,000. Once this system had been established, a local government could order data for its own jurisdiction at an additional cost depending on what data it wanted. Thus, a kind of two-part tariff was involved, with fixed costs to be covered by payments linked to the WTP responses, provided the project was accepted, and variable costs to be covered by user charges.

2.2 Payment Rules and Misrepresentation Incentives

The local governments were informed that the project would be carried out if their WTP statements for access to the project services exceeded the fixed costs. The 279 local governments in Sweden were stratified with respect to population size. Half were randomly allocated to group 1 and the other half to group 2. Group 1 was to state their WTP in a contract, and if the good was to be produced, they would pay a *percentage* of their stated WTP, no more than needed for the fixed costs to be covered exactly. (This percentage figure could be determined of course only after the responses hade been given.) Group 2 was to state their WTP in a slightly different contract which said that if the good was to be produced, they would pay a small fee of $100, identical for all who reported a WTP of at least that amount. Those in group 2 who stated a WTP below this figure would not be offered the services at all. The same was true for those in group 1 who reported a zero WTP. This implies that, if the services were to be provided, an exclusion mechanism would be used.

The incentives presented to these two groups were as follows. Respondents in group 1 had a reason to understate, but no reason to overstate, their WTP (the free-rider incentive). Respondents in group 2 with a true WTP above $100 would have a reason to overstate, but no reason to understate their WTP. Those in group 2 with a stated WTP below $100 would be excluded from consumption as well as from payments; hence, they were not exposed to any particular incentive to misrepresent their WTP. This means that group 2 as a whole was left with an overstatement incentive.

It was considered important that the payment for respondents in group 2 be small, so that a sufficiently large number of respondents would have a WTP in excess of the payment and hence an incentive to overreport their WTP. In this way, we would also limit the efficiency loss from excluding consumers with a non-zero WTP in this group. On the other hand, an extremely low payment level, e.g. zero, might jeopardize the quality of the responses because of the reduced checks on carelessness (in group 2) and because of feelings of injustice (in group 1).

One hundred dollars was considered low enough to fall short of the expected WTP of most local governments. Although it is a negligible part of their budget, the amount requires a reason for a government to spend it. Moreover, local governments in Sweden have been under heavy financial pressure for some time now, and this is likely to have created a high degree of cost consciousness.

Finally, two important details should be pointed out. The respondents (formally, the boards of the local governments) were informed about the reason for the different payment conditions ("to check possible attempts to respond by tactical WTP instead of the true WTP", thus indicating explicitly the different incentives that existed for the two groups). In addition, the respondents were told that the responses would be non-anonymous, i.e., that all responses would be publicized, the purpose being to make it harder for the respondents to misrepresent significantly their WTP.

2.3 *The Results*

As shown in Table 1, 274 out of 279 local governments responded (98%), the same absolute number in each group. The average stated WTP was SEK 827 in group 1 and SEK 889 in group 2. Multiplying by the total

Table 1

Aggregate and average WTP (in kronor, $1 = SEK 5 approx.)

	Number of govts		Total WTP (sum of responses)	Average WTP	Average WTP × 274	WTP interval	
	Total	Responded				in SEK	in percent of lower bound
Group 1	140	137	113,350	827	226,700	16,962	7,5%
Group 2	139	137	121,831	889	243,662		
Total	279	274 (98%)	(235,181)				

number of responding governments, we get an estimate of the lower bound
for the aggregate WTP as SEK 226,700, and an estimate of the upper
bound as SEK 243,662. In order to take into account that the composition
of the two groups may differ, we have to make an adjustment for the
sampling error. With a 95 percent one-sided confidence interval, we get the
lower bound as SEK 226,700 − 35,761 and the upper bound as SEK
243,662 + 36,956. The WTP interval that is directly observable is on the
order of SEK 17,000 or 7.5 percent of the estimated lower bound. Moreover, the lower bound exceeds the fixed costs of SEK 200,000 ($40,000),
which means that the project will be carried out and that the respondents
will have to pay according to the specified rules. (This has now been
accomplished).

The distribution of the responses are presented in Table 2. We note
that 30% of all local governments stated a WTP equal to zero and 9% a
nonzero amount below SEK 500, approximately the value of a couple of

Table 2

Distribution of WTP responses

SEK	Both groups abs. no. (%)	Group 1 abs. no. (%)	Group 2 abs. no. (%)
0	81 (30)	49 (36)	32 (23)
1–499	26 (9)	14 (10)	12 (9)
500	74 (27)	25 (18)	49 (36)
501–999	12 (4)	5 (4)	7 (5)
1,000	34 (12)	19 (14)	15 (11)
1,001–5,000	44 (16)	24 (18)	20 (15)
> 5,000	3 (1)	1 (1)	2 (1)
	93 (34)		
	274 (100)	137 (100)	137 (100)

publications. 27% responded with a WTP equal to the only figure mentioned, SEK 500 ($100), the payment relevant for group 2. 34% revealed a more noticeable interest in the project by stating a WTP > SEK 500, the maximum figure given being SEK 10,000.

Looking at the responses from each group, group 2 had a considerably larger number of SEK 500 responses than group 1 (36% as compared to 18% for group 1). Could this be interpreted as a reaction to the overstatement incentive provided to this group, from those with a true WTP below SEK 500? The answer is, of course, no. As governments in group 2 who gave a response of SEK 500 would have to pay exactly this amount, one can certainly assume that they have a *willingness* to pay this amount. Thus, if overstatements occurred in group 2, it would have to show up in the frequency of statements exceeding SEK 500. Yet, as we can see from Table 2, the number of responses with a WTP above SEK 500 was not larger in group 2 and did not increase in any significant fashion for higher WTP levels.

Instead, we see that the number of responses on each level was very similar for the two groups, except for the SEK 500 and 0 levels. Group 1 had a significantly higher percentage of zero responses than group 2 (36% as compared to 23%). As respondents in group 1 were confronted with an incentive to underreport their WTP, the question is whether the relatively large fraction of zero responses in this group could be a reflection of this fact. Here, however, we must note that all respondents stating a WTP = 0 were excluded from consuming the good in the future (which they knew in advance). Thus, a zero WTP could not be interpreted as a free-rider response.

2.4 Main Conclusions

1. The results—in particular, the small interval for aggregate WTP—do not reveal any extensive formation of coalitions of the type where a group 1 respondent asks someone in group 2 to state a very high figure in order to increase the chances of having the good produced, while he himself may state a low WTP and take a free ride. The non-anonymity condition may have been at work here. Another possible explanation, of course, is that the two groups were explicitly designed to act as "control groups" for one another, so that attempts by many to misrepresent preferences in this or other ways would be revealed by the method used. It should be noted that coalition behavior does not invalidate the interval method as such (as would be the case with many other methods); it just makes the interval wider and the method less useful for practical decision-making.

2. A clear-cut answer was given to the question as to whether the aggregate WTP exceeded the relevant costs or not.

3. The interval for the aggregate or average WTP was small, which means that the loss of accuracy was insignificant compared to a situation where it would have been possible to obtain *one* nondistorted estimate of aggregate WTP.

3. The Bus Line Project—The Test that Failed

The test discussed in the preceding section was carried out in the spring of 1982. Prior to that test, another one had been completed in 1980. The local government in Stockholm had agreed to let a new bus line be started if people in a given area, essentially people who worked in a large hospital and a large company, revealed a sufficiently high WTP for access to the bus line.

I shall not present the detailed results of this rather elaborate and cumbersome case because it eventually turned out to be a failure. Instead I shall try to explain why it failed, as this provides some insight into the problems of real-world experiments in this field. It had long been known that employees at the work places involved were dissatisfied with the public transportation facilities. In the summer of 1980 there was still no solution in sight and it was made explicit by the authorities that no additional bus service of the regular type would be provided within the next 12 months. Contacts with the administration of the work places revealed that they were favorably inclined towards using the interval method with the accompanying financial arrangements in an attempt to provide a new bus line. The time schedule and the bus route were determined on the basis of information from the personnel departments. Employees (and other people potentially interested in the bus line) were given extensive information about the whole procedure and were told that the bus line would be opened for a six-month trial period if the aggregate WTP exceeded costs. In order to establish an estimate of the aggregate WTP, the population of potential commuters was divided into two groups with different payment consequences (for the stated reason of possible misrepresentation of the WTP). In the event that the WTP interval exceeded costs, respondents in group 1 would pay their stated WTP per month (entitling them to a card which allowed them to ride on the bus) and each respondent in group 2 would pay a fixed, symbolic fee of $2 per month, provided the stated WTP exceeded that figure. In addition, a 20 cent fare was to be paid for each ride. Thus, the costs to be covered by the aggregate WTP equalled total costs minus the expected volume of fares.

Information meetings were arranged in such a way that all those likely to be interested in the bus line had the opportunity to attend. Their WTP statements could be given to us either after such a meeting or by mail. However, very few people responded, and the only people to turn up at the meetings were representatives of the local trade unions. They reported that they had held meetings of their own and had decided

(1) that they did not accept the local government's decision not to provide them with regular bus service on regular terms;
(2) that they did not accept the idea of having to pay in a way that differs from the way "everybody else" pays (bus service is subsidized in the area)—the implication being that they would rather go without this bus service, even if their members felt it would be worth the costs;
(3) that they would not like to help in realizing an arrangement that might reduce the level of public services provided free or at low costs. It was argued that such an arrangement, if accepted here, could spread to other parts of the public sector; and
(4) on these grounds, they advised their union members to abstain from participating in the project.

There are, of course, many possible reasons why so few people participated—actual demand may have been low, instructions may have seemed cryptic, the decision rule too uncommon, etc. But the position taken by the trade unions would, at least in Sweden, be reason enough for people to abstain from participating. Only 70 of an expected 400 or so potentially interested people responded with a non-zero bid. The results (which have, of course, no real interest given this conflict) can be stated briefly as follows. We got non-zero bids from about 35 persons in each group; the average WTP from group 1 (where people would have had to pay their stated WTP) was about $7 per month and the average WTP from group 2 (where people would have had to pay $2 per month) was about $8 per month. In order for the WTP from these 70 people to have been able to cover the costs, the minimum stated average WTP would have had to exceed $35–40 per month.

This test seems to have shown one important thing about applications of new mechanisms for decision-making with respect to public goods. If consumers of the public good in question are accustomed to a specific kind of financing, the responses to the questions posed and to the whole procedure may be essentially a political reaction to having the payment system and payment distribution altered. This may be particularly true when the respondents believe that they are now supposed to pay for something they would otherwise, or usually, get for "free" (i.e. which would be paid for by general taxes). Even if the reactions stop short of a boycott, the responses may very well be biased, hence introducing a systematic error in the estimation of the WTP. Specifically, it may increase free-rider behavior, hence reducing the lower bound of the WTP interval. It may even distort the incentives to overreporting, so that the upper bound of the WTP is no longer a relevant upper bound. The implication seems to be that attempts should be made to find applications to public goods where potential consumers are not strongly prejudiced in favor of a specific kind of (tax) financing. Such applications could be *new* types of public goods or local public goods new to the area, etc.

4. Summary

In spite of the extensive discussion of demand revelation in the literature, little has been offered by way of practicable instruments for decision-making with respect to real-world public goods in a real-world democracy. However, there seems to exist one approach capable of meeting the requirements of functional simplicity and misrepresentation checks that politicians are likely to make. This approach—the interval method—has been tested in two nonlaboratory, nonhypothetical cases briefly reported on here.

One application (a new bus line, a case provided by the local government of Stockholm) met strong opposition from local trade unions and may have failed for this reason. The outcome here indicates that trial applications of demand-revealing methods—which necessarily involve a new payment distribution—should probably avoid existing (types of) public goods where consumers have grown accustomed to a specific form of financing.

The other application (a case provided by the Swedish government) were completed satisfactorily with 98 percent participation from potential consumers. It proved successful in reaching a decision on the production of the public good (a statistics project) and gave an estimate of the interval of the aggregate WTP on the order of 7.5 percent of the lower bound. Thus, in the only real case where the interval method has been fully tested, there was little loss of accuracy in estimating the aggregate WTP.

References

Bishop, R. and Heberlein, T. (1979), "Measuring Values of Extramarket Goods", *American Journal of Agricultural Economics*, December.
Bohm, P. (1972), "Estimating Demand for Public Goods: An Experiment", *European Economic Review* 3, March.

Bohm, P. (1979), "Estimating Willingness to Pay: Why and How?" *Scandinavian Journal of Economics*, 81, pp. 1–12.

Brookshire, D.S. et al (1982), "Valuing Public Goods: A Comparison of Survey and Hedonic Approaches", *American Economic Review*, March.

Clarke, E. (1971), "Multipart Pricing of Public Goods", *Public Choice*, 8.

Green, J. and Laffont, J. (1979), *Incentives in Public Decision-Making*, Amsterdam: North-Holland.

Groves, T. and Ledyard, J. (1977), "Optimal Allocation of Public Goods", *Econometrica*, May.

Johansen, L. (1977), "The Theory of Public Goods: Misplaced Emphasis?" *Journal of Public Economics*, 7.

Johansen, L. (1981), "Review and Comments: J. Green and J.J. Laffont, Incentives in Public Decision-Making", *Journal of Public Economics*, August.

Marwell, G. and Ames, R.E. (1980), "*Economists Free Ride, Does Anyone Else?*", Disc. Paper, Univ. of Wisconsin.

Ng, Y.K. (1979), *Welfare Economics*, London: Macmillan.

Tideman, N. and Tullock, G. (1976), "A New and Superior Process for Making Social Choices", *Journal of Political Economy*, December.

Résumé

En dépit d'une large discussion dans les revues économiques de la demande révélée, peu d'instruments opérationnels sont disponibles pour la prise de décision sur des biens publics réels dans une vraie démocratie.

Cependant, on peut penser qu'il existe une démarche capable de répondre aux exigences de la simplicité fonctionnelle et aux erreurs de représentation que les politiciens sont susceptibles de faire. Cette démarche introduirait un intervalle pour la véritable disponibilité à payer, là où les limites supérieures et inférieures sont calculées de façon directe à partir de deux échantillons différents de la population (que des incitations opposées conduisent à une mauvaise représentation) et là où la dimension de l'intervalle donne la mesure de l'étendue totale de la mauvaise représentation. Cette dernière propriété est capitale, étant donné qu'aucune méthode, jusqu'à présent du moins, ne peut garantir qu'elle rend compte fidèlement de la disponibilité à payer (D.A.P).

Cet article présente deux applications à cette démarche qui ne sont ni hypothétiques ni de laboratoire, pour expliquer la demande de biens publics. L'une des applications qui concernait une nouvelle ligne d'autobus (cas fourni par le gouvernement local de Stockholm) a recontré une forte opposition de la part des syndicats locaux et a pu échouer pour cette ra on. Le résultat semble ici indiquer que des applications expérimentales 'es méthodes d'explication de la demande révélée—qui impliquent nécessairement une nouvelle répartition du paiement—devraient éviter les formes existantes de biens publics où les consommateurs se sont habitués à une forme spécifique de financement.

La seconde application concernait la production d'une nouveau modèle de statistiques (cas fourni par le gouvernement suédois). Ce test a pu être effectué de façon satisfaisante avec une participation à 98% des consommateurs potentiels. Il s'est avéré positif, dégageant une décision sur la production de biens publics et a donné une estimation de l'intervalle de l'aggrégat (DAP) de l'ordre de 7,5% de la limite inférieure. Cette perte de rigueur implicite dans la méthode de l'intervalle était insignifiante par rapport à une estimation, sans distortion, de la disponibilité générale à payer, si l'on avait pu obtenir une telle estimation.

The Demand for Public Goods and Services: Problems of Identification and Measurement in Western Countries*

Bernard P. Herber

I. Problems in Public Goods Measurement

The demand for public goods relates closely to the continuing debate in the Western industrial democracies concerning the appropriate economic role for government. Moreover, basic to any discussion of government's appropriate role in a mixed private and public sector industrial economy is the question of how to measure public sector economic activity. This paper will not be concerned with the process of public choice or the political mechanism through which preference for public goods is revealed. Instead, it will consider efforts to measure ex post the *demand* for public goods after these political decisions have already been made and implemented.

A number of difficulties may be observed in efforts to measure public goods demand. These include:

(1) The decision whether to include government nonexhaustive (distributional) expenditures as part of the demand for public goods, since only exhaustive (allocational) expenditures are consistent with the traditional allocational concepts used to measure aggregate output—gross national product and gross domestic product.
(2) The inability to apply the income elasticity of public expenditure concept, or other theoretical guidelines, so as to arrive at a universal, predictive, "positive theory of public expenditure."

*The author wishes to acknowledge the valuable contributions of his co-researcher, Dr. Paul U. Pawlik, to this paper. Moreover, the useful comments of the discussants, Professor Gunther Engelhardt and Professor Tetsuya Nosse, the session chairman, Professor Anthony Culyer, and various members of the audience are also appreciated.

Public Finance and the Quest for Efficiency. Proceedings of the 38th Congress of the International Institute of Public Finance. Copenhagen, 1982, pp. 141–153. Copyright © 1984 by Wayne State University Press, Detroit, Michigan, 48202.

(3) The confusion created by social accounting systems which automatically classify all government current expenditures as public consumption and all government capital expenditures as public investment.

(4) The failure of government exhaustive expenditure data to measure various *indirect* effects on private sector allocational behavior.

(5) The general absence of efforts to measure national economic output, including public sector output, along the lines of its *consumption benefit* characteristics.[1]

The last two areas of measurement difficulty will receive the primary attention of the present paper. One of these is the difficulty in estimating certain *indirect governmental allocation influence effects* on private sector decisions, effects which fail to show up in conventional government exhaustive expenditure data. That is, governmental influence on resource allocation may go well beyond direct resource-absorbing purchasing, and the resulting production of economic goods by the public sector. Thus, while government purchases of resources for the production of defense or public education are "directly" included in exhaustive expenditure data, the nonneutral substitution-type effects on private sector behavior exerted by a variety of "indirect" public sector activities is ignored. Such indirect activities include consumer safety regulation, worker safety regulation, public utility price and output regulation in natural monopoly industries, expenditure subsidies, and tax preferences. The exclusion of these indirect, but very real, allocational-influence effects from conventional exhaustive expenditure data results in an understatement of public sector allocational activity and, in this sense, understates the demand for public goods that has been revealed in the public choice process.

Another deficiency in conventional public goods measurement is that it tends to ignore the nature of the *consumption benefits* which flow from the public sector output. Nonetheless, the literature of modern public finance regularly classifies public goods (and private goods) on the basis of the characteristics of their consumption benefits. Is the consumption joint (indivisible, nonrival) across two or more persons, or is it private (divisible, rival) to a particular person? Related to this, are significant externalities present? The theory of public finance, following this line of analysis, arrives at a classification system for economic goods ranging from *pure public goods*, whose joint consumption benefits over a large group of consumers often make pricing difficult or impossible, to *pure private goods*, whose divisible consumption makes pricing to a particular purchaser feasible. Moreover, certain intermediate combinations of these two extremes characterize many other economic goods resulting in *quasi-public goods* and *quasi-private goods* classifications.

II. The Methodology: Measuring the Demand for Public Goods with Input-Output Data—United States Example

In order to improve upon the methods of measuring this demand, the present study will introduce a methodology utilizing the Input-Output Accounts compiled by the Bureau of Economic Analysis of the U.S. Department of Commerce. The years selected for the present study (1947, 1958, 1963, 1967, 1970, and 1972) were determined by the availability of the most comprehensive and most recently available I-O data. For the private sector, the I-O Accounts contain 79 separate industry categories and, for the years 1963 and 1967, many industries are further disaggregated into a total of 368 subcategories. The core of the I-O approach is the Transactions Table, which shows the dollar value on current account of the transactions between industries, thus revealing both the allocation of goods from a given industry to final users of the output as well as to other industries. Final use data are then further disaggregated into Personal Consumption, Private Fixed Investment, Government Purchases, Exports, and Net Inventory Change categories. The first three of these categories are emphasized in this paper. Moreover, the Government Industry component of the Transactions Table also provides useful data.

However, both the Final Demand (FD) data which measure the sales of each industry to final markets, and the Value-Added (VA) data which measure the increment to the value of output provided by each industry, contain government "nonlabor" purchases. Thus, only government "labor" purchases are found in the data for the Government industry category. Yet, this category, it would seem, should be representative of total direct public sector resource acquisition and output in the mixed economy. In order to compensate for this inconsistency in determining the publicness mix of GNP, the FD and VA data for each private industry are adjusted so as to exclude government "nonlabor" purchases. In turn, these "nonlabor" purchases are added into the government "labor" purchases data that are already contained in the Government industry category. Thus, a measure of *total public sector production* is attained, known as *Total Government Purchases* (ΣGP). These data are subsequently disaggregated into ten governmental functional expenditure categories. Meanwhile, either the Net Value Added (NVA) or the Net Final Demand (NFD) data, which remain after the subtraction of government "nonlabor" purchases from the industry data, could be aggregated across the 79 industries to represent private sector allocational activity. However, it is decided to use only *Total Net Value Added* (ΣNVA) as the measure of *total private sector production*.

III. Public Goods Demand Measurement for the United States under the "Government Allocation Influence" Criterion

Assignment of Publicness Ratings

The criterion developed in this paper to estimate the degree of overall governmental allocation influence in the economy, inclusive of both the "direct" resource-absorbing as well as the "indirect" substitution-effect varieties, will be referred to as the *Government Allocation Influence Criterion* (*GA*). Since allocational influence within the "aggregate" economy is the relevant consideration, it is necessary to use comprehensive data inclusive of both the private and public sectors of the mixed economy. To accomplish this broad measurement objective, the 79 private sector industry categories and the 10 public sector functional expenditure categories must be given "ratings" commensurate with their involvement with governmental allocative determination. Such a rating will be referred to as the *Publicness Rating* (*PR*) of the industry or government spending category. While such ratings are necessarily subjective in nature, it is believed that a careful investigation of the characteristics of each industry and expenditure category has made it possible to assign these ratings on a meaningful basis.

In the present study, the author and a co-researcher each made independent publicness rating estimates for the private industry and government expenditure categories, and then compared the results in order to arrive at a final rating value for each category. Clearly, subsequent studies could apply this so-called *Delphi*, quasi-scientific, research method in a more sophisticated fashion by arriving at a consensus from (say) 100 independent estimates. Ideally, this larger number of rating estimates would be drawn from a well-balanced cross section of persons, who could evaluate the categories from a specific relevant perspective (for example, persons from business, labor, government, universities, and the like).

The rating system follows an arbitrarily-selected range of *0 to 3*, whereby a rating of 0 signifies the absence of meaningful public sector allocational involvement and a rating of 3 depicts strong governmental presence in the financing and/or production of the economic good(s) represented in the particular industry or government spending category. Intermediate ratings between 0 and 3 will represent varying partial degrees of public sector allocational influence. This is a continuously linear scale with cardinal numbers. However, numbers other than a 0 to 3 range could be selected without a conceptual change in the conclusions.

Specific examples of the application of this rating system for *private sector* industry categories include the following: Industry Category #25—Paperboard Containers and Boxes—is given a "0" publicness rating under the GA criterion, since no appreciable influence is exerted on the industry's output by government. On the other hand, Industry Category #13—Ordnance and Accessories—is given a much higher publicness rating of "2.8," due to its close relationship to the defense industry which is dominated by the federal government. Meanwhile, Industry Category #1—Livestock and Livestock Products—is rated "1" due to such factors as the presence of governmental grading of meat by quality and subsidies to the industry. In turn, Industry Category #66—Communications—is rated "2" because of the presence of government price and output regulation in this industry.

In addition, industry publicness ratings are assigned to each industry subcategory, as data are available, for the years 1963 and 1967, so as to establish more sophisticated PR's for each of the 79 major industry categories. In doing this, the actual NVA data for each subcategory are used to weight its relative importance within the industry. As a result, the PR of each industry is representative of the "publicness rating" assigned to each industry subcategory, and of the "percentage of total industry value added" from each subcategory, as averaged across the two years (1963 and 1967). These PR figures may then be applied for all other years in a manner consistent with their direct application for the years 1963 and 1967. This disaggregated computation procedure for determining industry publicness ratings results in numerous "fractional" industry ratings rather than the "whole" numbers identified above (0, 1, 2, 3). For example, Industry Category #27—Chemicals and Selected Chemical Products—has a PR assignment of ".94."

Attention will now be given to the rating system as it applies to the 10 *public sector* functional expenditure categories. A rating of "3" is assigned to the National Defense, General Government, International Affairs and Finance, Education, Health-Labor-Welfare,[2] Veterans Benefits and Services, and Commerce-Transportation-Housing functions due to the presence of direct, and essentially complete, public sector provision of output. Meanwhile, the Space Research and Technology, Agriculture and Agricultural Resources and Natural Resources functions receive a "2" rating, since modest private sector allocation involvement is present. As an example, the Communications Satellite Corporation (COMSAT), under partly private ownership, interacts with the public sector Space Research and Technology function. Moreover, private sector purchases of timber grown on government land in relationship to the Natural Resources function of government represent a similar interaction. No functional expenditure category is given a rating of less than "2."

*Determination of the Publicness Value of GNP and of Its Private and Public Sector
Components in the United States: Government Allocation Influence Criterion*

The procedure necessary to achieve the ultimate objectives of this
study under the GA criterion may now be undertaken, that is, to estimate
the final *Publicness Value (PV)* for the private sector, for the public sector,
and for the aggregate economy (GNP).

The procedure for the *private sector:*

Step 1:   Industry Value Added
 − Government Nonlabor Purchases
 _____
 = Industry Net Value Added (NVA)

Step 2:   Industry Net Value Added
 × Industry Publicness Rating
 _____
 = Industry Weighted Net Value Added (WNVA)

Step 3: $\dfrac{\Sigma\text{WNVA for all industries}}{\Sigma\text{NVA for all industries}}$ = PV for private sector

The procedure for the *public sector:*

Since input-output data do not disaggregate government purchases into
all 10 functional expenditure categories, a labor/nonlabor disaggregation by
expenditure category is not available. Hence, the exact procedure applied to
the private sector of the economy cannot be applied to the public sector.
However, the Total Government Purchases value for all 10 spending categories combined can be ascertained (see ΣGP above). Moreover, non-I-O
data available from the U.S. Department of Commerce make possible a
disaggregation of Total GP according to the actual relative proportions of
each expenditure function by year. Thus, a Publicness Value can be determined for the public sector as a whole, inclusive of disaggregated data, even
though a specific labor/nonlabor division of government purchases by functional expenditure category is not attained. Accordingly, the following
procedure is used to determine the estimated PV for a given government
functional expenditure category, and subsequently for the entire public
sector:

Step 1:   Total Government Nonlabor Purchases
 + Total Government Labor Purchases
 _____
 = Total Government Purchases (ΣGP)

Step 2: Total Government Purchases
× Proportion of Total Government Purchases for a
given function
_____

= Government Purchases for a given function (GP)

Step 3: Government Purchases for a given function
× Expenditure Function Publicness Rating
_____

= Weighted Government Purchases for a given function (WGP)

Step 4: $\dfrac{\Sigma\text{WGP for all functions}}{\Sigma\text{GP for all functions}}$ = PV for public sector

The procedure for the *Aggregate Economy* (*GNP*):

Having estimated the Publicness Values of both the private and public sectors, the remaining step is to determine the Publicness Value for the aggregate economy or GNP. Since the two sectors constitute unequal proportions of GNP in terms of their resource allocation activities, a simple averaging of the PV's of each sector will not suffice. Instead, the following procedure is required in order to obtain the correct figure:

$$\frac{\Sigma\text{WNVA} + \Sigma\text{WGP}}{\Sigma\text{NVA} + \Sigma\text{GP}} = \text{PV for the aggregate economy (GNP)}$$

Empirical Results for the United States Economy

Table 1 summarizes the Publicness Values computed under the above procedures for the Government Allocation Influence Criterion. It may be observed that during the period 1947–1972, both the private and public sectors of the economy experienced increases in government allocational influence. More specifically, the PV of the private sector increased from 0.64 in 1947 to 0.84 in 1972, while that of the public sector grew from 2.91 to 2.95 during the same period. Meanwhile, the aggregation of the two sectors into GNP reveals a growth of PV from 0.90 in 1947 to 1.29 in 1972. In all cases, the growth was intermittent rather than steady.

Table 1

Private Sector, Public Sector, and Aggregate
Economy (GNP) Publicness Values under the
Government Allocation Influence Criterion
Selected Years 1947–1972

(0–3 scale of publicness)

Economic Sector	Year					
	1947	1958	1963	1967	1970	1972
Private Sector[1]	0.64	0.88	0.76	0.72	0.84	0.84
Public Sector[2]	2.91	2.95	2.93	2.94	2.95	2.95
Aggregate Economy (GNP)[3]	0.90	1.24	1.22	1.22	1.30	1.29

[1]Represented by Net Value Added data, as adjusted.
[2]Represented by Government Purchases data, as adjusted.
[3]Represented by Net Value Added plus Government Purchases data, as adjusted.

IV. Public Goods Demand Measurement for the United States under the "Joint Consumption" Criterion

Assignment of Publicness Ratings

The criterion developed in this paper to estimate the degree of output publicness (and privateness) in the economy, in consumption benefit terms, will be referred to as the *Joint Consumption Criterion (JC)*. As undertaken above for the GA Criterion, a Publicness Rating (PR) must be assigned for each private sector industry and public sector functional expenditure category. Again, the rating system will follow an arbitrarily-selected *0 to 3* range. A rating of 0 will signify the complete absence of joint consumption and/or externality characteristics in consumption, as well as the related absence of exclusion difficulties, while a rating of 3 will depict strong joint consumption-externality and nonexclusion traits. Intermediate ratings between 0 and 3 will represent varying degrees of joint consumption and/or externalities and possible exclusion difficulties.

For example, in reference to the *private sector*, Industry Category #25—Paperboard Containers and Boxes—receives a "0" PR, since no joint consumption-externality characteristics nor exclusion difficulties are apparent in relationship to the output of this industry. On the other hand, the extensive evidence of joint consumption and exclusion difficulties related to national defense result in a PR of "2.78" for Industry Category #13—Ordnance and Accessories. The joint consumption and partial nonexclusion

Table 2

Private Sector, Public Sector, and Aggregate
Economy (GNP) Publicness Values
under the Joint Consumption Criterion
Selected Years 1947–1972

(0–3 scale of publicness)

Economic Sector	Year					
	1947	*1958*	*1963*	*1967*	*1970*	*1972*
Private Sector[1]	0.28	0.30	0.29	0.31	0.33	0.32
Public Sector[2]	2.37	2.41	2.36	2.36	2.30	2.27
Aggregate Economy (GNP)[3]	0.50	0.70	0.73	0.84	0.77	0.74

[1]Represented by Net Value Added data, as adjusted.
[2]Represented by Government Purchases data, as adjusted.
[3]Represented by Net Value Added plus Government Purchases data, as adjusted.

characteristics of Communications Products result in a rating of "2" for that industry (Industry Category #66).

In the *public sector*, PR's for the 10 functional expenditure categories under the JC Criterion are assigned as follows: A rating of "3" is given to the National Defense, Space Research and Technology, and General Government functions, due to prevalent joint consumption-nonexclusion characteristics. On the other hand, a rating of "2" is given to the International Affairs and Finance, Education, Health-Labor-Welfare, Veterans Benefits and Services, Agriculture and Agricultural Services, and Natural Resources functions, in which these characteristics are less pronounced. Meanwhile, the Commerce-Transportation-Housing category receives a "1" rating, since considerable divisible consumption is apparent in this public sector expenditure function.

Determination of the Publicness Value of GNP and of Its Private and Public Sector Components in the United States: Joint Consumption Criterion

Next, following the procedure applied above under the GA Criterion, the final Publicness Value (PV) for each private industry and government functional expenditure category under the JC Criterion is computed, followed by an aggregation of these so as to determine the overall PV's of the private sector and public sector, respectively. In turn, the appropriate summation of the data for these two sectors results in the Publicness Value for the economy as a whole as represented by GNP.

Empirical Results for the United States Economy

Table 2 summarizes the Publicness Values computed under the Joint Consumption Criterion. It may be observed for the period 1947–1972 that the private sector PV increased from 0.28 to 0.32, and that of the aggregate economy (GNP) increased from 0.50 to 0.74. In the same period, the public sector PV declined from 2.37 to 2.27. In all cases, the trends were intermittent. Hence, the nature of consumption benefits increased in publicness between 1947–1972 both within GNP as well as within the private sector, despite a modest decline in public sector PV. However, this public sector decline did not cause an overall decrease in PV for the economy as a whole due to the following reasons: (1) government, with its higher PV values compared to those of the private sector, became a higher proportion of GNP between 1947 and 1972, and (2) the private sector, whose PV increased during the period, still represents a larger proportion of GNP than the public sector.

Disaggregation of United States Output by Type of Economic Good under the Joint Consumption Criterion

The final exercise in this paper will entail a classification of economic output by *type of economic good*, based on consumption characteristics. Thus, if a private industry or government functional expenditure category has been assigned a PR between 0 and 0.75 under the JC Criterion, its NVA or GP, respectively, will be entered within total output under the *pure private goods* classification since few, if any, joint consumption or externality and nonexclusion traits are present. A PR between 0.76 and 1.50 will result in a *quasi-private goods* classification; between 1.51 and 2.25 in a *quasi-public goods* classification, and between 2.26 and 3.0 in a *pure public goods* classification, as joint consumption or externality and nonexclusion characteristics become increasingly dominant.[3] After the NVA and GP values have been entered within their appropriate goods classifications, the NVA's are summed within each classification, resulting in a disaggregation of *private sector output* by type of economic good, and the GP's are summed within each of the four goods classifications, resulting in a disaggregation of *public sector output* by type of economic good. Finally, the summing of both NVA's and GP's within the goods classifications provides a profile of *aggregate economic output* (*GNP*), as disaggregated by type of economic good.

These results are presented in Table 3. As would be expected, most private sector output is of the pure private goods variety, followed by the

Table 3

Percentage of Total Output by Type of Economic Good
under the Joint Consumption Criterion, Private and
Public Sectors and Aggregate Economy (GNP),
Selected Years 1947–1972

Economic Sector	Type of Economic Good	*(Percent of Output)*					
		Year					
		1947	*1958*	*1963*	*1967*	*1970*	*1972*
Private	Pure Private	83	84	80	79	78	78
Sector	Quasi-Private	16	14	18	18	20	19
Output[1]	Quasi-Public	1	2	2	2	2	3
	Pure Public	<1	<1	<1	1	<1	<1
	Total	100	100	100	100	100	100
Public	Pure Private	<1	<1	<1	<1	<1	<1
Sector	Quasi-Private	5	13	13	12	12	12
Output[2]	Quasi-Public	52	34	38	40	46	49
	Pure Public	43	53	49	48	42	39
	Total	100	100	100	100	100	100
Aggregate	Pure Private	74	70	63	52	61	61
Economic	Quasi-Private	15	14	17	30	18	18
Output	Quasi-Public	7	7	10	9	12	13
(GNP)[3]	Pure-Public	4	9	10	9	9	8
	Total	100	100	100	100	100	100

[1]Represented by Net Value Added data, as adjusted.
[2]Represented by Government Purchases data, as adjusted.
[3]Represented by Net Value Added plus Government Purchases data, as adjusted.

quasi-private goods category. Yet, a modest trend in the private sector toward more publicness (less privateness) in consumption benefits is detected between 1947 and 1972. In turn, most public sector output falls within the quasi-public and pure public goods classifications, but unlike the private sector, the "quasi" classification ranks first in importance.[4] Moreover, also unlike the private sector, there is a modest trend toward more privateness (less publicness) in consumption benefits between 1947 and 1972. However, when the aggregate economy (GNP) is considered, the overall trend is away from the pure private goods and toward the pure public goods. Nonetheless, the greater part of total output remains in the "essentially privateness" range of pure private and quasi-private goods. This is consistent, of course, with the relatively greater allocational importance of the private sector within the mixed American economy.

V. Conclusions

This paper, using input-output data for the United States economy, provides further insight concerning: (1) the *total allocational influence* of the public sector, inclusive of various forms of indirect governmental influence on private sector decisions, and (2) the composition of aggregate economic output in terms of its *consumption characteristics*, inclusive of specific goods classifications. However, it is acknowledged that the present study constitutes only a beginning effort to improve measurement in these neglected dimensions of the demand for public goods. In the course of this research, numerous avenues for subsequent research have become apparent. For example, what particular government functional expenditure and/or private industry categories explain important trends? What expenditure categories and/or industries are, in any given year, most important in explaining the publicness and privateness results? Since technological and political changes over time may alter the appropriate publicness rating assigned to a given expenditure or industry category, subsequent research might adjust for such changes. In addition, attention might be paid to the intergovernmental implications of the data. Overall, the empirical results presented represent only a small portion of the potential analysis that could be pursued under this methodological approach. Furthermore, future research might utilize modelling as well as expanded application of the Delphi method for assigning publicness ratings.

In conclusion, it seems indisputable that the two measurement voids emphasized in this paper are worthy of attention. Moreover, it is obvious that any real effort to deal with these voids must follow a disaggregate approach. Input-output data are clearly of a disaggregate nature. It is hoped that the present research will prompt additional efforts by other researchers, using this and/or other disaggregate methods, to provide a more comprehensive and accurate measurement of the demand for public goods in Western countries.

Notes

1. The literature of public finance does contain some efforts to measure *subnational* government output along these lines.
2. The expenditure categories constitute only "government purchases," thus *not* measuring nonexhaustive (transfer) expenditures. Hence, the welfare component of the health-labor-welfare category would include only the resource-absorbing administrative costs of welfare programs.
3. The numerical bands used for classifying the four types of economic goods are arbitrarily set.

4. The low "<1" value for *pure private goods* in the public sector may seem initially surprising, in light of the substantial federal government financial involvement with divisible consumption in such programs as those related to food for the poor and housing. However, it should be pointed out that the I-O data used herein are "strictly *allocational*" in nature. Hence, the actual production of food and housing shows up largely in the data for the private sector rather than in public sector data.

Résumé

La demande de biens publics est étroitement liée à la question du rôle économique optimal qu'il convient à l'Etat de jouer dans les démocraties industrielles de l'Ouest. Toutefois, mesurer la demande de biens publics se heurte à un grand nombre de difficultés. On considère ici en tout premier lieu deux de ces difficultés: à savoir (1) l'échec de techniques de mesures conventionnelles susceptibles de rendre compte de diverses formes d'influence indirecte de l'Etat sur la répartition des ressources du secteur privé, et (2) l'absence générale d'efforts pour mesurer la production en terme de composition des avantages de la consommation selon qu'elle est privée ou conjointe, c'est-à-dire alternative ou complémentaire.

Afin d'améliorer ces deux insuffisances de mesure, on utilise des données d'"entrées" et de "sorties" pour l'économie des Etats-Unis conjointement à l'introduction d'une nouvelle méthodolgie de mesures. Après une description détaillée de cette méthodologie et de deux critères de mesures, on présente des résultats empiriques pour les Etats-Unis pour la période 1947–1972 (on sélectionne pour l'étude les années pour lesquelles on dispose des données les plus récentes et les plus complètes). On observe que le degré global d'influence du secteur public sur la production, tant pour celle de caractère étatique absorbant directement des ressources que pour celle de caractère indirect sur les décisions d'allocations des facteurs du secteur privé, a augmenté pendant la période considérée. En outre, la part publique de la production américaine a aussi augmenté pendant la même période.

Cet article ne constitue qu'une première tentative pour résoudre ces deux problèmes de mesures liés à la demande de biens publics. De nombreuses possibilités de recherche ultérieures apparaissent. Nous souhaitons que l'on encourage les efforts d'autres chercheurs qui utiliseront soit la méthode d' "entrées-sorties" présentée ici, ou d'autres méthodes, afin d'offrir le moyen de mesurer de façon plus complète et plus précise la demande de biens publics dans les pays de l'Ouest.

Enhancement of Public Sector Efficiency by Micro-Economic Control of Public Supply

Arthur Seldon

I. The Authority of Economics

The influence of economic science rests so far essentially on two centuries of micro-economic refinement of pricing since Adam Smith, especially the century of marginal analysis since Stanley Jevons, Carl Menger and Leon Walras in the early 1870s. Exchange in a 'market' between buyers and sellers produces the seal of voluntary agreement in the terms of exchange we call 'price', the successor of primitive barter. Since exchange between individuals or small groups is not only the most fundamental and potentially fruitful but also the most ineradicable form of human activity, the gradual but continuing refinement of pricing is designed to identify its imperfections and improve its efficiency in reflecting the preferences of the parties to exchange.

So far, 45 years of macro-economic refinement of models of whole national economic structures that analyse the relationships between totals or averages of incomes and expenditures, inputs and outputs, have yet to demonstrate comparable insight into economic processes or into the efficient use of scarce resources to reflect voluntarily-articulated preferences. Such macro-economic 'models' of economic relationships are flawed insofar as they do not rest on micro-economic foundations. Even if the macro-models can be refined to remove their imperfections, the heavy concentration of economists on them in almost all countries in the age of Keynes has exacted a high opportunity cost in the relative neglect of micro-economic controls. The neglect has been most costly in 'public supply', the provision of a wide range of goods and services by government at nil or nominal price bearing no link with average or marginal cost but with non-collective benefits.

Public Finance and the Quest for Efficiency. Proceedings of the 38th Congress of the International Institute of Public Finance. Copenhagen, 1982, pp. 155–165. Copyright © 1984 by Wayne State University Press, Detroit, Michigan, 48202.

Mathematical macro-modelling offers economists attractive scope for ingenious product differentiation, especially where they are financed by the state, and more in Western than in Eastern Europe, where there is an increasing appreciation of the role of pricing.

II. Pricing and Efficiency

The comparative efficiency and deficiency of micro- and macro-economic controls can be illustrated briefly from the recent effort of government in Britain to improve the efficiency of public supply by reducing expenditure on it. The disciplines have been almost entirely macro-economic: budgetary or discretionary expenditure ceilings or cash limits assigned to whole departments or services, decided centrally and administered locally, with relatively few or minor micro-controls by pricing (medicines, university fees for overseas students, etc.). The 'cuts' have applied more or less across the board over a wide range of supply from whole sections of the National Health Service and state education to art galleries, opera, home helps and refuse collection.

The general result has been arbitrary: from reductions in school and university budgets, justified by the falling numbers entering the relevant age groups, to closures of hospital casualty stations and libraries where trade unions have resisted staff pruning. The Universities, spearheaded by their Vice-Chancellors, have condemned the 'cuts' for damaging the fabric of British higher education, scholarship, learning and research to the lasting detriment of British living standards and social cohesion.

These macro-controls, enforced by both Conservative and Labour Governments, have been made by political judgement and bureaucratic advice almost entirely without assistance from micro-economic information. Yet many individuals would have paid more in taxes or charges to avoid reductions in services, not least in medical care, or even to secure improvement or extensions where they were thought deficient. Evidence from price-related surveys broadly supports this supposition.

The choice between micro- and macro-disciplines is a choice between imperfections. The imperfections of pricing have been analysed exhaustively by multitudes of economists almost since the birth of economics, not least the half century since the critiques of E.H. Chamberlin and Joan Robinson in 1933. The imperfections of the political process in providing tax revenue as the main source of finance for public supply have been analysed most penetratingly, despite Alfred Marshall and A.C. Pigou, by a relative handful of U.S.A. 'public choice' theorists for barely two decades since the late 1950s. And the "externalities' of tax-financing are still largely ignored by economists who concentrate on cost/benefit solutions for the externalities of pricing. ('Public' choice is a misnomer; the correct term is *political* choice, since the decisions are effectively made by political representatives· who misinterpret, overlook or frustrate the preferences of the public.)

Micro-controls are inefficient where they exclude externalities or the long view but are indispensable for efficiency insofar as they reflect personal knowledge of individual, family or local circumstances, requirements and preferences. Macro-controls are claimed to be superior for efficiency where they can take into account third-party effects by internalising externalities, and where they can overcome short-sightedness by discounting long-term consequences. But micro-controls, although imperfect, reflect real circumstances, requirements and preferences. Macro-controls are conceptually efficient but in practice are too crude to reflect individual valuations in a social welfare function; and in the real world their application is frustrated by vested interest and philosophic ideology.

Economists have bravely attempted to quantify externalities by cost-benefit analysis. The quantification rests on so many unverifiable assumptions that the estimates of costs and benefits they yield are largely spurious. But they are often dressed in scientific jargon impressive enough to induce politicians that they have scholarly support for policies they favour on ideological grounds for replacing market pricing in almost every conceivable human activity, for in the last analysis all human behaviour benefits or harms other agents. The conceptually interesting but often unworldly thinking of such 'externality" economists as E.J. Mishan is a seductive but dangerous guide for government facing real-life choices in the use of resources with opportunity costs (Cf. Mishan (1982, p. 246)).

Since individual citizens see the income effect on themselves as sellers of labour or producers more clearly than the price effect on them as buyers or consumers of labour, their pressure on government is predominantly as producers concerned with price as income rather than as a signal of scarcity or abundance to induce movement from lower to higher pay. In Great Britain, the price of labour in public supply is rarely used to encourage movement from declining services, such as from school-teaching, although it has been used to stimulate recruiting in the armed services and the police. It is because markets and market pricing put long-term consumer before short-term producer interests that it is properly regarded as a public good because people who 'drop out' cannot be charged for its benefits (as Russia and other non-market economies cannot be charged for the bench-marks of world commodity prices).

Still less is market price seen as the source of information about relative preferences. The allocation of resources to the social services in Britain is made with almost no reference to information on individual preferences.

Three further advantages of pricing should be recalled.

First, price is a teacher. By creating consciousness of opportunities foregone, price induces care in comparing values, caution in deciding between purchases, economy in managing money. Even in products as sensitive as drugs affecting health, where reduced purchase may induce ill-health or nil purchase cause death, countries with both capitalist and socialist economies have used pricing to penalise thoughtless over-purchasing and conserve supplies. Yet it is not used directly in pricing medical services to discourage life-styles or habits with no less certain consequences for health or life—over-drinking, over-smoking, over-eating, careless driving, risk-taking in sport.

Second, pricing is the alternative to paternalistic or authoritarian allocation, but it is not used much or at all to allocate resources in a wide range of public supply that yields non-joint, separable services or benefits—chiefly education, medical care, housing and more.

Third, price is the most pacific method of settling disputes over allocation of resources and over the values of their products. Pricing enables individuals to prefer some uses of scarce resources and thereby to exclude others. Where implicit exclusion is not performed impersonally by price, it has to be performed by visible authority whose decisions cannot be avoided except by rebellion or emigration. Pricing can resolve differences and disputes without physical conflict since it creates the invisible 'social' authority of the generality of consumers and producers, buyers and sellers, that is accepted because no individual or small group can be identified as exerting arbitrary authority.

Micro-controls to reduce the size of the public sector, help master inflation and reduce taxes and the bureaucracy as desired by public opinion, would have lessened the burden on macro-management which might have been more effective. The main failure of the Conservative Government elected in 1979 has been its inability to control the continuing growth in the public sector despite demonstrable inefficiency (mining, railways), reduced demographic demand (schools) and the superiority of private supply (local government services). Micro-controls would have been more acceptable since they transfer the decisions on 'cutting' services from politicians and officials, who are seen as autocratic, ill-informed and harsh, to the public newly-armed by pricing with information about the opportunity costs of buying less or more public services. Tensions could have been reduced, adaptations could have been made more gradually and public supply could have concentrated on activities where it was more efficient than private supply.

III. The Scope for Micro-Control

Until recent years only a handful of British economists were urging micro-controls in public supply as a systematic policy by substituting pricing for taxing where feasible. There had been intermittent studies of pricing for individual public services provided at nil or nominal price, and since the early 1960s the Institute of Economic Affairs has sponsored studies in the scope for pricing in housing, health care, libraries, transport, education, car parking, roads, water, fire services, refuse, seaside amenities, town planning, blood, animal semen, sports facilities and pollution protection.

An impressionist estimate some years ago suggested that public goods proper accounted for no more than half the expenditure on services in kind. The other half would be potentially controllable by pricing—fees, charges, etc. The ultimate incidence could be a transfer from public to private supply. The extent of the switch would turn essentially on the effect of the new competition from private supply on consumer sensitivity, producer efficiency and costs.

The structure of public supply in most countries, capitalist as well as nominally socialist, bears little relation to the broad distinction between public goods with joint benefits and non-public goods with separable benefits. The distinction is conceptually clear, although in practice public goods dispense some separable benefits. But the structure of public supply in Britain, and no doubt in other countries, is the result of historical accident, conservatism, resistance to reform by bureaucracies, confusion in the public mind sown by politicians (such as the British economist Anthony Crosland (1959)) who taught that 'public supply' was innately superior to private supply, and so on. The specific reasons for the growth of British public supply and tax financing are now almost entirely out-dated by social advance or discredited by experience: beginning with the late 19th century they are Booth's primary poverty, Rowntree's secondary poverty, R.H. Tawney's equality of access, the sociologists' parity of esteem, the Fabian economies of large-scale municipalisation or centralisation, natural monopoly, Pigou's external benefits and detriments, Keynesian demand management.

Consumption of the separable benefits is often a legal obligation, usually on the ground of externality: as in education, refuse and sewage disposal, precaution against communicable disease by vaccination. Even some of these are not immutable. A rising compulsory school-leaving age prevents some children from learning saleable skills more easily in industry. Pricing education, with tax rebates, vouchers and reverse taxes, would enable parents to make the decision for children better informed than teachers or educationists. Other separable benefits are optional—from employment services to art galleries. So financing by charging is not excluded even where consumption of a non-public good is mandatory by law.

The recent study of local government by Professor C.D. Foster and two co-authors (Foster et al. (1980)) suggested that only 10% or less of gross revenue expenditure on British local government services could be considered to be on public goods as generally understood (non-excludable and non-rival).

IV. The Externalities of Tax Financing Public Supply

The existence of externalities is, by itself, not sufficient to indicate the scope for tax-financing, since tax-financing creates external detriments of its own. To list them briefly does not do them justice but may suffice to recall at least their existence:

1. the costs of tax collection in billions of man-hours in assessing, reporting, collecting and minimising avoidance/evasion (much understated by official statistics);
2. the disincentives of taxation and the loss of output;
3. bureaucratic administration and the lowered *quality* of public services, especially in subjective and intangible aspects;
4. denial of individual choice even where practicable;
5. regressive effect of public supply distributed in response to cultural bargaining power: accent, family background, social connections, occupational influence;
6. monopoly and its insensitivity to consumer preference and repression of innovation;
7. the power of the strike threat in services paid for by remote taxpayers;
8. loss of resources overseas in a world market, not least of British doctors;
9. corruption in the sale of contracts, licences, permissions, etc.;
10. syndicalism in place of consumer sovereignty, resulting in over-consumption and under-investment;
11. social conflict: minorities (Catholics in Northern Ireland, Scotsmen in the United Kingdom, etc.) have to accept public services decided by majorities, and the result is regional separatism and national disintegration.
12. vested interest resistance to change.

V. A Rough Rule of Thumb

Some economists would concede the *a priori* case for a 'social' cost/benefit evaluation of the externalities of tax-financing. I would have no more confidence in it as a guide to policy than in a cost-benefit analysis of transport or any other economic activity. Instead, I propose a rule of thumb to test the theoretical hypotheses and obviate spurious calculations. It would do rough justice but would at least be administratively recognisable and could be refined by trial and error and corrected for undesirable side-effects by other measures. It is "Tax where you must, charge where you can".

To tax "where you must" because charging is not feasible is to confine taxing to essentially public goods with joint, inseparable benefits, from defence to local roads. To charge "where you can" is to identify separable benefits, from police convoying to motorways.

It remains to add two supplementaries: overt subsidies for public supply where beneficial externalities can be established, and income supplementation by tax refunds, reverse taxes or earmarked purchasing power to enable all (except the mentally incapable) to pay the charges.

VI. A Hypothetical Demand Curve for Priced Public Supply

If efficiency in public supply is related to individual preferences, how are they to be revealed? Short of insurance, veto or taxes as refined in the literature on public choice, sampling based on pricing might offer indications of preferences if other methods are not practicable.

The growing post-war doubts about the efficiency of nil-priced public supply were usually suppressed by the sociologists' reply that the welfare state was too young to judge and that opinion polling was indicating general public satisfaction—around 80–90%.

Such measures of 'approval' or 'acceptance', the nearest to 'demand', mean very little without reference to price. In 1962, to discover whether the British public could react to a market price, I proposed at the Institute of Economic Affairs in London that we go over the heads of politicians and discover the approval of ('demand' for) state education and medical care *at a price*. Two prices for the private alternatives were set as the amount required to top up tax, refunded in the form of an education voucher worth one-third and two-thirds of the current cost of (secondary, day) state schooling, and a health voucher worth one-half and two-thirds of the current cost of private insurance for non-public insurable health services. The results were entirely consistent with the laws of demand: 15% of the sample of heads of households would add to the lower-value school voucher (higher topping up) in 1965 and 30% would top up the higher-value voucher (lower net price). 23% would top up the lower-value health voucher and 30% the higher-value voucher. By the third survey in 1978, the figures had risen to 30% and 52% for schools and 51% and 57% for medical care. These figures would probably be higher in 1982, and higher still if the vouchers represented the full value of private supply.

These results are a measure of the rejection of public supply in the two main components of the British welfare state. The 57% *rejection* in 1978 for a two-thirds value health voucher contrasts with the 80–90% '*approval*' in priceless opinion polling.

A rough indication of price-elasticity is also indicated: unity in 1965 for schooling, less than unity in 1978 (and in the 1970 survey). For medical care, price-elasticity is relatively low in the three years. Further sub-analysis by socio-occupational group permits a rough measure of income-elasticity.

These results suggest that the market and consciousness of price is probably not far below the surface. What effect on the efficiency of public supply would follow pricing? What would be the *substitution* effect of pricing?

VII. Pricing, Private Competition and Efficiency in Public Supply

Micro-pricing public supply would stimulate its cost-consciousness by generating private competition. Public supply would be smaller but more efficient. Pricing public supply between marginal and long-run average cost would reduce the differential between public and private services and tend to shift demand from public to private supply, according to the price elasticities of supply and demand in both. If the long-run price elasticities were high, there could be a secondary shift varying with the income-elasticity of demand, since as incomes rise more individuals down the income scale demand (and pay for) better service than the state aims to supply equally out of taxation.

The common implicit assumption that elasticity of demand is nil prevents the objectors to charging from making their most cogent objection: that pricing the public supply (of schools, etc.) would increase the private supply. Yet the case for pricing the public supply of even as sensitive a service as medical care is precisely that it would increase its efficiency by competition.

VIII. Public Sector Efficiency and the Social Welfare Function

The public sectors of all economic systems are theoretically based on an implicit social welfare function. To see how far the British social welfare function reflected individual preferences a first approximation could be gained by a field survey that regarded the sample as individual Chancellors of the Exchequer. If there were a substantial bunching around the current structure of expenditure on public supply, its efficiency could be said to be higher than if there were wide dispersion. Professor J.M. Buchanan's *Public Finance in Democratic Process* investigated how the individual would choose to *pay* his taxes. My enquiry in 1978 (See Harris and Seldon (1979)) sought to discover how they would like their taxes *spent*. In this way I hoped to discover broadly how 'representative' contemporary British governments have been in spending the people's taxes (or frustrating their preferences).

Government expenditure was represented by three public goods: defence, roads and unemployment benefit, and four separable benefits: education, health, housing and pensions.

The first finding was that the British have almost no idea of how their taxes are spent.

To enable the sample to think micro-economically, it was told how taxes were spread over the seven main items; if changes were preferred, it was required to say whether taxes should be switched between the seven, or total taxes raised or lowered. Seventy percent wanted their taxes switched. Further research could refine this method, but on this showing, the British social welfare function is a *fiction*. The British public sector, on this evidence, is inefficient.

The question is, in public choice jargon, whether the replies were 'sincere' or 'strategic.' The ways to test their suitability as a guide to policy are by more extensive sample surveying, referenda and pricing of non-public goods—methods not open to a private researcher.

Further refinement was introduced by asking *how much* the sample would switch between the seven services. These adjustments correspond to the marginal changes made in everyday household purchases. Since daily adjustments cannot be made in public supply, it would be expected that substantial shifts would have accumulated. Predictably large shifts were recorded, from 20% for medical care to 100% for roads among the public goods.

Similar ground was covered for the four sub-divisions of state education (nursery, primary, secondary and higher), the four main branches of the NHS (hospitals, family doctors, prescriptions and public health services). Finally, individual welfare functions in local government were sought based on libraries, school meals, sports amenities and police.

Within state education, there was a switch of 100% to nursery schools, mostly at the expense of secondary education (recently in disfavour in Britain largely because of falling standards). In medical care, the largest switch was to hospitals, mainly at the expense of prescriptions. In local government services the largest proportion wanted a switch to the police, the smallest to libraries.

These findings, though tentative, seem unambiguous: they indicate that, with the guide of pricing, British public supply would have been more efficient.

References

Buchanan, J.M., *Public Finance in Democratic Process*, Chapel Hill, N.C.: University of North Carolina Press 1967.
Crosland, A., *The Future of Socialism*, London: Cape Jonathan Ltd. 1959.
Foster, C.D., R.A. Jackman and M. Perlman, *Local Government Finance in a Unitary State*, London: Allen & Unwin 1980.
Harris, R., and A. Seldon, *Over-Ruled on Welfare*, London: Institute of Economic Affairs 1979.
Mishan, E.J., *Introduction to Political Economy*, London: Hutchinson 1982.

Résumé

L'analyse micro-économique des prix fait toujours autorité en économie comme méthode permettant de rassembler des informations relatives aux préférences et aux coûts d'opportunité ainsi qu'au rationnement de ressources rares et, comme une méthode plus efficace que la planification autoritaire pour résoudre les conflits. Ces fonctions de la politique de fixation des prix sont plus appréciées en Europe de l'Est que dans l'Europe de l'Ouest, où il y a plus d'opposition envers elles du fait d'intérêts particuliers, d'opportunisme politique et de confusion intellectuelle. Les contrôles macro-économiques concernant l'offre publique se sont révélés inefficaces, arbitraires, injustes, une source de tensions sociales et ont eu d'autres graves inconvénients externes.

Le champ d'utilisation d'une politique des prix dans le domaine de l'offre publique est très large. En Grande-Bretagne, on pourrait l'appliquer à près de la moitié des dépenses publiques globales pour les services en nature, et bien plus pour les offres des autorités locales publiques.

Les difficultés que présente l'évaluation des externalités pour aider à l'utilisation relative des politiques fiscales et des prix pour le financement de l'offre publique conduisent à de larges approximations.

Mes recherches à l'Institut des Affaires Economiques de Londres sur les potentialités d'une évaluation micro-économique des prix montrent une courbe de demande hypothétique pour l'éducation et les soins de santé (et sans doute pour d'autres offres publiques) avec des indications sur les élasticités prix et revenu. Mes autres recherches basées sur un échantillonage de la réalité pour révéler les préférences du public montrent que la fonction de bien-être social en Grande-Bretagne est largement fictive. Le gouvernement britannique répartit les dépenses inefficacement. On pourrait largement augmenter l'efficacité de l'offre publique au moyen de la politique de tarification.

On peut éviter les effets défavorables sur le revenu de l'évaluation des prix en relevant les bas revenus en espèces ou en pouvoir d'achat déterminé (bons en timbres comme en Tchécoslovaquie) pour préserver les effets d'efficacité des prix et éviter les externalités du financement fiscal.

Government Shortcomings and the Conditions of Demand

Charles Wolf, Jr.

I. Criteria for Evaluation

To appraise the inadequacies in government performance, we need criteria for defining adequacy. As I have suggested elsewhere (Wolf (1979)) these criteria should be the same as those used to evaluate the adequacy of market outcomes.

The principal criterion is efficiency: according to this criterion, the results produced by government activities, or by market operations, are socially efficient if the same level of collective benefits yielded by those activities cannot be generated at lower cost, or, alternatively, if greater benefits cannot be generated with the same level of costs, and if, in either case, the resulting benefits exceed costs. Existing theories of market failure specify the conditions under which market outcomes will fail to satisfy this criterion. Such failures may occur due to externalities and public goods, increasing returns, and market imperfections, resulting in market outcomes that are inefficient (i.e., yielding excessive or insufficient levels of output, or inefficient modes of producing them). The theory of non-market failure suggests the corresponding conditions under which government activities will also predictably result in inefficiencies (See e.g. Wolf (1979), Niskanen (1971), Stigler (1971)).

The second criterion according to which outcomes can be judged inadequate is distributional equity. From this perspective, the outcome of either market or governmental activities may be inequitable in terms of one or another ethical norm favored by a particular evaluator.[1] Although invoking this criterion goes beyond the conventional boundaries of economics, it has profound significance with respect to the formulation, evaluation, and implementation of alternative public policies.

Public Finance and the Quest for Efficiency. Proceedings of the 38th Congress of the International Institute of Public Finance. Copenhagen, 1982, pp. 167–173. Copyright © 1984 by Wayne State University Press, Detroit, Michigan, 48202.

Realistic and relevant judgments about the shortcomings of governmental and market performance require that both be compared according to criteria embracing distribution, as well as efficiency. In the real world of public policy, distributional issues are usually more influential than efficiency considerations in shaping judgments about the performance of government and of the private sector—of both the "non-market" and the market.

With these criteria as a basis, I want to consider those inefficiencies and inequities that result from the conditions of demand for government activities in Western democracies, especially the U.S. These conditions of demand typically interact with the conditions of supply of governmental activities to produce outcomes that depart from the two criteria referred to above. Thus, the demand conditions are only one part of the explanation for shortcomings in government. The supply side inefficiencies are addressed elsewhere in this book. Supply and demand conditions thus interact to create the shortcomings associated with governmental performance.

In focusing on the inadequacies of governmental performance, I do not mean to imply that these shortcomings are either greater or less than those associated with market outcomes. Clearly, we should try to understand the shortcomings both of the market and of government, in order to be able to appraise potential remedies or palliatives or, simply, to pick the lesser among the two evils.

II. Conditions of Demand for Government Activities

Certain fundamental conditions of demand relating to government activities contribute to the inefficiency associated with these activities. These conditions differ sharply between the Western democracies and the centrally planned economies (CPEs). One of the differences lies in the differing process of adjustment by which each of the systems eventually tries to make corrections for the inefficiencies that arise. The principal focus of my remarks will be on the demand conditions characterizing Western democracies, and more specifically the U.S.

The principal conditions of demand contributing to inefficiencies in the delivery of government functions can be briefly summarized:

1. In recent decades, there has been a dramatic increase in public awareness of the market's shortcomings. This increase has been due both to the acknowledged failures of market outcomes to be socially optimal (e.g., the growth of toxic wastes and pollutants, the exercise of monopoly power by both business and labor, increased population density and its effect on congestion and on the generally

greater importance of externalities, etc.), and to wider dissemination of information about these lapses.

2. Market failures, and public awareness of them, have been reflected in, as well as influenced by, the organization and effective political enfranchisement of many groups and interests that formerly were less informed and less active in the political process, e.g., women's groups, minorities, students' groups, environmentalists, consumer groups, etc. And these groups have, especially over the last few decades, pressed for governmental legislation, regulation, and other programs, to remedy the failures of the market to produce desired outcomes.

3. In the political process which mediates these heightened public demands, rewards often accrue to legislators and governmental officials who articulate and publicize problems and legislate proposed solutions, but rarely assume responsibility for implementing them.

4. In part as a consequence of this reward structure, and of the short terms associated with elected office, the rate of time discount of political actors tends to be higher than that of society. There is often an appreciable disjuncture between the time horizon of political actors, and the time required to analyze, experiment, and understand a particular problem or market shortcoming, in order to see whether a practical remedy exists at all. The result is what Feldstein (1980, p. 6) has called "the inherent myopia of the political process". Future costs and future benefits tend to be heavily discounted or ignored, while current or near term benefits are magnified, and near term costs are especially distasteful.

A recent example of such myopia is provided by two of the four elements in President Reagan's economic policy proposals: tax reductions under the Economic Recovery Tax of 1981, and tight monetary policy. The tax reductions proposed in ERTA received overwhelming support in the Congress and among the public, until pressure on interest rates and unemployment was experienced in 1982. Assuming that these latter costs are short-run, and that the tax reductions are valuable for the health of the American economy in the longer run, the gulf between short-run costs and long-term benefits may well turn out to be politically unacceptable to the detriment of the original policy proposals.

Other examples of the perverse effects of high time discounts implicit in the political process (i.e., "myopia") abound: for example, the failure to realize that Medicare and Medicaid, introduced to help the elderly and the poor, might lead to the subsequent explosion in health care costs that we now face; or that welfare programs, such as Aid for Families with Dependent Children, although intended to provide help for poor families, might have the subsequent effect of seriously weakening the structure of the family [Feldstein (1980, p. 4)].

5. Finally, there is a distortion of demand that arises from the decoupling between those who receive the benefits, and those who pay the costs, of government programs. The classical "free-rider" problem is a special case of decoupling: benefits are received regardless of whether any particular individual pays. Where benefits and costs are borne by different groups, incentives for effectual political organization and lobbying by prospective beneficiaries often lead to politically effective demands that are economically inefficient. Examples are provided by agricultural price supports, in both the American and Western European economies, as well as other forms of protection and subsidy to particular interests and sectors: tariffs; import quotas; concessional loans for Soviet purchases of European equipment; etc.

The decoupling between beneficiaries and victims can also explain the absence of government intervention, as well as its occurrence. For example, in the case of gun control in the United States, prospective beneficiaries of such control, namely the public at large, are numerous and dispersed, while those who would incur the costs of control are a concentrated, well-organized group of gun enthusiasts, i.e., the National Rifle Association. Even though aggregate social benefits from gun control may exceed the costs that would be imposed on the gunners, control by government does not occur.

Two different aspects of this decoupling phenomenon are worth distinguishing. What might be called "micro-decoupling" arises where the benefits from an existing or prospective government program are concentrated in a particular group, while the costs are broadly dispersed among the public, as taxpayers or consumers. The beneficiaries may thus have stronger incentives and may make politically more effective efforts, to initiate, sustain, or expand the program, than the victims have or make to oppose it. The result may be a government program or regulation that is inefficient (aggregate costs exceed benefits), or inequitable, or both. Examples include the agricultural price supports in the U.S. mentioned earlier, the Common Agricultural Policy of the EEC countries, and those increases in Social Security benefits over the past 20 years which have made the income of retirees more fully protected against inflation than that of most of the employed, tax-paying labor force.

By "macro-decoupling," I refer to what may be the fundamental and inherent problem of demand for government programs in Western democracies. Macro-decoupling is quintessentially a problem of political economy, and is also a source of inefficiency over time, rather than at a particular point in time. Macro-decoupling arises because, on the one hand, political power rests with the voting majority while, on the other hand, most public revenues come from taxes paid by a minority of upper income recipients, due to the "progressive" character of prevailing tax systems. So the base of political power rests with the majority, while a minority provides most public revenues. This decoupling provides a political opportunity and an economic incentive to expand redistributive programs. Whereas micro-decoupling implies that a well-organized minority exploits the majority, macro-decoupling implies the majority's exploitation of the minority.[2] The result of macro-decoupling, in the absence of restraint by the majority, can be erosion of the mainsprings of investment, innovation and growth, if the lower-income majority's temptation to redistribute weakens the upper-income minority's incentive to invest and innovate. (It may be equally true that limiting the minority's affluence is essential if social harmony is to be maintained.)

The enormous expansion of "entitlement" and other social programs in the United States (and also in Western Europe) since the mid 1960s is, to some extent, a reflection of this decoupling: student loans and scholarships; subsidized housing programs for low income families; Medicaid and Medicare; food stamps and legal aid to indigents; disability insurance; comprehensive employment and training programs; urban transit; etc. The results of this expansion are extraordinary. By 1980, 36 million Americans received monthly Social Security checks. Benefits were received by 22 million from Medicaid, 28 million from Medicare, 18 million from food stamps, 15 million from Veterans' programs, 11 million from Aid for Families with Dependent Children, etc.

Both types of decoupling may contribute to "excess" demand for government activities (programs, regulations, redistribution)—"excess" either in the sense that they entail greater social costs than benefits, or that they are not sustainable because they diminish incentives for productivity and growth in the economy.

Such excessive demands may, in turn, contribute significantly to inefficiencies in the *supply* of government activities if, as I have argued elsewhere, governmental production functions are subject to diseconomies of scale (Wolf (1982)).

In sum, conditions of demand in Western democracies can lead to profound distortions in politically effective demands for government action or inaction. The principal culprits are: (1) the often excessively high time discounts of elected officials, resulting from the relentless pressure of their relatively short terms and their pending reelection campaigns; and (2) the decoupling between those who benefit from and those who pay for, government programs, frequently resulting in stronger incentives to expand than to confine government programs. As a result, government programs may be initiated or expanded even though they are inefficient in a micro-economic sense (e.g., tariffs, agricultural price supports, etc.), as well as inequitable in conferring special gains and privileges on politically effective groups, while imposing greater costs on politically less effective ones. Other programs may be expanded to a level where they become inefficient in a dynamic sense (e.g., "entitlement" programs) by undermining the incentives on which the economy's longer-term growth depends.

Notes

1. For a brief discussion of six or seven plausible interpretations of "equity" see Wolf (1981).
2. I am indebted to Horst Hanusch for this formulation.

References

Feldstein, Martin (ed.), *The American Economy in Transition*, Chapter 1, Introduction, Chicago: University of Chicago Press 1980, pp. 1–7.
Niskanen, William A., *Bureaucracy and Representative Government*, Chicago: Aldine-Atherton 1971.
Stigler, George J., The Theory of Economic Regulation, *Bell Journal of Economics and Management Science*, 2 (1971), pp. 3–21.
Wolf, Charles, Jr., A Theory of Nonmarket Failure: Framework for Implementation Analysis, *Journal of Law and Economics*, 22 (1979), pp. 107–139.
Wolf, Charles, Jr., Ethics and Policy Analysis, in *Public Duties: The Moral Obligations of Government Officials*, edited by J.L. Fleishman, L. Liebman and M.H. Moore, Cambridge, Mass.: Harvard University Press 1981.
Wolf, Charles, Jr., Policy Analysis and Public Management: Strengths and Limits, *Journal of Policy Analysis and Management*, 1 (1982), pp. 546–550.

Résumé

Les conditions qui caractérisent la demande de biens et services publics peuvent contribuer à la fois à l'inefficacité de ces activités et à leur répartition inéquitable.

Cet article souligne deux conditions particulières de la demande:

1—Le fort taux d'actualisation qui prévaut dans le secteur public découle d'un grand nombre de facteurs propres au contexte politique des démocraties de l'Ouest, y compris l'horizon de temps relativement court dont disposent les élus et la nécessité qui s'en suit pour eux d'accumuler des résultats impressionnants avant leurs prochaines campagnes électorales. Ceci a pour effet d'encourager les programmes publics qui semblent avoir des avantages à court terme malgré leurs coûts élevés à long terme, et de décourager à tort des programmes à fort coûts à court terme et à larges avantages à long terme.

2—La distinction entre ceux qui reçoivent les bénéfices des programmes publics et ceux qui supportent leurs charges. On distingue deux variétés d'un tel découplage: "les micro-découplages" lorsque les bénéfices des programmes existants prévus sont concentrés sur un groupe social particulier alors que les coûts sont largement répartis entre les contribuables ou les consommateurs; et des "macro-découplages" découlant de l'attribution du pouvoir politique à une large majorité d'électeurs, tandis que les recettes publiques proviennent principalement d'impôts payés par une minorité d'entre eux. Ce découplage fournit une incitation propre à élargir les programmes de redistribution, car la demande effective relève de la majorité tandis que les coûts sont payés par une minorité; même quand les groupes bénéficiaires sont de petit nombre, des alliances politiques peuvent leur permettre de s'allier pour former une majorité politiquement efficace.

Ces sources de distorsions de la demande peuvent interférer avec des économies d'échelle dans les fonctions de production du secteur public et engendrent des gaspillages de la fourniture des services publics.

The Role of Elected Representatives in Parliamentary Forms of Government

Guy Kirsch

There is an obvious and most common answer to the question of what the role of representatives is: They have to take decisions on behalf of the electorate without distorting the will of the sovereign citizens. The role of elected representatives is to make exactly the same decisions the citizens would have made if they were not hampered by the heaviness of the direct participation by all in the democratic decision-making process.

There can be no doubt that reality rarely, if ever, corresponds to this ideal. The representatives do not only react to what the electorate wants them to do. In many cases they do have the possibility to act on their own. This is often seen as a deplorable perversion of the democratic process and the diagnosis and therapy of such a state of affairs make up a large part of the scientific literature in this area. This paper does not concentrate on this problem, but aims at bringing into focus another aspect of our subject.

1. The Thesis

Following an old and venerable tradition, public finance usually starts its theoretical discourse by referring to the citizens' wants that are to be satisfied by public goods. It is implicitly taken for granted that the wants and needs are pre-existent to the collective decision-making process. This paper puts forward the thesis that this is an oversimplified view of the problem and that an important function of the elected representatives is to help the individual citizens to generate those operational wants that are to orient government activity and in relation to which the efficiency of the public sector is to be measured. Wants are considered to be not only an

Public Finance and the Quest for Efficiency. Proceedings of the 38th Congress of the International Institute of Public Finance. Copenhagen, 1982, pp. 175–186. Copyright © 1984 by Wayne State University Press, Detroit, Michigan, 48202.

input, but also an output of the collective decision-making process. The thesis is that the quality of democracy, as a libertarian democracy, depends on whether the elected representatives play that role and how they do it.

2. Wants are the Result of Experience-Based Learning Processes

Economists normally assume potentially unlimited and given wants and scarce resources. It may, therefore, seem somewhat surprising to say that the existence of wants is a problem; they just seem to be the one thing we have in abundance. But on closer examination, we discover that man is not born with definite wants. A person's wants, at any moment of time, are the result of a learning process based on experience: you do not just have wants, you acquire, you learn to have them. Now, this seems to be a rather adventurous statement, since wants are thought to be the ultimate criterion for efficiency measures and for evaluating individual welfare situations. Nevertheless this statement can be more easily accepted if we consider that this welfare itself consists in a reduction of the discomfort caused by psychological tension, resulting from the lack of something. What this something may be is at first absolutely unclear. What man is first aware of is a sense of lacking, of unspecified uneasiness. He feels uncomfortable without knowing why and without knowing what to do about it.

Here enters the experience-based learning process. It is through experience that man learns to combine his welfare, that is the relief of his discomfort caused by a certain lack, with definite means to reduce this discomfort. Wants are the result of a combination of a vague sense of uneasiness and the knowledge of how to fight it. The complaint no longer runs "I lack something", but "I want this."

One might feel that, as a rule, just one instrument suffices to relieve the discomfort, i.e. in a given situation, at a given moment an individual can lower the tension by just *one* determinate means, the only problem being whether he knows about this and whether he can get hold of that means. Now, this view corresponds within certain limits to reality; however it neglects the fact that man is much more flexible than that. In many instances man may lower his psychic tension, may decrease his discomfort by relying on one out of a list of known and available instruments. That is to say man may transform his rather vague sense of uneasiness into more than one determinate and operational want.

The impression that these considerations are very remote from our topic vanishes if we consider what they imply. First, if we accept what psychology tells us about the development of individual wants we have to agree that an individual may impair his welfare by having the "wrong" wants. He may for instance spend his money very judiciously on beer which he—very judiciously—should not buy.

There is more to it. We just may be in a situation where we don't know of any way to relieve our discomfort. We feel uncomfortable without knowing why. We miss something without knowing what. In this case we don't see any way to increase our welfare. "Wunschloses Unglück" is the title of a play by Peter Handke.

Second it is by experience that we learn what instrument to combine with our discomfort in order to achieve an increase in our welfare. This is true on the individual level; it also applies when we look at the formation of collective wants.

Now, before having a closer look at these, it is to be noted that the experience of an individual may rest on what he had experienced in the past. It may also be based on what happened to others in the past. Educating children for instance consists mainly in transmitting to them the experiences of their forefathers, i.e. to allow them to have the results of some experiences without actually having experienced it. Another way to achieve the same result is for the individual to watch what happens to others, i.e. to make use of their experience without having to pay for it. This is important, because undergoing an experience can be a very expensive affair, and it may be very useful to take advantage of the experience others have paid for.

There is still another way to experience things, without actually participating in them. It consists of creating intellectual experiences. Without being able to rely on *real* experiences, one tries to imagine what will happen to one's welfare situation if a certain course of action is taken.

The production of fictitious experiences is in most cases not very costly. Unfortunately this advantage is compensated by the probability that the real experiences ex post will not correspond to the ex ante fictitious experiences. You must have some strong imaginative power in order to be able to produce these fictitious experiences and it is this imagination that may mislead you. This danger will be the greater the less elements of past real experiences you have to rely on, when it comes to check the results of your imagination. So, the less real experiences you have, the more you must rely on your ability to produce fictitious experiences. The more this is true, the riskier that production is.

A good example illustrating this point is the government activity related to national defense in the nuclear age. Though two A-bombs have been dropped in a real war, nobody has any real experience as to what a nuclear war might be like.

3. Having Private Wants . . .

Our topic is the role of elected representatives in generating the demand for government activities, but as the analysis of private wants is less complicated, it may be useful, first, to consider the formation of private wants, in contrast to public wants.

If somebody coming home after a long day's work feels uneasy without knowing why, without knowing what he wants, he may try successively a can of beer, a shower and ring up a friend. In doing this, he may realize that talking to someone is what he badly needed all the time. Realising what a chat with a friend does for his welfare, he comes to know what he wants, namely to talk with his friend.

Now, trying out these different experiences until one hits at what relieves the discomfort may not be expensive, in which case quite a series of such experiences may be made. 'If however the pursuit of private experiences is costly, one also has to rely on others' or on fictitious experiences in this area.[1]

4. . . . . is less Difficult than Having Collective Wants

This digression from the government activities to the generation of private wants should prove its usefulness when we turn to the question how public wants originate and what the role of elected representatives is in this business.

The citizen desires to increase his welfare, he even speaks about promoting the common good. Whether this should be attained by government activity X or Y is very often unclear. The citizen knows, at best, that something should be done. He is not always capable of saying what he wants done.

This does not come as a surprise. The possible reasons for this can be summarized as follows: it is not very expensive to try a new brand of beer in order to know whether one "wants" it or not. In contrast to this, it is very costly to try a new social security system, a new military strategy, a new transport system. If you build a highway system you spend billions and you get stuck with it for a long time. It is yours even if, after having experienced what it means to have that system, you realize that you do not want it. Thus, as far as public goods are concerned, decisions very often have to be made without having the necessary experience; and when at last you have had the experience it is no longer needed, because no similar decision is to be made in the future.

Even if the costs of going back on a decision about public goods are not prohibitive, the relation connecting a specific government activity to a specific policy result, i.e. to a change in individual welfare situations may be so complex as not to allow the vast majority of the electorate to be correctly informed about it. This will most probably be the case when changing conditions do not allow enough time for citizens to discover, even if looking actively for it, which government activities are beneficial and which are not. In traditional societies time-honored and time-proven policies may evolve; in fast-changing societies this is much more difficult.

It is difficult and dangerous to make use of experiences with certain public goods that have been made in foreign countries. What is bliss for one country may be blight for another. Not to be misguided by foreign experiences requires to take into account all the circumstances relevant to the overall effect of a given government activity. These may differ from one nation to another.

To imagine fictitious experiences with certain public goods and formulating wants on that basis requires a great amount of technical information, much strength of imaginative power and much energy and time. To expect all of this as a rule from an individual citizen is dubious.

Now, all this seems to be a very disappointing result. It is evident that if this pessimistic view is valid, the quest for efficiency will be in vain. Fortunately the situation is not that hopeless. The reason is that we do not have to rely exclusively on the informational and motivational capacities of the individual citizens, but that the interaction such as it exists in a parliamentary democracy between voting citizens and canvassing representatives contributes to the solution of the problem at hand.

5. The Role of Elected Representatives in a Democratic System

There is some plausibility to the hypothesis that political candidates, more often than not, are all-round amateurs rather than all-round specialists. This encourages them to present their voters with programs that are vague, full of catchwords implying everything and saying nothing. Being without technical information themselves, they are initially unable to formulate more precise and concrete programs. Besides, they most probably are not eager to do so, because the more precise a candidate's programs and promises, the easier it is for the citizens to control him and the easier it is for other candidates to criticize him.

In order to bring out the essence of our thesis we limit our argument to a very simple situation, neglecting many specifications and details. We start with two candidates, A and B, offering two different platforms. Both are

vague and without any concrete content. Empirical investigation and theoretical reflection suggest that a political candidate tends to criticize his
competitor more than to stress his own qualities and highlight the virtues of
his own program. Candidate A puts the program B into a concrete form, or
still better: he depicts in concrete terms the negative aspects of that program. The picture A draws of B's program will be one-sided, stressing only
its negative aspects, its costs. In all probability this will be inaccurate,
insofar as it relies on a limited and distorted knowledge of what consequences will emerge, what policy instruments will generate what under
which circumstances.

This puts candidate B into a defensive position. He is confronted with
a very negative interpretation of his plan, and, more important, his program
is by now more concrete than he wanted it to be. In this situation, candidate B must try to counterbalance the negative aspects of his plan by
stressing its positive consequences. He must show that the negative aspects
stressed by his opponent have been grossly exaggerated and that by looking
"objectively" at reality, one can see that A's interpretation of B's program is
based on an erroneous analysis of reality.

In order to undertake the defense of his own program, candidate B has,
at the very least, to acquire a certain minimum of technical information,
and he must put his program into a concrete form.

The process, however, does not stop here. Candidate B is not only
urged to react defensively on A's offensive; he himself may, and most
probably will, attack. He will stress the negative aspects of A's program,
and in doing this, he will make use of the technical information he has
acquired so far. This will give his interpretation of A's program a more
realistic, if only highly selective, character. A's interpretation of B's program will be just as one-sided as B's interpretation of A's proposal; nevertheless B's picture of the costs of A's program will be more accurate
because B had to acquire a knowledge A did not possess. Candidate B
having counter-attacked, A is now in the very position into which he had
put B.

It is easy to imagine that this process tends to continue as if feeding on
itself. An attack calls for a counter-attack which calls for a counter-counter-
attack. The better A is informed about the technicalities of the activity
under discussion, the more B must endeavour to reach a higher level of
information, which in turn is a spur to A. The more A highlights the costs
of B's proposal, the more B must point out the positive consequences. The
more concrete A's attack on B's position, the more B has to defend himself
by referring to precise technical aspects instead of general statements.

It is most important that the continuation of this process does not
depend on the good will of the candidates involved. In a certain sense, we
may identify here an invisible hand that makes democracy a functioning

affair, although, as will be explained below, pathological degeneracies may hinder this functional mechanism.

6. The Production of Fictitious Experiences

Political competition that characterizes parliamentary democracy is a social and organizational device to mobilize, to produce and to confront the information that is an indispensable ingredient of fictitious experiences. Indeed, under ideal conditions the political competition stages, in a highly dramatized form, scenes of what is going to happen if program A or program B is to be implemented. It means that political competition mobilizes the energies of the opponents, the imaginative powers that are necessary if experiences are to be had, without someone having undergone them. The political competition also mobilizes the available information that must be taken into account, in order not to let imagination create fictitious experiences that, for lack of realism, are just nice dreams or bad nightmares.

Thus, even if neither candidate A nor candidate B is interested in generating a concrete offer of government activity, both are compelled to do exactly that, if they want to have any chances to be elected.

Yet there is more to it. Though it is important that the political candidates are able and willing to come up with a rich *supply* of realistic proposals for government action, it is indispensable that the sovereign citizens are able to develop an enlightened *demand*. This is equivalent to saying that in a libertarian democracy the citizens must be willing and able to connect their own sense of discomfort with various ways the candidates propose to reduce that discomfort. The citizens must be able to transform their feeling of uneasiness into determinate wants. And that is exactly what can be expected from the democratic process *under ideal conditions:* the political competition with its speeches, round-table-discussions, TV-appearances, brochures, articles, etc. is a dramatic display of a wide range of instruments to reduce individual discomfort.

The expected result from this set-up, or at least the desired one, is that by watching the display of political alternatives or even by participating in them this way or another, the citizens acquire in the competitive process the information which permits them not only to feel that they lack *something*, but to know what they *want*.

Thus in a democracy the political process connects the candidates and the citizens in a *system* that mobilizes imaginative energies and the search for information, in order to produce the fictitious experiences that are necessary if concrete wants are to be formed.

What is most important in this context is that this is brought about, no matter what the motives of the representatives are. It is hardly an exaggeration to say that politicians, candidates in a parliamentary democracy, as individuals, are unimportant. All that matters is that a wide range of political alternatives is presented, that the pros and cons of these alternatives are brought to the fore, that the interplay of the different candidates, whoever they are and whatever they want, provides the electorate with experiences it would not or could not acquire by itself.

If we look back at what our considerations have been concerning this point, we realize that starting from a rather pessimistic view we have moved to a very optimistic one. The spelling out of wants should be guaranteed thanks to the role a democracy compels the representatives to play.

7. There are Constraints Limiting the Functioning of the Democratic System

Unfortunately this optimistic outlook is as unjustified as its pessimistic counterpart. If competition among the political candidates is to bring about the expected result, the range of political alternatives likely to be discussed must not be curtailed by the censorship of a self-appointed authority or by a tacit conspiracy of silence. Any such taboos diminish the choice of ways and means to increase the individual welfare situation.

It would be unrealistic to assume that such taboos do not exist. There are good reasons to believe that institutional and organizational barriers as well as psychological obstacles keep politicians and citizens in given collectivity at a given moment from considering all the alternatives that could be imagined and that would be possible. Furthermore sociological and sociopsychological research (see Hertzler (1965, p. 275), Devereux (1970, p. 13), Badura (1971, pp. 109–110), Friedländer (1975, p. 159)) tends to corroborate the hypothesis that in a given society at a given moment certain value judgements are taboo. This means that positive and/or negative consequences of political alternatives that would be relevant to these values cannot be discussed openly. A political candidate who would mention these consequences referring to the forbidden values would simply exclude himself from the political competition.

This is not to say that political taboos have no positive function; however, it is not to be overlooked that they are disfunctional because they shorten the list of politically debatable, hence possible alternatives of government activity (see Kirsch (1977)).

Though in a democracy it is the role of representatives as political leaders to follow the citizens, I feel that it is their duty to resist the fear-ridden taboos of the electorate, to function, as it were, as a therapist fighting his patients' neuroses.

Unfortunately here no invisible hand can be identified that urges the political candidates to assume that role. On the contrary: Howard S. Becker (1963) has made a point by showing that political competition may not only consist in presenting alternative proposals for government activity, but also in preventing decision problems from entering the public discussion. This amounts to saying that candidates may try to have the upper hand by manipulating the taboos of their electorate. The difference between a politi-cian and a statesman is probably that the latter knows how to get around, reshape, and use the taboos of his electorate, whereas the former just ac-cepts them as a limiting constraint. The statesman increases the range of possible and debatable political alternatives in spite of the citizens' timid narrowness of mind, the politician accepts to be, to become and/or to remain just as narrow-minded and neurotic as his electors are.

In this context the Downsian dynamics which push, under certain con-ditions, political programs to become more similar in order to meet in the center of the political spectrum, appear to be ambivalent. Though they reduce the political tensions and make it less difficult to reach a consensus, they limit the fictitious experiences political competition generates. However it must be admitted that, insofar as the democratic process within the com-peting parties allows for the discussion of a wider range of political alterna-tives than is finally discussed between these parties, this negative side-effect of Downsian party dynamics is, at least partly, counter-balanced.

There is another obstacle that prevents voters from gaining experience by watching the political debate between competing candidates. Insofar as alternative government activities cannot be discussed publicly, e.g. because national defense reasons call for a certain degree of secrecy, voters are denied the possibility to give their vague political orientations a concrete form. Not knowing themselves what to want they cannot but retire in an apolitical apathy, in a total disinterest in the Republic, or else express, in a more or less inarticulated way, what they feel. It does not come as a surprise that this very often takes the form of emotion-ridden demonstra-tions and rioting. In a libertarian democracy collective decisions are made by exchange of words. The throwing of Molotov-cocktails and the use of the policeman's club is a serious symptom of degeneration in a democracy.

There is a kind of symmetry between political taboos and political secrets. The former originate in the refusal of the electorate to consider certain policy aspects, the latter are important because they conceal subjects the citizens vaguely feel they should know about in order to be able to take them into consideration when making their political choice, when determin-ing their collective wants. In both cases the political candidates occupy a strategic position. They should not accept, without any further thinking, the narrow-minded taboos of their voters, and they should not withhold information from these voters that can be discussed publicly, without preju-dice for the collectivity.

Yet, there are important differences between taboos and secrets. Com-petition among the political (would be) representatives does not seem to be an adequate instrument to transcend these taboos. On the contrary, candi-dates most probably will mutually reinforce their respect of these taboos. On the other hand, it is most plausible that political competition favors the disclosing of secrets because a candidate may take advantage of using secret information he has come to know, and because the top secret stamp is usually handled by the public administration, and not by the legislative. This is not to say that the legislative never uses that stamp. If Puviani's thesis is right that the "classa politica" has interests of its own, that these may differ from and are possibly conflicting with many or all electors' interests, then secrecy is a very useful, or even necessary, instrument to create and to perpetuate "illusioni finanziarie" (Puviani (1973)). Fortunately there are others on whom to rely when taboos and secrets are not to be too formidable obstacles in the production of fictitious experiences, to wit the free press.

Summing up, we may say that the role of representatives in the forma-tion of the electors' wants in the democratic process can only be played when certain conditions exist: the political debate must be *open*.

Besides being open, the political debate must be *public:* the perfor-mance of the political drama can only enter the learning process, and hence contribute to the production of fictitious experiences and the formation of collective wants if the audience is admitted.

Up to this point we have concentrated on the process relating candi-dates to one another and generating, under certain conditions, a full range of fictitious experiences that are both realistic and innovative. Now, lest these experiences be lost, it is necessary that the citizens confront the information which the political debate mobilizes with their feeling that something is to be done. Only if they did this, can one expect that concrete and determinate collective wants emerge. Unfortunately, theoretical reason-ing and empirical research cause little optimism as far as the citizens' ability and readiness to inform themselves on political subjects are concerned. Anthony Downs' thesis that rationality commands citizens not to incur information costs beyond a certain level still holds.

There is still more. People are socialized, that is, educated to be a member of society, in small groups, such as families, Kindergartens, college fraternities, etc. This makes it difficult for them to grasp the sociopsycho-logically different reality of large collectivities. On an intellectual and emo-tional level they are not too good at understanding that (and how) their individual welfare is affected by і. _ competing political alternatives. Precisely because collective goods are collective goods the individual member of the collectivity may feel that the outcome of political decisions affects him, yet at the same time he may consider the political decisions themselves as events so remote as not to affect his welfare. The outcome of government activities is seen as a God-given—or at least as an inescapable manifestation of a fate that is a kind of abstraction—compared to the concreteness of the limited circle of everyday life.

The hypothesis that for many people events on the state level are less real or not real at all, is at least as plausible as its counterpart which enters, as a rule, without questioning into our theory of public finance. If our hypothesis is right, the consequences of our interpretation of parliamentary democracy as a learning and teaching institution are important. The abstractness and remoteness of what is debated in the political discussion prevents citizens from integrating that what they assist in, if ever they are aware of it, into the whole of their experiences. Consequently the political debate is lost as a factor in determinating concrete collective wants.

One might object to this rather pessimistic anti-Jeffersonian view of the electorate that though there may be something in it, it is not the whole story. People are not *totally* uninformed about what goes on in the Republic. This is surely right. However, it is to be pointed out that the information people have about political matters is often very fortuitous. They are not looking actively for information in order to give a concrete and determinate shape to their craving for welfare. Often enough they just passively swallow the information that is easy and pleasant to swallow. The information that is presented in a nice way reaches them, whereas the other information that might be much more important for them is neglected. The selection criterion being the consumptive as contrasted to the investive value of information, citizens tend to be informed because receiving and having information is pleasant, not because getting and being informed is useful.

There is another misdirection affecting the information citizens tend to have. As has been stated above, people living in a society are trained in small groups. This is a source of constant misunderstandings. Citizens transpose their attitudes and expectations, their hopes and fears from the world of face-to-face relations into the universe of impersonal (or rather a-personal) connections in large groups, such as states. Instead of realizing that (1) in the system of political decision making a politician, or a candidate is someone playing a role, that (2) this politician, as an individual can be replaced by almost any other, that (3) what is important is the *role* he plays and not the person he *is*, citizens tend to personalize politics. They love or they hate politicians, instead of evaluating coolly and rationally what these politicians stand for, what role they play and what proposals they make.

This certainly is justified insofar as, confronted with an uncertain future, the spelling out of wants is not only impossible, but may be even harmful. In this situation, the citizens are compelled to personalize politics. They look for politicians they want to follow. It is then not so much the quest for efficiency but the quest for persons to be trusted.

Note

1. For example: Needing a home is a very vague desire as opposed to wanting a particular kind of house. Now, most people have a certain experience with this or that kind of house; but this experience may be too limited to provide them with a clear and precise idea of what kind of house they will want in their present situation. So they have to look at the experiences other people (seem to) have with all kinds of houses. Lately this aspect has been given a special attention as far as private goods are concerned. See Ehrenberg (1972).

References:

Badura, B. (1971), Sprachbarrieren. Zur Soziologie der Kommunikation, Stuttgart: Fromman-Holzboog.
Becker, H.S. (1963), Outsider: Studies in the Sociology of Deviance, New York: Free Press of Glencoe.
Devereux, G. (1970), Essais d'ethnopsychiatrie générale. Paris: Gallimard.
Ehrenberg, A.S.C. (1972), Repeat-Bying. Theory and Applications, Amsterdam—London—New York: North Holland Publishing Company.
Friedländer, S. (1975), Histoire et psychanalyse, Paris: Seuil.
Hertzler, J. (1965), A Sociology of Language, New York: Random House.
Kirsch, G. (1977), Fonctions et disfonctions de tabous politiques, in: G. Gaudard et al. (ed.), La politique économique de la Suisse, Fribourg: Editions Universitaires, pp. 65–80.
Puviani, A. (1973), Teoria della illusione finanziaria, Milano: Istituto Editoriale Internazionale.

Résumé

Comment les citoyens en arrivent-ils à connaître de façon opérationelle les besoins qu'ils entendent satisfaire par la production de biens collectifs? La présente étude analyse comment et dans quelles conditions le processus politique engendre l'expérience fictive qui, à défaut d'expérience réelle, doit permettre aux gens de passer du "Il me manque quelque chose" au "Je veux ceci ou cela". Elle analyse aussi certaines pathologies du processus démocratique qui immobilisent soit l'imagination créatrice, soit le savoir technique et qui par là empêchent la transformation d'un vague sentiment de malaise en besoins collectifs opérationels.

THE SUPPLY OF
GOVERNMENT OUTPUT

Inefficiencies in Public Transfer Policies in Western Industrialized Democracies*

Victor Halberstadt, Robert H. Haveman, Barbara L. Wolfe and Kees P. Goudswaard

I. Introduction

During the 1970's, almost all Western industrialized democracies experienced unprecedented economic and social changes for a peace-time period. For many countries, economic growth, which seemed so vigorous in the early postwar period, seemed to disappear in the early 1970s. Unemployment rates rose rapidly, wage and price inflation were rampant, export markets were unstable and shrinking, and rates of productivity growth stagnated. Recently, there have been numerous, sometimes highly speculative, hypotheses put forth regarding the causes of this poor economic performance. These include high and growing tax rates, increasingly generous income transfer programs, increasingly stringent environmental controls, and the structural changes required to accomodate radical increases in oil prices.

Because various causal factors have probably played some role in accounting for poor economic performance, the ultimate need is to quantify the contribution of each. The methodological and data requirements for making such an identification are enormous. Any causal factor not only has a direct impact on performance, but it also interacts with other factors. Discerning the full quantitative contribution of a factor through both direct and indirect channels of impact is not possible given available data and estimation procedures. We have undertaken a more limited task: to evaluate the role played by one of these causal factors—growing cash and in-kind income transfers—in impeding economic performance during the past decade.[1]

*The authors would like to thank Willem Drees, and their discussants, Jorge Macon and K.D. Grüske, for helpful comments.

Public Finance and the Quest for Efficiency. Proceedings of the 38th Congress of the International Institute of Public Finance. Copenhagen, 1982, pp. 189–208. Copyright © 1984 by Wayne State University Press, Detroit, Michigan, 48202.

The post-war era in industrialized democracies can be characterized by the development of the welfare state.[2] Through state measures, individuals have become collectively insured against a wide variety of private risks: the loss of income upon retirement, the loss of support upon the death of parents or spouses, the loss of income if unemployment strikes, and support of income if one has low earnings capacity. Similarly, firms have become protected against the loss of business due to declining export markets or low aggregate demand. Income and capital transfers to industry have become part of the welfare state broadly considered.[3]

This support has been provided to individuals in a variety of guises—pensions, cash income transfers, and in-kind transfers for food, housing and medical care. Industry subsidies have been even more varied—employment creation and preservation subsidies, a wide variety of investment subsidies, tariffs, public loans to foreign purchasers of domestic production, and regional employment programs.

In this paper, we will focus on transfers directed at individual citizens. These transfers take a variety of forms in all industrialized democracies, but in each country some basic similarities exist:

All countries have social insurance measures for retirement and disability.

All countries have unemployment benefit programs, and programs to compensate workers for injuries on the job.

All countries have programs to assist families to purchase necessities such as food, housing, and medical care.

Most countries provide support contingent on the number of children in a family.

All countries have programs providing an income "safety net" to individuals with low earnings capacities.

We will proceed as follows: First, we will identify the incentives for behavioral change implicit in these transfers, in particular, their effect on work, saving, investment, and economic growth. This discussion will have to be impressionistic, at best. There are numerous incentives; some contribute to economic growth, others do not. Second, we will use evidence from economic literature to assess the extent to which transfer programs and the taxes required to finance them have discouraged labor supply and savings. This section closes with some observations on macroeconomic efficiency effects of income transfer programs. The fourth section is the most speculative. There we present some evidence on both the declining economic performance and growth of the public transfer programs in five Western democracies: The Federal Republic of Germany, The Netherlands, Sweden, the United Kingdom, and the United States. The purpose of this discussion is to establish the basis for assessing a causal link between growing transfer policies and the poor performance of the economies. Finally, we will present some tentative policy suggestions consistent with our assessment of the contribution of growing income transfers to lagging economic performance.

II. The Potential Effects of Income Transfers on Economic Efficiency

The catalogue of the potential impacts of income transfers on individual behavior is a long one. By their very nature, these programs change relative prices and incomes confronted by those who may be eligible to receive income support, and those liable for the taxes to support these measures. If price and income elasticities are greater than *de minimus*, these effects will induce changes in individual behavior which may or may not contribute to efficiency or economic performance. These incentives have been discussed in many places; here we will mention several of them, separating those with a positive efficiency impact from those with a negative effect on productivity and economic performance.

Potential Positive Efficiency Effects of Transfers

— By providing income support targeted on the poor, nutrition, health (through increased medical care and better housing) and, hence, work effort may be supplemented.
— By providing an income cushion, individuals may be more willing to engage in job search and inter-regional and inter-occupational mobility.
— By providing income support, individuals may more readily accept technological change or bear risks.
— By providing income support for young children, they may have increased nutrition, medical care, and thereby human capital.

Potential Adverse Efficiency Effects of Transfers

— Income transfers provide an income cushion and, if work conditioned, reduce effective wage rates. Both effects encourage the substition of leisure for work effort, if leisure is a normal good.
— Savings may be reduced as individuals believe that public pensions reduce the need to privately provide for future needs.

— High taxes and high marginal rates required to finance income transfers may discourage work, earnings, and risk taking.

— Generous transfers supported by high taxes shift the terms of trade away from participation in market activities and toward do-it-yourself and "underground economy" activities.

— Provision of income support which is untaxed gives incentive to change one's position, characteristics, or status so as to qualify for benefit recipiency.

The literature on the adverse incentive effects of income transfers and their associated taxes has focused primarily on the factor supply effects of these measures. Individuals respond to changes in expected net income or wealth or the net prices of working and saving brought about by transfer programs. In the discussion of labor supply and savings effects that follows, we assume that the incentive structure of the private economy with public transfer programs in place is similar to the structure that would exist without the programs.

Labor Supply

The effect of income transfers on labor supply is generally analyzed within standard consumer theory. An individual maximizes utility by choosing among income-leisure options, given a budget constraint. Because most transfer programs provide income support without requiring work and reduce benefits when earnings increase, the recipient's budget constraint is shifted in position and slope. Hence, two program parameters—the income guarantee and the marginal tax (or benefit reduction) rate—are the most important in analyzing work incentive impacts. The guarantee produces an income effect; the tax rate, both an income and a substitution effect. If leisure is a normal good, a transfer with a positive guarantee and tax rate creates income and substitution effects which unambiguously reduce labor supply. A program with a zero tax rate has only an income effect that reduces labor supply.

Transfer programs may also induce an intertemporal labor supply response. A permanent, age-related transfer program may tend to induce earlier retirement or a decrease in labor supply in pre-retirement years because potential beneficiaries require less private pre-retirement savings to support consumption during their retirement years [Feldstein (1974)].

This standard model has been extended to account for the nature of real world constraints, the complexity of actual income transfer programs, and the nature of utility functions. For example, when the budget constraint is kinked because of either peculiarities in program design or the simultaneous existence of several transfer programs, labor supply functions may be discontinuous, have both forward and backward-bending segments, or have kinks [Hanoch and Honig (1978)]. As a result, increases in the guarantee or tax rate may bring about aggregate responses different from those suggested above. While the standard model treats work effort as a continuous variable, an individual's response may be discontinuous (e.g., withdrawal from the labor force, as in early retirement). Constraints on work time flexibility (e.g., employer-imposed constraints on work hours) also produce discontinuous responses.

Moreover, the standard model does not yield predictions about any individual family member's labor supply if this decision is made jointly with those of other household members [Killingsworth (1976)]. Finally, "entitlement effects" may induce some persons to enter the work force to qualify for social insurance programs, or to work more to raise their future benefits from such programs [Hamermesh (1979)]. In spite of these reservations to or extensions of standard theory, aggregate work effort is, on balance, expected to be lower with than without transfers, but the size of this effect remains unclear.

Private Savings

The price and wealth effects of public transfers, especially those which are age-related, may also affect consumption behavior. In the life-cycle framework of Harrod (1948), Ando and Modigliani (1963), and Modigliani and Brumberg (1954), saving is undertaken during working years to support consumption during retirement. Within this framework, compulsory Social Security benefits provide an alternative to private savings. If private savings were reduced by the same amount as public savings from Social Security tax revenues were increased, there would be no net reduction in aggregate savings. However, because most programs operate on a pay-as-you-go basis, there is no public saving, only a transfer from current workers to current retirees. Hence, if the present value of benefits appears larger than the present value of social security taxes in such a system, private (and therefore aggregate) savings may decrease.

An extended life-cycle framework can be used to analyze the simultaneous impacts of an age-related transfer program on both labor supply and savings [Feldstein (1974)]. In such a framework, the potential negative savings impact due to life-cycle considerations can be distinguished from the incentive for retirement at younger ages. As a result of the retirement effect, saving during working years may increase in order to support consumption over a now-longer retirement period. This effect offsets at least in part the reduced savings impact from the simple life-cycle model.

Age-related transfers may also induce a reduction in saving if they are perceived as an increment to net wealth and hence, result in increased consumption. While the future tax liabilities required to finance an actuarially fair program would appear to offset this benefit-related wealth effect, the offset may not be equivalent.

While the above discussion has focused on the savings effects of age-related transfers, other redistributive transfers can also affect savings. Consider, for example, transfers such as unemployment benefits, workers' compensation, or survivors' benefits which reduce temporary losses of income. If savings are undertaken for precautionary motives in addition to life-cycle considerations, these transfers may also alter private savings decisions.

In sum, economic theory provides no clear prediction on the direction of the private savings response to transfer programs. While theoretical considerations can guide research into behavioral responses, the uncertainty can only be resolved examining the empirical evidence.

Macroeconomic Efficiency Effects

Income transfer programs have macroeconomic as well as microeconomic efficiency consequences. First, programs such as unemployment and disability insurance provide a built-in stabilizing element in the economy. In a slack economy, aggregate consumption demand which may stimulate investment is sustained by income transfer payments. In the *short term* these transfer programs are likely to contribute to the achievement of full employment. However, the effects of employment benefits on consumption appear to be smaller than might be expected because unemployed recipients tend to maintain their consumption even with reduced benefits [Hamermesh (1982)].

In the *long run*, investment, employment, inflation and the balance of payments will be influenced by taxes needed to finance income transfer programs. In the absence of backward shifting, higher employers' statutory contributions to social security programs (including sickness benefit programs) lead directly to increased (non-wage) labor costs. Instead, higher taxes on employers might be partially shifted backward, leading to reduced real wages. But to the extent it is only partial, higher wage and labor costs will result.[4] The possible consequences of rapidly rising wage and non-wage labor costs include: 1) higher final goods prices and/or 2) reduced profit margins. In the former case, formal price-wage links cause higher final goods prices to be reflected in higher wages in the next period, thus fueling inflation and harming international competitiveness. In the latter case in which forward shifting of rising labor costs is not (or only partially) possible, the reduced profit margins directly affect investment and economic growth. In both cases, the price of labor rises relative to other inputs, stimulating substitution and a reduced demand for labor. The resulting growth in unemployment increases the number of transfer benefit recipients (in particular, unemployment and disability recipients)[5] which again necessitates higher social security taxes.

III. Have Income Transfers Reduced Work and Saving?

A large number of recent, largely U.S., studies has sought to quantify the magnitude of the negative work and savings incentives of income transfers. This literature provides a basis for judging the extent of the behavioral responses generated by income transfer policies. From these studies, it is possible to estimate the total impact of the income transfer system on work effort. This estimate must be rough because the studies tend to focus on individual programs and not on the entire income support system. When the entire system of many programs is put into place, some fundamental behavioral and institutional changes may well occur. People's evaluation of the benefits and costs of working (or working hard), the benefits and costs of entering the labor force early when young (or leaving later when old), the benefits and costs of avoiding layoffs or terminations, the benefits and costs of hurrying back to work when laid off, and the benefits and costs of seeking advancement and promotions may all be altered. In addition, peoples' attitudes toward the quality of their work and their pride in it may decrease, and as a result the incidence of absenteeism, delays, and shoddy products may increase.[6] All of these changes must be considered in evaluating the total effect on work of the support system.

The expansion of U.S. social welfare expenditures from 1950 to 1976 has been "guesstimated" to have caused total hours worked to decline by 7 percent from what they would have been if the system had not expanded [Lampman (1978)]. This rather high number also includes the effects of some programs (e.g., public education) not in the income transfer system. Moreover, the effect on work of the taxes required to finance the expansion was also included. Thus, is likely to be an overestimate of the effect of the transfers alone.[7]

More recently, statistical estimates of the work responses of various groups to the guarantees and benefit-reduction rates in specific programs have been applied to programs targeted on specific groups in order to measure the work reduction attributable to each program [Danziger, Haveman, and Plotnick (1981)]. The aggregate labor supply effect obtained from this procedure applied to the major income transfer programs suggests a total work reduction of about 5 percent attributable to the post-war growth in income transfers. This result is consistent with the 7 percent figure cited above in that some major components of total social welfare expenditures are excluded. Moreover, the 5 percent estimate does not include the disincentive effect of the increased taxes required to finance the outlays.

Neither of these estimates supports the view that increased income support or social welfare spending has seriously disrupted the functioning of the labor market. Indeed, the percentage reduction in total economic activity caused by these disincentives will be less than either the 7 percent or 5 percent reduction in time worked because the earnings of most recipients are well below the average of U.S. workers.

The effect of the income support system on thrift and savings has also been estimated. The expansion of benefits has been found to decrease total savings. This occurs because income is transferred to lower-income people, who have higher propensities to consume, and away from higher-income people, who tend to save more.

In recent years a large number of researchers have investigated the effect of Social Security on savings.[8] An impressive array of variables and empirical equations have been mustered in "regression wars" among these contenders. The general result—and perhaps the current consensus among economists—is that income transfers have depressed private savings by a small amount, but that this amount cannot yet be measured precisely. These studies, it should be noted, focus on social security retirement programs, and not on the effect of the entire income support system, and they do so in the context of a fully employed economy. For a slack economy the case may be quite different.

In sum, past growth of the system appears to have modestly reduced work effort, savings, and GNP growth. Proportional expansion of existing programs may, however, cause a larger erosion of work effort and savings.[9]

In interpreting these estimates however, it is important to keep in mind that they are "best guesses" made in a partial equilibrium framework. A number of other factors may have caused the GNP slowdown and these are likely to be correlated over time with the growth of income transfer policies. Indeed, income transfer policies may have been employed as an instrument to reduce the labor supply of older and less productive workers, hence increasing employment opportunities for women and youths entering the labor market. Moreover, maximizing GNP may not be the only relevant goal of a country.

Thus, to appropriately measure the role of income transfers in the economic slowdown would require estimating a longitudinal general equilibrium model, utilizing an extensive (and unavailable) data base. Even if this could be done, however, it would be necessary to recall that other social objectives exist in addition to maximizing GNP. Citizens may care about the income distribution, or about the distribution of certain merit goods, suggesting that the concept of efficiency should be broadened from the narrow notion of GNP. With such a broader notion of efficiency, reductions in GNP required to achieve, say, reduced poverty, reduced inequality, or increased income security may be quite consistent with an increase in aggregate economic well-being.

IV. Income Transfers and Economic Performance: Coincidence or Causation

The poor pattern of economic performance in Western industrialized nations is by now well recognized. This performance has been accompanied by rapid growth in the generosity and accessibility of income transfer programs—and in total expenditures, beneficiaries, and taxes required to finance them—as well as substantial demographic changes such as the increasing proportion of elderly people in the population.

Table 1 shows some selected indicators of income transfer growth and economic performance in five countries—the Federal Republic of Germany (FRG), The Netherlands, Sweden, the United Kingdom, and the United States.

These data are clearly too restrictive to permit reliable cross-national analyses, or to estimate the quantitative contribution of income transfer growth to poor economic performance. They are suggestive, however.

The patterns presented in Table 1 are as follows:

(1) For all of the countries, expenditures on income security programs as a percent of GNP increased from 1963 to 1977. In 1963, the median percentage was 12.3; by 1977, the median percentage was 23.3. Sweden experienced the greatest growth in social program expenditures over the period, U.K. the smallest. The U.S. program remained the smallest (in percentage of GNP) throughout the period. Sweden became the country with the largest program, while The Netherlands ranked second in both 1963 and 1977.

(2) This program growth was accompanied by an increasing fiscal burden in financing social insurance through employer-employee contributions. Median contributions as a percent of GDP grew to 14.4 in 1977, from 8.6 in 1963. The pattern does not precisely correspond to the growth in social insurance as a percent of GNP since financing of programs differ across countries.

Table 1

Selected Indicators of Income Security and
Economic Performance in Five OECD Countries

	1963	1966	1971	1974	1977	1980
1. Expenditures for income security programs[1] (% of GNP)						
FRG	16.9	18.4	18.8	22.5	26.5	NA
Netherlands	14.4	16.9	21.5	24.7	28.4	NA
Sweden	12.2	14.5	20.6	24.4	30.7	NA
U.K.	11.1	12.3	13.5	14.1	17.1	NA
U.S.	6.8	7.7	11.1	12.1	13.7	NA
2. Total employer-employee contributions to income security programs[1] (% of GNP)						
FRG	11.8	11.8	13.1	15.0	16.2	NA
Netherlands	12.8	16.6	20.2	22.9	23.3	NA
Sweden	5.8	6.9	9.3	10.3	15.4	NA
U.K.	7.9	6.4	6.3	7.3	8.7	NA
U.S.	4.7	6.1	5.3	7.8	8.4	NA
3. Growth of real GNP						
FRG	3.0	2.5	3.2	0.5	3.0	1.9
Netherlands	3.6	2.7	4.3	3.5	2.4	0.6
Sweden	5.2	2.1	0.8	4.3	-2.0	1.4
U.K.	3.9	2.0	2.7	-1.0	1.3	-1.4
U.S.	3.9	6.0	3.4	-0.6	5.4	-0.1

4. Gross fixed capital formation (% of GNP)

FRG	25.5	25.4	26.4	21.9	20.7	23.6
Netherlands	23.8	26.2	25.9	21.8	21.1	21.0
Sweden	24.2	24.8	22.1	21.5	21.2	20.3
U.K.	16.7	18.3	18.4	20.3	17.9	17.8
U.S.	17.9	18.6	18.1	18.4	18.4	18.2

5. Productivity (GDP/Employment) (% change)

FRG	NA	NA	2.7	2.5	2.9	0.9
Netherlands	NA	NA	4.0	3.4	2.5	0.2
Sweden	NA	NA	−0.8	2.2	−2.1	0.0
U.K.	NA	NA	3.4	−1.2	2.2	0.5
U.S.	NA	NA	3.6	−3.8	1.7	−0.5

6. Gross saving (% of GNP)

FRG	26.4	26.6	27.3	25.1	22.7	23.1
Netherlands	25.5	26.5	26.8	27.9	22.4	20.1
Sweden	24.7	25.2	24.1	23.0	17.6	17.3
U.K.	17.4	18.9	19.7	16.9	18.9	19.2
U.S.	19.3	20.3	18.4	19.3	18.7	18.3

7. Unit labor costs (manuf., % change)

FRG	NA	NA	10.4	8.9	3.3	5.3
Netherlands	NA	NA	9.5	12.3	5.6	4.9
Sweden	NA	NA	10.8	10.7	17.0	10.0
U.K.	NA	NA	9.4	21.5	11.1	21.9
U.S.	NA	NA	3.2	11.2	6.4	10.9

Continued on next page

Table 1—Continued

	1963	1966	1971	1974	1977	1980
8. Consumer prices (% change)						
FRG	NA	3.5	5.3	7.0	3.7	5.5
Netherlands	NA	5.8	7.5	9.6	6.4	6.5
Sweden	NA	6.4	7.4	9.9	11.4	13.7
U.K.	NA	3.9	9.4	16.0	15.8	18.0
U.S.	NA	2.9	4.3	11.0	6.5	13.5
9. Labor force participation rates (males aged 25–54%)						
FRG	96.5[2]	NA	97.1[3]	94.1[4]	NA	NA
Netherlands	98.0[2]	NA	96.9[3]	94.2[4]	NA	93.6
Sweden	95.7[2]	NA	94.8[3]	NA	NA	NA
U.K.	NA	NA	97.8[3]	95.8[4]	NA	96.1
U.S.	95.7[2]	NA	94.8[3]	93.5[4]	NA	93.5
10. Labor force participation rates (males 55–64%)						
FRG	NA	NA	86.8[5]	NA	85.8[5]	NA
Netherlands	NA	NA	68.8[5]	NA	47.9[5]	NA
Sweden	NA	97.8[5,6]	86.9[5]	89.7[5,4]	79.9[5]	NA
Sweden		83.0[5,6]	73.9[5]	74.0[5,4]	58.0[5]	
U.K.	NA	NA	91.0	90.8[4]	NA	NA
U.S.	NA	85.2[6]	81.5[3]	74.8[4]	73.0	NA

200

11. Standardized unemployment rates (% of labor force)

FRG	NA	0.2	0.9	1.6	3.7	3.1
Netherlands	NA	0.8	1.3	2.8	4.2	4.9
Sweden	NA	1.6	2.5	2.0	1.8	2.0
U.K.	NA	2.3	3.7	2.9	6.2	7.4
U.S.	NA	3.6	5.7	5.4	6.9	7.0

[1] These statistics include old-age, survivors and disability, public health insurance, worker's compensation, unemployment insurance, family allowances, public employee programs, and public assistance
[2] 1960
[3] 1970
[4] 1975
[5] The upper numbers are for 55–59 year olds, the lower number for 60–64 year olds
[6] 1965

Sources: 1,2: *Social Security in Europe: The Impact of an Aging Population*, An information paper prepared for use by the special committee on aging, U.S. Senate, U.S. Government Printing Office, Washington, December 1981
3,4,6,8,11: OECD, *Economic Outlook*, December 1981
5,7: OECD, *Economic Outlook*, various years
9: OECD, *Demographic Trends 1950–1990*, Paris 1979
10: ILO, *Yearbook of Labor Statistics*, various years

(3) At the same times as expenditures and contributions have grown, the rate of growth in GDP fell in all five countries. The median growth among the countries declined from 3.9 percent in 1963 to 0.5 percent in 1980.

(4) Among the remaining indicators of economic performance, changes in three are consistent with the explanation that the growth of income transfers contributed to poor economic performance: gross fixed capital formation as a percent of GDP; gross savings as a percent of GDP; and labor costs in manufacturing. For these three indicators the patterns of poor economic performance roughly followed the pattern of income transfer growth as a percent of GDP across the five countries.

(5) Changes in other indicators do not correspond closely with the pattern of growth in income transfers. For example, while the labor force participation rate for older males declined in all of the countries, the rate of decline across countries does not closely parallel the rate of program growth. Thus, there is some limited evidence of a link between income transfer growth and economic performance, but evidence of a large impact is not present.

What, then, can be concluded? First, the theoretical linkages between income transfer growth and economic performance have been comprehensively identified. While the primary links involve labor supply, savings, and macroeconomic effects, other channels of impacts, though less closely linked to economic performance, are also important. Second, we have documented the empirical relationship between income transfer program growth and economic performance in five western industrialized countries. As transfer program expenditures and recipients grew, labor supply productivity and economic growth fell. This pattern persisted over all of the countries studied. Third, on the basis of microeconomic studies, it can be concluded that while some of the blame for the poor economic performance can be attributed to growing transfer benefits, the magnitude of the effect so allocated is not large—surely not in the range above 25 percent.

In sum, then, by exploring the linkages between the structure, growth, and incentives of income transfers and economic performance, we hope to have increased understanding of this important issue, and to have stimulated further research on the role of welfare state growth on economic performance. We have, however, once again emphasized the complexity of the factors which interact to determine economic performance—factors as diverse as exogenous oil price increases and poor harvests, the growth of environmental and health-safety regulations, demographic changes, shifts in international relationships and their associated capital flows, the efficiency with which investments are undertaken, and the adequacy of economic coordination among the western countries.

V. Some Tentative Policy Suggestions

The problem of the linkage of transfer growth and economic performance is a classic "chicken and egg" problem: Poor economic performance surely leads to an increase in the demand for public transfers—for example, in the demand for unemployment, disability, and early retirement benefits. Conversely, increasingly generous transfer benefits, more lenient elgibility requirements, and higher marginal tax rates are likely to lead to higher costs, reduced labor supply, and decreased savings and investment.

One way of identifying causation would be to estimate the growth of transfer recipients and expenditures over the past decade assuming no change in policy parameters such as eligibility or generosity. If the estimated pattern of program growth was the same as the actual growth in terms of both beneficiaries and expenditures, poor economic performance would be the "cause" of the growth in public transfers and not the reverse. If the estimated growth were substantially less than the actual increases, program generosity and leniency could be viewed as causal, at least to some degree.

But even establishing such causality has little normative significance. Perhaps the political decisions taken to reduce eligibility requirements were designed to encourage reductions in the labor supply of older workers so as to open up job opportunities for youth and, hence, avoid disillusionment or social unrest. Perhaps the decisions to increase benefits reflected distributional preferences, and hence were decisions which in fact increased economic well-being. Moreover, it makes a difference if the consequences of the changed policies were anticipated, or if they were unexpected. If the latter, poor economic performance may have been both induced by increasingly generous transfers, and *ex post*, at least, inefficient.

Irrespective of the direction of causation, however, ways exist to increase the efficiency of income transfer policies. Thus, public transfer policies could be redesigned to minimize a wide range of adverse consequences which might result—in terms of labor supply, savings, productivity, tax burdens, family stability—irrespective of whether or not these disincentives have increased through time.

Consider the following suggestions:

First, attention should be given to maintaining strong work incentives for those who receive or might receive benefits. For example, the benefit structure could be changed so that all those eligible for disability benefits could maintain benefits, at some level, even though they worked. Benefits could be paid until the individual's earnings were equivalent to his (her) predisability earnings, making up all or part of the deficit until this point is reached. A preferred alternative would base benefits on the earnings of the person's cohort with and without specific limitations. The payment would thus be all or part of the difference in expected earnings due to a specific limitation for a person's age, sex cohort, adjusted for the person's relative position prior to limitation. Again, the payment would cease when the pre-limitation level of earnings was reached. A proposal along these lines has recently been made by Nagi (1982).

A second suggestion, applicable only to countries where benefits in-kind are tied to the receipt of cash transfers, is to provide income-conditioned, in-kind benefits to all those with low money incomes, regardless of the source. For example, in countries where medical care is not nationalized or where insurance is not universally provided by the government, the government could provide income-conditioned medical care vouchers so that those with low income would have health subsidies. As it stands now in systems where public provision of medical insurance or other benefits are tied to transfer recipiency, the medical insurance component and/or other benefits are an added incentive to either get on or remain on the transfer program. Removing this link would reduce this program inefficiency.

A third suggestion is designed to potentially reduce part of any negative effect of public transfers on savings. Economic theory suggests that Social Security benefits might substitute for private savings for retirement years, or might be perceived as an increment to net wealth resulting in increased consumption and lowered savings. A suggestion is to tie retirement benefits not solely to earnings but also to savings. In such an arrangement, benefits would increase at some rate in relation to the amount the individual contributes to savings—in, say, a benefit account set up to contribute to the retirement transfer system, a separate retirement account, or some other special plan. In such a scheme, retirement benefits would either be the minimum amount or a greater, more generous amount based on earlier saving behavior. Net social security wealth would thus be directly tied to an individual's own lifetime savings behavior. One version of this plan might be to "subsidize" savings by making certain savings tax free, as is the case now in some countries. The individual might forego the right to early (pre-retirement) withdrawal, or incur a penalty on such withdrawal, in order to gain from this tax incentive. These possibilities are only suggestive, and individual governments might well wish to impose a variety of restrictions or regulations designed to fit the country's own objectives or institutional arrangements.

Fourth, to reduce the adverse labor supply consequences of public transfers, increased rehabilitation, employment, or labor market incentives could be attached to income transfer recipiency. These efforts would include training, employment counseling and job placement, provision of medical services, and the stimulation of job sharing. If training, rehabilitation, additional schooling, or employment counseling can increase the probability that low skill or disabled workers can find jobs at reasonable wages, work may appear more attractive to them than non-work along with the receipt of income transfers.[10]

A much discussed alternative to improve efficiency is to substitute a credit income tax for the existing set of income transfer programs. [See, for example, Garfinkel (1982)]. All persons would file an income tax form. Those below a certain level (adjusted for family size) would receive cash transfers from the government, those above would pay taxes. The tax-transfer schedule for this plan would incorporate low marginal tax rates throughout the earnings range. All citizens, both existing transfer recipients facing high benefit reduction rates and higher income tax payers would face lower "tax" rates on marginal income, thereby increasing incentives to work. Moreover, increases in earnings for transfer recipients would not entail (as in many current systems) the loss of all benefits, plus the applicable income tax rate.

All of the above labor market policies work on the supply side—they are designed to improve labor productivity. However, as suggested above, a major part of the current problem of poor economic performance concerns a lack of job opportunities (at least given sticky or regulated wages), and can only be undone by a substantial acceleration of growth of both final demand and plant capacity. Evidence suggests that employment subsidies made directly to firms can work directly in stimulating jobs. Because the payments are generally a part of the salary of any new hires, they reduce the cost of hiring additional workers, encouraging firms to increase their employment. From society's point of view, as long as the cost of the subsidy does not simply replace payments the firm would make even without the subsidy, and the subsidy is less than the income transfer (or the present value of the subsidy plus any further government payments are less than the present value of the income transfers), this is a more efficient policy than income transfers. [For extensive analyses of both the economic theory of and empirical research on employment subsidies, see Haveman and Palmer (1982)].

These labor market-based suggestions, however, are made cautiously. In a period of high unemployment, large amounts of resources devoted to such labor market policies may reap little success. This apparently has been the conclusion reached in a number of countries. [See, for example, Haveman (1978) on the Dutch Social Employment Program, and review of the Conference on European and American Labor Market Policies by Haveman (1982)].

In the past most, if not all, proposals to increase the efficiency of income transfers have met with considerable resistance in industrialized democracies. This resistance is not only of a technical nature, but apparently finds a strong basis in both acquired rights and the electoral weight of the number of recipients of public transfers. However, the current problem of poor economic performance and its interaction with growing income transfers may force more serious consideration of such policy alternatives.

Notes

1. The major socialist countries have also experienced a reduction in productivity and economic growth over this period, suggesting that causes in addition to those discussed here may have been at work.

2. For a recent overview of contemporary critical issues, see: OECD, *The Welfare State in Crisis*, Paris, 1981.

3. The effects of these policies will not be discussed in this paper, even though some of them are, technically, income transfers.

4. In the case of backward shifting, increased contributions can partially or wholly be compensated by a decrease in nominal wages.

5. Recent empirical research shows that the number of disability benefit recipients is clearly influenced by economic circumstances. See Halberstadt, Haveman, Wolfe, and Goudswaard (1981).

6. These institutional and more subtle attitudinal changes have been discussed by Lindbeck (1980, 1981) in a series of papers.

7. Lampman's approach, in which the simultaneous effect of income transfers and the taxes required to support them is evaluated, is consistent with the analytical framework urged by Lindbeck (1980, 1981) for evaluating the efficiency effects of income transfers.

8. See Danziger, Haveman and Plotnick (1981) for an extensive review of these studies.

9. However, a cross-national study by Cameron (1982) suggests that the very dramatic increases up to 20 percent of GNP in government spending in countries such as Sweden, Netherlands, and Denmark would have reduced economic growth by only one percent.

10. In the U.S. a number of pilot demonstrations on public employment which includes job placement assistance and work training have recently been conducted. See Bishop, Farkis, Keeley, Munson and Robins (1982) for a full description of the design.

References

Ando, A. and F. Modigliani. "The 'Life-Cycle' Hypothesis of Saving: Aggregate Implications and Tests," *American Economic Review*, March 1963, 53(1), pp. 55–84.

Bishop, J., G. Farcus, M. Keeley, C. E. Munson, and P. Robins. "A Research Design to Study the Labor Market Effects of the Employment Opportunity Pilot Projects," *Evaluation Studies Review Annual*, Volume 5, eds. E. W. Stromsdorfer and G. Farkas. Los Angeles: Sage Publications, 1980.

Cameron, D. R. "On the Limits of the Public Economy." *Annals of the American Academy of Political and Social Sciences*, 459, January 1982. pp. 46–62.

Danziger, S., R. Haveman, and R. Plotnick. "How Income Transfer Programs Affect Work, Savings and the Income Distribution." *Journal of Economic Literature*, September 1981, 19(3), pp. 1015–1028.

Feldstein, M. "Social Security, Induced Retirement and Aggregate Capital Accumulation." *Journal of Political Economy*, Sept./Oct. 1974, 82(5), pp. 905–26.

Garfinkel, I., ed. *Income-Tested Transfer Programs: The Case For and Against*. New York: Academic Press, 1982.

Halberstadt, V., R. H. Haveman, B. L. Wolfe, and K. P. Goudswaard. "The Economics of Disability Policy in Selected European Community Countries: A Preliminary Study and a Proposal for Further Research," Center for Research in Public Economics, Report 81.20, Leyden, The Netherlands, 1981.

Hamermesh, D. S. "Social Insurance and Consumption: An Empirical Inquiry," *American Economic Review*, March 1982, 72(1), pp. 101–113.

Hamermesh, D. S. "Entitlement Effects, Unemployment Insurance and Employment Decisions," *Economic Inquiry*, 17(3), July 1979, pp. 317–332.

Hanoch, G. and M. Honig. "The Labor Supply Curve Under Income Maintenance Programs." *Journal of Public Economics*, February 1978, 9(1), pp. 1–16.

Harrod, R. F. *Towards a Dynamic Economics*. London: Macmillan, 1948.

Haveman, R. "European and American Labor Market Policies in the Late 1970s: Lessons for the United States." Technical Report T-82-1, National Commission for Employment Policy, January 1982.

Haveman, R. "The Dutch Social Employment Program," in *Creating Jobs: Public Employment Programs and Wage Subsidies*, edited by J. Palmer. Washington, D.C.: Brookings Institution, 1978.

Haveman, R. and J. Palmer (eds.). *Jobs for Disadvantaged Workers: The Economics of Employment Subsidies*. Washington, D.C.: Brookings Institution, 1982.

Killingsworth, M. "Must a Negative Income Tax Reduce Labor Supply? A Study of the Family's Allocation of Time." *Journal of Human Resources*, Summer 1976, 11(3), pp. 354–365.

Lampman, R. "Labor Supply and Social Welfare Benefits in the United States," in National Commission on Employment and Unemployment Statistics, *Concepts and data needs: Counting the labor force. Appendix Volume I*. Washington, D.C.: U.S. Government Printing Office, 1978.

Lindbeck, A. "Disincentive Problems in Developed Countries." Institute for International Economic Studies Reprint No. 171. Stockholm, November 1981.

Linkbeck, A. "Work Disincentives in the Welfare State." Institute for International Economic Studies Seminar Paper No. 164. Stockholm, November 1980.

Modigliani, F. and R. Brumberg. "Utility Analysis and the Consumption Function: An Interpretation of Cross-Section Data," in *Post Keynesian Economics*. Edited by K. K. Kurihara. New Brunswick: Rutgers University Press, 1954, pp. 388–435.

Nagi, S. "Decision Criteria and the Question of Equity in the Distribution of Disability Benefits," in: H. Emanuel, ed., *The Determinants of Access to Disability*, Greenwich, Conn.: JAI Press, forthcoming.

Organization for Economic Co-operation and Development,
—*Demographic Trends 1950–1990*, Paris, 1979;
—*Economic Outlook*, various years, Paris;
—*The Welfare State in Crisis*, Paris, 1981.

Résumé

On évalue, dans cet article, le rôle des transferts croissants de revenus qui sont l'un des nombreux facteurs susceptibles d'avoir causé une entrave à l'activité économique des années 1970.

Dans les premières sections on étudie de façon "impressioniste" quelques effets micro et macroéconomiques des systèmes de transferts. Les transferts de revenus peuvent avoir un impact important sur le comportement des individus. Il se créé des effets de revenu et de substitution qui, en général, réduisent la propension à travailler. Il se peut aussi que l'épargne constituée pour faire face aux besoins de consommation pendant la retraite se réduise. De plus, les impôts perçus pour financer des programmes de transferts de revenus conduisent à des coûts accrus du travail non-salarié qui peuvent réduire la demande de travail et aussi, par le biais de marges bénéficiaires réduites, les investissements et la croissance économique. On montre à partir d'études empiriques que la propension à travailler et l'épargne sont réduits par le système des transferts mais à un faible degré seulement.

Dans la quatrième section de cet article, on présente des indicateurs de la croissance des transferts de revenus et des résultats économiques dans cinq "Etats providence" (la République Fédérale d'Allemagne, la Hollande, la Suède, le Royaume-Uni et les Etats-Unis). Ces indicateurs montrent une corrélation entre la croissance des dépenses de transfert et la diminution de l'offre de travail, de la productivité et de la croissance économique. Toutefois, il faut observer que d'autres facteurs peuvent contribuer à ralentir la croissance du P.N.B.; ils sont susceptibles d'être reliés au cours du temps avec la croissance des transferts de revenus. De mêmes, de mauvais résultats économiques conduisent sûrement à une augmentation de la demande pour des transferts publics. De plus, des programmes de transferts de revenus peuvent, par exemple, avoir été utilisés comme instrument d'une politique tendant à encourager des réductions de l'offre de travail chez les travailleurs âgés. Mais sans tenir compte de l'origine de la cause et des intentions politiques, il existe des moyens d'accroître l'efficacité des politiques de transferts de revenus. Dans la dernière section de cet article on propose quelques suggestions.

Le problème actuel qui découle des intéractions entre des résultats économiques médiocres et des transferts de revenus croissants conduit plus que jamais à considérer avec sérieux des politiques alternatives.

Regulation in a Democracy: Inefficiency or Efficiency?

Suphan Andic and Ramón J. Cao-García

Introduction

The economics of regulation has its normative and positive constructs. The normative theory considers regulation as one policy option among many, and attempts to establish which activities should be regulated and to what extent. Its fundamental assumption is that the government is an impartial ethical observer and a benevolent welfare maximizer. Since market failures of distinct types are inevitable in a capitalist economy, regulation is one of the means whereby such failures should be redressed to the extent determined by the welfare function of the society articulating the preferences of its individual members. The task of the normative theorist is then to identify which failures are best suited to be redressed by regulation, rather than some other form of public policy and government intervention. It is also to determine the quantity of regulation, given the value norms embedded in the social welfare function, by locating that point where the marginal benefit of an added unit of regulatory activity will just equal its marginal cost.

One difficulty with the normative theory of regulation is the important contradictions between its prescriptions as to what should be done to remedy a given undesirable situation, and what the regulatory agencies, set up to remedy the failure, actually do. A second difficulty is that it fails to explain why a specific type of regulation occurs at the time that it does. In other words, it tells us nothing about the decision as to when a regulatory activity should begin to be implemented. For instance, the teaching profession goes back to the beginning of civilization, yet the licencing of the profession is fairly new, although there is no ground for the argument that the externalities associated with teaching are today greater than what they have been in the past.[1] This is an extremely relevant point to which the normative theory has not addressed itself.

Public Finance and the Quest for Efficiency. Proceedings of the 38th Congress of the International Institute of Public Finance. Copenhagen, 1982, pp. 209–222. Copyright © 1984 by Wayne State University Press, Detroit, Michigan, 48202.

The positive theory of regulation is a logical outcome of the contradictions between the normative prescriptions and actual regulatory behavior. The positive theory is, in principle, independent of "what ought to be" and deals with "what is". It should provide a system of generalizations that would lead to correct predictions about the consequences of any change in circumstances, about the phenomena it intends to explain, so that it can be 'accepted' as valid or 'rejected'. The predictions, by which the validity of the conclusions of the traditional positive theory of regulation has been asserted, have been far from flattering for the theory and have not had profound effects on its normative counterpart of the desirable regulation. This stems essentially from the fact that the 'what is' has been treated in a far too limited scope, and the analyses and ensuing policy recommendations have largely been made in an environment devoid of political and bureaucratic processes, without taking into consideration how political and bureaucratic behavior may violate and alter the normal welfare criteria.

The present paper looks at regulation within a political process, and is, therefore, essentially one within the general framework of the economic analysis of political processes and bureaucracy. It builds on the contributions of those who have already taken steps in the same direction.

It begins with a brief survey and critique of the current theory. It then develops an analysis which forms the core of a positive theory of regulation, with no normative implications. The aim is to harmonize the existing views on the effects of regulation and be able to predict its quantity and direction. The theory is woven around the point that in a democracy citizens, politicians, and bureaucrats all demand regulation in their self-interest. The citizens in the winning coalition demand regulation because it helps maintain the status quo with respect to income redistribution, and hence reduces their uncertainty. The politician demands regulation because it simplifies his task as a coalition manager and provides him with monopoly power over his coalition. The bureaucrats are 'high demanders' of regulation because it generates fiscal illusion which facilitates budget expansions. The interactions among the three forces create the feedback effect of regulation breeding further regulation. The paper then reaches the conclusion that under the circumstances the efficiency or inefficiency of regulation cannot be judged by its standard measurement as the difference between actual output and the value it would have had in the absence of regulation.

THE CURRENT THEORY

The current fragmented positive theory of the economics of regulation focuses principally on four sets of variables: the political process within which it functions; the bureaucratic machinery which implements it; the Congressional system that legislates it; and the fiscal illusion it gives rise to. Naturally the interdependence among the four is not denied.

The Political Process

There have been numerous attempts to predict the outcome of regulatory policies within a political process. Stigler (1971, 1974), Posner (1971, 1974), Peltzman (1976), Mendeloff (1974), Mackay and Reid (1979), Downing and Brady (1979), Aranson and Ordershook (1981) have basically considered regulation as a device to transfer income to well-organized groups in exchange for political votes. Dissatisfied with the consumer protection model of regulation, where the mere existence of market failure is sufficient to generate demand for regulation and according to which regulation, as a free good, is costlessly supplied by the political process, Stigler took the improvement of the economic status of economic groups as constituting the basis for demand and located its supply in the theory of the optimum size of effective political coalitions. Constituents demanded regulation; political representatives supplied it, and the 'market' distributed it among the demanders. Since the market distributes more of a good to those whose effective demand is high, and since political effective demand is high where groups are large, the explanation of small producer groups benefiting from regulation was found in the inverse relationship of size to costs. Costs consisted of information costs—finding out the costs and benefits of a political decision; of organization costs—translation of interests into effective action (campaigning, lobbying); and 'political heed' costs—quieting down the opposition to the transfer.

The extension of the analysis, however, led to the general proposition that the rational politician will be concerned with the appropriate structure of benefits and costs to be able to exploit the differences within the winning and losing group as a whole. As a result, regulation will not necessarily be identifiable with a single economic interest (Peltzman, 1976), and political equilibrium will not necessarily result in either pure producer protection or pure consumer protection. Rather, since his objective is to maximise his own welfare function, the politician will be inclined to compromise. He will not ignore the opportunities to increase producer wealth, but will not fully exploit them either for fear of narrowing the consumer base of the coalition. He will not give the entire benefit to the producers, but let them share it with the consumers.

Obviously then the current consideration of regulation within the political process does not allow the *a priori* prediction of the redistributive implications of regulation.

The Bureaucratic Machinery

Attempts to explain the behavior of regulatory agencies as part of the rational behavior of bureaucrats have also predicted outcomes favorable to organized interests. The reasons are many but not fully explained. One is the excessive cost of the regulatory process and the imperfection in information costs it creates. A second uses a life cycle theory according to which the individuals become more conservative as they grow older and swing their interest towards those of organized groups. A third is a training cycle explanation: once their term of appointment is over, regulators get to be employed by regulated industries and, given their prior knowledge of the functioning of the bureau, serve the interests of the group. A final reason takes the form of the prisoner's dilemma (Noll, 1971).[2]

The difficulty with all these approaches is that they fail to explain the pro or anti regulation attitude of the bureaucrat, which is precisely what is needed if it is going to form part of the positive theory of the economics of regulation and explain the types, timing, the magnitude, and predict the consequences. Why do two separate regulatory bureaus pursue totally different objectives? Why does a regulator's behavior change at a given moment of time?

The experiences of the Civil Aeronautics Board (CAB) and of the Interstate Commerce Commission (ICC) illustrate two opposite approaches to regulation in the same political system at the same particular time, and beg the answer to the question why the attitude towards regulation changes within one and the same political system. CAB's price fixing behavior up until 1968 appears to lend support to the political support maximization theory of cross subsidizing and averaging fares (Peltzman, 1976, pp. 238–9). In 1968, CAB changed its policy and adopted the system of setting fares according to costs. Since costs decline sharply over long distances, prices were not permitted to rise as fast over long distances as over short distances. Economic efficiency criteria were thus introduced into rate setting and the consumer coalition was favored.

On the other hand, because of the broad concept of equity—among the carriers and shippers, rural and urban interests, small and large shippers—which has permeated all the acts relating to the transportation industry since the ICC Act of 1887, the ICC, by setting joint rates, has served to protect the smaller, weaker, and less efficient parts of the railroad industry, has charged high fares on short haul and spread the profit effects to long haul. It pursued a policy of welding a consumer and producer coalition with the balance being tilted to the latter. And, as recently as 1978, a broad ranging railroad deregulation bill was stymied in the US Congress.[3]

The Congressional System

Although still in their infancy, the theories that explain regulatory behavior through congressional behavior stress first, that a Congressman's objective is to be re-elected; second, that it is through his own individual preference for a specific assignment, in this case regulation, that he opts to become a member in the regulatory committee; and third, it is through his activities in this committee that he perceives his opportunity for re-election (Shepsle, 1978). Obviously, the theory does not explain how re-election depends upon the Congressman's activity in the committee, nor why the committee (or the Congress) takes the regulatory decisions that it does.

Fiscal Illusion

Finally, the 'fiscal illusion' explanation of regulation rests on the manipulation of the perceived costs and benefits of the regulatory measures. Essentially, the costs will be 'understated' and the benefits overstated. Explicit taxes and expenditures are replaced by regulation; they are not explicitly reflected in the public budget or in private books or pocketbooks. Costs, in general, go unrecognized (with the exception of some groups who are adversely affected). Since cost structures differ among producers and income types and levels among consumers, and since taxes are not uniform, there is no one-to-one correspondence in the replacement of taxes by regulation. Hence, the economic effects of regulation differ from those of a tax which it presumably represents; in other words, the substitution effects differ. Moreover, the increase in the perceived ratio of benefits to costs creates a tendency to overregulate and causes public production to expand to levels beyond the 'optimal'.

The fiscal illusion aspect of regulatory behavior becomes all the more significant in a period of inflationary developments when the tax bite is felt directly, while the regulatory bite is not. This is precisely what happened in the U.S. in the seventies. Cost considerations, which were pushed into the background in the name of the virtue of all the programs legislated in the sixties, became imminent in the seventies, and hence regulation, and a very complicated one at that, became the increasing order of the decade.[4] It pervaded the entire economic, social and community structure. It divided the population into numerous groups, each distinguished by some discernible characteristic (ethnic, sex, color, national origin, etc.) and made them more easily recognizable. It forced the formation of interest groups, formally as well as in the perception of the individuals themselves. It gave rise to further entitlements and rights. It, in fact, redistributed, but not in the traditional producer-consumer distinction of the classical regulation theory, rather in a new way that distinguished between producer-producer (black vs. white; minority vs. majority); producer-consumer (Naderism); producer-employee (sex and racial quotas); and consumer-consumer (smokers vs. non-smokers).

This brief overview shows that, in its present state, the positive analysis of regulation lacks integration: it needs to integrate into a coherent whole all the forces that operate within itself and give shape to the present state of regulation. But it also needs to be integrated with the rest of the economic theory of the public sector as it deals with externalities, public goods problems, and market failures. The more so, since there is a growing literature on collective failures—non-market failures—which promote countervailing action within the private sector and spread the collective failure beyond the confines of government organizations (Wolf, 1979; Peacock, 1980).

The development of such an integrated positive theory is beyond the scope of this paper. The purpose here is much more limited: it is to identify some of the key elements such a positive theory should incorporate in a democratic society. This requires the examination of some of the characteristics of a democratic regime, in order to pinpoint those that are relevant in the formulation of a positive theory of economic regulation.

Uncertainty, Regulation, and Political Systems

It has been argued that a necessary pre-condition for the emergence of a democratic constitution is the existence of uncertainty in society about the socio-economic position any particular member will hold in the future (Buchanan & Tullock, 1962; Cao-García, 1983). Uncertainty tends to arise when there is mobility among groups in society, which makes it impossible to predict to which group the individual will belong at any given moment in the future. There must not be any dominant group which can impose its hegemony over the long run; and there must be no permanent coalition in society based on externally distinguishable permanent characteristics, such as race, religion, ethnic differentiation etc.

The existence of uncertainty in the planning horizon of the individual leads to constitutional rules that are unbiased, in the sense that the long run benefits expected from them are distributed evenly among all citizens. This does not imply, however, that in the short run the members of the dominant coalition have no interest in maximizing the present value of the gains to be derived from their position of dominance. The members of the ruling coalition have an interest in reducing the level of uncertainty within their planning horizon, which is equivalent to saying that they are interested in maintaining the status quo and the prevailing distribution, or redistribution, of social benefits. Regulation thus provides an instrument to attain this goal within the constraints of a democratic constitution.

It is interesting to note that the non-discriminatory feature of democratic decision-making rules will tend to force the winning coalition to use indirect methods to increase the welfare of its members, rather than directly transferring income from the members of the losing coalition. Since the amount of the benefits to be derived is directly associated with some set of variables which differs among the various members of the coalition, those who receive less than a proportional share will push for other special policies, and the tendency will be generated towards their proliferation in democratic regimes.

Moreover, such indirect policies cause behavior modifications. If the perceived cost of regulation is lower than that of a tax which could achieve the same effect, the relative price of the benefit will be reduced. The change in the relative price will have the consequence of modifying the solution vector for the market. This is not costless and hence reduces gross benefits. For the winning coalition it presents a waste of resources, and it promotes the creation of more indirect government policies to compensate for the cost, and thereby reinforces the tendency towards the proliferation of governmental policies in democracies. The argument that non-market failures induce further market failures (Peacock, 1980) can be looked upon as a natural outcome of the private sector's reactions to indirect policies that are necessarily adopted in democracies to bestow benefits upon its winning coalition.

And regulation is one such policy. As a result, all the interpretations of regulation—as an instrument of income redistribution, of expanding the public sector activities, and for maintaining the status quo (Moore, 1981)— can now all be integrally harmonized within this democratic setting, since all are part of, or specific objectives within, the overall goal of the dominant coalition to maximize the present value of its benefits. Such a view also permits the formulation of a hypothesis on the expected timing of regulating a new activity or of modifying existing regulations. This, unfortunately, is a highly neglected area in the theory of regulation. We hypothesize that a new regulation will be enacted, or the behavior of a regulatory agency will be modified,[5] whenever the composition of the dominant coalition changes.

The Politician's Demand for Regulation

Any attempt to construct a general theory of regulation based upon the behavior of the ruling coalition must account for the coalition formation process. The existence of transaction and information costs prevents a winning coalition from being organized spontaneously; a political entrepreneur is required who will organize and manage a coalition of an optimal size so that his election will be assured.[6] Once elected, he will obtain rents from being in office and will have to redistribute income to benefit his supporters, while simultaneously holding together a winning coalition.

To do this, he must be able to identify properly the members of his supporting coalition and their wants. This creates a typical public goods provision with free riders. For, if the citizens were organized in clubs or lobbying groups in line with their vested interests, there would be no need for proper identification, and a coalition of 'political groups' would be formed instead of a coalition of individual voters. However, to be a member of a political group is not costless, and non-members cannot be excluded from the political benefits the organization may obtain from the government. Because of the political—or public good—aspect of the lobby group, there will not be adequate incentive for its organization (Olson, 1971).

Hence, to encourage the members of his supporting coalition into organizing is in the interest of a politician in office. For, thereby, the proper identification of his coalition members will be made easier; he himself will be better informed of his supporters' wants; and, as a result, he will become a more efficient coalition manager.

Because of its peculiar characteristics, regulation becomes especially attractive to the politician in his task as coalition manager in a democracy. In fact, according to some students of the subject, regulation itself creates interest groups. Many organizations that benefit from the regulations have in fact been created after the regulatory legislation (Moore, 1981, p. 102).

Others have asserted that regulation itself creates groups that, once organized, may influence regulation. Certification of an occupation, for example, may lower the costs of organization for members of that occupation who consequently may succeed in obtaining licencing (Zerbe & Urban, 1980, p. 19). If so, the politician's task in political group formation is vastly facilitated and, through regulation, he is able to spread part of the organization and information costs on to the society as a whole.

Regulation has yet another characteristic which is of vital interest for the politician: it makes it costlier for the coalition members to replace him as their manager. In their eyes the drafting of a regulation act vests the politician with the expertise on the regulated activity. It is irrelevant whether the expertise is real or merely imaginary. It suffices for the interested citizens to perceive it as relevant. Then, the particular politician stands out over his competitors. He becomes more difficult to replace in the eyes of the concerned voters; the stability of the coalition is increased and, as a result, the probability of an electoral defeat is lowered. This raises the monopoly power of the politician over his clients (i.e. his supporting coalition) and enables him to increase the rents from holding the office.

In summary, a politican will find in regulation properties which make it more attractive compared to other forms and types of income redistribution through the political process. For one, the managerial function of the politician is made easier, since the incentives for group formation are increased. Secondly, it enhances the polician's monopoly power, while at the same time it reduces the probability of electoral defeat. It can, therefore, be hypothesized, that first the quantity of regulation will increase with the complexity of the political process—with the concomitant increase in the politician's demand for information. Second, the more unstable the coalitions, the higher the quantity of regulation. The observed tendency for regulation to increase in times of economic instability can then be explained by the generation during economic crises of social and political non-conformity and hence unstable coalitions. Similarly, the spread of regulation into all aspects of social life during the sixties and its perception as being "costless" may also be explained by the social and political non-conformity rampant during the period.

Bureaucratic Interests

Once enacted, regulatory rules will have to be implemented. And it is the bureaucrat that will implement, administer, and enforce them. A theory of regulation will, therefore, have to incorporate into its reasonings the expected behavior of the bureaucracy as it affects regulatory activities.

Economic theory has come to accept the monopoly bureau construct in the provision of public goods and services, with differences from its counterpart in the private sector. It is generally recognized that a bureau behaves quite differently from manufacturing firms in the market, partly because the bureau's output is technically different, making it very difficult to monitor productive efficiency and even to determine whether or not the output corresponds to the wants, and partly, because the set of institutions within which the private and public producers function differ significantly.[7]

Briefly, the monopoly bureau construct leads to the conclusion that in a democracy the bureaucrat will maximize his budget in the interest of maximizing his own utility function, which includes, in addition to pecuniary income, the benefits he derives from the bureau's activities, private (social prestige, leisure time, upward mobility etc.) as well as public (provision of public goods which the bureaucrat values). Since regulation is one instrument that enables the expansion of bureaucratic activities, the bureaucrat can be expected to use it in attaining his maximization objective.

Regulation has a characteristic which is of particular interest for the bureaucracy: it redistributes income through fiscal illusory devices, so that the transfers are not explicitly registered in the public accounting budget (Posner, 1971; Jordan, 1972; Aranson and Ordershook, 1981), and the perceived costs of government services are reduced. The result is a relative ease in expanding the budget. The bureaucrat would, therefore, become a high demander of the types of regulation its bureau enforces.

It is to be noted, however, that the use of regulatory devices within the monopoly construct enables us to theorize on the forces that lead to extending the coverage and enforcement levels of existing regulatory activities, but not to derive hypotheses as to the emergence of regulation, simply because high bureaucratic demanders do not come into existence until after a regulatory agency is born.

Feedback Effects

All the arguments so far tend to indicate that there results a strong feedback effect from the forces that help hypothesize the emergence and/or the expansion of regulated activities: regulation breeds more regulation.

First of all, the enactment of a regulatory legislation induces individual voters to organize in groups. Members of the regulated trade or activity find themselves in a situation whereby benefits from being organized are increased, while frequently the law itself includes provisions that reduce the costs of getting organized. As a result, net benefits increase, and the base for Stigler's (1974) negative correlation between size and organization costs is eroded. The benefits of regulation are not limited any more to a small group with effective power of their own to demand regulatory benefits; but high demand now comes to be equated to high number of demanders. Once individuals become members of a regulated group, they also discover that they now possess an effective ability to voice expanded political wants. And since they are 'high demanders' of regulation, they will turn into a force which seeks the expansion of the scope and levels of enforcement of the regulatory legislation which is relevant to their particular interests.

Secondly, as argued above, the new regulation itself creates a new breed of 'high demanders', and these are the employees of the bureau which is in charge of administering and enforcing the rules. They too tend to become a political force that is not uninterested in having regulatory activities expanded, since thereby they will attain higher utility levels.

Thirdly, the passage of new regulatory law could very well ignite a new force which would be a potential for an expanded demand for regulation. This force would be those trades and activities who, though unregulated, could be motivated to seek regulation actively upon observing the regulation of some other economic sector. A new regulation that would redistribute benefits away from the already regulated groups will increase the benefits of those seeking regulation and hence increase the demand for regulation. No doubt, their success in having benefits redistributed will depend, among others, on their potential electoral strength, as well as on the availability of a politician who is recruiting members to create a winning coalition.

Is Regulation Inefficient?

What is the relevance of all the above in the judgment of efficiency (or inefficiency) of regulation in a democracy?

To be able to pass such a judgment, the litany of the literature on estimating the efficiency losses created by regulatory rules has largely emphasized the comparison of the value of the output as it is with what it would have been in the absence of regulation and yielded an extremely long list on efficiency losses.

Although such comparisons are necessary, they are insufficient. First of all, as Wolf so aptly puts it: "(Public) policy formulation properly requires that the realized inadequacies of market outcomes be compared with the potential inadequacies of non-market efforts to ameliorate them" (Wolf, 1979, p. 107). Market failure provides the rationale for public policy remedies, yet the remedies themselves may fail for reasons similar to those of market failure.

These reasons lie fundamentally in the supply and demand characteristics of the public sector, as opposed to those of the private market. The output of the public sector is difficult to define in principle and in practice; often it is impossible to measure and, for convenience sake, it is expressed as the cost of the inputs used in its production, which tells nothing about its efficiency; it is produced by legislatively mandated agencies with no competitors; it commands no unit price, a total output is produced at a total cost with no accounting profit and loss. The measurement of the allocative impact of regulation on the economy must, therefore, also consider the difference between the loss of welfare generated by market failure and that caused by non-market failures.

Secondly, non-market inadequacies promote countervailing action within the private sector and spread the inadequacy beyond the confines of the public agencies. This can be seen in regulated firms' inflation of their cost estimates which they submit to the regulatory agencies, in order to be able to negotiate a higher rate. Once the rate is ratified, it then becomes quite logical for the firms to arrange their actual costs to be as close as possible to the submitted estimates.[8]

A third point to consider is whether the redistribution of the benefits generated by regulation is actually Pareto inefficient. To answer the question in the affirmative requires that we know precisely what the allocative configuration was prior to regulation. If profit maximization by a cartel is taken to be optimal, and if regulation in a political process leads to lower profits (hence misallocation of resources), this is considered to be a violation of optimality (Peltzman, 1976). But this is much too narrow a view of optimality because it refers to a specific industry, and because it assumes profit maximization as the only condition to determine optimality, when economic literature is replete with theories of the firm that try to explain why in real life firms do not necessarily practice profit maximization, for reasons other than regulatory constraints. Hence, a judgment of the efficiency or inefficiency of regulation begs the determination of the sub-optimality. But this can only be done if we have a standard of optimality against which the deviations from it can be gauged. Economic theory has as yet to come up with such a standard to replace the almost obsolete Pareto norms.

Fourthly, the core of a positive theory of regulation we have presented leads to the conclusion that regulation is but another instrument through which the scope of public sector activities expands. The ensuing increase in the share of the public sector, in the total output of the economy implies an efficiency loss, which results from the differential change in productivity in the public and the private sectors of the economy, as evidenced historically (Andic and Veverka, 1964) and as powerfully argued theoretically (Baumol, 1967, and Baumol & Oates, 1975). Since productivity growth in the public sector is slower than in the private sector, the costs of producing a unit of output in the public sector increase relative to the costs of producing a unit of output in the private one.

Finally, whether regulation is efficient or not will depend upon how wide a lens we use as we assess its costs and benefits and its redistributive impacts. A narrow lens shows up inefficiencies, as indicated by the empirical estimates referred to above, because it is adjusted to the view that distribution through regulation yields no benefit to those that bear its cost. But, if interdependence is admitted between the utilities of the so-called 'winners' and 'losers' in the regulatory process, then it is quite conceivable the regulation might cause everyone's welfare level to rise. This requires empirical investigation of utility interdependence in a regulatory process, and remains beyond the scope of this paper.

Notes

1. After all, Socrates was sentenced to death because the Government of Athens was of the conviction that he was generating negative externalities.

2. Accordingly, a single legislator is one among many in the welfare of all voters, but a monopolist among all of his constituents. Hence he would reward the helpful bureaucrat by not opposing his policy. The voter, even though he may not favor regulation, would nevertheless vote for the proponent of regulation, since the opponent, as a single voice, is unlikely to change the policy and the proponent would do well for the district. As a result, the voter would get at least some return rather than none.

3. It is interesting to add that a new bill will be effective as of July 1, 1982, which will tilt the welding of the coalition somewhat towards the consumer.

4. The social regulatory agencies grew from 12 in 1970 to 18 in 1980 and their budget from $1.4 bill to $7.5 bill. The Code of Federal Regulations expanded from 54,482 pages to nearly 100,000 over the same time span (White, 1982).

5. The modification of the distribution of the benefits does not require that new regulation be enacted; it can just as well be attained by mere modification of the behavior of the regulatory bureaus. The cases of CAB and ICC are cited in the text. A change is also taking place in electric utility regulation which in the sixties benefited the companies, but since the early seventies, is tilted towards the consumers.

6. For a discussion of the optimal coalition size under different levels of uncertainty see Cao-García (1983), Ch. 4.

7. For an analysis that focuses on the behavioral implications of the differences in these institutional constraints see Niskanen (1971, Chs. 9–12).

8. One of the authors has personally observed a tendency towards such a practice in shipping.

References

Andic, S. and Veverka, J. (1964), "The Development of Public Expenditures in Germany: 1871–1958", *Finanzarchiv*, 23, pp. 169–278.

Aranson, P.H. and Ordeshook, P.C. (1981) "Regulation, Redistribution, and Public Choice", *Public Choice*, 37, pp. 69–100.

Baumol, W. (1967), "Macroeconomics of Unbalanced Growth: The Anatomy of the Urban Crisis", *American Economic Review*, 57, pp. 415–426.

Baumol, W. and Oates, W.E. (1975), *The Theory of Environmental Policy*, Englewood Cliffs, N.J.: Prentice Hall.

Buchanan, J.M. and Tullock, G. (1962) *The Calculus of Consent*. Ann Arbor: The University of Michigan Press.

Cao-García, R.J. (1983) *Explorations Toward an Economic Theory of Political Systems*. Lanham, Maryland: University Press of America.

Downing, P.B. and Brady, G.L. (1979), "Constrained Self-Interest and the Formation of Public Policy", *Public Choice*, 34, pp. 15–28.

Jordan, W.A. (1972), "Producer Protection, Prior Market Structure, and the Effects of Government Regulation", *Journal of Law and Economics*, 15, pp. 151–176.

Mackay, R.J. and Reid, J.D., Jr. (1979) "On Understanding the Birth and Evolution of the Securities and Exchange Commission: Where Are We in the Theory of Regulation", in G.M. Walton, ed., *Regulatory Change in an Atmosphere of Crisis: Current Implications of the Roosevelt Years*. New York: Academic Press.

Mendeloff, J. (1979) *Regulation Safety: An Economic and Political Analysis of Occupational Safety and Health Policy*. Cambridge: MIT Press.

Moore, T.G. (1981) "Comments on Aranson and Ordeshook's Regulation, Redistribution, and Public Choice", *Public Choice*, 37, pp. 101–105.

Niskanen, W.A., Jr. (1971) *Bureaucracy and Representative Government*. Chicago: Aldine-Atherton.

Noll, R.G. (1971) *Reforming Regulation: An Evaluation of the Ash Council Proposals*. Washington D.C.: Brookings.

Olson, M. (1971) *The Logic of Collective Action: Public Goods and the Theory of Groups*. New York: Schocken.

Peacock, A.T. (1980) "On the Anatomy of Collective Failure". *Public Finance*, 34, pp. 33–43.

Peltzman, S. (1976) "Toward a More General Theory of Regulation". *Journal of Law and Economics*, 19, pp. 211–248.

Posner, R.A. (1971) "Taxation by Regulation", *Bell Journal of Economics and Management Sciences*, 2, pp. 22–50.

Posner, R.A. (1974) "Theories of Economic Regulation", *Bell Journal of Economics and Management Sciences*, 5, pp. 335–358.

Shepsle, K.A. (1978) *The Giant Jigsaw Puzzle: Democratic Committee Assignments in the U.S. House of Representatives*. Chicago.

Stigler, G.J. (1971) "The Theory of Economic Regulation", *Bell Journal of Economics and Management Sciences*, 2, pp. 3–21.

Stigler, G.J. (1974) "Free Riders and Collective Action: An Appendix to Theories of Economic Regulation", *Bell Journal of Economics and Management Sciences*, 5, pp. 359–365.

White, T.H. (1982) *America in Search of Itself: The Making of the President, 1956–1980*, New York: Harper and Row.

Wolf, C. Jr. (1979) "A Theory of Non-Market Failure: Framework for Implementation Analysis", *Journal of Law and Economics*, 22, pp. 107–139.

Zerbe, R. and Urban, N. (1980) *Towards a Public Interest Theory of Regulation*, Cambridge: NBER Conference Paper 70.

Résumé

La théorie positive de la réglementation n'a pas fourni de réponses satisfaisantes quant aux raisons pour lesquelles la quantité, le modèle et la direction de la réglementation changent, principalement parce qu'elle n'a pas suffisamment prêté attention à la façon dont le comportement politique et bureaucratique peut violer et altérer les critères sociaux normaux.

Cet article rend compte d'un tel comportement dans un régime démocratique. Cette théorie est centrée sur le fait que dans une démocratie tous les citoyens, politiciens et bureaucrates demandent une réglementation conforme à leur propre intérêt. Ces demandes qui réagissent les unes sur les autres expliquent que la réglementation s'auto-alimente. Dans ces conditions il devient impossible de juger de l'efficacité ou de l'inefficacité d'une réglementation selon le critère habituel, c'est-à-dire la différence entre la production effective et la valeur qu'elle aurait eue en l'absence de réglementation.

Motivations and Constraints in the Supply-Cost of Government Services: A Game Theoretic Analysis

Harvey Leibenstein

I. Introduction

The above is a fancy title for a set of concerns about which we know rather little. In fact, had I been completely aware of the requirements and complexities of the subject,[1] I probably would not have accepted the invitation to write this paper.

While in general we can usually presume that economic motivations and constraints are fairly well known, this is not the case with respect to governments. In this section we will argue that because motivations and constraints can be highly variable, and because governments are monopolies that have unique characteristics, it becomes extremely difficult to simplify the problem sufficiently to build a model that yields determinate and reasonable results.

Let us speculate for a moment on what an ideal paper might look like. Such a paper would spell out the significant considerations. Somehow it would combine these considerations in such a way that a functional relation could be established between certain visible and measurable characteristics of government and the supply cost of government services. Ideally the relation would give unique results in the sense that there would be a one-to-one correspondence between every subset of characteristics and the cost of the services provided. Finally, it would be nice if there were enough factual data around so that the basic relationship could be tested. But alas we are at present very far from being able to do anything of the sort. At best some of the ideas suggested may be useful in indicating further directions of research.

The nature of the difficulties may be readily perceived if we compare the analysis of supply by governments and the counterpart analysis for a representative firm in a competitive setting. Four motivational forces can be

Public Finance and the Quest for Efficiency. Proceedings of the 38th Congress of the International Institute of Public Finance. Copenhagen, 1982, pp. 223–240. Copyright © 1984 by Wayne State University Press, Detroit, Michigan, 48202.

discerned: (a) profit maximization, (b) competition, (c) survival, and (d) demand. We consider each briefly and inquire whether such a motivational force, or some substitute, exists in the case of government.

Profit maximization is usually deemed to be sufficient to determine cost minimization if the owners control all of the variables that determine costs. However, governments as such are not run by profit maximizing owner-management groups. The citizens are not in the same relation to government as stockholders in a closely held corporation. We need not belabor this point.

Even if some private enterprises were not controlled by profit maximizing managers, the force of competition would operate in the same direction. Competition would place the non-cost minimizing firms at a disadvantage. Here too the analogy with government fails. Governments are not subject to competition, and they do not lose revenue, or anything else that they might desire, as a consequence of not being able to supply services at a sufficiently low cost.

A motivational force related to competition is survival. If a firm does not meet competitive standards long enough, it persumably will not survive. The fear of not surviving may be sufficient to eliminate high level costs. However, governments need have no such fear. There may be no connection between the knowledge of costs and voters' reactions to governments so that survival as such may not be a major issue. But some cost considerations may enter indirectly via the budgeting process. We will take that into account later.

Obviously every firm is concerned with demand, and with survival through meeting market demand. However, since most forms of taxation do not depend on voluntary behavior, demand as such does not enter directly as a factor where governments are concerned. Even the *nature* of the product is not assured under government supply. The motivations and constraints on governments are not such as to lead to either minimum costs, or to any clear-cut level of costs so that on the basis of the neoclassical paradigm we can make simple supply assertions. In other words, the cost level can be highly variable; and it can differ considerably from the minimum necessary.

What criteria should we use in order to assess the value of government services? In some sense or other we would have to try to determine some ideal cost as determined in the market or by comparison with the most efficient governments available as against the actual. But the value of government services will depend in part on the nature of the interests being served by the bureaucracy. If the interest or purpose being served decreases welfare, then we may argue that there will be an inverse relation between the effectiveness with which the service is carried out and its value. More services of an undesirable nature are obviously less valuable than less services of this type. In the second part of this paper we will consider some of the problems raised by considerations of this sort.

The paper is divided into two major parts. In the first we sketch the theory of effort determination and examine the relation between the degree of effort and the cost of supplying government services. In the second part we will be concerned with a variant of the agent-principal problem and try to show how services for various interests are connected with their value. In both cases a theory of games approach will be used, although the main aim is to show how such an approach helps us to delineate the nature of the problem rather than to produce clear-cut and determinate results or theorems and proofs.

The spirit in which game theory is to be used is well expressed in a recent book by another writer. A quotation indicates what I have in mind. "The concepts and general approach of game theory serve as a helpful tool, suggest useful techniques, and help channel sources of insight; it is taken here as a diving board, but by no means as a binding framework" (Ullman-Margalit (1977)). This is similar in spirit to the way game theory was used by Thomas Schelling (1960) in his seminal work on bargaining. It is especially important to note these points in connection with an aspect to be considered later, namely, the relaxation of the maximization postulate as a universal motivating force behind behavior.

II. A Game Theory Approach to Effort Determination

The basic idea to be sketched in this section is that the supply of government services depends on the supply of effort by members of the bureaucracy, and that effort supply is a game-theoretic problem. Effort is viewed as a discretionary variable. Interactions within groups influences the supply of effort. While in essence it is a game theory problem, in particular, it is usually a *latent* prisoner's dilemma (PD) problem. Furthermore, we will argue that the latent PD problem is solved by effort conventions, and finally that such solutions are usually non-optimal.[2]

Much of the material in this section has already been presented elsewhere, especially in connection with the determination of effort in private enterprise firms. (See Leibenstein (1980), and (1982b)). In the interest of having this paper be somewhat self-contained, the basic ideas are repeated in very brief form. In addition, this may be looked upon as an exercise in translation. That is to say, can we substitute civil servants for employees, and bureau directors for private enterprise managers and still get similar but certainly not identical results to those obtained in the private firm?[3] This will then serve as a basis for raising some significant questions. Are the results the same, weaker, more ambiguous, or stronger than in the somewhat competitive private enterprise case?

Our basic assumptions are: (1) individuals make non-maximizing decisions based on habit or conventions when pressure is low, but that they move towards fully calculating behavior (i.e., approximate maximization of utility) when pressure increases up to some point. Beyond some point if pressure is too great decision making may once again become suboptimal.[4] An additional element is the concept of inert areas which states that within the inert area bounds individuals will not shift from one effort position to another despite changes in relevant independent variables. (2) The organization membership contract is viewed as incomplete. Usually salary is specified but not all aspects of effort are specified.

One of the important insights that we obtain from game theory is that it involves a different decision problem than is used in standard economics. In standard microtheory agents are assumed to control all the variables. Hence, choice and maximization are straightforward individual decision problems. In game theory the outcome depends on the strategic choices of all agents. We will argue that effort determination within organizations such as a bureaucracy is a game theory problem. Effort is not determined by the contract, nor by the employees alone, or the bureau managers alone. By effort we have in mind each member's choice of his *activities* (A), the *pace* (P) level and the *quality* (Q) with which the activities are carried out. While effort is a discretionary variable, the civil servants do not arbitrarily decide their effort level completely because they care about other people's reactions to their effort. On the other hand, rules surrounding effort, such as rules about hours of work, will not completely control the effort level. Thus, in part employees will make strategic decisions which will help to determine the effort level outcome.[5]

The bureau managers also do not control the effort levels of the employees. The bureau manager cannot foresee everything and hence must leave some room for discretion. Furthermore, the civil servant may have some special knowledge which the bureau manager may not possess. In addition, the bureau manager, who is himself a civil servant, also uses his effort with discretion.

What does each side provide? The employees provide different levels of effort. The bureau management, which is part of the overall bureaucracy, provides salary schedules, career schedules, retirement provisions, and conditions of work which determine (in part, and only in part) the internal motivational system of the bureaucracy. Obviously, there are alternative bundles of salaries, promotion schemes, etc. Furthermore, each bundle will bear a different cost per employee ranging from M_1 to M_n. For the purpose of this paper we will assume that a higher cost bundle is worth more to employees than a lower cost one. For simplicity consider the ex-

Table 1
Bureau Managers

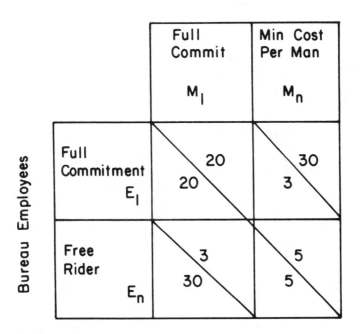

		Full Commit M_I	Min Cost Per Man M_n
Bureau Employees	Full Commitment E_I	20 / 20	30 / 3
	Free Rider E_n	3 / 30	5 / 5

treme 2×2 case (Table 1). By "full commitment" we mean that the employees choose the effort level E_1, i.e. to work in as devoted a manner as possible in the interest of the bureaucracy. By "full free rider" we have in mind a relatively low effort level E_n under which the individual pursues his personal interest to the maximum extent possible. We show in the 2×2 payoff table the presumed utilities to representative members of the employees and the bureaucratic managers. As the utilities are chosen the payoff table represents a prisoner's dilemma (PD) problem. If we look at the southeast, northwest diagonal (and if we had intermediate payoffs between the extremes), the payoffs would increase as we go towards full commitment on both sides. Since effort and output increase as we move towards full commitment, this should be associated with higher utility to the manager. Let us assume that the working condition bundles are chosen in such a way so that the value of the effort for every symmetric pair is worth more than the increase in the cost of the bundle. We also assume that the employees prefer to use effort more for their own purposes than that of the bureaucracy. At the same time, the bureau managers would prefer, for each effort level provided by the employees, that the costs be as low as possible. This would mean that they could increase their *power* by employing more people

Figure 1

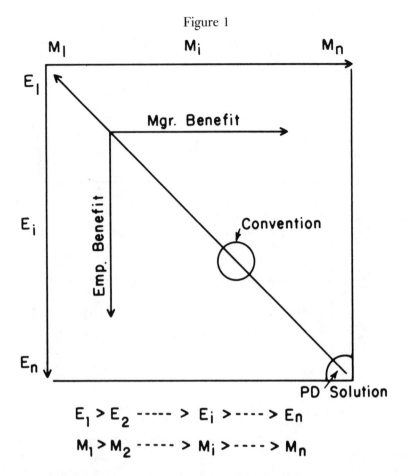

$$E_1 > E_2 \text{ ----- } > E_i > \text{ ---- } > E_n$$

$$M_1 > M_2 \text{ ----- } > M_i > \text{ ---- } > M_n$$

on a given budget. If these assumptions are correct, then the outcome would be a prisoner's dilemma situation. For each choice made by the bureaucratic management, the employees would prefer the "free rider" choice. For each effort choice offered by employees, the bureau managers prefer the maximum effort per dollar. If both sides tried to make individual maximizing choices, the PD outcome $E_n M_n$ results. This outcome is Pareto inferior to full commitment on both sides.

In Figure 1 the same ideas are presented as in Table 1, except that we are now concerned with either an n × n option table (say n segments on both the X and Y axes), or by two sets of continuous options. In addition to the extreme options shown in table 1, we also show the n−2 intermediate options. These intermediate options involve emulative "convention commitments." What this means is that employees copy roughly the effort level and effort quality of other employees. The bureau chiefs accept these emulative conventions as representing roughly proper effort levels and provide pay and working conditions roughly commensurate with effort. Note that the values in the payoff space are intermediate between the extreme values in Table 1. Along the diagonal shown in Figure 1, we move from Pareto inferior to Pareto superior solutions. Given a lower effort convention, there is above it a higher one which reflects both greater effort and better pay and working conditions offered by the bureaucracy. We assume that along the diagonal (and diagonals parallel to the one shown in the figure), there exists a sequence of Pareto superior payoffs as we move from the southeast towards the northwest corner. As we move from bottom to top we assume that employees provide higher effort levels. As we move from right to left along the top we assume that the bureaucratic managers provide more valuable internal motivational systems. For any effort level there is a desire for the bureacracy to obtain it at lower costs per dollar (or more men per budget and hence more status or power). For any M_i (set of working conditions) there is a desire for the representative employee to move towards the bottom. Clearly this is an n × n PD case. The end result is the prisoner's dilemma solution.

We should note that there is really a multiple PD problem. Within each peer group, or approximate peer group, there are strong free rider incentives. For non-management employees of a given bureau, *as a group*, it is desirable that the group work effectively so that no one challenges the budget or the working rules. However, if the group is fairly large, no individual, as an individual, need have such an interest. In fact, any specific individual should use his "effort space" to pursue his own interest, and leave it to all others to achieve bureau objectives. Of course, every member of the group faces the same motivations. In addition, the same holds for bureau managers as a group. All this seems to increase the likelihood of the PD solution; we shall see that this is not the likely outcome. The argument which we shall sketch below is that conventions can dominate prisoner's dilemma solutions and themselves become the solutions to an *augmented* game which includes within it the PD game. In addition, conventions can *simultaneously* solve the free rider aspects of the problem which exist for members of each peer group.

By a convention we have in mind a particular solution (i.e., regularity of behavior) to a coordination problem of which there are a number of equilibria. People adhere to the convention because they need the solution, and because adherents will use sanctions (e.g., approval and disapproval) against deviants. The consequence of a convention is that adherents count on other people using the convention. Thus, if an effort convention exists, then everyone assumes that others will use it; and, if it is superior to the PD outcome, then the convention becomes the dominant solution.

Consider how the convention might be chosen. It is as if the parties were

Table 2

	M$_i$	M$_2$	M$_3$
E$_i$	2 2	—	—
E$_2$	—	3 3	4 0
E$_3$	—	0 4	1 1

permitted two choices each. Each can choose or not choose the convention, but if one of them does not choose the convention then this nullifies the convention as a choice. The basic idea is indicated in the payoff tables below. The convention choice is marked E$_i$M$_i$. In Table 2 the convention is obviously the best choice. While *individual* choosing would lead to the prisoner's dilemma, the convention permits "group rationality" to triumph over individual rationality.[6] The convention E$_i$M$_i$ is inferior to the choice E$_2$M$_2$ but superior to E$_3$M$_3$. Will such a convention be chosen? We will argue that it obviously will be since otherwise individuals are reduced to the prisoner's dilemma choice which is worse for them. However, we note that the convention is Pareto inferior to the co-operative choice marked E$_2$M$_2$, but the cooperative choice cannot be reached by individual rationality.

III. Effort Conventions

The basic idea is that conventions are solutions to coordination problems where there are *multiple* equilibria.[7] Coordination requires that *one* of the multiple equilibria be chosen. An example will indicate what is involved. Table 3 indicates the choice between group A and O (for others) of the starting time for work. While 8, 9, or 10 a.m. are equally good, one *and only one* of these must be chosen. The payoffs not along the diagonal indicate that *non-coordinated* hours of work are much inferior. The payoff utili-

Table 3

	10	9	8
10	10 / 10	2 / 3	3 / 2
9	3 / 3	11 / 11	2 / 2
8	3 / 3	3 / 3	10 / 9

ties on the diagonal are not all equally good, but all on the diagonal are very much superior to anything off the diagonal. Can a non-optimal choice be made? There is nothing to prevent 8 rather than 9 o'clock being chosen. Once 8 o'clock is the convention, it would be foolish for anyone to try 9 o'clock. The non-conventional payoff is very much lower. The main point is simply that, once developed, any convention which solves the coordination problem and which is clearly superior to the non-coordinated payoffs is a possible solution.

Should one join, or behave according to a convention which is non-optimal? Clearly yes. It is not a matter of whether the convention is the best possible convention, but rather the value of the convention versus the value of non-conventional behavior. As long as the convention is greatly superior to non-conventional behavior that is all that matters. This suggests that non-optimal conventions can persist. A case in point is that of language. A specific language is a complex convention which associates sound with meaning. It is immaterial that this particular association is not the best possible language on the basis of some criterion. Usually the real choice is to use the language in question or not to use language at all. We must distinguish weak from strong conventions. By a weak convention we have in mind one that exists without sanctions. By a strong one we have in mind one which is supported by sanctions even if the sanctions are no more than a sense of approval or disapproval of others. Effort conventions are usually strong conventions.

Now consider the determination of the convention effort level. Suppose that an individual's effort depends on the observed effort of his peers, and secondly, that the effort depends on the sanctions that individuals impose on deviation to the convention. In addition, the sanctions depend on the effort levels of the past.[8] In other words, tradition and history are strong factors in determining how things are done. This is similar to saying that the argument "we've always done things this way" is very frequently compelling.

We assume that the following relationships hold:

(1) $E_i = E_i (O, S)$ where
(2) $S = S (E_i, O_{t-1}, \ldots, O_{t-n})$, for all i,
(3) $O_{t-1}, O_{t-2}, \ldots, O_{t-i}, \ldots, O_{t-n}$ are given.
(4) $E = E (O, S)$, the average reaction function for all i.

E_i is the effort level for individual i, in response to O, the effort level he observes when entering the bureau, and S the sanction efforts (e.g., signs of approval and disapproval) imposed on i for deviation from the existing standard. For simplicity we also assume that pace is the only effort variable. The nature of the relations are illustrated in Figure 2. The fact that we have the function E_i rising with the observed effort level (i.e., not a horizontal line), means that the individual is motivated to fit in with the behavior of others. If the level of observed effort is very low, then i would put forth a somewhat greater effort, and vice versa when the observed effort is very high. However, beyond some level of observed effort the function flattens out to indicate that there is a maximum effort that i would put forth no matter how hard other people work. Now, the position of the function E_i, and of E, the *average* of all individuals' reactions, depends also on the level of sanctions, which in turn depends on history. If the observed level is below i's effort level, then we would expect that sanctions would induce i to lower his effort, and vice versa. In general the individual will shift his effort level, in part because he wants to fit in with the group, and in part because he is responsive to sanctions from the group when a sufficient deviation from group behavior occurs.

Different personalities will react differently to group sanctions. Some will try to merge their effort completely with that of others, some will deviate to some degree on the low side and others on the high side. Thus, a distribution around the average will exist. In Figure 2 the vertical axis represents the *average* reaction to the average observed pace of *all* economic agents. After all jockeying for position in response to sanctions has ceased, E(O, S) will then be a stable reaction function. The intersection of E(O, S) and the 45° line will determine the equilibrium level of effort. It is the level at which the reactions to the observed rate and the observed rate are the same.

Figure 2

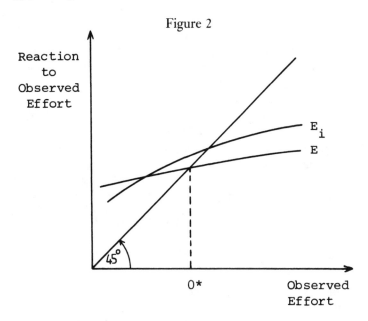

We should not expect individuals to fine tune their effort levels around all deviations from equilibrium. The postulate of inert areas says that for small deviations no reactions would take place. This can be shown by "fat" curves. If both the reaction curve and the 45° lines have certain magnitudes, then the intersection becomes an area. This area reflects the idea that within it there are no deviations that come as a reaction to a change in observation O. Thus, if a few people change their effort level somewhat, this does not result in any reaction from others, and hence there is no return to the initial equilibrium. Beyond the inert area boundaries, reactions and adjustments occur.

Perhaps the best way to think about conventions is to view them as decision processes that do not involve calculation. Rather, they operate on the basis of a stimulus response mechanism. Once the environment requiring the convention presents itself, the response, in terms of the conventional form of behavior occurs. The small probability that it will not occur is ignored by most or all agents. We may view such a way of choosing as an individual "non-rational" or individual non-maximizing approach. But it does the job. It enables both parties to choose an outcome that is Pareto superior to the PD solution. The convention, and non-maximizing behavior, permits group rationality to triumph over individual (maximizing) rationality.

Where there are more than two options, the actual convention can be Pareto optimal, but it is more likely to be non-optimal. Even if in the past

234   HARVEY LEIBENSTEIN

the convention was optimal, circumstances change but conventions are
sticky. Hence, in the new circumstances the convention is likely to be
non-optimal. Furthermore, if n is large, the initial developers of the convention, using trial and error methods, are more likely to hit on a non-optimal
convention. Will those who adhere to a non-optimal convention attempt to
improve it so that a Pareto improvement could occur? This will depend on
incentives and costs. If the group of adherents is large, then the costs of
change for any individual are likely to be high compared to the value of the
gain discounted for risk. The costs that come to mind are those of gathering
and distributing information, persuading others, and the cost of facing
sanctions by strong adherents. There is also a free rider disincentive since
anyone who takes the initiative suffers a cost, but if the Pareto improvement occurs then those who did not put forth any effort gain just as much.

IV. Value of Effort

It is one thing for the bureaucrats to put forth effort, but something
else for that effort to be valuable. Consider a 3 × 3 payoff table in which
three types of groups exist whom the bureaucrats, and their chiefs, can
possibly aim to please: the citizens, the politicians, and outside interest
groups. The bureaucrats are the row choosers and the bureau managers are
the column choosers. As indicated in the table, the payoffs are arranged so
that we have a simple cooperative game; all conflict choices yield lower
utilities to both sides. Both the bureaucrats and the managers will want to
cater to the interest groups. The question that arises is how do the citizens
come out in such a situation.
Professor M. Aoki (1981), in an interesting paper, has argued that the
Japanese bureaucracy operates in such a way that the citizens are well
served under such a setup. Essentially this becomes a bargaining problem
between the bureaucratic representatives of different groups, and some
critically placed governmental bureaus, such as the budget bureau or the
treasury, acting in such a way so that it arbitrates or referees between the
different interest groups. The argument is that this works out efficiently in
the sense that the bureaucrats use the optimal amount of information available for the purpose, and the "referee" has no interest in working out a
biased compromise, since the bureaus do not work for the interests and
cannot be fired by the interests. On the other hand it is, at least in principle, possible to visualize a payoff system to citizens which is inversely
related to the payoffs to the three groups in the diagonal.
Leif Johansen (1979) has examined intragovernmental bargaining
procedures; but he argues, having Scandinavia in mind, that this is likely to
be an inefficient process. Each agent in the bargaining process will find it to

Table 4

Bureau Managers

	Cits	Pols	Int
Citizens	10 / 10	5 / 5	6 / 6
Politicians	5 / 5	15 / 15	7 / 7
Interest Groups	6 / 6	7 / 7	20 / 20

(Rows labeled **Bureau Employees**; for each cell the upper-right number is the payoff to Bureau Managers and the lower-left number is the payoff to Bureau Employees.)

his advantage to give the wrong information; and, as a result, the outcome is likely to be non-optimal. If everyone was sincere and gave the right information, a more efficient outcome would result. This aspect of the problem can probably be interpreted as a prisoner's dilemma game in the sense that whatever options between sincerity and insincerity one party chooses, it pays to be insincere to an equal or greater degree than the other party. Thus, within certain bounds of credibility, the information used is the most exaggerated that can be used as a consequence of the process. There are too many special cases and possibilities to consider. As far as the present writer is aware, there are no easily obtainable generalizations. All that can be said at present is that if the checks and balances are not so delicately poised that the outcome is a fair representation of what the citizens want, and if the bureaucracy plays a role in giving a biased result, then the value of bureaucratic activity must be discounted to reflect this fact.

V. Comments and Conclusions

A basic notion is that the conventional effort level is stable in the small. The convention is imbedded within an inert area so that small perturbations do not influence effort. However, if the shock to the system is sufficiently great then the system itself, as well as the conventions under which it operates, will be destabilized. It is through such means, i.e., the external shocks, that changes can occur and that improvements in efficiency can take place. The general vision is that we have an internal motivation system and a related internal set of conventions which determine bureaucratic productivity, but that the shocks can produce changes in the internal motivational system. The difficulty for our analysis is that there is nothing systematic about these external motivational elements. With respect to private enterprise, the X-inefficiency elements are modified by such *external* motivating forces as the nature of the competitive environment, changes in demand, the introduction of new products, etc. These elements usually can be analyzed in a systematic manner. But governments, by their nature, usually have unassailable monopoly positions. There are, however, some external changes that do in fact have strong motivational impacts. Some which come to mind are: reductions in the real value of tax revenues, or reallocations towards some strong claims (e.g., defense) which reduces the real value of budgets to other bureaus. In addition, the political representational system can through legislation influence the bureaucracy. In the U.S. some anti-tax referenda (Proposition 13 in California, and Proposition 2 in Massachusetts) also put great pressure on the effort levels of the bureaucracy. Thus, even with respect to government these external motivational forces unquestionably exist; but they seem to arise more in an ideosyncratic rather than a systematic manner. In addition, the bureaucracy can attempt to use its favorable position with the legislature to avoid fully facing the external motivational pressures. The bureaucracy can argue that there is a need for the services, that they are not responsible for the high costs, and that hence it is the job of the legislature to find the additional revenues through taxes or borrowing to support the current effort conventions. This is not to argue that such means always work but only to argue that external pressures may not be sufficient to change fairly persistent non-optimal effort conventions. Professor Helga Pollack, in commenting on this paper, made an excellent point to the effect that the low points in the business cycle might also reduce revenues and put pressure towards making the bureaucracy more efficient.

Part of the difficulty of changing effort levels in both public and private enterprises might be called the production function mentality. This is the view that there exists some given relationship between inputs and outputs, and especially between services rendered and labor employed. This was very clear in some of the arguments produced both against Proposition 13 in California and Proposition 2 in Massachusetts. In each case it seemed to be taken for granted that if less revenues were available then a *proportionate decrease in services would have to* take place. The view that effort levels are based on conventions appears to support this approach. However, our argument is that if the budget constraints are sufficiently strong then the pressures on bureaucracy become sufficient to induce a change in the conventions. However, some budget constraints may be *too* tight and lead to undesirable substitutions of greater pace for lower quality of effort.

We did not mean to imply that a single effort convention holds sway in the system. A limitation of the foregoing is that it does not consider more complex situations in which different conventions dominate in different bureaus. It is even possible for different conventions to rule in the same bureau if some of the bureaucrats follow a convention established by a profession which goes beyond the bureaucracy, as against conventions which hold wholly with it. For example, lawyers or economists may operate at very different conventional effort levels than other civil servants in part because they are motivated by professional standards. Even more important than matters of pace and quality may be the differences in the activities chosen by those who are trained to follow professional procedures.

In relaxing the utility maximization postulate, we assumed that when pressure is low non-calculating procedures are employed. A few comments on this score are in order. First, and most important, it is easier for various individuals to choose a convention which solves the prisoner's dilemma problem if the choice procedure involves a non-calculating stimulus-response mechanism. Thus, our manner of relaxing the maximization assumption makes it easier for us to see how we obtain convention solutions since the stimulus-response mechanism makes it easier for each individual to believe that others will choose in the same way. Second, once the convention exists the non-maximization aspect allows us to believe that few people would flout the convention even if there is a calculated advantage in doing so. The fact that people under normal low pressure conditions do not calculate enables them to stick to the convention with ease. Third, it becomes easier to see that people will go to the trouble to support the convention with sanctions against others if non-maximization is postulated. Imposing sanctions is frequently unpleasant. But if the sanctions are imposed as a consequence of a response to strong emotions (i.e., stimulus response) rather than part of a cooly calculated activity, then it becomes reasonable to expect that individuals will do so.

To summarize: if we assume that there are two sides in a bureau which we may roughly designate as the ordinary civil servants and the bureau managers, then there may be adversarial relations between these groups. The bureau managers may be interested in having low budgets per employee or maximum effort per salary unit, while the operating civil servant may desire to shift effort towards their own interests rather than the bureau's or citizens' interest. It is reasonable to presume that such adversarial behavior on both sides should lead to lower productivity levels than would otherwise be the case. Thus, we would have under these circumstances a hidden or partially hidden prisoner's dilemma problem. However, the prisoner's dilemma solution is avoided by the adoption of conventional effort levels.

These levels may represent high or low productivity depending on (a) the nature of the convention, and (b) the choice of activities which determines the value of effort. The latter depends in part on the "interests" towards whom bureau members and bureau managers direct their efforts, and on the political processes that determine the interests. In addition, the value of effort will depend on the system of checks and balances through which the government operates as a whole.

Equilibrium effort levels are likely to be imbedded in inert areas, which possess attainable destabilizing boundaries. Thus, they are likely to be stable in the small but not in the large. External motivating factors may destabilize the convention and in some cases lead to new conventions with higher effort values. Among the possible destabilizing forces are (a) reduction in the real value of tax revenues, (b) increased competition for budgets from other bureaus or ministries, (c) pressure brought by the legislative or political process, (d) competition of services from the private sector, (e) direct citizen referenda, and in rare cases (f) government permitted or created competition between bureaus offering similar or substitutable services. Unfortunately, low effort conventions do not call such external motivating forces into play in any systematic manner. Hence, a wide range of performance levels are likely to be possible and to persist in governmental bureaucracies.

Notes

1. A review of a few of the major textbooks leads to the conclusion that there is very little on this subject compared to other topics. See especially the excellent book by Dennis Mueller (1979), and see also Brown and Jackson (1978).

2. For a more extensive treatment of this approach as applied to the private enterprise, see my paper, "The Prisoner's Dilemma in the Invisible Hand," *American Economic Review* (1982), and my *Beyond Economic Man*, Ch. 9.

3. See Footnote 2.

4. This idea is consistent with a well-established law in Psychology known as the Yerkes-Dodson law. The Yerkes-Dodson law is usually illustrated by a bell shaped curve. If we view decision making as the *performing* activity, then we would expect it to be non-optimal at low pressure levels, rise towards optimality as pressure increases, and fall again as pressure grows beyond its optimal values. This law is so well established amongst psychologists that the citations to the original experiments (1908) are rarely made. For a general treatment see Atkinson and Birch (1978).

5. On this point see Rapoport (1970), Ch. 3.

6. On the theory of conventions see Schelling (1960), Lewis (1969), Ullman-Margalit (1977), and Schotter (1981).

7. My own approach to conventions emphasizes both the informational and the sanction aspects. Lewis (1969) and Schotter (1981) emphasize primarily informational coordination.

8. Standard economics seems to ignore the influence of the past. "Bygones are bygones" is basic to analysis. Of course, here the past is critical in determining current effort levels.

References

Aoki, M. (1981), "The Function of Economic Planning: A Reconsideration," *New Streams in Economics*, Y. Murakami and K. Hamada, eds., Tokyo: Toyo-Keizai.

Atkinson, J. W., and O. Birch (1978), *Introduction to Motivation*, New York: Van Nostrand.

Aumann, R. J. (1981), "Survey of Repeated Games," *Essays in Game Theory and Mathematical Economics*, Mannheim: B-I Wissenschaftsverlag.

Brown, C. V. and P. M. Jackson (1978), *Public Sector Economics*, Oxford: Martin Robertson and Co.

Chammah, A. and A. Rapoport (1965), *Prisoner's Dilemma*, Ann Arbor: University of Michigan Press.

Johansen, Leif (1979), "The Bargaining Society and the Inefficiency of Bargaining," *Kyklos*, Vol. 32, No. 3, pp. 497–522.

Leibenstein, H. (1976), *Beyond Economic Man*, Cambridge: Harvard University Press.

Leibenstein, H. (1982a), "On Bull's-Eye Painting Economics," *Journal of Post Keynesian Economics*, Vol. IV, No. 3, pp. 460–5.

Leibenstein, H. (1982b), "The Prisoner's Dilemma in the Invisible Hand: An Analysis of Intrafirm Productivity," *American Economic Review*, Vol. 72, No. 2, pp. 92–97.

Lewis, D. (1969), *Convention: A Philosophical Study*, Cambridge: Harvard University Press.

Mueller, Dennis C. (1979), *Public Choice*, Cambridge: Cambridge University Press.

Rapoport, Anatol (1970), *N-Person Game Theory*, Ann Arbor: University of Michigan Press.

Schelling, T. S. (1960), *The Strategy of Conflict*, Oxford: Oxford University Press.

Schneider, Friedrich and Werner Pommerehne (Nov. 1981), "Free Riding and Collective Action: An Experience in Public Macroeconomics," *Quarterly Journal of Economics*, Vol. XCVI, No. 4, pp. 689–704.

Schotter, A. (1981), *The Economic Theory of Social Institutions*, Cambridge: Cambridge University Press.

Simon, H. A. (May 1978), "Rationality as Process and as Product of Thought," *American Economic Review*, Vol. 68, No. 2, pp. 1–16.

Ullman-Margalit, Edna (1977), *The Emergence of Norms*, New York: Oxford University Press.

Résumé

On peut séparer les travailleurs dans un bureau en fonctionnaires d'exécution d'une part et dirigeants d'autre part. Il existe en général des relations d'opposition entre ces deux groupes. Les dirigeants peuvent souhaiter avoir des budgets peu élevés par employé ou un effort maximum par salarié, tandis que les fonctionnaires d'exécution peuvent désirer le réduire au minimum dans leur propre intérêt plutôt que dans celui du bureau ou des clients. Il est raisonnable de penser qu'une telle attitude oppositionnelle des deux parties conduit à des niveaux de productivité plus faibles qu'il n'en serait autrement. Ainsi, nous aurions dans ces conditions un problème caché ou partiellement caché du "dilemme du prisonnier". Toutefois on évite d'avoir à en trouver la solution en adoptant des niveaux d'effort conventionnels.

Ces niveaux peuvent représenter une productivité faible ou élevée. La nature de la convention et le choix des activités retentissent sur la valeur de l'effort. Cette dernière dépend en partie des "intérêts" sur lesquels les membres du bureau et les dirigeants concentrent leurs efforts et des processus politiques qui déterminent ces "intérêts". De plus, le valeur de cet effort dépendra du système de mesure sur la base duquel fonctionne le gouvernement dans son ensemble.

Ces niveaux d'efforts d'équilibre peuvent être fixés dans des régions inertes ayant des limites que l'on peut atteindre en destabilisant le système. Ainsi, ils ne sont susceptibles d'être stables que dans une marge étroite.

Des facteurs de motivation externes peuvent destabiliser la convention et dans certains cas conduire à de nouvelles conventions offrant des valeurs d'effort plus élevé. Parmi les forces de destabilisation possibles on trouve (a) des réductions dans la valeur réellé des revenus fiscaux, (b) une concurrence accrue pour les budgets venant d'autres bureaux on ministères, (c) une concurrence des services relevant du secteur privé, (d) une pression exercée par des procédés législatifs ou politiques, (e) des référenda au suffrage universel des citoyens et, dans de rares cas, (f) une concurrence permise ou créée par le gouvernement entre les bureaux offrant des services similaires ou substituables. Malheureusement, les conventions à faible valeur de l'effort ne font pas jouer systématiquement de telles forces de motivation externes. Ainsi, on est susceptible de trouver et de voir persister un large éventail de niveaux d'activité dans les bureaucraties étatiques.

Public Sector Productivity and Relative Efficiency: The State of Art in the United States*

Donald M. Fisk

The number and diversity of governments in the United States confounds any attempt to simply and accurately summarize the state of the art of U.S. government productivity. There are about 80,000 distinct units of government in the United States which employ about 16.2 million individuals, not including military. These governments, in total, spend about $1 trillion of which about half is for purchase of goods and services (all figures are for 1981). Government functions cover not only the usual services such as defense, education, police and fire but also liquor stores, cemeteries, grain elevators, lotteries and even a State bank.

Several recent studies have examined parts of the government productivity puzzle in the U.S. They provide the basis for the following discussion which addresses five productivity-related subjects: the production process, measurement, comparison of public and private efficiency, economies of scale, and technological diffusion.

The Production Process

Specification of the production process has long been a problem for those studying government productivity. While there is still considerable disagreement concerning the process the research community has increasingly come to rely on the following model: Government draws on a series of *inputs* to produce a series of *activities* which result in one or more *outputs* which are intended to produce a series of desirable *consequences*. In this model inputs consist of labor and capital; activities are intermediate services or processes; outputs are the final goods or services produced by the gov-

*The views in this paper are those of the author and do not reflect the views of the U.S. Bureau of Labor Statistics.

Public and Finance and the Quest for Efficiency. Proceedings of the 38th Congress of the International Institute of Public Finance. Copenhagen, 1982, pp. 241–249. Copyright © 1984 by Wayne State University Press, Detroit, Michigan, 48202.

ernment; and consequences, or outcomes and impacts, are the intended results of government action (Burkhead and Hennigan (1978)). In its more sophisticated form the model includes the citizen, who is a producer as well as a consumer, and community conditions which affect service production techniques (Whitaker (1982)).

For some government services, such as sanitation, the production model can be applied in a relatively straightforward manner. In the basic model sanitation organizations use laborers, drivers, trucks, brooms, gas, and uniforms as inputs. These inputs are deployed to produce a series of activities such as training, service and repair. Outputs, in this case, might be the trash collected and streets swept. The consequences should be cleaner streets and neighborhoods, fewer fire and health hazards and presumably happier citizens. The more sophisticated model would also include citizen inputs such as reporting of missed collections and dirty streets, separating and preparing trash for recycling and disposal and carrying trash to the curb for pickup.

For a few services, such as sanitation, there is general agreement as to what constitutes inputs, activities, outputs and consequences. For many services, however, the distinction is not obvious. Police and fire service inputs, activities and consequences are reasonably clear cut but not outputs. For other services, such as electric power, the inputs, activities and outputs are clearcut but not the consequences. Public transit officials, for example, argue that their job is to provide service to a community and its residents (Tomazinis (1975)). Their output is the operating transit vehicle, and the community's use of the service is the outcome or consequence. This concept, of course, is at odds with the view of the private sector transit manager who would argue that the capacity provided to a city is an activity while use of that capacity is the output.

Measurement

Disagreement over outputs and consequences, as well as multiple goals and conflicting objectives, has led to considerable confusion in the measurement and interpretation of government productivity. Multiple criteria and measures are common. Ostrom suggests four criteria—effectiveness, responsiveness, equity and efficiency—when assessing police services (Ostrom (1979)). Most public administrators use efficiency and effectiveness criteria with effectiveness defined as equity, responsiveness, outcome and impacts. Efficiency is usually defined as technical efficiency.

Technical efficiency, which is the focus of this section, is simply output divided by input. Output is final organizational output and input is the labor used in producing the output. Labor accounts for about half of all government expenditures in the U.S., and as much as 80 percent for some services such as fire and police. For most services labor consumed is a good measure of resource use. Thus far there has been little interest in multi-factor or total factor government productivity measurement in the U.S.

The preferred measure of output is a physical measure. For most government services it is the only possible measure. However, for a few services, such as postal, water and sewer, there is a market price and it is possible to measure output using value. These services are commonly known as enterprise funds and account for about 10 percent of all U.S. Federal, State and local government civilian employment.

For many years productivity trends have been calculated for enterprise funds and included as part of U.S. national private sector productivity statistics. Between 1967 and 1981 outputs for these services increased at an annual rate of 2.2 percent, labor input increased at 1.3 percent and labor productivity increased at 0.9 percent. There are serious questions concerning the use of value to measure outputs when prices are set administratively and occasionally heavily subsidized as they are with government enterprises.

The difficulties in using physical counts to measure service output is often discussed (Mark (1982)). Government service output measurements present additional problems in the U.S. Some services, like police and fire, lack both the required conceptual framework and national data. Other services, such as sanitation, are supported by good conceptual research but no national time series data. There are a few services, such as electric power, for which conceptual work and aggregate national data exist which can be used to calculate government productivity (Fisk (1981)).

Individual government productivity measurements, as contrasted to aggregate national statistics, are somewhat more common. One survey of local governments in the U.S. found that over three-quarters of the responding governments calculated and used efficiency measures in their operations (Fukuhara (1977)). Another survey of State governments found wide use of efficiency measurements although as with the local governments they varied markedly by government and service area (Urban Institute (1975)). Furthermore, several local governments have moved to institute comprehensive measurement systems (Hatry (1982)).

The Federal government also tracks labor productivity (efficiency) trends. Currently 67 percent of the workforce, about 1.8 million employee years, are covered. The Federal index is a ratio of work accomplished divided by labor used to produce the output. Output measures are a combination of final outputs such as mail delivered and intermediate services such as buildings and grounds maintained. There are about 3800 different output measures covering about 455 organizational units. The measurements are grouped into 28 functional categories such as audit, communications, postal and library service. Long term productivity trends for these 28 functions range from a plus 11.6 percent for communications to a minus 0.8 percent for printing and duplicating. The overall increase for all functions in 1981 was 2.2 percent, the long term trend is 1.5 percent (Mark (1981)).

Comparison of Public and Private Service Efficiency

Notwithstanding the problems in measuring government productivity there are a number of studies of comparative efficiency of public and private delivery. These studies, almost without exception, focus on a single service, quite often on one part of one service and most often on "hard, tangible" services. Most studies are cross sectional.

Sanitation: The service that has been examined most often is sanitation, particularly solid waste collection. There are literally dozens of studies. The most extensive study of this area was undertaken by E.S. Savas who concluded from a sample of 340 governments that the individual private household collection contract was more expensive than municipal production which was more expensive than the municipal contract with a private firm (Savas (1977)). A study by Kemper and Quigley of 128 cities in one State (Connecticut) found much the same results: Individual private collection was 30 percent more expensive than municipal collection but municipal collection was 25 percent more expensive than private contract collection (Kemper and Quigley (1976)).

Electric Power: There have been a number of studies of public power, and comparisons of public and private power generation and distribution. De Alessi summarized the existing research as follows: municipal utilities charge less, spend more on construction, have higher operating costs, change price less frequently, do not innovate as often, favor business over residential users, offer fewer services and show greater variation in the rates of return. Despite the studies there is still considerable debate over the relative efficiency of public and private power organizations (De Alessi (1974)).

Hospitals and Nursing Homes: There is little concrete information on the relative cost of government and private hospitals and nursing homes. One study did find that for-profit homes had lower costs than government-operated facilities, but it did not control for type of illness. Another study found that the Veterans Administration operated nursing homes were 83 percent more expensive than privately operated homes for comparable care for comparable patients. Yet another study of the quality of care in 118 nursing homes found that there was no difference between the types of provision.

Finally, a study of hospitals in New York City found no cost difference between profit and non-profit institutions (Savas (1982)). After examining the available research, Spann concluded that the quality of care in the two types of institutions is quite comparable but the costs may be slightly lower in private, for-profit operations (Spann (1977)).

Fire Services: There is only one important private fire company in the United States and only one in depth study of its efficiency. This study, which was conducted by Ahlbrandt, concluded that the private fire service was about half as expensive as government service (Ahlbrandt (1973)). The reasons for the cost savings were the use of part-time personnel to supplement full-time firefighters; development and use of new equipment and technology; and the realization of economies of scale.

Education and Other Services: Education accounts for about half of all State and local government expenditures in the United States, and there are both private and public schools but little research into relative costs of provision. Likewise there are a number of other services including custodial services, food service, tree trimming, data processing, water supply and legal aid for which there are statistics on comparative efficiency, but little hard evidence as to whether private or public provision is cheaper (Savas (1982); and Fisk, Kiesling and Muller (1978)).

Unpublished Studies: In addition to the published studies there are a number of unpublished studies conducted by individual governments. The Federal government, for example, requires that agencies periodically examine their services to ascertain if private contractors can perform them more efficiently (U.S. Office of Management and Budget (1979)). Some local and State governments also undertake comparisons (Fisk, Kiesling and Muller (1978)).

Comparison Through Provision: Government efficiency is increasingly being tested in the market place. In some cases multiple contractors are employed, in other cases government personnel and private contractors are used (Savas (1981)). The usual approach is to divide a jurisdication into geographic areas and contract for each area separately. One recent innovation permits government personnel to bid against private contractors for the right to provide service with the lowest price winning (Hughes (1982)).

Economies of Scale

There are numerous studies of economies of scale in government production in the United States, same dating from the 1930's but most are of more recent vintage (Fox (1980)). A few address theoretical considerations but most are empirically based. Many examine both short and long term economies.

Capital-Intensive Services: There are a number of studies of the provision of drinking water, and most have found economies of scale. Clark found that large system unit costs were about half that of small systems (Clark (1980)). Five other studies found both short and long term economies of scale (Fox (1980)). The major economies appear to be in water treatment, not storage and distribution.

There are far fewer studies of wastewater (sewerage) treatment. Two found economies of scale but neither study examined the impact of the number and location of customers, an important issue in wastewater. There are also a few studies of economies in road maintenance. Fox identified three but found serious defects in each study. No studies were found of economies of scale of municipal electric power systems. However, studies of private electric systems found major economies present (Fox (1980)).

Labor-Intensive Services: Labor-intensive services, such as education, fire and police, demonstrate far fewer economies of scale than do capital-intensive services. Fox (1980) examined 19 studies of educational economies and concluded: (1) size economies exist for elementary schools up to about 300 students; (2) size economies exist for high school up to about 1500 students; and (3) size economies exist for administrative expenditures up to 30,000–40,000 students. Fox found 2 major deficiencies in the educational studies. First, they focus on school costs only, ignoring such costs as transportation, and second, they fail to come to grips with the quality issue. Most simply use the number of students, or some variant, as the measure of output.

Fire and police studies of economies of scale show mixed results. Ahlbrandt (1973) found constant returns to scale for paid departments and decreasing returns for volunteer departments. Others, including Hirsch, concluded that there are size economies but that they are quite small. Fox concluded, after examining five studies, that there are few economies for fire services for cities above 10,000 population. Fox also examined seven police studies and found that the studies which used population as the output measure did not find economies of size, but those which used a scale of services index did find significant economies. Fox concluded that as city size expands new services are added which offset any cost savings that flow from expanding existing services (Fox (1980)).

There is considerable research into the economies of sanitation. Recent studies of solid waste collection conclude that economies occur in the small size cities, up to about 20,000 population, but not in the medium and large size cities where there may be diseconomies (Fox (1980)). Research on solid waste disposal operations is less plentiful but there is general agreement in the literature that there are major economies until the population reaches about 100,000 (Sorg and Hickman (1970)). Beyond that point the costs decrease but at a lesser rate.

Technological Diffusion

The overall impact of technology and innovation on public productivity has been given scant attention by the research community although there has been a modest amount of research into the adoption of technological innovations by government. Probably the most interesting overall finding of this research has been the similarity between government and private diffusion (Feller (1978)).

Recent research into government innovation, which relied primarily on the case study approach, found the traditional "S" shape diffusion curve. In a study of 43 government innovations Feller and Menzel identified the same stages of adoption found in the private sector (Feller and Menzel (1978)).

Recent studies have suggested that government innovations have accelerated since the mid-1960's, and that innovations are much more prevalent today than was previously thought. Also, it now appears as if innovation leadership is much more diverse. Current evidence also suggests that government innovation frequently does not result in improved government performance (Feller and Menzel (1978)). Yin (1978) explains this last finding by suggesting that two different engines drive government innovation. One engine is traditional production efficiency, the other bureaucratic self-interest.

Lastly, several studies have compared the speed in adopting new technologies by the public and private sector. The results of this research are mixed with some showing no difference and others showing faster adoption by the private sector (Russell and Burke (1975); Roessner (1977); and Savas (1982)).

Conclusions

Several points stand out in this brief survey of productivity and efficiency in U.S. government services. First, there has been a large amount of research and analysis of government productivity. Second, despite the large amount of research there are still great gaps in our knowledge. A particular problem is absence of a unifying theory. Third, studies of the rate of innovation diffusion and economies of scale in government yield results similar to those found in the private sector. Finally, many of the difficulties in measuring public output—its intangible nature, its externalities and its quality assessment problems—are similar to those encountered in measuring private sector services.

References:

1. Ahlbrandt, Roger, Jr., "Efficiency in the Provision of Fire Services," *Public Choice*, 1973, pp. 1–15.

2. Ahlbrandt, Roger, Jr., *Municipal Fire Protection Services: Comparison of Alternative Organizational Forms*, Beverly Hills, California: Sage Publications, 1973.

3. Burkhead, Jesse, and Patrick J. Hennigan, "Productivity Analysis: A Search for Definition and Order," *Public Administration Review*, January/February, 1978, pp. 34–40.

4. Clark, Robert M., "Small Water Systems: Role of Technology," *Journal of Environmental Engineering Division*, February, 1980, pp. 19–35.

5. De Alessi, Louis, "An Economic Analysis of Government Ownership and Regulation: Theory and the Evidence from the Electric Power Industry," *Public Choice*, Fall, 1974, pp. 1–42.

6. Feller, Irwin, "Research Findings and Issues in the Design of an Intergovernmental Science System," Unpublished paper, State College, Pennsylvania: Pennsylvania State University, November, 1978.

7. Feller, Irwin, and Donald C. Menzel, "The Adoption of Technological Innovations by Municipal Governments," *Urban Affairs Quarterly*, June 1978, pp. 475–77.

8. Fisk, Donald M., "Pilot Study Measures Productivity of State, Local Electric Utilities," *Monthly Labor Review*, December, 1981, pp. 44–6.

9. Fisk, Donald M., Herbert Kiesling and Thomas Muller, *Private Provision of Public Services: An Overview*, Washington: Urban Institute, 1978.

10. Fox, William F., *Size Economies in Local Government Services: A Review*, Washington: U.S. Department of Agriculture, August, 1980.

11. Fukuhara, Rockham, "Productivity Improvement in Cities," *Municipal Yearbook— 1977*, Washington: International City Management Association, 1977.

12. Hatry, Harry P., "The Status of Productivity Measurement in the Public Sector," in Frederick S. Lane (editor), *Current Issues in Public Administration*, New York: St. Martin's Press, 1982.

13. Hughes, Mark, "Contracting Services in Pheonix," *Public Management*, October, 1982, pp. 2–4.

14. Kemper, Peter, and John M. Quigley, *The Economics of Refuse Collection*, Cambridge, Massachusetts: Ballinger Publishing Company, 1976.

15. Mark, Jerome A., "Measuring Productivity in Government: Federal, State and Local," *Public Productivity Review*, March, 1981, pp. 21–44.

16. Mark, Jerome A., "Measuring Productivity in Service Industries," *Monthly Labor Review*, June, 1982, pp. 3–8.

17. Ostrom, Elinor, et. al., "Evaluating Police Organization," *Public Productivity Review*, Winter, 1979, pp. 3–27.

18. Roessner, David, "Incentives to Innovate in Public and Private Organizations: Implications for Public Policy," *Administration and Society*, 1977.

19. Russell, Louise, and Carol Burke, "Technological Diffusion in the Hospital Sector," Washington: National Planning Association, 1975.

20. Savas, E.S., "Intercity Competition Between Public and Private Service Delivery," *Public Administration Review*, January/February, 1981, pp. 46–52.

21. Savas, E.S., "Policy Analysis for Local Government: Public versus Private Refuse Collection," *Policy Analysis*, Winter, 1977, pp. 49–74.

22. Savas, E.S., *Privatizing the Public Sector*, Chathan, New Jersey: Chathan House Publishers, 1982.

23. Sorg, Thomas J., and H. Lamier Hickman, *Sanitary Landfill Facts*, Washington: U.S. Department of Health, Education and Welfare, 1970.

24. Spann, Robert M., "Provision of Government Services," in Thomas E. Borcherding, *Budgets and Bureaucrats*, Durham, North Carolina: Duke University Press, 1977, pp. 87–88.

25. Tomazinis, Anthony R., *Productivity, Efficiency and Quality in Urban Transportation Systems*, Lexington, Massachusetts: Lexington Press, 1975.

26. U.S. Office of Management and Budget, "Policies for Acquiring Commercial or Industrial Products and Services Needed by the Government," Washington: U.S. Office of Management and Budget, March 29, 1979.

27. Urban Institute, "The Status of Productivity Measurement in State Government: An Initial Examination," Washington: Urban Institute, 1975.

28. Whitaker, Gordon P., et al., *Basic Issues in Police Performance*, Washington: U.S. National Institute of Justice, 1982, pp. 94–104.

29. Yin, Robert, "Changing Urban Bureaucracies: How New Practices Become Routinized," Santa Monica, California: RAND Corporation, 1978.

Résumé

La recherche sur la productivité des activités gouvernementales et son efficacité relative aux U.S.A. est à la fois abondante et fragmentaire. Un problème majeur est l'absence d'une théorie qui donnerait une direction à cette recherche, en particulier comment intégrer l'efficacité technique et économique. Les études qui comparent l'efficacité étatique et l'efficacité technique privée ont trouvé, pour la plupart, que la production privée est moins chère, mais une bonne partie de cette recherche est discutable et pour de nombreux services il n'existe pas de recherche rigoureuse. Les études des économies d'échelle et de diffusion technologique dans les activités publiques montrent en général des modèles semblables à ceux que l'on trouve dans le secteur privé. Des statistiques nationales globales font en général défaut, sauf pour les évolutions à long terme de la productivité des entreprises qui sont partie intégrante des calculs sur le secteur privé.

Productivity in the Local Government Sector— A Framework for Empirical Research*

*Klaus-Norbert Münch, Wolfgang Länger and
Gerhard Rauscher*

1. Introduction

The continuous growth of the public sector has increasingly stimulated the interest of scientists and the public. Both desire deeper economic understanding of public sector activities. It is of interest to know whether transfers of resources from the private to the public sector lead to increases in welfare. Many economists express doubts, arguing that the market is more productive than the public sector (Baumol (1967)). Unfortunately, empirical research, especially on efficiency and productivity in the public sector, gives only inadequate answers to such crucial questions. The fundamental problem is: does government carry out the right activities and is it doing so efficiently?

Thus, we must find answers to the following questions:

— Has the best allocation of resources been attained by the provision of a certain public service?
— What is the quality of the services offered from the point of view of the producer and the consumer? Has the quality of services improved over time? Will similar public institutions provide comparable services with the same input-output relations?

* This paper reports about the research project: "Produktivität im kommunalen Sektor—Eine empirische Untersuchung in ausgewählten Gemeinden", sponsored by the Stiftung Volkswagenwerk and carried out by a research group at the University of Augsburg under the direction of Prof. Horst Hanusch.

In preparing the paper, we profited greatly from helpful comments and assistance in editing by Prof. Wolfgang F. Stolper. We are indebted to our colleague Karl-Heinz Weiss who presented the paper on the 38th IIPF-Congress at Copenhagen. It is needless to say that remaining infirmities or errors are evidently ours.

Public Finance and the Quest for Efficiency. Proceedings of the 38th Congress of the International Institute of Public Finance. Copenhagen, 1982, pp. 251–265. Copyright © 1984 by Wayne State University Press, Detroit, Michigan, 48202.

— Has there been a difference in the development of productivity of the market and the public economy? Have all possibilities to improve the public production process been utilized?
— What are the determinants of productivity changes in the public sector? What are the possibilities of improving the productivity in the public sector?

To answer these questions, it is useful to carry out input-output analyses, cost accounting studies, cost-benefit analyses etc. Each of these studies has its own purpose. We can only concentrate on one of these analyses. As there is an urgent need to gain insights into the public production process, we work on productivity analyses.

With this in mind, the main focus of our research relates to the question of the development of productivity. In this context, output and input in real terms have to be measured and related to each other. The thus developed framework for public productivity analysis will be applied to selected local services in the Federal Republic of Germany.

The methodological part of the study will investigate the following problems:

— the definition and measurement of input and output of local services.
— the factors which determine the level and the development of productivity of the service sectors under consideration.

Public goods can be differentiated according to the extent in which the criteria of non-exclusion, non-rivalry, merit wants and external effects apply (Hanusch (1972) and (1981a)). With these criteria in mind, the following community services have been chosen to investigate public services with substantially different characteristics.

— Public utilities and waste collection characterized by possible total exclusion of and rivalry among consumers
— Public mass transit and high schools characterized by possible exclusion and limited non-rivalry
— Theaters and recreation services characterized by possible exclusion, limited non-rivalry and merit wants
— Hospital-care systems characterized by limited exclusion and rivalry in medical treatment
— Fire protection where exclusion is not possible and non-rivalry exists because of the characteristics of the preventive service

2. Procedure

In order to study the development of productivity of the mentioned local services it is necessary to define input and output indicators and to solve the problem of how to relate these indicators to each other.

2.1. Inputs

The major inputs into the public production process are labor and capital.

Labor. To measure the quantity of labor, we use, as usual in productivity analyses, the number of employees and the hours worked. Two main problems arise from this procedure.

First, as a rule, indicators needed for the empirical research are available only for the public authority as a whole. The share of employees involved in the provision of the specific service under consideration must therefore be somehow calculated.

Second, it is essential to allow for differences in the skills of the employees. In order to derive a single indicator for the input, these various qualities must somehow be combined. This can be done by using the methods developed by Kendrick (1961) or Denison (1962). Denison weighs man-hours according to education, training, age, and sex of the employees. Kendrick on the other hand weighs the number of employees or man-hours by specific wages at constant prices, in order to express the different qualifications resulting from education, experience, skill etc. We have adopted Kendrick's method because it is the only one for which data are available.

Capital. Capital consists of all material goods necessary for the specific public production process. As with labor, the problem arises how to combine the different capital goods into a single measure (see Craemer (1972)). It is normally impossible to restrict oneself to measure capital in physical units. As a rule, a single indicator for capital must be constructed aggregating the capital goods by using their prices as weights. In order to deflate the nominal prices we have used indices for capital good prices by the *Statistisches Bundesamt*.

2.2. Output

One of the most difficult problems in public economics relates to the identification and measurement of public sector outputs (see e.g. Fisk and

Winnie (1974), Bahl and Burkhead (1977), Brüngger and Orga (1978), Hjerppe (1980), Hanusch (1981b)). There is no generally accepted opinion as to what the output of such services as schools or theaters or hospitals really is. Depending on how the output is defined, different indicators must be constructed. An example will illustrate this problem.

Assuming that teachers have the task of training interested people as technicians, the following output indicators can be derived:

— The number of potential participants
— the actual number of participants
— the number of participants who successfully passed the final examination
— the number of participants who got an adequate job
— the increase in income resulting from the training.

Each of these output measures is of interest. They differ in the level at which they are defined. Understanding public output requires therefore an exploration of the public production process which covers several transformation processes from the input level up to the welfare level as illustrated in figure 1 (for a similar approach see Berczi (1978) and Gäfgen (1980)).

The different transformation levels can be characterized as follows:

Transformation Level I.   At the basic level labor and capital are inputs for an output proper which can be considered under the aspects of both supply and individual use. Stressing supply, the potential use of publicly provided goods (output (a)) is the adequate output indicator of this level. On the other hand, if the individual use is seen to be the purpose of public production, then the actual use (output (b)) becomes all the more important. Both output indicators can be measured in real terms.

Transformation Level II.   Impacts on goals of a higher level must be considered because public production is not a goal in itself. Its purpose is to increase individual utility by changes in the fulfillment of individual needs (output (c)).

Transformation Level III.   The fulfillment of individual needs is closely connected with the ultimate purpose of public production: to increase social welfare (output (d)).

A comprehensive productivity analysis should include all transformation levels. The welfare approach is an appealing framework for measuring public output. In most public service sectors, however, it cannot be quantified at all, or only in a rudimentary manner. In addition, measuring welfare requires a preceding analysis of transformation levels I and II, but, it is impossible to obtain information on which of the outputs (a) to (c) have to be examined. These outputs, however, are of central interest for an analysis that concentrates on public production in real terms.

Figure 1: *The production structure of local government services*

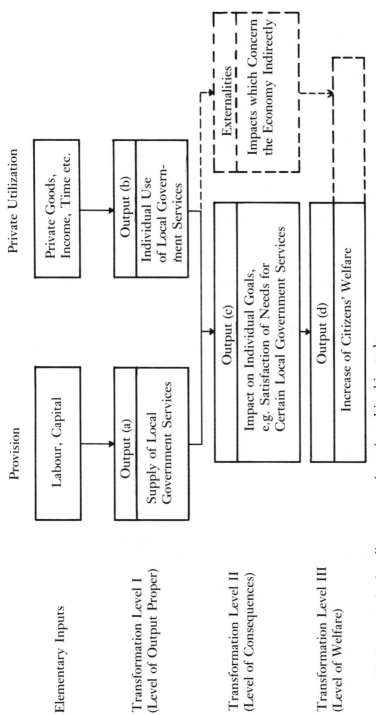

Note: The boxes in broken lines are not investigated in this study.

255

We therefore study, as far as possible, the type of local public output supplied, emphasizing both quantity and quality. Environmental impacts (external effects) will not be considered because they are of little importance in this context.

Problems arise in general because, in most cases, each of the outputs (a) to (c) cannot be described by quantitative indicators only. Qualitative aspects are important too, and these may be additive or multiplicative. Both methods of measurement can be found in the literature (see Balk (1975) and Hatry/Fisk (1971)). Both methods raise, however, problems of weighing and double counting. Although there is no commonly accepted solution, amalgamation techniques found in cost-effectiveness analyses can lead to pragmatically acceptable solutions. We minimize this problem by analysing different quantity and quality indicators separately, and combining them only for supplementary information.

3. Measures of Productivity

Measures of productivity are defined as the ratio of output to input. According to our objectives, there are two possibilities for deriving productivity measures (Berczi (1978)):

— to relate the output of one of the discussed transformation levels to the basic factor inputs; or
— to relate the output at a higher level to the output at the preceding level (ending with output at transformation level I to factor inputs).

As mentioned above, an analysis of the public production process has to concentrate on the relationship of output at transformation level I to factor inputs.

Because in most cases labor is the dominant input factor (see for example Orzechowski (1974)), it seems reasonable to analyse primarily labor productivity. Yet in order to discover whether there has been a process of factor substitution, we also examine capital and total factor productivity. All these measures can be defined both for actual and potential use. If one relates actual to potential use, one gets an indicator of capacity utilization for a specified time period. This makes it possible to analyse both peak and average utilization. A step further would be to find the determinants of productivity on the input and the output side. They can influence both quantity and quality. The establishment of such determinants requires regression analysis and similar statistical methods (Hanusch (1982)).

4. Empirical Results

The analysis of public mass transit in a German city in a pilot study made it possible to test this concept of productivity measurement. In this section, we present the first empirical results. Similar methods will be applied to other public services.

4.1. Data Base

General statistics did not provide sufficient information for a detailed analysis. We therefore had to gather some data from special local statistics like municipal budgets, organisation charts and annual reports of public service suppliers. Additional information was available only from unpublished internal statistics.

a. Inputs For the inputs of transformation level I we used the following indicators:

Labor
— number of total employees weighed by the index of contracted working time for each year
— operating staff (drivers and conductors) weighed by the index of contracted working time for each year.

Capital
— the main components of the capital stock are vehicles and tracks. For accounting and aggregating the various capital assessments, we use deflated prices. Thus, for the years under consideration, we have comparable values of the gross capital stock.

b. Outputs The outputs are defined as follows:
Output (a): potential passenger kilometers (seats and standing-room times vehicle kilometers)
Output (b): actual passenger kilometers

To include quality aspects, the following indicators were selected:

— average speed
— hours of operation
— number of stops per kilometer en route

Figure 2: *The development of output (1970 = 100)*

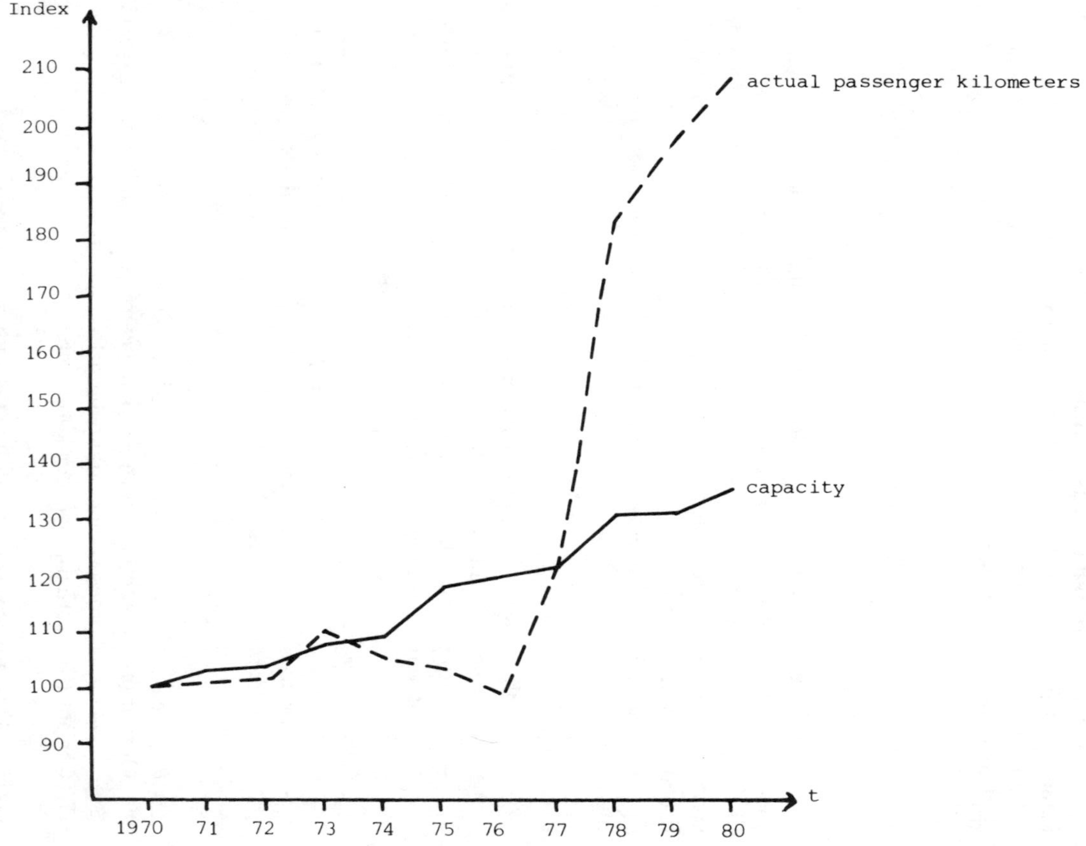

actual passenger kilometers

capacity

— frequency of vehicles
— density of the network (total length of network/service area)

All these indicators are cardinally scaled. They can therefore be weighed and combined in a one-dimensional value.

Significant changes over time could not be detected, therefore, a quality adjustment can be neglected in the community under consideration.

In the following, we want to show in some figures the development of output and of total and single factor productivities for public mass transit in a German community. For each indicator the base is 1970 = 100.

4.2. Single Factor Productivity

In figure 2, we show the development of potential passenger kilometers (capacity) and actual passenger kilometers.

While capacity has steadily increased during the research period, actual passenger kilometers remained nearly constant to 1976, but they have more than doubled to 1980. The reasons for this different behavior have not yet been investigated.

Figure 3 indicates the average utilisation of capacity. Lack of data prevents us from computing the relation of peak load to capacity.

Up to 1976 there are no significant changes: if anything, capacity utilization has a little declined, but after 1976 the ratio increased.

Figure 4 illustrates the development of the input factors capital and labor. For labor both total staff and operating staff are shown.

Capital inputs have increased continuously. In the first half of the research period both labor inputs have declined about 12%, in the second half they have increased to a slightly higher level than in 1970.

Figure 5 illustrates the development of capital, total staff and operating staff productivity. Potential passenger kilometers serve as the output indicator.

Capital productivity declines, while both measures of labor productivity increase during the whole period. There has been clearly a substitution of capital for labor. It is therefore important to analyse total factor productivity to answer the crucial questions of whether there has been an increase in productivity.

4.3. Total Productivity

For aggregating input factors, the measures must be made comparable. For this purpose the quantitative labor input is multiplied by per capita

Figure 3: *Average utilisation of capacity*

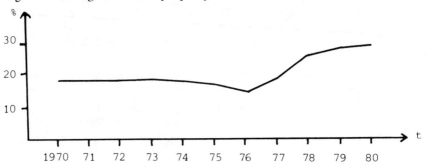

Figure 4: *Development of inputs (1970 = 100)*

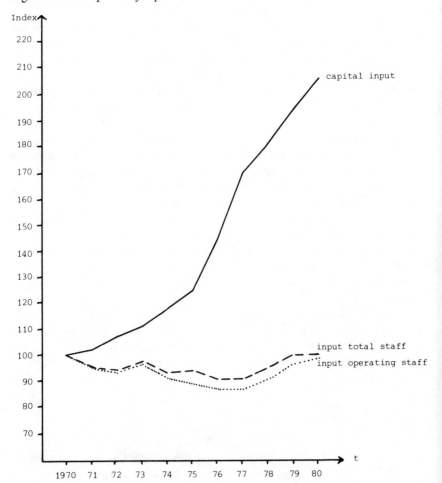

Figure 5: *Development of single factor productivities (1970 = 100)*
Index

261

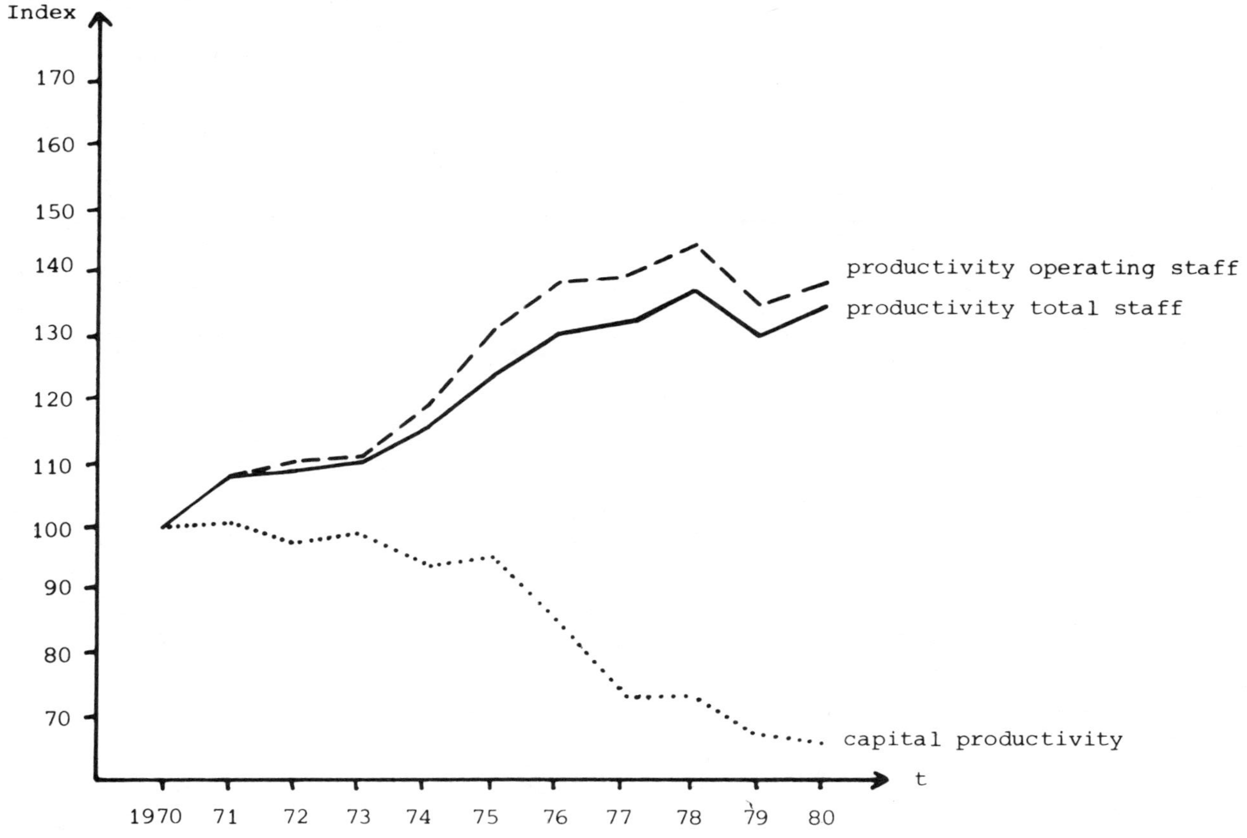

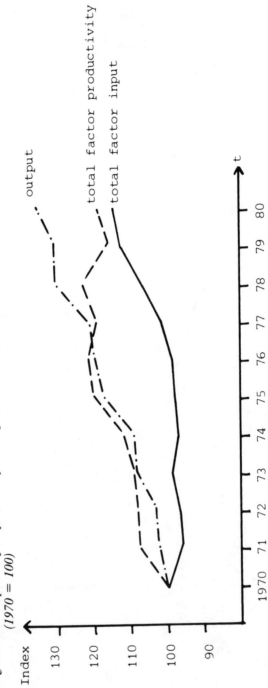

Figure 6: *Development of output, total factor input, and total factor productivity (1970 = 100)*

262

personnel expenditures in 1970. For aggregating labor and capital, the capital stock has to be transformed into a capital flow by multiplying the former term with the average depreciation rate for the years 1970 to 1980. The output is measured by the capacity indicator. Figure 6 shows the development of output, total factor input, and total factor productivity.

Over the whole period, output as well as total factor inputs increase. Total factor productivity shows a positive trend despite the declines in 1977 and 1979.

5. Conclusions

Our first results show that labor and total factor productivity in the local government sector has increased which is, in our opinion, already important enough to point out. The assumption that there has been no or only a very small productivity increase in the public sector seems to be a mere hypothesis. It has been refuted for at least some local public services. We expect to expand our research to additional local public services and cities. Moreover, it will be necessary to discover the determinants of productivity changes and the possibilities for improvement. For this, cross section analyses have to be carried out and more municipalities must be included into the study.

References

Bahl, R.W., Burkhead, J., Productivity and the Measurement of Public Output, in: Levine, C. (ed.), Managing Human Resources, A Challenge to Urban Governments, Urban Affairs Annual Reviews, Vol. 13, Beverly Hills—London: Sage Publications 1977, pp. 253–261.

Balk, W.L., Technological Trends in Productivity Measurement, in: Public Personnel Management, March/April 1975, pp. 128–133.

Baumol, W., Macroeconomics of Unbalanced Growth: The Anatomy of Urban Crisis, in: American Economic Review, Vol. 57 (1967), pp. 415–426.

Berczi, A., Improving Public Sector Management through Systematic Measurement of Operational Performance, in: Management International Review, Vol. 18 (1978), No. 2, pp. 63–76.

Brüngger, H., Orga, C., Ansätze zur Messung des Outputs des Staates, in: Schweizerische Zeitschrift für Volkswirtschaft und Statistik, 114. Jg. (1978), pp. 375–388.

Creamer, D., Measuring Capital Input for Total Factor Productivity Analysis: Comment by a Sometime Estimator, in: Review of Income and Wealth, Series 18 (1972), pp. 55–78.

Denison, E.F., The Sources of Economic Growth in the United States and the Alternatives Before Us, Supplementary Paper No. 13, New York: Committee for Economic Development 1962.

Fisk, D., Winnie, R., Output Measurement in Urban Government: Current Status and Likely Prospects, in: Social Science Quarterly, Vol. 54 (1974), pp. 725–740.

Gäfgen, G. Leistungsmessung im Gesundheitswesen—Ein Beispiel für die Ökonomie des

Dienstleistungssektors, in: Hamburger Jahrbuch für Wirtschafts- und Gesellschaftspolitik, 25. Jahr, Tübingen 1980, pp. 177–196.

Hanusch, H., Theorie des öffentlichen Gutes. Allokative und distributive Aspekte, Göttingen: Vandenhoeck & Ruprecht 1972.

Hanusch, H., Äquivalenzprinzip und kollektive Güter—Allokations-theoretische Aspekte, in: D. Pohmer (ed.), Beiträge zum Äquivalenzprinzip und zur Zweckbindung öffentlicher Einnahmen, Berlin: Duncker & Humblot 1981a, pp. 37–91.

Hanusch, H., Output Measurement of Local Government Services, Paper prepared for a Conference on "Measuring the Size and Growth of the Public Sector", Berlin 1981b.

Hanusch, H., Determinants of Public Productivity, in: R. Haveman (ed.), Public Finance and Public Employment. Proceedings of the 36th Congress of the International Institute of Public Finance. Jerusalem 1980, Detroit: Wayne State University Press 1982, pp. 275–288.

Hatry, H.P., Fisk, M., Improving Productivity and Productivity Measurement in Local Governments, Washington D.C.: The Urban Institute 1971.

Hjerppe, R.T., The Measurement of Real Output of Public Sector Services, in: Review of Income and Wealth, Series 26 (1980), pp. 237–250.

Kendrick, J.W., Productivity Trends in the United States, Princeton: Princeton University Press 1961.

Orzechowski, W.P., Labor Intensity, Productivity and the Growth of the Federal Sector, in: Public Choice, Vol. 17 (1974), pp. 123–126.

Résumé

L'état actuel des connaissances économiques ne peut répondre que de façon imparfaite à des questions aussi controversées que:

(1) Est-ce que des transferts supplémentaires de ressources du secteur privé au secteur public engendrent des gains sociaux?

(2) Y-a-t-il des différences dans le développement de la productivité entre l'économie de marché et l'économie publique et quels sont les facteurs qui déterminent la croissance ou la diminution de la productivité dans le secteur public?

Pour discuter de ces questions, la démarche de notre analyse de la productivité demande une exploration du processus de la production publique dans son ensemble qui couvre plusieurs processus de transformation depuis le niveau des intrants productifs jusqu'au niveau du bien-être social.

Tandis qu'une analyse complète de la productivité se doit considérer tous les niveaux de transformation, une étude basée sur la production comme celle que l'on présente ici devrait plus généralement prendre en compte les intrants élémentaires, l'offre des services et leur utilisation individuelle par le consommateur. Ainsi l'analyse examine le type, la quantité et la qualité des intrants et des extrants publics. On discute pour savoir s'il faut combiner les aspects qualitatifs et quantitatifs et quelles sont les relations entre capacité de production et demande effective.

On considère plusieurs mesures de productivité, productivités en terme d'un facteur (travail ou capital) aussi bien que productivité totale.

Partant de leurs modifications dans des séries statistiques temporelles et de différences dans des analyses comparatives, on tente d'extraire des facteurs explicatifs.

Les premiers tests empiriques montrent que le développement de la productivité dans le secteur étatique local révélait des tendances positives significatives pour les dix dernières années.

New Concepts for the Supply of Government Services*

Christoph Badelt

This paper aims (1) to demonstrate that alternatives to the supply of government services cannot be investigated simply within the framework defined by the literature on governmental versus market failure, and—based on this perception—(2) to analyze the possible role of the "voluntary nonprofit sector" as an alternative to the provision of goods and services by the public sector. It will be pointed out that any discussion of alternatives to existing schemes of providing services should deal with a comparative analysis of institutions rather than sectors. We will demonstrate this approach by comparing a specific kind of voluntary organization—which will be labeled "volunteer group"—with other institutional arrangements, particularly with those prevailing in the public sector.

Section I recapitulates briefly the arguments which are emphasized in the discussion of market failure versus governmental failure. The ensuing sections deal with shortcomings of this line of arguments. Section II reviews the literature on voluntary organizations, pointing out that the "third sector" can be an alternative both to the public sector and to the private for-profit sector. Section III adopts a comparative view of institutions and outlines the manner in which volunteer groups (an example of an institution in the voluntary sector) could serve as alternative providers of services which are usually conceived of as government services. Section IV discusses possible policy implications.

* I would like to thank Burton Weisbrod (University of Wisconsin-Madison) for comments on earlier drafts. In addition, a considerable number of conference participants, in particular G. Brosio, A. Peacock, and K.E. Schenk, made helpful suggestions which are gratefully acknowledged. This is a substantially shortened version of the original paper which is available from the author on request.

Public Finance and the Quest for Efficiency. Proceedings of the 38th Congress of the International Institute of Public Finance. Copenhagen, 1982, pp. 267–278. Copyright © 1984 by Wayne State University Press, Detroit, Michigan, 48202.

268   CHRISTOPH BADELT

I. Market Failure Versus Governmental Failure—A Wrong Question?

Economists often justify the existence of government services by market failures. On the other hand, in analyzing "new concepts for the supply of government services", the increasing counter-revolution, represented by the "theory of governmental failure", cannot be ignored.

Main Arguments of the Current Controversy

The main cases of private market failure have already entered the textbooks of economic theory and public finance. Though terminology varies, there is no doubt that public goods, externalities, economics of scale and imperfect markets—in particular, imperfect information—are the most important examples of why a market economy could fail to achieve an optimal allocation of resources. In addition, market failure is sometimes seen more broadly, in that "failure" is defined not only with regard to allocative efficiency, but also with respect to other socioeconomic goals, especially equity (see, e.g., Wolf, 1979: 110–112), sometimes also full employment and a target growth rate of an economy. Finally, the concept of merit goods has been used as an additional justification for governmental activities.

The rapid increase of governmental activities in Western market economies has brought growing criticism of the performance of government agencies as well. The outlines of a more complete "theory of governmental failure" are developing (see e.g. Rowley, 1978; Weisbrod, 1978: 30–41; Wolf, 1979; Peacock, 1980; Recktenwald, 1980). Again, the details of criticism differ among the authors; nevertheless, there are some elements which are common to most theories of governmental failure. Strong emphasis is placed on the inefficiencies of bureaucratic systems, which can be explained by a number of reasons, among them the objectives of individual decision makers in collectivities, inadequate information, lack of feedback between consumers and public producers of services, missing or wrong incentives, unanticipated long-term effects of governmental actions, etc. In addition, the success of governments in reaching other socio-economic goals than efficiency is challenged. Governments are, for example, accused of generating distributional inequity (e.g. Wolf, 1979:128).

Shortcomings

Why is this kind of discussion not a sufficient basis for an analysis of new concepts of governmental services? To begin with, at least a part of the literature seems to assume that market failure automatically justifies government activities, and vice versa. Thus, it is implicitly argued that the failure of one institution implies the capability of another institution to correct this failure. As far as the justification of governmental activities is concerned, this logical inconsistency can be observed in Pigouvian welfare economics as well as in the German tradition of defining the role of government within a "Social Market Economy" (see, for example, Borchardt's (1981:42) critique of Eucken's "Theory of Economic Policy"). Although the perception of this inconsistency is not new (see e.g. Demsetz's (1969) "Nirvana-Approach"), it can still be found in current criticisms of a market system, in particular in political discussions. Similar logical mistakes can also be observed in the opposite direction. A considerable part of the criticism of public bureaucracies seems to imply that governmental failures can be remedied by markets (see e.g. Geissler, 1978; Engels, 1979).

Nevertheless, there are also counterexamples in the more recent controversy over the failures of markets and governments, where it is argued that certain problems may exist both in markets and in governmental decisions (see e.g. Wolf, 1979: 123). This implies a first step toward a comparative approach. But even in this position, two crucial problems jeopardize the applicability of the theory of governmental failures to a thorough investigation of new concepts of government services.

First, even in the comparative contributions the range of discussion is usually confined to the public sector and the private (for-profit) sector. With very few exceptions (e.g. Weisbrod, 1978) the existence of a "third sector" (voluntary sector) apart from market and state is ignored.

Second, the theory of governmental failure in particular usually focuses on behavioral aspects that are not limited to the public sector. This leads to the question, whether the controversy between market failure and government failure is relevant at all. Perhaps it should be replaced by a discussion about alternative *institutions*, which may be located in the public, the private, or the "third sector".

This second objection can be illustrated by two examples.

(a) In Wolf's (1979: 112–115) approach, some of the "nonmarket failure" is ultimately explained by demand and supply characteristics which are said to be typical of the nonmarket sector.[1] To illustrate, nonmarket outputs are "usually hard to define in principle", or "evidence of output quality is elusive" (Wolf, 1979: 113). Later, these arguments are used to explain governmental failure. It is not correct to create the impression that the problems that follow from the impossibility of measuring outputs are necessarily the problems of government. If, for example, the output of education cannot be measured exactly, which may lead to "inefficiencies" in the production of educational outputs, it is not obvious why the institution which provides education is to blame for the lack of efficiency. In other words, the source of the "failure" may lie in the character of the good rather than in the institution which provides it. It remains a matter of further (empirical) investigation to find out whether governmental institutions can cope better or worse with the problems a specific good may cause than a for-profit firm or a voluntary organization.

(b) A similar bias can be noted in the critique of bureaucracy which is a fundamental element of the "theory of governmental failure". For simplicity's sake, let us assume that all the charges concerning the inefficiency of bureaucracies are justified. Why is it, then, correct to equate failures of bureaucracies with "governmental failures", given the fact that bureaucracies are also observed in the for-profit (and in the voluntary) sector? Of course, the theory of governmental failure admits the existence of bureaucracies outside the governmental sector. It would, however, point out that bureaucracies in the market sector will not suffer from the same problems as public bureaucracies, because they are subject to what Mises (1945:47) called the "incorruptible judgement of that unbribable tribunal, the account of profit and loss". In other words, the market will not allow any inefficiency to occur.

Although this argument seems to be impressive, it is not necessarily valid, because it represents a kind of reciprocal "nirvana approach". Advocates of this argument compare existing imperfect governments with ideal enterprises in ideal markets, ignoring, for example, problems of X-Inefficiency or imperfect competition which occur in reality and which may weaken the argument substantially. While it is correct to criticize the "nirvana approach" when the interventionistic bias of early critics of private market failure is being examined, it is only fair to use the same term also where this mistake is made in the opposite direction.

If these considerations are correct, the controversy between market failure and governmental failure might be of secondary interest. The discussion should rather be concentrated on a comparison of institutions which are, for example, defined by criteria like size, objective function, constraints, etc. Instead of globally evaluating the performance of "the government" or "the for-profit firm" the more relevant question would be to investigate the capability of various types of institutions to achieve aims like efficiency, equity, a certain level of provision of goods and services, etc.

The following sections will elaborate on the two shortcomings we have identified. Section II reviews the main arguments about the capability of the "voluntary sector" to provide services alternatively to the public sector. Section III examines the comparative (dis)advantages of voluntary organizations by adopting a comparative view of institutions.

II. The Voluntary Sector as Provider of Goods and Services

There is no question that goods and services are also provided outside the public and private (for-profit) sectors of an economy. This is why the voluntary sector (Weisbrod, 1975) sometimes is conceived of as a residual set of institutions which are not included in the other sectors of an economy. However, in this paper we will *define* the voluntary sector as the set of nongovernmental institutions providing goods and services for other than profit reasons. According to this definition the voluntary sector is itself heterogeneous and, therefore, contains a variety of institutional forms, differing widely in size, constitution, aims, and other characteristics. Note that the voluntary sector cannot be confined to large nonprofit organizations, since our definition also applies to more informal networks of service provision, on which we will concentrate in Section III.

One important measure of the *quantitative importance* of the voluntary sector is the number of volunteers.[2] According to a recent survey in the USA (Gallup Organization, 1981), 52% of the American adults volunteered time between March 1980 and March 1981, forming a non-negligible hidden labor force. In addition, British surveys related the volunteer labor force in specific industries to the respective labor force in the public sector. To give an example, 270,000 hypothetical full-time volunteers were active in the provision of personal social services, while there were only about 200,000 public employees in these fields (Hadley and Hatch, 1982: 93–98; Wolfenden Committee, 1978: 35–36).

While there is a considerable literature in sociology, political science, and social work, on the performance of voluntary organizations, this cannot be said for economics. Apart from a few examples (e.g. Weisbrod, 1977; Hansmann, 1980; Badelt, 1980; White, 1981) the role of voluntary organizations as providers of goods and services does not receive much attention from economists. Nevertheless, the existing literature has already worked out a number of *arguments in favor of voluntary organizations*. In particular, it has been pointed out that voluntary organizations

— can supplement, or even substitute for, the services provided by public sector institutions;
— can identify needs that are not recognized by the other sectors, in particular not by the government;
— can improve the quality of statutory services, for example in the field of social services (which is particularly pointed out for voluntary organizations employing volunteer labor);
— may be more "trustworthy"—an important argument in a world of asymmetric information;
— can make use of the benefits of "non-professionalism".

Not all of the claimed advantages of voluntary sector institutions are empirically well documented, although for nearly all of them some support can be provided by systematic case studies or at least by "anecdotal evidence". However, if these arguments are to be used to investigate possible alternatives to the public provision of services, two main lines of criticism have to be overcome.

(1) Even if all the mentioned advantages are valid, there are some problems voluntary organizations encounter, which may eventually jeopardize their benefits (see Badelt, 1983). To begin with, many voluntary organizations are exposed to bureaucratization and professionalization. Furthermore, problems of independence, control—and—last but not least—the question of the "efficiency" of voluntary organizations have to be touched on.

(2) The second line of criticism is more fundamental. The discussion about success and failure of the voluntary sector stresses the advantages and (sometimes) disadvantages of voluntary sector institutions without comparing them sufficiently with the institutions in the other sectors. Even when comparative elements are introduced (see, e.g. Hadley and Hatch, 1981), it is often not clear why certain advantages should be ascribed exclusively to institutions in the voluntary sector, in particular if they are explained by arguments like decentralization, participatory rather than bureaucratic decision making structures, etc.

All this is to say that the capability of voluntary sector institutions has also to be investigated within a framework which defines institutions by a set of criteria which may or may not be observed across the borders of the private for-profit, the public, and the voluntary sectors in an economy. Only with this approach can it become clear whether advantages which are claimed for voluntary organizations are to be explained by characteristics which can be found necessarily and exclusively in the voluntary sector. Whether or not this is the case is not only of theoretical interest but also important for policy implications.

III. "Volunteer Groups" as an Alternative to Governmental or Private (For-Profit) Service Provision: A Comparative View of Institutions

In what follows we will analyze specific institutions in the voluntary sector and discuss their role as a possible alternative to the governmental provision of services. We will have to define a *set* of discriminating characteristics of the institution we investigate independently of whether *single* characteristics can also be observed in the for-profit or in the public sector. The discussion cannot be confined to a comparison of volunteer groups and public sector institutions but has to take all sectors of an economy into account.

Definition of Volunteer Groups

Volunteer groups are a well-known phenomenon in the political and social life of many countries. According to the recent Gallup survey 23% of American adults donated volunteer labor outside the big voluntary organizations. A popular example of volunteer groups are the "self-help groups" active mostly in health and other personal social services. The number of these groups in the USA is close to 500,000 (Gartner and Riessman, 1977: 6).

Volunteer groups are not active in the health services alone. They also run neighborhood day care programs, organize recreation programs, provide clean-up of streets and parks, form babysitting cooperatives or private transport schemes. Typically, volunteer groups operate on a decentralized level; sometimes they are also called "grass-root groups" or "neighborhood organizations".

In the abstract, volunteer groups can be seen as one specific type of institution within the voluntary sector. They are defined by the following discriminating attributes:[3]

(a) the groups rely to a large extent on volunteer labor, in particular as far as direct service provision is concerned;
(b) the main purpose of their activity consists in meeting directly the demand for certain goods and services;
(c) every individual group member can directly participate either in production decisions or in consumption decisions, whichever the group is focused on;
(d) the number of group members is small.

In this paper we will investigate only volunteer groups which provide collective goods (pure public or mixed goods) to meet the demand of group members.[4] An example is a neighborhood organization which provides a playground for the children living in the area.

Having defined the type of institution on which we focus we can now proceed to investigate whether volunteer groups may have comparative advantages over other institutional arrangements. For simplicity's sake we will concentrate on only two possible aspects: benefits to consumers and transaction costs.[5]

Benefit Aspects

A neighborhood playground may be provided by a public sector institution (e.g. the local community), by a for-profit firm, or by a volunteer group formed by the residents of the neighborhood. The benefit aspect of our problem, then, has to answer the following question: Is there a difference in the utility local residents gain from the playground if (a) the playground is built and operated by themselves (i.e. provision by a volunteer group), or (b) if the playground is provided by the local government or by a for-profit firm?

A possible answer to this question can be provided by the theory of discriminatory clubs (Tollison, 1972; DeSerpa, 1977) which points out that the utility of a volunteer group member is not only affected by the consumption of the club good (i.e., the playground) but also by the group member's characteristics an individual member has to "consume".

That is to say that members of a volunteer group may gain benefits not only from the good they produce, but, for example, also from the social integration group members "consume" when joining the group, from the participation in the decision on how the playground will look, or from the mere fact of doing volunteer work for a reasonable aim. Of course, some of these elements are also valid if a public sector institution provides the playground. "Consumption of members' characteristics", which can be positively interpreted as social integration, also takes place during the mere consumption process. A certain degree of participation in production decisions can in principle also be granted by a public sector institution. However, it is plausible to assume that in a volunteer group the degree of interaction, the degree of participation, and the engagement in volunteer work will be higher, because in this case the volunteers are assumed to plan, build, and operate the playground themselves.[6]

Transaction Costs Aspect

Transaction costs considerations have to be made separately for three elementary classes; for (a) search and information costs, (b) bargaining and decision costs, (c) policing and enforcement costs.

(a) In volunteer groups, potential group members have to search for other individuals with similar preferences. This search may be facilitated by the fact that these groups are often formed by individuals living in a similar situation (e.g. living in a neighborhood). This may indicate comparative advantages in information costs for neighborhood organizations over any other form of institutional arrangement.

On the other hand, for-profit firms and public sector institutions usually have developed more sophisticated techniques to identify potential consumers and to discover their tastes, not to mention that governments often do not have to search actively for consumers of their services. Thus, it is hard to generalize about which institutional form would minimize search and information costs.

(b) Bargaining and decision costs depend on the decision-making structures. Since volunteer groups are defined in part by their participatory decision-making structure they are likely to have higher bargaining and decision costs than hierarchical institutions. Hence, if we assume that decisions both in public-sector institutions and in for-profit firms are made hierarchically, this would imply a comparative disadvantage for volunteer groups.

(c) Policing and enforcement costs usually are assumed to be high when individuals have strong incentives to "shirk" in the production process or to "free-ride" in the consumption process (see e.g. Alchian and Demsetz, 1972). There are some characteristics of volunteer groups that apparently reduce the incentives to shirk, in particular the small group size, the direct demand orientation, and the ownership arrangement. Hence, we could expect comparative cost advantages for volunteer groups, particularly over public sector provision.[7]

IV Summary and Policy Implications

The analysis of volunteer groups as an example of an institution in the voluntary sector indicated that the provision of services in this institutional form may lead to benefits apart from those stemming from the service itself. Some of these benefits may be reduced or even offset by transaction costs, although at least in some categories of transaction costs, savings can be expected so that the final balance of the transaction cost considerations is ambiguous.

Since a predominant advantage of volunteer groups turns out to be a matter of participants' utility, a final evaluation of their performance depends on assumptions (or knowledge) of prevailing tastes. Wherever the non-material aspects that we mentioned are appreciated, volunteer groups can be an important alternative to the governmental provision of services. One area where this alternative is most promising is that of personal social services, such as care for the elderly or handicapped, youth work, nursery schools, and other forms of education.

Note, however, that virtually all the comparative advantages of volunteer groups can be traced back to single characteristics none of which is exclusively found in the voluntary sector. This refers both to the benefits and the transaction cost sides of our analysis. For example, volunteer work can be done outside the voluntary sector, for-profit firms can be small, direct influence on producer decisions can occur outside the voluntary sector, etc. One important insight following from a comparative view of institutions is that the *combination* of certain single characteristics (*each* of which is *not exclusive* to the voluntary sector) can be responsible for the advantages that the voluntary sector has over the public sector under specific circumstances.

If this theoretical perception is correct, some fundamental policy implications can be drawn.

(1) The discussion of new concepts for the supply of "government" services should be extended to the voluntary sector; it must not be confined to the debate of for-profit versus public sector institutions.

(2) When considering the voluntary sector, we should also consider informal volunteer work (done in "volunteer groups") as an alternative to the public provision of government services. Volunteer groups can play a particular role in the provision of social services where indicators of a changing structure of needs can be observed. To the extent that non-material needs are not taken care of sufficiently by the "Welfare States", volunteer groups could gain importance.

(3) Many failures of the governmental provision of services, and much success of volunteer groups can ultimately be explained by characteristics that are neither necessary nor exclusive to the public and the voluntary sectors. Hence, for example, "failures" of the government sector that result from bureaucratization, centralization, or professionalization need not necessarily be healed by a devolution of tasks to another sector. At least in part, improvements can also be made by altering the institutional structure within the public sector.

(4) Insofar as the advantages we have identified for volunteer groups are true, new concepts of the supply of government services can also be based on decentralization, participation of clients, employment of volunteers, and initiating and fostering self-help activities.

(5) Finally, strategies of reorganizing the governmental provision of services and devolving tasks to voluntary organizations are not mutually exclusive. There are a number of examples (in particular in social work, but also in other service areas) which demonstrate that a close cooperation between voluntary sector institutions and (mostly local) governments can lead to a cumulation of benefits.

Notes

1. In a footnote Wolf admits that the "nonmarket sector" should not be confined to governments. But in the ensuing discussion he mostly deals with governments (1979:112)

2. For an overview of other indicators in Germany, Britain, and the USA, see Badelt, 1980: 241–252.

3. It is important to note that volunteer groups are characterized by all four of these attributes since some of them also apply to other economic institutions.

4. For a more extensive discussion from a club theoretical standpoint, including also groups providing private goods and working for the demand of non-members, see Badelt 1982.

5. Among other ceteris paribus conditions we assume that production costs do not vary among the investigated institutional alternatives.

6. Note that these considerations imply comparative advantages of volunteer groups only if the total utility gained from components other than the consumption of the club good is positive.

7. The situation is not that clear if we recall that for-profit firms may be small as well and, therefore, can enjoy the same advantages. On the other hand, the possibilities for public sector institutions to reduce shirking are much more limited.

References

Alchian, A. and Demsetz, H., (1972), "Production, Information Costs, and Economic Organizations", *American Economic Review*, 62 (5), pp. 777–795.

Badelt, C., (1980), *Sozioökonomie der Selbstorganisation*, Frankfurt, New York: Campus

Badelt, C., (1982), *A Public Choice View of Volunteer Groups*, Midwest Economic Association, Chicago, Ill., (mimeographed).

Badelt, C., (1983), "Community Action: Success, Failure, Prospects", in: *Public Transfers and Some Private Alternatives during the Recession*, ed. by Pfaff, M., Berlin: Duncker & Humblot, pp. 242–257.

Borchardt, K., (1981), "Die Konzeption der Sozialen Marktwirtschaft in heutiger Sicht", in: *Zukunftsprobleme der Sozialen Marktwirtschaft*, ed. by Issing, O., Berlin: Duncker & Humblot, pp. 35–55.

Demsetz, H., (1969), "Information and Efficiency: Another Viewpoint", *Journal of Law and Economics*, XII, 1, pp. 1–22.

DeSerpa, A., (1977), "A Theory of Discriminatory Clubs", *Scottish Journal of Political Economy*, 24 (1), pp. 33–41.

Engels, W., (1979), "Die Rolle des Staates in der Wirtschaftsordnung", in: *Staat und Wirtschaft*, ed. by Weizsäcker, C.C., Berlin: Duncker & Humblot, pp. 45–63.

Gallup Organization, (1981), *Americans Volunteer 1981*, Princeton.

Gartner, A., and Riessman, F., (1977), *Self Help in the Human Services*, San Francisco: Jossey-Bass.

Geissler, H. (ed.), (1978), *Verwaltete Bürger-Gesellschaft in Fesseln*, Frankfurt: Ullstein.

Hadley, R., and Hatch, S., (1981), *Social Welfare and the Failure of the State*, London: George Allen & Unwin.

Hansmann, H.B. (1980), "The Role of Nonprofit Enterprise", *Yale Law Journal*, 89, 5, pp. 835–901.

Mises, L.V., (1945), *Bureaucracy*, Glasgow et al.

Peacock, A., (1980), "On the Anatomy of Collective Failure", *Public Finance*, 35, pp. 33–43.

Recktenwald, H.C., (1980), "Zur Theorie des Staatsversagens", *Public Finance*, 35, pp. 72–78.

Rowley, D., (1978), "Market 'Failure' and 'Government Failure' ", in: *Economics of Politics*, ed. by Institute of Economic Affairs, London.

Tollison, R., (1972), "Consumption Sharing and Non-Exclusion Rules", *Economica*, 39 (155), pp. 276–291.

Weisbrod, B., (1975), "Toward a Theory of the Voluntary Nonprofit Sector in a Three Sector Economy", in: *Altruism, Morality and Economic Theory*, ed. Phelps, E., New York: Russell Sage Foundation, pp. 171–195.

Weisbrod, B., (1977), *The Voluntary Nonprofit Sector, An Economic Analysis*, Lexington, Toronto: Lexington Books.

Weisbrod, B., (1978), "Problems of Enhancing the Public Interest: Toward a Model of Governmental Failures", *Public Interest Law*, ed. by Weisbrod, B., Handler, J., Komesar, N., Berkely, et al.: University of California Press, pp. 30–41.
White, M., (ed.), (1981), *Nonprofit Firms in a Three Sector Economy*, Washington: The Urban Institute.
Wolfenden Committee, (1978), *The Future of Voluntary Organisations*, London: Croom Helm.
Wolf, C., (1979), "A Theory of Nonmarket Failure: Framework for Implementation Analysis", *Journal of Law and Economics*, XXII, 1, pp. 107–139.

Résumé

Cet article montre que l'on ne peut étudier des alternatives à l'offre de services publics de façon satisfaisante à l'intérieur du cadre fourni par les publications disponibles sur les faiblesses respectives des productions privées et publiques. Les limites à ce type d'arguments sont de deux sortes: (1) On ignore souvent l'existence d'un "troisième secteur" qui s'ajoute aux productions privées et publiques, (2) bien des échecs, en particulier ceux imputés au secteur public, apparaissent en réalité comme des faiblesses de caractère institutionnel que l'on peut observer dans tous les "secteurs" de l'économie.

C'est pourquoi, cet article adopte une vue comparative des institutions avec par exemple une analyse des "groupes volontaires associatifs" comparés à la fourniture de services par des institutions du secteur public ou par des entreprises du secteur privé. On souligne que la fourniture de services par des groupes de volontaires associatifs peut conduire à des "bénéficies" pour les membres du groupe distincts de ceux issus du service lui-même. Bien que ces bénéfices puissent se trouver réduits par des coûts de transaction, les groupes de volontaires associatifs peuvent se révéler comme une alternative favorable aux institutions étatiques, en particulier dans le domaine des services sociaux de caractère personnel. En dehors du soutien apporté à des groupes de volontaires associatifs, de nouveaux concepts sur l'offre de services étatiques devraient être basés sur la décentralisation, la participation des clients et l'emploi de bénévoles.

PROBLEMS IN THE FINANCING OF PUBLIC GOODS AND SERVICES

Some Simple Analytics of the Laffer Curve*

James M. Buchanan and Dwight R. Lee

I. Introduction

Our purpose in this paper is to present some analytics of the tax rate-tax revenue relationship (summarized in the rubric "Laffer curve") embodied in the supply-side economics that dominates macropolicy discussion in the early 1980's. In order to simplify our exposition, we ignore the serious complexities involved in conceptualizing a single rate-revenue relationship in a tax system that includes many separate bases for taxation, along with many rates, including progressive (nonuniform) rates on important revenue-producing sources. What is *the* rate of tax in the United States? We simply assume that this question may be satisfactorily answered.

In order to bring the analysis to the simplest possible level, we shall assume that there is only one well-defined base for taxation, and, further, that there is a single uniform rate of tax imposed on the generation or use of this base. Throughout the analysis, we shall utilize a demand theory construction. We consider the behavior of the potential taxpayer as a potential "demander" of the tax base. This construction is self-evident if we think of the base as an ordinary commodity, say, beer. It is less familiar, but nonetheless fully appropriate, to think of the taxpayer as demanding units of income when he supplies resource inputs. With an income base for tax, it is, of course, possible to examine the taxpayer's behavior in supplying labor or other resources to produce the base. Most of the analysis of taxpayer response has taken this supply-side approach.[1] The two constructions are reciprocals of each other; they describe the same behavior and yield identical results.[2] Our demand-side approach, however, will enable us to draw on

*We are indebted to our colleagues, Geoffrey Brennan, Nicolaus Tideman, Robert Tollison and Gordon Tullock for helpful suggestions on an earlier draft.

Public Finance and the Quest for Efficiency. Proceedings of the 38th Congress of the International Institute of Public Finance. Copenhagen, 1982, pp. 281–295. Copyright © 1984 by Wayne State University Press, Detroit, Michigan, 48202.

familiar propositions in orthodox demand theory that tend more readily to be overlooked when the supply-side approach is taken.

The objective is to examine the possible relationships between tax rates and tax revenues. There will be a direct and proportionate relationship when the base is invariant to changes in rate. In terms of familiar Marshallian coordinates, the direct and proportional rate-revenue relationship exists when the elasticity of the demand for base is zero throughout the range of possible tax rates.[3]

In all nonextreme conditions, we should expected that the "demand curve" for the base would be downsloping throughout the range of possible tax rates, thereby generating nonlinear relationships between rates and revenues. For simplicity in exposition, we shall utilize linear relationships between price (including tax) and quantities demanded. The so-called Laffer curve becomes fully analoguous to the price-total revenue curve and can be derived from the most elementary of price-theory diagrams, the downsloping demand curve, along with a pretax price assumed constant over quantities. Commencing with a zero tax rate, and then allowing this rate to increase incrementally, we can trace out a range over which total tax revenue increases, reaches a maximum, and then a range over which total tax revenue decreases, until, at some rate, revenue falls to zero.

Why should a rationally-motivated political decision process generate a result that is located on the range where the relationship between rates and revenues is inverse? Regardless of how we might model the objective function of the politician, whether as a revenue-maximizing Leviathan or as a genuine public servant who devotes all revenues to the financing of public goods, there would never seem a logical reason for increasing rates beyond maximum revenue limits.

Careful application of the tools of demand theory will help us explain why political decision-makers may find themselves located on the negatively-sloping portion of a Laffer curve, and we shall also show why they may face a dilemma of sorts in extricating themselves from such a position. The familiar and long-recognized distinction in the value of the elasticity coefficients between short-run and long-run periods of adjustment is central to the analysis. Although the relevance of the time period has been recognized in popular discussion of the Laffer relationship, no attempt has been made, at least to our knowledge, to demonstrate the behavioral implications. Governments tend to operate with short-time horizons, much shorter than the period required for individuals to adjust patterns of behavior to changes in tax rates, and for institutions facilitating such adjustments to become fully operative. Consistently rational short-run maximizing behavior in setting tax rates may well generate an ultimate political equilibrium that is on the downsloping side of a long-run Laffer curve.

II. A Model of Government

If we are to explain how a position on the downsloping part of a tax rate-tax revenue curve is attained, we need some model of governmental or political decision-making. In our initial model, developed in Part III, we specify only that government always seeks to obtain additional tax revenues. Note that this specification of the government's objective need not imply that politicians and/or bureaucrats expect to secure private-personal gains from increased tax revenues. They may or may not do so. In the latter case, they may seek additional tax monies solely for the purpose of financing additional supplies of public schools and services or transfers. In Part IV, we modify this strict revenue-maximization objective for government by allowing politicians to incorporate taxes as "bads" in their own utility functions.

A second characteristic of our model for governmental behavior involves the time horizon relevant for tax decisions. Governments, as such, may have very long lives, but political decision makers, as such, tend to have relatively short lives, in either democratic or nondemocratic regimes; at best they possess extremely attenuated property rights in the income streams generated by their policies. Politicians will not, therefore, maximize the present value of total tax collections through time in a calculus that incorporates any "reasonable" rate of discount (perhaps approximating the private rate of return on capital in the economy). Political decision-takers will tend to maximize the present value of tax revenues in accordance with a very high discount rate, reflecting the length of their own political horizons in some probabilistic sense.[4]

Our analysis will enable us to describe a position of "political equilibrium" in the tax rate-tax revenue relationship, given the model of government postulated. In order to present the argument in terms of a plausible scenario, we impose a zero tax rate-tax revenue starting position, from which we allow government to increase the tax rate (the variable directly under its own control) up to but not beyond a defined amount in any single period. The politician's time horizon is assumed not to extend beyond a single period, with this period being shorter than the time necessary for full taxpayer adjustment to a tax rate change. The analysis develops the dynamic adjustment process through which the tax rate approaches the equilibrium through a sequence of discrete steps. In the text it will be assumed that the adjustment process converges to the equilibrium and that the equilibrium is stable.[5]

Figure 1a

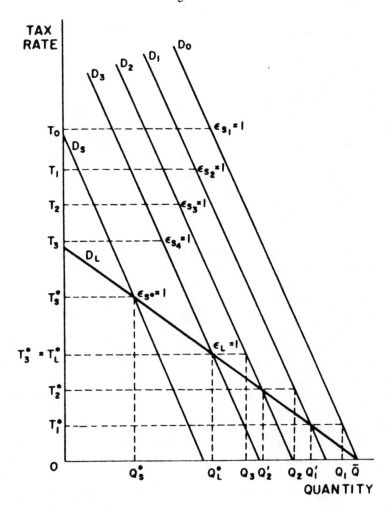

III. Geometrical Analysis[6]

We introduce a highly simplified geometrical construction depicted in Figures 1(a) and 1(b). The abscissa is drawn at the level of the pretax price, which, for a money-income base is simply $1. In Figure 1(a), the heavily-drawn curve D_L is defined as the truncated long-run demand curve for the base with "long-run" being specifically defined to be a period sufficiently long to allow for full behavioral adjustment to each rate of tax on base, and for the attainment of the full institutional equilibrium subsequent to such behavioral adjustment. In his work on the Swedish tax structure, Charles

Figure 1b

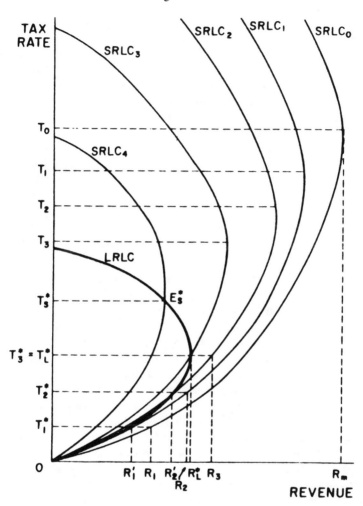

Stuart has suggested that the calendar length of such a period, for Sweden at any rate, may be up to ten years (see Charles Stuart (1981)). The short-run, long-run distinction clearly seems more important in the tax-adjustment context than it does when we are considering demands for ordinary commodities, in part at least, because governments tend to levy taxes on those bases that are relatively immune to easy adjustment by potential taxpayers (as indeed they are advised to do so by orthodox normative tax theorists).

The same relationship as that shown in the demand curve (heavily drawn) in Figure 1(a) is traced out in Figure 1(b) by the heavily-drawn

curve, with total tax revenues being measured along the abscissa. The two
end points of this curve correspond to the origin (at zero tax rate) and to the
intercept of the demand curve in Figure 1(a), at which point the tax rate
becomes sufficiently high so that, given time for complete adjustment, no
base is demanded at all. If prices are converted to percentage rates, this
intercept value may lie close to one-hundred percent, although it may
readily fall below or even go above this level.

As noted above, we start the adjustment process from the zero rate-
zero revenue position. In this fiscal setting, the quantity of base demanded
is $\overline{Q}$, all of which seems potentially taxable. The goverment desires to
impose taxes on this constitutionally-allowable base, but we stipulate that
the increase from zero must proceed in discrete steps, each amounting to a
maximum of $\overline{T}$. The rate could, of course, be increased by less than this
amount.

In the initial setting (zero rate-zero revenue), the government with a
short time horizon will not face the long-run demand curve described by
D_L in Figure 1(a) or the long-run Laffer curve depicted as LRLC in Figure
1(b). It will, instead, face a rate-revenue relationship appropriate to its own
planning horizon (discount rate), and to the particular historical equilibrium
established at the zero rate-revenue starting position. For simplicity in exposition here, we shall incorporate only one short-run relationship in the
analysis. We shall work with a two-period adjustment; the first-period adjustment is given by the politically relevant short-run relationship; the full
adjustment is assumed to take place at the beginning of the second period.

The short-run relationship, as viewed from the zero rate-revenue equilibrium and as defined by the behavioral adjustments from this equilibrium,
is shown as D_0 in Figure 1(a), with the accompanying short-run Laffer
curve drawn as $SRLC_0$ in Figure 1(b). Note that this is the *only* one of the
several short-run Laffer curves depicted (as well as any others that might be
drawn) in Figure 1(b) that lies wholly outside the long-run Laffer curve
throughout its range.

By imposing the tax rate, $T_1^* = \overline{T}$, the government takes maximum
allowable advantage of the fact that short-run elasticity is less than 1 and
expects to secure total revenues measured by $T_1^*Q_1$ (Figure 1(a)) or R_1
(Figure 1(b)). We assume that these expectations are fulfilled in the first
period; taxpayers respond behaviorally by reducing their demands along D_0
in immediate response to the tax increase. As the time sequence extends to
the second period, however, they make more extensive adjustments. By our
assumption, full adjustment is reached at the beginning of the second period. If the tax rate remained at T_1^*, total revenue in this period would be
$T_1^*Q_1' = R_1'$ which is below $T_1^*Q_1 = R_1$.

We can now examine the period two rate increase, from T_1^* to T_2^*,
which is motivated by the same consideration of short-run inelasticity that

motivated the first increase and is followed by the same pattern of adjustments. And, similarly, for a third rate increase from T_2^* to T_3^*. Note, that when full taxpayer adjustment to any rate is attained, the government, in contemplating a further increase, will again face a short-run demand curve, analogous to that faced at the initial position, but drawn through the long-run demand curve. These short-run demand curves are shown at D_1, D_2, and D_3 in Figure 1(a), with corresponding short-run Laffer curves in Figure 1(b). Note that, as drawn, the relevant short-run Laffer curve, for any rate above zero, will lie inside the unique long-run Laffer curve at all rates below the rate to which behavioral adjustments have been made, and above the long-run Laffer curve at all rates above the rate to which behavioral adjustments have been made. These relationships between the short-run and the long-run Laffer curves emerge directly from the postulated increase in response to rate-changes through time.

Once the tax rate indicated by T_3^* (or also as T_i^*) is reached, a tension between short-run and long-run considerations comes into play. Up to this point, a revenue-seeking government will tend to increase rates by the allowable limits, regardless of its planning horizon. Assume that full behavioral and institutional adjustment to this rate, T_3^*, has been achieved. Government will still face the short-run demand curve D_3, corresponding to the short-run Laffer curve $SRLC_3$ in figure 1(b). Tax revenues can be increased in the period immediately following by pushing the rate beyond T_3^*. If the planning horizon of governmental decision-makers is at all limited, rational behavior suggests increasing the rate above that which maximizes total revenue in the full-adjustment context. The rate of tax will be increased beyond the level at which the tax or revenue elasticity of the fully adjusted demand for the base is unitary.

The tension between short-run and long-run maximizing considerations will continue to exist for rate increases between T_3^* and T_s^*, the point at which the relevant short-run Laffer curve indicates maximum revenue limits at its intersection with the long-run Laffer curve. At this point, labeled E_s^* in figure 1(b), governmental decision-makers have no incentive to increase tax rates, even if their planning horizon extends only to one period. Beyond this point, there would seem to be no rational maximizing behavior that could be adduced to explain rate increases. We label this position to be one of "political equilibrium." Those who determine levels of tax rates have no incentive to increase rates further, and persons who pay taxes have fully adjusted to the rates in being.

The position of political equilibrium is on the downsloping part of the long-run Laffer curve, but it is also at the maximizing point on the relevant short-run Laffer curve. There is no political incentive for rates to be *reduced* or *increased*. A reduction in rates of tax would reduce revenues in the short-run while increasing revenues over the long run. This model allows us to explain quite easily the positions of the two adversaries in the current economic policy debates relevant to the effects of tax decreases. Those who argue that government would never operate on the downsloping part of "the Laffer curve", and who adduce evidence to suggest that revenues would indeed fall with cuts in rates—these persons are implicitly adopting a short-run perspective. On the other hand, those who argue that reduction in rates will stimulate supply-side responses sufficient to generate increases in total tax revenues are implicitly adopting the long-term perspective and, in addition, they are implicitly assuming that initial rates in the critical range between T_L^* and T_s^*. By its very nature, any supply-side response is a long-term response. Given the incentive structure faced by modern politicians, on the other hand, rational behavior in governmental decision processes may be oriented toward short-term objectives. The supply siders and the revenue-maximizing politicians may both be correct.

IV. Taxes as "Bads" in Governmental Objective Functions[7]

Perhaps the most familiar objection that may be raised to the analysis of Part III above is one directed at the model of government. Political decision-makers need not always seek to maximize tax revenues, although the spending of such revenues must be acknowledged to be positively-valued arguments in the relevant objective functions. Such politicians, it may be claimed, may also recognize that taxes impose costs on members of the polity, and these costs may cause decision-makers to incorporate taxes as "bads," directly into the objective function.[8] In this modified model, under any given constraints, governments will not seek to achieve the revenue maximum, but will maximize utility by holding rates of tax below that level which will generate highest total revenues.

This change in the basic model for governmental behavior can still find the equilibrium tax rate above that which maximizes revenue on the long-run Laffer curve and will leave completely unaffected the long-run—short-run political dilemma that is central to this paper. Figure 2 depicts this new setting. The additional set or family of curves in Figure 2 are indifference contours derived from government's postulated objective function, and reflect the internal trade-off ratios within this function between tax rates and revenues. The analogous set of indifference contours (not drawn) in figure 1(b) would be a set of vertical lines.

Through a process of adjustment analogous to that traced out in some detail in the construction of Part III, the tax rate will be sequentially increased to T_1^*, T_2^* and T_3^*, leading to the political equilibrium $\hat{E}$ in figure 2, where indifference curve I_4 is tangent to the relevant short-run Laffer

Figure 2

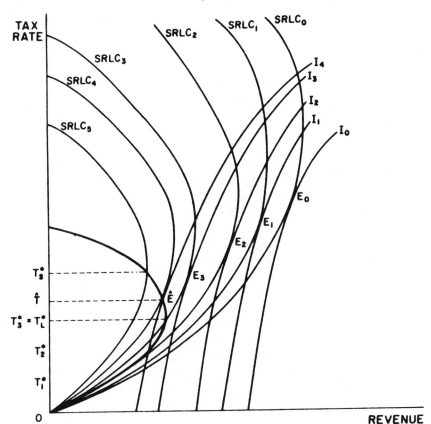

curve, $SRLC_4$, at the point of intersection with the unique long-run Laffer curve. As the construction indicates, this equilibrium may be located similarly to that in figure 1(b), along the downsloping portion of the long-run rate-revenue relationship. The only difference between the construction in figure 1(b) and Figure 2 is that, in the latter, the strict "Laffer range" between the point of possible political equilibrium and long-run revenue maximization is somewhat narrower than it is in the former. With the inclusion of taxes as bads directly in the objective function, the conceptualized "ideal point" would not, in general, be that of long-run revenue maximization. But regardless of the location of the political equilibrium, it will always generate less long-run utility, if not revenue, than the equilibrium based on the tangency between the long-run Laffer curve and an indifference curve. This follows directly from the fact that the long-run Laffer curve is nowhere tangent to a short-run Laffer curve. So going from the political equilibrium to the long-run utility maximizing "equilibrium" would necessitate a temporary reduction in utility; a reduction that is not politically acceptable given the political time horizon.

V. Expectations and a Tax Constitution

Up to this point, we have assumed that taxpayers are passive responders both in short-run and long-run settings to tax rates that are exogenously imposed on them by government. Taxpayers do not attempt to make predictions about how government will operate in future periods and adjust their own behavior in anticipation of government's tax actions. It will be useful to see how the introduction of expectations will modify the analysis.

Suppose that each taxpayer models government as a short-run revenue maximizer. How will this set of expectations modify taxpayer behavior? The answer seems straightforward. Taxpayers will predict convergence to the political equilibrium: assuming the requirements for convergence hold. They will predict the tax rate appropriate to such an equilibrium, T_s^*, and will immediately adjust their behavior to that rate, with the response to rates that differ from T_s^* given by the short-run demand curve D_s, even though enough time has elapsed to allow full adjustment. Instead of a convergence process that may require a long sequence of periods, the system moves quickly to the position of equilibrium which may be, as the construction in Parts III and IV indicate, located on the downsloping part of the long-run Laffer curve.

At this equilibrium, governmental decision-makers and the group of taxpayers, as a set, find themselves in a dilemma of sorts. Both would be better off if rates could be reduced and revenues increased. The taxpayers would have reduced excess burdens of taxation, and government would have more revenues to spend. Escape from this dilemma may be difficult, however. Under expectational equilibrium, taxpayers would not respond completely to a reduction in tax rate because they would predict that the pattern of convergence would merely be repeated, at some net cost to them. Government cannot increase tax revenues by moving down the long-run Laffer curve by cutting tax rates until and unless it can convince taxpayers that the rate reduction will be permanent. But taxpayers will not predict permanence in rate levels so long as they postulate the short run maximizing behavior on the part of government. The dilemma here is in many respects analogous to that between the monopolist of money issue and those persons who hold cash or money balances.[9]

In this expectational setting, there are "mutual gains from trade" to be exploited by governmental decision-makers and members of the taxpaying public. These gains can be secured only if government can somehow bind itself through some form of constitutional commitment to lower tax rates below political equilibrium levels (in the short-run model), and to hold rates at these lower levels. The recognition of the dilemma here offers a logical basis for the Reagan administration's insistence on multi-year versus single-year tax reductions, although it would have seemed more efficient to introduce a genuine constitutional commitment incorporating tax-rate or revenue ceilings.

VI. Revenue Generation and Length of Adjustment

Regardless of the validity or the invalidity of the claim that pre-1981 tax rates in the United States were sufficiently high to be located along the downsloping part of the long-run Laffer curve, there must always be a predictable relationship between revenue generation and the time period allowed for adjustment. As noted earlier, at all rates of tax above that for which behavioral adjustments have been completed, more revenues will be generated in the short-run than in the long-run, whether revenues will increase in both cases, whether short-run revenues will increase and long-run revenues decrease, or whether both short-run and long-run revenues will decrease. Conversely, for all rates of tax below that for which behavioral adjustments have been completed, more revenues will be generated in the long run than in the short run, whether revenues will decrease in both cases, whether short-run revenues will decrease and long-run revenues increase, or whether both short-run and long-run revenues will increase.

As we noted earlier, the supply side approach to tax policy that calls for rate reduction is necessarily long-term in perspective if the revenue objective remains important to government. In a relative sense, rate cuts always reduce revenue potential in the short-term, provided that we assume governments have not erroneously wandered off into the downsloping range of even the relevant short-run Laffer curve. The critical question is perhaps "how long is the long-run"? To the extent that we allow for all behavioral and institutional adjustments, the period may be long indeed, perhaps decades. In this case, relatively low rates of tax on base may be required to generate maximum revenues on a sustaining basis. Our use of a two-period model may be overly constraining, in the sense that some intermediate period becomes most relevant for policy considerations.

The importance of the period allowed for adjustment may be summarized in the simple geometry of Figure 3. Assume that the previously-existing tax rate, T, had been fully adjusted to individual behavior patterns.

Figure 3

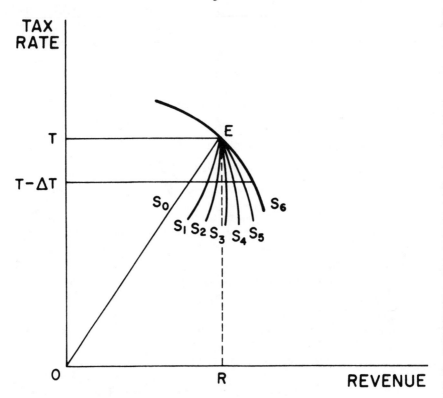

This rate generates a total revenue of R. Assume, now, that this rate is reduced to $T-\Delta T$. In the instantaneous short-run, taxpayers can make no behavioral adjustments to the rate cut. Revenues will maximally fall in direct proportion to the cut in rate. The instantaneous rate-revenue relationship will be shown by the straight line drawn through the previous equilibrium position to the origin. As some period is allowed for behavioral and institutional adjustment, revenues will increase, as shown by the other members of the family of rate-revenue curves (Laffer curves) drawn in Figure 3. For example, if the period is specified to be a half-year, the appropriate response might be that shown along S_1; if one-year, along S_2; if two years, along S_3, etc. The S_6 curve may, for example, only depict the response for an extremely long period, say twenty years.

Once the necessary existence of the whole family of taxpayer response curves to any tax cut is recognized, the difficulties involved in any meaningful prediction as to the direction of effect on total revenues should be obvious. The person who suggests that tax cuts must reduce total revenues is asserting that, no matter how long the period for adjustment, the positive relationship will not emerge. In terms of Figure 2, S_6, the long-run Laffer curve, will lie to the left of the vertical line from E. The person who suggests that tax cuts must increase total revenues cannot be referring to the instantaneous relationship; he must be allowing for a sufficiently long adjustment period. He is asserting that, given such a period, S_6 will slope outward from E.[10]

VII. Conclusions

In our title, we promised "some simple analytics" of the rate-revenue relationship. A coherent analytical framework is a necessary and preliminary requirement for meaningful empirical inquiry. Was the United States fiscal setting in 1981 described by a location analogues to either E_s^* or $\hat{E}$ in Figures 1(b) and 2 respectively? Many economists have disputed this underlying presupposition of the Reagan tax policy thrust. As our analysis should make clear, however, empirical evidence, on the other side, may be difficult to adduce.

Much of the existing empirical work on input elasticity is inconclusive in judging the long-run impact of a tax cut on government revenues. For example, in an effort to address this impact, Fullerton makes use of thirteen empirical investigations of labor supply elasticities (see Don Fullerton (1982)). Of the thirteen studies all were cross sectional except two, leaving inconclusive any means of assessment concerning the completeness of the adjustments. All thirteen studies generated estimates based on uncompensated responses to changes in the return to labor. This is reasonable when, as in the cases in most of the studies, the response of particular subsets of the labor force is being investigated. However, when the response of the aggregate labor force is to be estimated, as it necessarily must be when considering the results of a general tax change, the more reasonable assumption is that at least some compensation takes place. What workers gain (lose) from a tax reduction (increase) will be offset to some degree by a reduction (increase) in benefits from governmental services.[11] To ignore this offset is to understate labor supply elasticity when leisure is a normal good.

It is also true that input supply elasticities will generally be smaller than the output elasticities that are of ultimate concern. The positive effect of an increase in the return to labor may not come primarily from the motivation it provides to work more hours, but from the motivation to work more productively. Labor supply elasticities fail to pick up the output effects that flow from human capital increases induced by an additional return to labor. This output effect is further enhanced through the symbiotic interaction that exists between a growing stock of human and physical capital.

The definitive empirical work remains to be done. Not only does such work call for the estimation of long-run input elasticities (where long-run may extend to a decade or more), but also for the inclusion of these elasticities into a model that recognizes the dynamic interactions and feedbacks that exist between inputs in the generation of measured output. The simple analytics we have presented in this paper offer the challenges to those who would either refute or corroborate the claims of the Lafferites.

Notes

1. Specifically related to the Laffer-curve relationship, see Don Fullerton (1982). By contrast, in their recent book, Geoffrey Brennan and James Buchanan (1980a) utilize a demand-theory construction throughout their analysis.
2. For a discussion of the reciprocal nature of the demand and supply relationship, see James M. Buchanan (1971).
3. In our construction, we apply the rate of tax directly to the base, with base defined in units of ultimate consumable "goods", whether a single commodity like "beer" or the bundle of commodities and services that the taxpayer might purchase with post-tax income units. This procedure allows us to convert the percentage rate of tax readily into an increment to pretax price, and to utilize orthodox demand analysis straightforwardly. Note, however, that this construction differs from the standard definition of a tax "rate" under income taxation, which involves applying a percentage rate to the generation of base, *inclusive* of tax. In terms of a simple numerical example, if the pretax price of a unit of consumable goods is $1, a 10 percent tax, in our construction, becomes equivalent to a 10 cent addition to pretax price. In order to generate $1's worth of final consummable goods, the taxpayer would have to generate $1.10's worth of income including tax, to which a "rate" of 9.99 pecent would be applied to secure the 10 cents. Hence, a rate of 10 percent, in our construction, is equivalent to the lower rate of 9.99 percent on the inclusive base.

The distinction here is important with respect to the dimension in which responses to changes in rate are measured. Invariance in the generation of base, net of tax, in our construction, necessarily implies a positive relationship between rate and generation of base, defined gross of tax. More generally, any range of adjustment over which the demand for base, net of tax, is inelastic by definition implies a positive relationship between rate and base, gross of tax.
4. The importance of the time horizon for the political decision-maker emerges because of the nonmarketability of what might be called "political capital," both for the decision-makers themselves and for their electoral constituents. The political decision-maker who acts so as to maximize the present value of the whole fiscal system cannot, at the end of his projected tenure in office, "sell off" a share of the accumulated value that his actions have generated, as could his counter-part in a proprietary enterprise. And his very tenure in office may depend critically on meeting demands of constituents who similarly could not "sell off" enhanced capital values of a "sound finance regime" generated by their own rationally planned long-term "investments".
5. The specific parametric conditions necessary for convergence have been analysed and this analysis is available from the authors.
6. This section is based on the model developed in Buchanan and Lee (1982a).
7. This section is based on the model developed in Buchanan and Lee (1982b).
8. The aversion to tax increases may be mild when these increases can be enacted in ways that appear independent of political action: e.g., inflationary induced bracket creep.

9. For an extended discussion of the money-monopolist's dilemma, see Geoffrey Brennan and James Buchanan (1980a), Chapter 6. For an elementary treatment, see Geoffrey Brennan and James Buchanan (1980b).

10. Note that the family of curves in Figure 3 is derived from the fan-like array of demand curves drawn from a *single* price-quantity equilibrium, the array that is found in the textbooks to illustrate varying elasticities of demand with time period. See, as an example, Milton Friedman (1976), p. 16.

11. For a theoretical investigation of this consideration, see Assar Lindbeck (1980).

References

Brennan, Geoffrey and James Buchanan (1980a) *The Power To Tax*, Cambridge: Cambridge University Press.

Brennan, Geoffrey and James Buchanan (1980b), *Monopoly in Money and Inflation*, London: Institiute of Economic Affairs.

Buchanan, James M. (1971), "The Backbending Supply Curve of Labor: An Example of Doctrinal Retrogression?," *History of Political Economy*, 3, pp. 383–390.

Buchanan, James M. and Dwight R. Lee (1982a), "Politics, Time and the Laffer Curve," *Journal of Political Economy*, 90, pp. 816–819.

Buchanan, James M. and Dwight R. Lee (1982b) "Tax Rates and Tax Revenues in Political Equilibrium: Some Simple Analytics", *Economic Inquiry*, 20, pp. 344–534.

Friedman, Milton (1976), *Price Theory*, Chicago: Aldine.

Fullerton, Don (1982), "On the Possibility of an Inverse Relationship Between Tax Rates and Government Revenues," *Journal of Public Economics*, 19, pp. 3–22.

Lindbeck, Assar (1980), "Tax Effects Versus Budget Effects on Labor Supply," Seminar Paper No. 148, Institute for International Economic Studies, Stockholm, Sweden.

Stuart, Charles (1981), "Swedish Tax Rates, Labor Supply and Tax Revenues," *Journal of Political Economy*, 89, pp. 1020–1038.

Résumé

Pourquoi un processus politique rationnel augmenterait-il toujours le taux d'imposition au-dessus du niveau qui maximise les recettes fiscales? Sans tenir compte de la fonction objective du politicien ou du citoyen qui l'élit, on ne trouverait pas d'explication à l'augmentation des taux d'imposition au delà des limites du revenu maximum. Le but de cet article est de l'expliquer. Il est reconnu qu'un gouvernement dont l'objectif est la maximisation des recettes, augmentera, selon des hypothèses vraisemblables, le taux d'imposition jusqu'à cette zone où une relation inverse existe entre taux d'imposition et recettes fiscales. Un équilibre politique caractérisé par cette relation inverse est aussi possible quand le taux d'imposition joue une rôle négatif sur la fonction d'utilité du gouvernement. On montre aussi qu'une fois que cet équilibre politique inverse impôt-recette est atteint, un climat d'anticipation peut avoir été créé dont il est difficile de sortir.

La Relation Entre Recettes Fiscales et Taux D'imposition Dans Le Temps: Quelques Résultats Analytiques Simples*

Guy Gilbert

I. Introduction

Le présent article se propose d'examiner dans quelle mesure l'analyse statique comparative de l'évolution du niveau des recettes fiscales en fonction des taux d'imposition, donc de l'existence et des caractéristiques éventuelles d'une "courbe de Laffer", peut être étendue à une perspective temporelle.

Dans son principe, l'analyse de Laffer ne fait référence qu'à des phénomènes instantanés. Aux décalages de perception près, la relation qui décrit l'évolution des recettes fiscales en fonction du taux d'imposition n'est définie que pour un instant donné. Elle indique notamment si le taux actuel n'est pas trop élevé, c'est-à-dire s'il ne serait pas possible d'obtenir le même montant de ressources fiscales à partir d'un taux plus faible. Or, le niveau actuel d'un taux d'imposition peut être apprécié dans deux perspectives qui sont souvent confondues ou du moins insuffisamment séparées. Dans une perspective synchronique, le niveau du taux d'imposition sera envisagé du point de vue de ses conséquences *instantanées* sur le rendement de l'impôt, sur l'efficacité ou l'équité. Dans une perspective temporelle, le taux d'imposition sera apprécié par rapport à ses valeurs passées ou futures; l'on parlera alors de pays sous-imposés ou sur-imposés par référence à l'évolution passée ou par comparaison avec des pays plus ou moins "avancés" en termes de croissance économique. L'abondante littérature sur l'évolution historique des prélèvements obligatoires fourmille d'exemples de la combinaison entre ces deux perspectives (voir par exemple Musgrave (1978)). Bien que la littérature sur la

*L'auteur tient à remercier J.P. Decaestecker et P.H. Derycke pour leurs commentaires sur une version précédente de l'article, ainsi qu'un lecteur anonyme.

Public Finance and the Quest for Efficiency. Proceedings of the 38th Congress of the International Institute of Public Finance. Copenhagen, 1982, pp. 297–312. Copyright © 1984 by Wayne State University Press, Detroit, Michigan, 48202.

courbe de Laffer ne se soit pas orientée principalement dans cette direction, quelques développements concernent cet aspect temporel (voir Fullerton (1981), p. 1 et p. 22, Greffe (1980), p. 95, Wanniski (1978), p. 13–16). La distinction entre "prohibitive range" et "normal range" à un moment donné, pour un impôt donné et une structure fiscale déterminée permet-elle de fournir des indications sur l'évolution souhaitable du niveau de la fiscalité dans le temps? Telle ne semble pas être l'opinion de Hemming et Kay (1980); ". . . it is only possible to define a Laffer curve at one particular point in time for a country with a particular tax system and a particular distribution of skills within a country, such a curve cannot be identified by analysis of the development of tax revenues over time" (p. 84). Rien n'interdit pourtant d'examiner l'évolution temporelle de la courbe de Laffer en fonction de paramètres qui la déterminent et de la rapprocher de l'évolution à long terme de tout ou partie des recettes fiscales. Cet article s'interroge précisément sur les conditions d'existence et les caractéristiques d'une "courbe de Laffer de longue période" et sur sa pertinence comme cadre d'analyse de l'évolution de longue période des recettes obligatoires. Pour ce faire, on partira d'un modèle simple de courte période développé ensuite sous deux aspects différents dans la longue période.

Un premier point étudie les conditions d'existence et la forme d'une courbe de Laffer de courte période au moyen de deux modèles d'équilibre partiel, l'un relatif à la production agrégée, l'autre au marché du travail (II). La relation entre recettes fiscales et taux moyen d'imposition y est schématisée à l'extrême: seul le côté production est examiné; les effets-revenu sont ignorés, tout comme les dépenses publiques. Enfin, un seul impôt est envisagé, dont la base est alternativement la production et les revenus du travail; la prise en considération d'une pluralité de pré-lèvements fiscaux est donc exclue (voir sur ce point les modèles de Canto, Joines et Laffer (1978) et Fullerton, Shoven, Whalley (1978).

Un second point envisage le passage des courbes de Laffer de la courte période à la longue période, c'est-à-dire celle où les paramètres des marchés des biens taxables et les taux d'imposition sont susceptibles de varier (III). Deux aspects différents sont alors étudiés. L'influence de l'évolution tempo-relle de l'élasticité de l'offre de travail donne lieu à un premier modèle (III.1) où l'offre *et* la demande de travail varient conjointement dans le temps. Ce premier modèle s'interprète aisément en termes d'évolution tem-porelle des préférences individuelles en faveur des biens à financement fiscal. Un autre modèle est présenté ensuite qui s'appuie sur un fondement alternatif de la courbe de Laffer: la substitution entre travail taxé et travail non taxé (III.2). Ce second modèle reprend le modèle d'équilibre du marché du travail étendu à deux secteurs et met en jeu des anticipations imparfaites du taux d'imposition. Une dynamique chaotique de l'évolution des recettes fiscales est ainsi mise à jour.

Un dernier point (IV) revient sur les perspectives d'application empirique des modèles exposés.

II. Les conditions d'existence et la forme d'une courbe de Laffer de courte période: le rôle de l'élasticité de la base d'imposition.

Ainsi qu'il est bien connu la "courbe de Laffer" est l'expression graphique de la relation qui définit le montant des recettes fiscales en fonction du taux d'imposition et de la base imposable.

Si T est le montant des recettes fiscales, θ le taux moyen d'imposition et $Q(\theta)$ la base taxable, elleh même fonction continûment dérivable du taux d'imposition, la relation considérée s'écrit:

$$T = \theta \cdot Q(\theta) \qquad (1)$$

En courte période, on suppose $\delta Q(\theta)/\delta\theta$ négatif. Une augmentation du taux d'imposition diminue la base taxable. La forme de la "courbe de Laffer" dépend donc uniquement de la spécification de la fonction $Q(\theta)$, donc de l'élasticité ϵ de la base imposable au taux de l'impôt comme il apparaît ci-après

$$\frac{\delta T}{\delta\theta} = Q(\theta) + \theta \cdot Q'(\theta) \qquad (2)$$

$$= (1 + \epsilon)\, Q(\theta)$$

avec $\epsilon = \theta Q'(\theta)/Q(\theta)$ et ϵ^*, l'élasticité qui maximise le montant des recettes fiscales collecté, est égale à -1. Si $\delta Q/\delta\theta < 0$ et si ϵ est inférieure à -1, l'augmentation du produit de l'impôt consécutif à l'augmentation du taux d'imposition est plus que compensée par la réduction de la base, soit $Q(\theta) < -\theta \cdot Q'(\theta)$, donc $\theta > - Q(\theta)/Q'(\theta)$ et la recette globale diminue: la courbe de Laffer est décroissante. Lorsqu'il existe, un point particulier de la courbe de Laffer attire néanmoins l'attention; la valeur θ^* du taux d'imposition qui maximise les recettes fiscales. Ce point existe-t-il en toute généralité? Si l'on admet que si $\theta = 100\%$, $T = 0$ (désincitation totale à produire une base d'imposition positive) et que si $\theta = 0$, $T = 0$, alors le théorème de Rolle permet d'affirmer qu'il existe au moins un extremum de la fonction $Q(\theta)$ pour des valeurs de θ comprises entre 0 et 1. L'existence, sinon l'unicité, du maximum étant établie, il reste à préciser la forme exacte de la courbe de Laffer. L'on peut déjà préciser l'évolution de la valeur de θ^* en fonction de $Q(\theta)$;

$$\theta^* = - \frac{Q(\theta)}{Q'(\theta)} \qquad (3)$$

Pour ce faire, nous partirons de l'exemple développé par Fullerton (1981).

Considérons un marché du travail en équilibre (partiel) instantané relatif à un bien homogène (L) et taxé au taux θ. La demande de travail (L_d) est fonction du taux de salaire avant impôt, w, et l'offre de travail, L_0, du taux de salaire après impôt $(1-\theta)$w; on supposera les élasticités des fonctions d'offre et de demande constantes soit

$$L_d = Aw^\alpha, \ \alpha < 0 \tag{4}$$

$$L_0 = B[w(1-\theta)]^\beta, \ \beta > 0 \tag{5}$$

Le taux de salaire d'équilibre est donc:

$$w = \left[\frac{B}{A} (1 - \theta)^\beta\right]^{\frac{1}{\alpha-\beta}} \tag{6}$$

En combinant (4), (5) et (6), il vient la "relation de Laffer":

$$\log T = \log \theta + \log A \tag{7}$$
$$+ \frac{1+\alpha}{\alpha-\beta} \log \frac{B}{A} + \frac{1+\alpha}{\alpha-\beta} \beta \log (1 - \theta),$$

où $T = \theta$wL est le montant des recettes fiscales. Si l'on pose pour simplifier $A = B = 1$,

$$\log T = \log \theta + \frac{1+\alpha}{\alpha-\beta} \beta \log (1 - \theta) \tag{7'}$$

Le graphique 1 donne un exemple de courbes de Laffer correspondant à $\alpha = -2$ et β variant de 1 à 5. Le taux d'imposition θ^* qui maximise les recettes fiscales est égal à:

$$\theta^* = \frac{\alpha - \beta}{\alpha(1 + \beta)} \tag{8}$$

Quelle est l'évolution du taux d'imposition θ^* lorsque α et β varient?

$$\frac{\delta\theta^*}{\delta\alpha} = \frac{1}{\alpha^2} \frac{\beta}{1 + \beta} \tag{9}$$

$$\frac{\delta^2\theta^*}{\delta\alpha^2} = \frac{-2}{\alpha^2} \frac{\beta}{1 + \beta} \tag{9'}$$

$$\frac{\delta\theta^*}{\delta\beta} = \frac{-1}{(1 + \beta)^2} \frac{1 + \alpha}{\alpha} \tag{10}$$

$$\frac{\delta^2\theta^*}{\delta\beta^2} = \frac{2}{(1 + \beta)^3} \frac{1 + \alpha}{\alpha} \tag{10'}$$

Les expressions (9), (9'), (10) et (10') montrent que si la demande de travail est fortement élastique ($\alpha < -1$), et l'offre peu élastique, les taux

Graphique 1: *Courbes de Laffer pour une élasticité donnée de la demande de travail*
(α = −2)

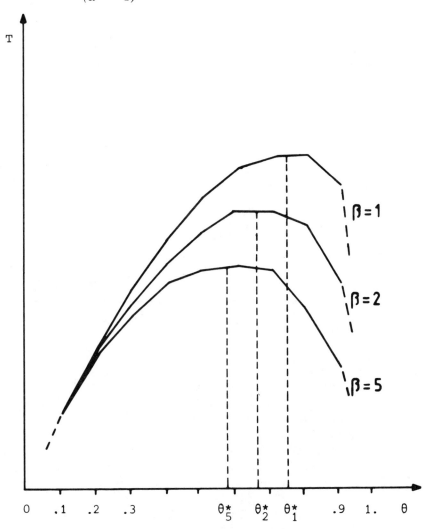

d'imposition optimaux θ* sont d'autant plus faibles que l'élasticité de l'offre de travail est faible et que celle de la demande de travail est forte. Si la demande de travail est faiblement élastique (−1 <α< 0), alors θ* tend vers +∞ quand α→0.

Ainsi, conformément à l'intuition, le taux optimal approche de 100% quand β tend vers 0 et il tend vers 0 quand β devient infiniment grand. *Pour que ε* soit compris entre 0 et 1 et pour l'exemple choisi, il convient toutefois*

Graphique 2: *Relation entre le taux d'imposition et l'élasticité/impôt de la base taxée*

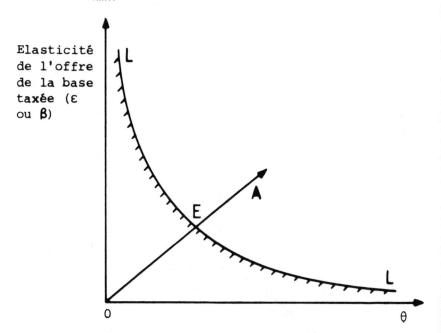

que α soit inférieur à −1. En effet, θ* >0 implique que α(1+β) < 0 soit α < 0; pour que θ*<1, il faut α(1+β)< α−β soit α <−1. Cette seconde condition est relativement forte et demanderait à être soigneusement étudiée dans le cas d'une application empirique. Il existe donc une relation entre θ et β dont la forme précise dépend de celle de Q(θ), mais qui peut prendre, en particulier, l'allure de la courbe du graphique 2. En effet, on vérifie aisément que $\epsilon' = \delta\epsilon/\delta\theta < 0$ pour tout θ apppartenant au voisinage de θ* ce qui assure bien que les recettes fiscales sont décroissantes au voisinage de l'optimum θ* du taux de pression fiscale.

L'on peut alors tirer de (7′) et de (8) la valeur maximale des recettes fiscales T* pour toutes valeurs de θ*

$$\log T(\theta^*) = \log \frac{\alpha - \beta}{\alpha(1 + \beta)} + \frac{1 + \alpha}{\alpha - \beta}\,\beta\,\log \frac{\beta(1 + \alpha)}{\alpha(1 + \beta)} \qquad (11)$$

Cette expression constitue en quelque sorte l'équation d'une courbe de Laffer avec adaptation optimale des autorités fiscales, celles-ci ayant comme objectif permanent la maximisation absolue des recettes fiscales lorsque α et β varient.

Graphique 3: *Lieu des courbes de Laffer dans l'espace* β, θ, T.

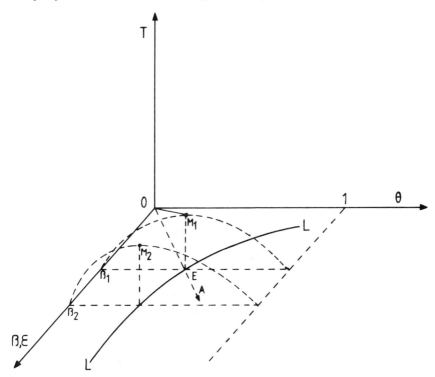

La courbe ci-après peut être interprétée comme le lieu des maxima des courbes de Laffer correspondant chacune à une valeur déterminée de l'élasticité-impôt de la base d'imposition, et peut se représenter sur un diagramme à 3 dimensions θ, T et ε de la façon suivante (Graphique 3).

Le point E est la projection sur le plan βOθ du maximum de recettes fiscales Mβ₁ obtenu pour une élasticité β₁. Par extension, la courbe LL est le lieu des maxima des courbes de Laffer correspondant à des valeurs déterminées de ε projetées sur le plan 0εθ. Si l'on qualifie, à la suite de Laffer, de "normaux" les taux moyens d'imposition compris entre 0 et θ, la portion hachurée du graphique 2 correspond à l'espace de ces taux d'imposition "normaux".

Il ressort de tout ceci que le débat autour de l'existence et de la forme de la courbe de Laffer se résume à des hypothèses divergentes sur l'élasticité de la base d'imposition: une courbe décroissante ("prohibitive range") implique une élasticité inférieure à − 1 et/ou des taux d'imposition élevés. Une courbe croissante ("normal range") suppose une élasticité supérieure à − 1 et/ou des taux d'imposition faibles.

III. Deux modèles simples de courbes de Laffer dynamiques

En dépit de leur extrême simplicité, les modèles présentés au paragraphe précédent constituent un point de départ commode pour l'étude dynamique de la courbe de Laffer. Dans un premier modèle, les élasticités de l'offre *et* de la demande de travail seront supposées varier dans le temps en fonction des préférences des agents, ce qui permettra de revenir sur la désutilité de l'effort comme fondement de la courbe de Laffer. Dans un second modèle, nous supposerons que la dynamique des recettes fiscales dépend entre autres éléments du partage entre travail taxé et travail non taxé et nous recalculerons les courbes de Laffer correspondant à ces modèles.

1. Recettes fiscales et évolutions temporelles des élasticités de l'offre et de la demande de travail.

L'on supposera que α et β ne prennent plus de valeurs fixes mais sont respectivement des fonctions du temps:

$$\alpha = X(t), \text{ avec } \alpha < -1 \tag{12}$$

$$\beta = Y(t), \text{ avec } \beta > 0. \tag{13}$$

L'on supposera en outre que X'_t, la dérivée de X_t par rapport à t, est soit positive, soit négative: le cas (H1) où X'_t est positive peut correspondre à la situation où la redistribution de fonds publics en faveur des entreprises s'accroissant au cours du temps, celles-ci sont encouragées à demander plus de travail; par contre, le cas (H2) où $X'_t > 0$ suppose que la fiscalité sur le revenu est supportée en définitive par les entreprises, ce qui se traduit par une baisse des profits et une hausse tendancielle des coûts donc une réduction de la demande du travail.

Par ailleurs, $Y'_t = \partial Y(t)/\partial t$ peut être supposé négatif (H1), si l'on considère que l'impôt réduit le niveau d'utilité de l'individu et qu'en conséquence, ce dernier doit fournir un effort plus intense pour compenser la diminution de son revenu disponible; ou bien que l'individu représentatif apprécie de moins en moins les biens publics financés par l'impôt par rapport aux biens non financés de cette façon. Y'_t pourra être supposé positif au cas inverse (H2) de préférence croissante pour le financement fiscal des biens publics notamment.

En combinant (12), (13), et (7'), il vient:

Tableau 1

	X't	
Y't	positif (H1)	négatif (H2)
Positif (H1)	Indéterminé en général	$\dfrac{\partial \log T_t}{\partial t} > 0$
Négatif (H2)	$\dfrac{\partial \log T_t}{\partial t} < 0$	Indéterminé en général

Signe de l'expression (15)

Soit
$$T_t = [\theta(1 - \theta)]^{\dfrac{1 + X_t}{X_t - Y_t} Y_t} \tag{14}$$

$$\frac{\delta \log T_t}{\delta t} = \frac{X_t Y_t'(1 + X_t) - X_t' Y_t(1 + Y_t)}{(X_t - Y_t)^2} \log (1 - \theta) \tag{15}$$

Le signe de l'expression (15) n'est clairement déterminé que dans deux cas comme il apparaît au tableau 1.

La courbe des recettes fiscales de longue période obtenue de la sorte est donc susceptible d'être ou décroissante si l'élasticité de la demande de travail est négative et l'élasticité de l'offre positive, ou croissante si les signes des deux élasticités sont inversés. En tout état de cause, l'analyse de longue période confirme en partie les conditions posées sur α et β au paragraphe précédent. Les recettes fiscales ne seront durablement croissantes ou décroissantes que si une élasticité positive de l'offre de travail rencontre un comportement inverse de la demande et vice versa. Hormis ces cas simples, ce sont les valeurs des élasticités qui détermineront le signe de l'évolution des recettes fiscales.

L'on remarquera que l'expression (14) ne fournit pas le lieu des recettes fiscales maximales dans le temps. Elle décrit simplement le lieu de recettes fiscales correspondant à des équilibres successifs sur le marché du travail. La courbe $T(t, \theta^*)$ qui relie les maxima d'imposition instantanés serait de la forme:

$$T(t, \theta^*) = \frac{X_t - Y_t}{X_t (1 + Y_t)} \left\{ \frac{Y_t(1 + X_t)}{X_t (1 + Y_t)}^{\dfrac{1 + X_t}{X_t - Y_t} Y_t} \right\} \tag{16}$$

ce qui permet de dériver la relation entre t et θ^*. Il apparaît donc là encore possible d'obtenir l'expression d'une courbe de Laffer de longue période au moyen d'hypothèses simples sur le signe et la valeur des élasticités d'offre et de demande du bien taxé. La variation temporelle de ces élasticités semble naturellement découler d'hypothèses sur les préférences des agents taxés: les préférences des offreurs et des demandeurs devant évoluer de manière continûment divergente pour que l'on puisse être assuré du signe de l'évolution de longue période des recettes publiques. Ces premiers modèles ne garantissent pas que la courbe de Laffer de longue période passe par un maximum à une date finie pour des valeurs de θ comprises entre 0 et 1.

Un autre aspect de l'évolution tendancielle de la courbe de Laffer peut être exploré grâce à l'aptitude du modèle sous-jacent à représenter l'arbitrage entre travail taxé et travail non taxé. Un second modèle illustrera cette propriété.

2. *L'évolution du partage travail taxé/travail non taxé et le niveau des recettes fiscales.*

Il est maintenant bien connu qu'une courbe de Laffer présentant un maximum de recettes fiscales pour des taux compris entre 0 et 1 peut être obtenue à partir de modèles fondés sur des fonctions d'utilité où l'utilité marginale du revenu est supposée positive et celle de l'effort (taxé) négative. Ces conditions sont nécessaires mais pas suffisantes, car même dans ce cas, la spécification exacte des fonctions d'utilité conduit à des effets de revenu et de substitution très différents en importance relative. Si ces deux effets se compensent exactement, la base d'imposition sera indépendante du taux d'imposition et la courbe de Laffer sera toujours croissante: si l'effet revenu, dont le signe est souvent indéterminé, est positif et supérieur à l'effet de substitution, la courbe de recettes sera toujours croissante: dans le cas contraire (effet revenu négatif), la courbe sera toujours décroissante comme dans le cas où l'effet revenu est positif, mais inférieur à l'effet de substitution (voir d'Autume (1981), Hemming et Kay (1980)).[1]

Un autre fondement à la courbe de Laffer peut être présenté à partir d'une économie à deux secteurs. On supposera que l'offre totale de travail en t se partage entre le travail taxé (LT_t) et le travail non taxé ($\overline{LT}_t$):

$$L_{0,t} = LT_t + \overline{LT}_t = LT_t (1+\gamma_t) \qquad (17)$$

$$\gamma_t = \gamma\hat{\theta}_t \qquad \hat{\theta}_t = \tau\theta_{t-1} \qquad (18)$$

L'on suppose en outre que la propension à offrir du travail non taxé est une fonction γ du taux d'imposition perçu par l'agent, elle-même fonction du taux de la période antérieure et à partir duquel il va répartir son offre de travail. Par souci de simplicité, les fonctions γ et τ seront assimilées ici à des scalaires. Si l'illusion fiscale[2] est nulle, $\hat{\theta}_t = \theta_t$; mais si l'illusion est non nulle, quel qu'en soit le sens, les anticipations des agents seront incorrectes et les autorités fiscales pourront tirer parti de cet état de choses puisque l'on suppose que leur information est parfaite[3]. Une double dynamique caractérise donc ce modèle. Une première dynamique correspond à l'évolution des taux d'imposition effectifs θ_t dans le temps; une seconde, dépendante de la première découle de l'illusion fiscale et des erreurs d'anticipation des agents.

L'on supposera en outre que les salaires avant impôts sont supérieurs dans le secteur taxé WT à ce qu'ils sont dans le secteur non taxé $\overline{WT}$, et que les demandeurs de travail sont indifférents à l'utilisation de travail taxé ou non taxé.

L'équilibre des deux marchés du travail stipule que:

$$L_{d,t} = L_{o,t} = L_t^* = LT_t(1 + \gamma_t)$$

D'où
$$LT_t = \frac{L_t^*}{1 + \gamma_t} \qquad \text{soit}$$

$$\gamma_t = \phi \cdot \frac{\overline{WT}}{WT(1 - \hat{\theta}_t)} \qquad (19)$$

$$Lt_t = \frac{L_t^*}{1 + \phi \cdot \dfrac{\overline{WT}}{WT(1 - \hat{\theta}_t)}} \qquad (20)$$

Puisque $T_t = \theta_t \cdot WT_t \cdot LT_t$ et puisque le salaire et les quantités de travail total restent inchangés par rapport au modèle initial (équation (6)), il vient par combinaison de (6) et de (20).

$$\log T_t = \log A + \log \theta_t + \frac{\alpha + 2}{\alpha - \beta} \log\left[\frac{B}{A}(1 - \theta_t)^\beta\right]$$
$$+ \log(1 - \hat{\theta}_t) - \log[\phi\,\overline{WT} + (1 - \hat{\theta}_t)WT] \qquad (21)$$

L'expression (21) constitue une autre forme de courbe de Laffer, dont l'évolution par rapport à θ est complexe. Le signe en est positif si l'on maintient les conditions de signe sur α, β, θ, et que l'on pose $\phi(WT) > 0$. On retrouve naturellement l'influence négative du taux de salaire "au noir" sur le rendement des impôts.

Au cas où les agents anticipent parfaitement ($\theta_{t-1} = \theta^*_{t-1}$, $\hat{\theta}_t = \theta_t$, $\forall t$), et où α et β sont constants, le modèle conduit à une évolution optimale de T (maximale). Mais si les agents anticipent avec erreur et si l'on part d'une situation où $\theta_t \neq \theta_t^*$, ceci produira deux effets:

(i) les autorités fiscales réviseront leur calcul en t+1,

(ii) si l'optimum fiscal est atteint en (t−1), soit $\theta_{t-1} = \theta^*_{t-1}$ et que les anticipations des agents ne sont pas statiques ($\hat{\theta}_t \neq \hat{\theta}_{t-1}$), le processus décrit par la courbe de Laffer est susceptible de se produire. Le taux d'imposition va pouvoir osciller comme le suggère la version dynamique de la relation (21).

$$\log T_t = \log A + \log \theta_t + \frac{\alpha + 2}{\alpha - \beta} \log \left[\frac{B}{A}(1 - \theta_t)^\beta\right]$$
$$+ \log (1 - \tau\theta_{t-1}) - \log [\phi \, \overline{WT} + (1 - \tau\theta_{t-1})WT] \tag{22}$$

Cette relation de récurrence fournit là encore la relation dynamique entre l'évolution des taux, des bases d'imposition et du produit de l'impôt.

IV. Remarques de Conclusion

1. Les résultats présentés ici avaient pour ambition de fournir un cadre d'analyse simple à une étude de l'évolution des recettes fiscales dans la longue période qui parte de relations du type Laffer. Les modèles développés à cette occasion se sont fondés sur l'élément essentiel de l'analyse de Laffer: l'élasticité de la base d'imposition au taux d'impôt comme résultante d'un double mécanisme de substitution: substitution travail/loisir et travail taxé/travail non taxé. Selon que cette élasticité sera fortement négative ou non, le profil de l'évolution des recettes fiscales au cours du temps sera régulièrement croissant ou non. Tant que l'on suppose des lois simples de variation en fonction du temps des élasticités/impôts de l'offre et de la demande de produit taxé et que l'on ignore les effets de revenu, l'on observe en général des évolutions régulières du niveau d'imposition (optimal ou non), croissante notamment lorsque les préférences pour les biens financés par l'impôt s'accroissent, décroissantes au cas contraire. Ceteris paribus, la portion "prohibée" de la courbe de Laffer tendrait alors à se déplacer vers des valeurs de plus en plus élevées du taux moyen d'imposition. Dès que l'on complique un peu le schéma d'analyse en introduisant notamment des anticipations imparfaites de la part des agents, ou des effets de seuil, la dynamique n'a plus de raison d'être régulière comme le suggèrent les résultats du dernier modèle présenté.

2. La portée des résultats obtenus reste toutefois limitée en raison de l'extrême simplicité des modèles étudiés. Sur certains points, des travaux théoriques antérieurs sont beaucoup plus complets (voir notamment la revue de littérature dans Fullerton (1981), pp. 3–6, Fullerton, King, Shoven, Whalley (1978) (1981), Hausman (1981)). En effet, nos modèles se situent en

équilibre partiel; ils négligent les effets de revenu, de même que ceux liés à la répartition des dépenses publiques entre agents; a fortiori, ils ignorent les effets positifs d'une intervention de l'Etat destinée à corriger les défaillances du marché ou à mettre en action la complémentarité entre biens financés par l'impôt et les autres biens.

3. L'exercice présenté ici est exclusivement théorique, mais pourrait faire l'objet d'estimations empiriques. La littérature empirique autour de la courbe de Laffer s'est sensiblement accrue dans les années récentes et dans des directions très diverses; Canto, Joines et Webb (1979) ont évalué l'efficacité en termes de rendement fiscal du programme de réduction d'impôt de Kennedy en 1964. Stuart (1981) a utilisé un modèle à deux secteurs pour calculer une courbe de Laffer pour la Suède, Hemming et Kay (1980) ont insisté sur l'influence de la progressivité du barème d'impôt sur le revenu dans la détermination des recettes fiscales dans le cas du Royaume-Uni, Minarik (1981) et Feldstein, Slemrod et Yitzhaki (1980) ont étudié l'effet des taux d'impôt sur le niveau des gains en capital et en conséquence sur les recettes fiscales assises sur ces gains. Enfin, la courbe de Laffer a été testée au niveau local (Grieson et al. (1977) pour le cas de New York et (1980) pour Philadelphie).

L'estimation empirique des courbes de Laffer de longue période pose néanmoins divers problèmes. Le premier concerne la prise en compte des caractéristiques internes du système fiscal (progressivité, répartition des dépenses fiscales . . .). La modification de celles-ci dans le temps affecte le taux moyen d'imposition θ_t, ce qui peut être aisément pris en compte, et la valeur des paramètres α, β, γ, τ, . . . ce qui complique alors singulièrement le modèle.

L'opinion négative de Hemming et Kay sur la possibilité d'établir une relation de Laffer sur la longue période ne vaut donc que si ces deux effets sont ignorés.

Le second problème est celui de la mesure de l'évolution des élasticités: non seulement, la variation de α et β résulte d'un changement de préférences, mais encore faut-il préciser la place de la fiscalité et des dépenses publiques dans ce changement de préférences, afin que le modèle soit complet. Le degré d'intériorisation des préférences pour les biens publics pose notamment le problème de savoir dans quelle mesure des préférences croissantes pour les biens publics entraînent l'acceptation par les agents du financement fiscal correspondant. Par ailleurs, la mesure agrégée des élasticités fût-elle simplement synchronique est loin d'être totalement satisfaisante (voir Fullerton (1981) et Killingsworth (1982)). Par ailleurs, les estimations fondées sur des observations de séries temporelles ne sont pas parmi les plus fiables (voir Lucas et Rapping (1970), Owen (1971), Godfrey (1975).

Si ces obstacles peuvent être surmontés, il est possible d'envisager des estimations économétriques des modèles présentés ici. Un point particulièrement intéressant consisterait à évaluer la convergence/divergence des niveaux de fiscalité en fonction des paramètres d'élasticité et de réaction des contribuables retenus. La dynamique chaotique du dernier modèle présenté semble en effet bien s'accorder avec la réalité de l'évolution *réciproque* des niveaux de fiscalité dans les pays industriels (Gilbert (1979)).

4. La mécanique simple des modèles utilisés ne doit pas conduire à ignorer l'importance des caractéristiques politico-institutionnelles dans l'évolution à long terme des niveaux de fiscalité et des taux d'imposition.

L'évolution des paramètres d'élasticité qui conditionnent la dynamique des recettes fiscales ne rend que très imparfaitement et très indirectement compte de ces phénomènes. Peut-on ainsi supposer sans précautions que le comportement fiscal de l'Etat reste en longue période la maximisation des recettes fiscales possibles (objectif d'efficacité interne ou "bureaucratique") ou du moins le souci de se maintenir dans la portion "normale" de la courbe de Laffer, sous prétexte que des taux "prohibitifs" conduisent à une désincitation généralisée à l'effort ou un encouragement à la fraude fiscale? De même, le comportement fiscal du contribuable ne saurait être modélisé "ne varietur" de façon aussi rudimentaire; l'influence des structures de vote, les effets d'illusion sont déterminants (Pommerehne et Schneider (1978)). Finalement, la mise en évidence d'une "portion normale" de la courbe de Laffer de plus en plus étendue ne doit pas être interprétée sans nuances en termes de seuls effets de revenu et de substitution. Les réactions du contribuable vis-à-vis de l'évolution tendancielle de la fiscalité sont autant sinon plus du domaine de l'économie des choix publics que de celui de la mécanique des effets de revenu et de substitution.

Notes

1. D'Autume (1981) a mis en évidence un cas particulier où la courbe de Laffer passe par un maximum entre $\theta = 0$ et $\theta = 1$. Il suffit de supposer que "l'ensemble de consommation" de l'individu représentatif est borné, c'est-à-dire qu'il existe une consommation minimale, ainsi qu'une limite à l'effort. Dans ce cas, le taux maximum d'imposition θ^* dépend de ces deux paramètres et prend la signification d'une barrière physiologique. On remarquera toutefois que rien n'exclut a priori la possibilité que ce taux maximal soit très élevé. D'autre part, il se peut que la courbe de Laffer soit constamment croissante jusqu'à ce θ^* physiologique; enfin, la courbe de Laffer n'est plus définie au-delà de θ^*.

2. Au sens de perception systématiquement erronée du taux de l'impôt (voir Buchanan (1964), Wagner (1976) sur ce point).

3. Ce sera par exemple le cas si les contribuables anticipent faute d'information, que $\hat{\theta}_t = \theta_{t-1}$.

References Bibliographiques

Autume, A. d' (1981), "La courbe de Laffer: quelques éléments d'analyse", Université Paris X-Nanterre, G.R.E.F.I., Manuscript.

Buchanan, J. (1964), "Public Debt, Cost Theory and the Fiscal Illusion", *Public Debt and Future Generations*, Chapel Ill, ed. J.P. Ferguson.

Canto, V.A., Joines, D.H., Laffer A.B., (1978), "An Income Expenditure Version of the Wedge Model", mimeo, University of Southern California.

Canto, V.A., Joines, D.H., Webb (1979), "Empirical Evidence on the Effects of Tax Rates On Economic Activity", Proceeding of the Business and Economics Statistics Section, American Statistical Association, Washington, D.C.

Fullerton, D. (1981), "On The Possibility Of an Inverse Relationship Between Tax Rates and Government Revenues", Dec. 1981, *NBER Working Paper*.

Fullerton, D., King, A.T., Shoven, J.B., Whalley, J. (1978), "General Equilibrium Analysis of U.S. Taxation Policy", in: 1978 Compendium of Tax Research, U.S. Treasury Department Office of Tax Analysis, pp. 23–58.

Fullerton, D., King, A.T., Shoven, J.B., Whalley, J. (1981), "Corporate Tax Integration in the United States: A General Equilibrium Approach", *American Economic Review*, 71, September, pp. 677–691.

Gilbert, G. (1979), "Economie politique des structures fiscales", Thèse Doctorat de Sc. Eco., Université Paris x-Nanterre, mimeo.

Godfrey, M.L. (1975), "*Aspects théoriques et empiriques des effets de la fiscalité sur l'offre de main-d'oeuvre*", O.C.D.E., Paris.

Greffe, X. (1980), "Les révoltes de contribuables aux Etats-Unis", Cahiers du Laboratoire d'Economie Sociale, Université de Paris I, mimeo.

Grieson, R.E., Hamovitch, W., Levinson, A.M., Morgenstern, R.D. (1977), "The Effects Of Business Taxation On The Location Of Industry", *Journal of Urban Economics*, 4, April, pp. 170–185.

Grieson, R.E. (1980), "Theoretical Analysis And Empirical Measurement of The Effects of The Philadelphia Income Tax", *Journal of Urban Economics*, 8, July, pp. 123–137.

Hausman, J.A. (1981), "Labor Supply" in, Aaron, H.J. et Pechman J.A., eds. *How Taxes Affect Economic Behavior*, The Brookings Institution, Washington D.C.

Hemming, R., et Kay, J.A. (1980), "The Laffer Curve", *The Journal of the Institute for Fiscal Studies*, 1, n° 2, mars.

Killingsworth, M.R. (1982), "*Labor Supply*", Cambridge University Press.

Lucas, R.E. et Rapping, L.A. (1970), "Real Wages, Employment And Inflation" in Phelps E.S. et al.: *Microeconomic Foundations of Employment And Inflation Theory* Norton, New York, pp. 257–305.

Musgrave, R.A. (1978), "Notes On Fiscal Sociology", Discussion Paper, Harvard University, Institute of Economic Research.

Minarik, J.J. (1981), "Capital Gains", in Aaron H.J. et Pechman J.A., eds; *How taxes affect economic behavior*, The Brookings Institution, Washington, D.C.

Owen, J.D. (1971), "The Demand For Leisure", *Journal of Political Economy*, Janv-Fev, pp. 56–76.

Stuart, Ch. (1981), "Swedish Tax Rates, Labor Supply and Tax Revenues", *Journal of Political Economy*, 89, 5, pp. 1020–1038.

Pommerehne, W.W. et Schneider, F. (1978), "Fiscal Illusion, Political Institutions and Local Public Spending", *Kyklos*, 31, 3, pp, 381–408.

Wagner, R.E. (1976), "Revenue Structure, Fiscal Illusion and Budgetary Choice", *Public Choice*, 25, 1, pp. 45–61.

Wanniski, J. (1978), "Taxes, Revenues And The "Laffer Curve" ", *The Public Interest*, 50, Winter, pp. 2–16.

Summary

The paper investigates several long-run theoretical relationships between tax revenues and average tax rates (Laffer curves). Three simple partial equilibrium models allow the derivation of the relationship between government revenues and tax rates in the long run, assuming that both the elasticities of demand and supply of labor and the reactions of tax-payers vary over time.

Under these assumptions, simple analytic formulations were obtained, which show that the "normal range" of the Laffer curve could possibly extend over time. Changing public good preferences of tax-payers, and substitution between taxed and untaxed labor explain the growing "normal range" over time.

Tax Financing and the Shadow Economy*

Hannelore Weck and Bruno S. Frey

I. The Burden of Taxation and Existing Research on the Shadow Economy

Over the last twenty years, the burden of taxation in all industrial countries has greatly increased. The rising burden of taxation is commonly taken to be one of the dominant reasons for the existence and growth of the shadow or underground economy. The shadow economy may be defined as that part of income creating (value adding) economic activities which is presently not included in official statistics.[1]

Up to now, economists' research on the shadow economy has concentrated almost exclusively on measuring the size of this sector in the economy. In view of the importance attached to taxes as the cause of the shadow economy, it is surprising to note that (with one exception) the measurement approaches used so far completely disregard this determinant.[2] The purpose of this paper is to show that it is indeed useful to explicitly consider the role of taxation when the size of the shadow economy is evaluated. However, it will also be argued that it is not sufficient to consider only taxation and to disregard other possible causal influences, since this may result in a serious misspecification and distortion of the estimates.

Part II of this paper reviews the role of taxation in current measurement approaches. In part III the *multiple* causes leading to a shadow economy are discussed, and the method of "soft modelling" used in order to derive an estimate of the size and the development of the shadow economy, for example in the Federal Republic of Germany, is described. Part IV

*Part of the research in this paper has been presented at conferences and research seminars at N.I.A.S. in Wassenaar, The Netherlands; the Università di Torino, Italy; the University of Basel, Switzerland; the University of Aarhus, Denmark; and the Evangelische Akademie in Tutzing, Germany. We are grateful for helpful suggestions to Han Emanuel, Francesco Forte, Hiromitsu Ishi, Gebhard Kirchgaessner, Alan Peacock, Pierre Pestieau, Werner W. Pommerehne, Kurt Schmidt, Friedrich Schneider, Rupert Windisch, Vito Tanzi and Peter Zweifel.

Public Finance and the Quest for Efficiency. Proceedings of the 38th Congress of the International Institute of Public Finance. Copenhagen, 1982, pp. 313–327. Copyright © 1984 by Wayne State University Press, Detroit, Michigan, 48202.

considers both multiple determinants and multiple effects (indicators) of the shadow economy which makes it possible to *test* the influence of taxation on the shadow economy econometrically. Part V offers concluding remarks.

II. The Role of Taxes in Current Measurement Approaches

There is only one approach in the literature, the (sophisticated) currency demand approach, which explicitly considers the causal effect of taxation on the size and development of the shadow economy. The currency demand approach assumes that all "black market" transactions are done in cash. This assumption does not seem to be unfounded; a survey undertaken in Norway by Isachsen, Klovland and Strøm (1982, p. 220) finds that about 80% of all shadow sector payments are indeed in cash. The *simplistic* currency demand approach further assumes that the "normal" currency-demand deposit ratio in the official economy is constant over time, so that all increases in the C/D-ratio can be attributed to the growth of the shadow economy (Gutmann, 1977, 1979).

However, the currency-demand deposit ratio (or any similar ratio of currency to the monetary magnitude such as M_2) does not only depend on the growth of cash transactions in the "black" sector, but is also influenced by a great many other factors, such as the rate of interest, the level of income, the rate of inflation etc. The *sophisticated* currency demand approach evaluates what increase in currency demand is due to an increase in the rate of taxation, keeping all other influences constant. A full-scale currency demand equation is estimated, taking the general form

$$\frac{C}{M} = f (i, Y, \ldots, \tau),$$

where $\dfrac{C}{M}$ = currency relative to some money magnitude;

i = interest rate;
Y = (per capita) income;
τ = tax burden.

(The points indicate that there may be other factors influencing the demand for cash which are not further considered). The size and development of the shadow economy is evaluated by considering the partial effect of taxation on the demand for cash, $\partial(M/C)/\partial\tau$. Most authors compare the "excess" currency demand brought about by the increase of the tax rate over its lowest level in the period considered (e.g. Tanzi 1980, Klovland 1980).

Having no independent knowledge about the (relative) velocity of currency, it is assumed that it is the same in the shadow as it is in the official economy.

The (sophisticated) currency demand approach is based on various crucial assumptions. It is in particular very sensitive to the choice of the velocity of the circulation of cash in the shadow economy, about which little or nothing is presently known. What matters most in the context of our study is the implicit assumption that the size of, and increase in, the shadow economy depends exclusively on the increase of taxes. If there are other causes inducing people and firms to become active in the shadow economy, the approach involves a serious misspecification: the influence of the burden of taxes is incorrectly measured, and what is measured is not the total size of the shadow economy, but instead that part of it which is due to taxation.

III. Taxes and other determinants of the shadow economy

The burden of taxation is not the only factor which causes individuals and firms to become active in the shadow economy. Considering the decision process on the micro level we may distinguish the following set of incentives (or disincentives) to move to the shadow economy:

(*a*) *The higher cost of working in the official economy.* Besides taxes, the increasing amount and intensity of government regulations are an important reason to switch to the shadow sector. In many countries it has, for example, become difficult, if not impossible, to dismiss workers once they are hired. In order to adjust to the varying demand conditions, many firms therefore resort to the "black" labour market, where they are able to hire people just for the period they need them. Recently, a great many regulations have been introduced with respect to health, safety, and environmental standards which a job or production process must meet. Though such regulations may be beneficial to the society as a whole, both individual workers and producers often find it advantageous not to keep to the rules— which means that they have to enter the shadow economy.

(*b*) *The legal and moral cost of working in the shadow economy.* To be active in the "black economy" is generally illegal. Individuals and firms therefore have to consider the probability of being detected and punished. The more extensive and effective the controls, and the higher the punishments, the larger is the expected cost of being in the shadow economy. This factor works as a disincentive to leave the official economy. Undertaking an illegal activity also imposes a moral burden in addition to ex-

316 HANNELORE WECK AND BRUNO S. FREY

pected punishment. There is a barrier to "black" market work even if the legal sanctions are considered to be negligeable. The readiness to commit an illegal act by being active in the shadow economy depends on the population's attitude towards the government. If the government is considered to be an 'oppressive and alien entity not caring for the welfare of its citizens, people will have fewer moral qualms to violate the law and to cheat on taxes. If, on the other hand, the state's activities are mainly seen as being in the interest of the citizens, and if the subjects are satisfied with the exchanges between the taxes they pay and the benefits in terms of goods and transfers they get, they will incur higher moral costs when moving into the shadow economy.

(c) *The opportunity cost of time.* The longer the official *working time* per week (or year), the higher the opportunity costs of additionally working in the shadow sector are. (In most countries, one usually keeps one's job in the official sector in order to remain within the social security system and to make detection more difficult for the tax authorities). A decrease in official working hours on the other hand enlarges the capacity to enjoy both more leisure time *and* to work in the shadow sector.

In some countries, especially in Italy[3], some "black" workers leave the official sector completely. We therefore expect that a decrease in the official (age-specific) participation rate indicates an increased participation in the shadow economy.

(d) *Structural influences.* The factors outlined which give an incentive to work in the shadow economy do not work with the same intensity for all individuals and firms. There are economic sectors (in particular those with low capital intensity and changing location such as construction), occupations (e.g. craftsmen), types of goods (in particular services), types of workers (in particular foreign "gastarbeiter"), which are more likely than others to be involved in the shadow economy. It is useful to identify such activities, because participation in the "black" sector may increase even with the cost factors (a), (b), (c) staying constant, if their share in total (official) employment and value added increases (structural effect).

We have now identified seven determinants of the shadow economy, namely: the burden of taxation; the burden of regulation; the expected legal punishment; the moral cost of working illegally; the length of the working day; the age specific sex participation rates, and structural influences. Normally, one would regress these determinants D on the size of the shadow economy, S. In the simplest case of linear multiple regression, we would have

$$S_j = \sum_{i=1}^{n} \hat{\alpha}_i \cdot D_{ij} + \epsilon_j,$$

the $\hat{\alpha}_i$ representing the coefficients estimated on the basis of time-series or cross-section data.

Such an approach is, of course, not possible here, because it is the dependent variable S_j whose size is to be determined. Unlike in regression analysis, given the determinants D_{ij}, the coefficients α_i have to be determined on the basis of outside knowledge, in order to derive the size of the shadow economy S_j (at a given moment of time $j=t$, or between regional units $j=r$). As the determinants indicate the various factors increasing the incentive to become active in the shadow economy, it is useful to interpret the coefficients α_i as weights, satisfying the conditions $0 \leq \alpha_i \leq 1$, $\Sigma \alpha_i = 1$.

The size of the weights α_i of the various determinants is not exactly known, but the scientific as well as the popular literature on the shadow economy gives some indication about their relative size. Using this information makes it possible to employ the "soft modelling" approach which has recently been developed (see Kofler and Menges 1976) to facilitate decision making when only the ranking, but not the probabilities of the underlying variables are known.

Empirical Application

The determinants of the shadow economy discussed, and the sketched "soft modelling" technique, have been empirically analyzed for various purposes. A *cross-section* study of 17 OECD countries has been done, establishing the expected relative size, and the expected relative increase in size of the shadow economy between 1960 and 1978 (Frey and Weck 1983a, 1983b)[4]. A *time-series* study for the Federal Republic of Germany has been made for the period 1960–1978 (Frey, Weck and Pommerehne 1982). It reaches the conclusion that the incentives for joining the shadow economy have noticeably increased over this period, and that one can therefore safely expect that the income produced in the shadow economy has grown as compared to the official GNP.

The "determinants" approach sketched emphasizes that there are a number of causes motivating individuals and firms to take up work in the shadow economy, over and besides taxation. The approach does not, however, allow one to test this hypothesis econometrically, because the size of the shadow economy is unknown. In order to be able to use econometric estimation, it is necessary to approximate the size of the shadow sector by several *indicators*, and then to relate the determinants to these indicators by way of the "unobserved variable" method. This approach is discussed in the following section.

IV. Testing the Influence of Taxation on the Shadow Economy

In the ordinary regression analysis there is only one indicator for the dependent variable, and the various determinants can be regressed on this indicator. In our case, as the shadow sector size cannot be observed, we have to take more than one indicator into account ($k > 1$), and a more sophisticated estimation procedure is in order. The "unobserved variables" method, which is an extension of factor analysis, may be used for this purpose[5], the size of the shadow economy being the unobserved variable.

Indicators for the size of the shadow economy may be observed in three different areas:

(a) Value added. As an increase in the shadow economy involves a relative outflow of resources from the official economy, official GNP is lower than it would be if no shadow economy existed. Real GNP, or its rate of growth, compared to its "normal" size or trend, is thus an indicator of the shadow economy's growth.

(b) Labour. One may concentrate on one, and the most important, factor of production (at least in the "black" sector), labour. A decrease in official labour supply in terms of hours worked and persons is an indicator of the size of the shadow economy.[6]

(c) Money. As suggested by the monetary approaches (see the discussion in section II and Feige (1979)), the size of total money or of currency supply may serve as an indicator of the size of the shadow economy.

Empirical Application

The "unobserved variables" approach has been used to estimate the relative size of the shadow economy in 17 OECD countries over the period 1960–1978 in a pooled cross-section time series analysis. The estimation model and the estimated parameters are shown in figure 1.

The determinants of the size of the shadow economy comprise eight variables: The impact of taxation (tax burden) is captured by the share of direct taxes, of indirect taxes, and of social security contributions in GNP. Taking into account that individuals react to perceived rather than actual taxes, the increase of the (direct) tax burden is included among the determinants on the assumption that people get used to levels of taxation and note increases on the tax share more fully. The share of public officials in total employment is taken to represent the (unknown) burden of regulations. The moral cost of working illegally is captured by an index of "tax morality" based on survey research in public finance[7]. In order to have an increase of this index "push" for a larger shadow economy, this variable is introduced in the form of "tax immorality". The final two variables are designed to

Figure 1: *The unobserved variable estimate. 17 OECD countries, 1960–1978*

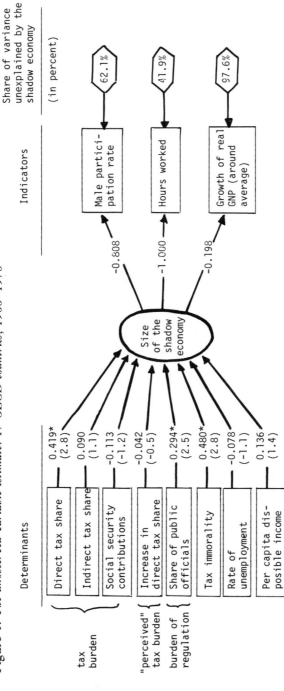

(The figures in parentheses below the parameter estimates indicate the t-values; an asterisk indicates statistical significance at the 99%-level).

pick up structural variables: as is often argued, unemployed persons have a higher propensity to work clandestinely. Per capita disposable income is designed to allow for the idea that workers in poor countries have a higher "need" to supplement their official income in the "black" sector.

The empirical study for the pooled analysis of OECD countries results in three of the determinants having a statistically significant influence, only: Direct taxes (parameter value 0.42), regulation (0.29), and tax immorality (0.48). These parameters have the theoretically expected positive sign. It is interesting to note that an increase in the share of indirect taxes does not tend to increase the size of the shadow economy, possibly because it is not fully noticed by the population. The same is true for social security contributions, in this case the reason being that they are conceived as "prices" for which one "buys" a particular service. The variable with which "tax perception" is measured may well be so inadequate as to explain the insignificance of the respective parameter. The same may be true for the two structural determinants.

The result of estimating the influence of the various determinants thus suggests that taxation is indeed an important cause of the existence and rise of the shadow economy, but that is not the only one. Tax morality may be even more important. The incentive to leave the official economy due to overly tight regulations is a third crucial cause.

The methodology of the "unobserved variable" estimate requires that the coefficient of one of the determinants is normalized. In figure 1, the effect on the hours worked is taken to be -1. By comparison, the effect on the rate of participation (of males) is smaller (the coefficient is -0.8), and the effect on the rate of growth of real official GNP is even smaller (-0.2). (Due to the basic differences in the monetary arrangements among countries, no indicators appearing in the money market have been considered in this pooled cross-section time-series estimate). The figures at the right-hand side of the table show the share of variance of the respective indicators not explained by the size of the shadow economy. As may be seen, this share varies between 42% and 98%.

The size of the shadow economy S in one country relative to that in each of the other countries can be calculated by considering the statistically significant determinants shown in figure 1. The coefficients of the share of direct taxes, τ_d (0.42), of regulation R (0.29) and of tax immorality IM (0.48) are normalized to add up to one in order to be interpretable as weights. This yields the equation

$$S = 0.35\tau_d + 0.25R + 0.40 \text{ IM},$$

with all variables measured in terms of z-values. Figure 2 shows the resulting *ranking* of the size of the shadow economy (conceived as share of official GNP) of 17 OECD countries for the final year of our study.

Figure 2: *The relative size of the shadow economy in 1978. 17 OECD countries.*

z-values

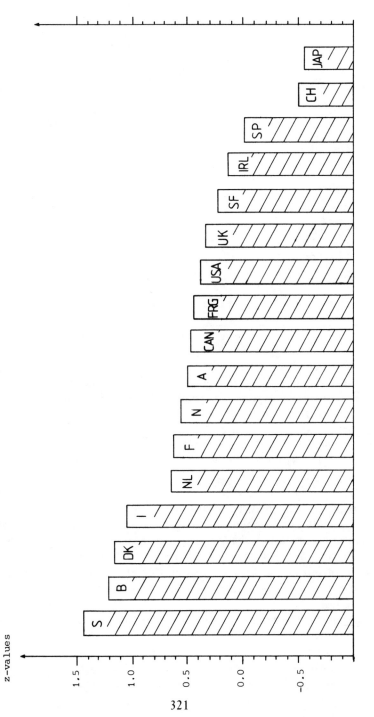

Table 1

The size of the shadow economy as percent of GNP.
17 OECD countries, 1960 and 1978.

	1960	1978
Sweden	5.4	13.2 (base)
Belgium	4.7	12.1
Denmark	3.7	11.8
Italy	4.4	11.4
Netherlands	5.6	9.6
France	5.0	9.4
Norway	4.4	9.2 (base)
Austria	4.6	8.9
Canada	5.1	8.7
Germany (F.R.)	3.7	8.6
United States	6.4	8.3
United Kingdom	4.6	8.0
Finland	3.1	7.6
Ireland	1.7	7.2
Spain	2.6	6.5
Switzerland	1.1	4.3
Japan	2.0	4.1

The Scandinavian countries (except Finland) turn out to be on top, together with the Benelux countries and Italy. A comparatively small shadow sector is attributed to Japan and Switzerland, Ireland and Spain. The Anglo-Saxon countries (U.S. and U.K.), and the German speaking countries (Austria and the F.R.G.), are calculated to have below average size shadow economies, a result which strongly conflicts with some of the (fantastic) estimates which have been put forward particularly for the United States[8].

The relative measures (rankings) of the size of the shadow economy shown in figure 2 may be transformed into absolute measures (shares of official GNP) if two points are fixed (to determine the level and the distances of one country's shadow economy from the next). For that purpose, the currency demand estimates undertaken by Klovland (1980) for Sweden (13.2% of official GNP) and Norway (9.2%) for the year 1978 are used. Table 1 shows the resulting estimates for the beginning and the final year of our study.

According to table 1, the shadow economy occupies in all countries an increasing share of total economic activity. In some countries such as Sweden, Belgium, Denmark, Italy and Ireland, the share in official GNP has increased more than 5 percentage points while in Japan the rise is only 2 percentage points. The increase is also relatively small for the United States which is mainly due to the small increase in direct taxes.

V. Policy Relevance and Future Research

The estimates presented are preliminary; they are subject to various shortcomings, three of which will be mentioned here. The first is the weak data base especially with respect to internationally comparable figures. As has been pointed out, there is (to our knowledge) no internationally comparable data available on the extent of controls. Our figures capturing the extent of regulation and of the moral cost of illegal work are also quite weak. The second shortcoming is the estimation method employed, which is not robust with respect to alternative specifications, though it certainly employs a measurement approach which is in principle well suited to the problem at hand. The third shortcoming is the weak theoretical basis of the model. The micro-economic, i.e. the behavioral base of the model must quite clearly be improved. Also, the concepts such as "moral cost of working illegally" or of "tax morality" must be put into a rigorous framework. What matters even more, is that important links of interdependence are neglected by our (and all other) approaches. As is shown in figure 3, it should be taken into account that the government (as well as other institutional decision makers) may react to changes in the size of the shadow economy, as reflected by the indicators.

Two possible reactions of the government should in particular be explicitly modelled: when the government observes that the shadow economy increases and that its tax revenue is thereby reduced (compared to a situation with no shadow sector) it may well decide to raise tax rates in order to make up for the loss. Such a policy would, of course, raise the incentive to leave the official economy. Alternatively, or in addition, the government may decide to intensify the controls.

Another feedback which may be of importance is transmitted through the taxpayers: when they observe an increase in the shadow economy, this may reduce or even destroy their tax morality; the intrinsic motivation to contribute to financing the public goods offered by government is impaired.

There are many other such feedbacks which may and should be taken into account when modelling the shadow economy. It is in effect necessary to put the inofficial sector within the framework of a whole politico-economic system which explicitly models the political sector's reactions. To neglect this aspect means that the estimates may be seriously distorted, and that the policy conclusions drawn on the basis of the estimates may be mistaken.

Despite the shortcomings just discussed, the measurement approaches presented in this paper constitute an advance over the currently existing approaches, since they explicitly take into account the multiplicity of deter-

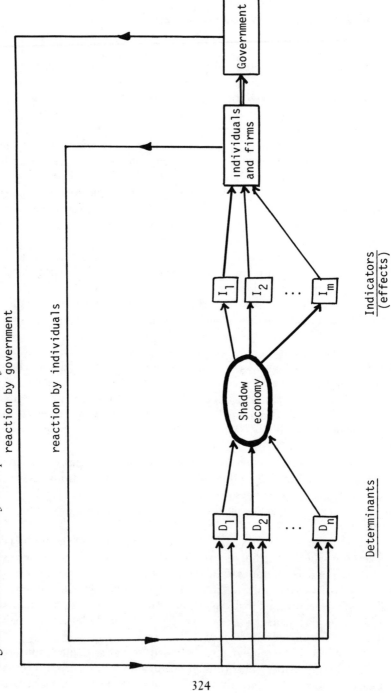

Figure 3: *The shadow economy in the politico-economic system.*

reaction by government

reaction by individuals

Government

individuals
and firms

I_1 I_2 ... I_m

Shadow
economy

Indicators
(effects)

D_1 D_2 ... D_n

Determinants

324

minants as well as of indicators. *Taxation* is indeed an important cause for the existence and rise of the shadow economy, but there are in addition other crucial causes, in particular regulation and tax morality, which should not be overlooked. This knowledge has important policy consequences. The studies considering the burden of taxation as the only cause are of little use for policy purposes. They implicitly suggest that there is only one way to influence the size of the shadow economy, i.e. by changing the tax rates. Our approach on the other hand points to several avenues through which the shadow economy can be influenced if so desired. It may well be that when taxes are reduced, the government and the public administration react by intensifying regulations. The effect on the individuals' and firms' incentives to work in the official economy may thereby be counterbalanced.

Notes

1. See, for example, Macafee (1980), Smith (1981) and Feige (1982).
2. No survey of the methods is intended here, for that purpose consult, for example, Frey and Pommerehne (1982) or Pommerehne and Frey (1982).
3. See Fuà (1976), L. Frey (1978), Contini (1982).
4. These papers discuss extensively the way the determinants are quantitatively measured. It must suffice here to point out that some of the variables are extremely difficult to measure adequately for an inter-country comparison. No information at all is available for the intensity and effectiveness of controls. Quite weak evidence is available on the burden of regulation (it is approximated by the share of public officials in public administration, assuming that there is a fixed relationship between number of regulators and effects of regulations). The same applies to the moral burden of joining the shadow economy.
5. See the LISREL (*Linear Interdependent Structural Relationship*) procedure as developed by Jöreskog and Van Thillo (1973), which is in turn a generalization of the MIMIC (*Multiple Indicators Multiple Causes*) approach, see Jöreskog and Goldberger (1975).
6. It may be observed that the working time and the participation rate are now identified as indicators, while they were taken as determinants in section III. Indeed, both interpretations make sense, because both aspects are present. See the discussion in the concluding section.
7. For the derivation of the index, see Weck (1983).
8. Feige (1979) estimates the U.S. to have a shadow economy amounting to 33% of the official GNP (later revised to 27%; Feige 1982).

References

Contini, Bruno (1982), "The Second Economy in Italy", *Taxing and Spending* 3, (Nov./Dec.), 17–24.
Feige, Edgar L. (1979), "How Big is the Irregular Economy?", *Challenge* 22, (Nov./Dec.), 5–13.
Feige, Edgar L. (1982), "A New Perspective on Macroeconomic Phenomena. The Theory and Measurement of the Unobserved Sector in the United States: Causes, Consequences, and Implications", in Michael Walker (ed.), *The International Burden of Government*, Vancouver, forthcoming.

Frey, Bruno S. and Werner W. Pommerehne (1982), "Measuring the Hidden Economy: Though this be Madness, yet there is Method in it?", in Vito Tanzi (ed.), *The Underground Economy in the United States and Abroad*, Lexington, Heath, 3–27.

Frey, Bruno S. and Hannelore Weck (1983a), "Estimating the Shadow Economy: A 'Naive' Approach", *Oxford Economic Papers*, 35 (March), 23–44.

Frey, Bruno S. and Hannelore Weck (1983b), "What Produces a Hidden Economy? An International Cross Section Analysis", *Southern Economic Journal*, 49/3, 822–832.

Frey, Bruno S., Weck, Hannelore and Werner W. Pommerehne (1982), "Has the Shadow Economy Grown in Germany? An Exploratory Study", *Weltwirtschaftliches Archiv*, 118, 499–524.

Frey, Luigi (1978), "*Il lavoro nero in Italia nel 1977: Tendenze dell' occupazione*", Foundation CERES, Turin, June.

Fuà, Giorgio (1976), *Occupazione e capacità produttive: La realtà italiana*, Il Mulino, Bologna.

Gutmann, Peter M. (1977). "The Subterranean Economy", *Financial Analysts Journal*, (Nov./Dec.), 24–27, 34.

Gutmann, Peter M. (1979), "Statistical Illusions, Mistaken Policies", *Challenge* 22, (Nov./Dec.), 14–17.

Isachsen, Arne J., Klovland, Jan T. and Steinar Strøm (1982), "The Hidden Economy in Norway", in Vito Tanzi (ed.), *The Underground Economy in the United States and Abroad*, Lexington, Heath, 209–231.

Jöreskog, Karl G. and Arthur S. Goldberger (1975), "Estimation of a Model with Multiple Indicators and Multiple Causes of a Single Latent Variable", *Journal of the American Statistical Association* 70, (Sept.), 631–639.

Jöreskog, Karl G. and Marielle Van Thillo (1973), "LISREL: A General Computer Program for Estimating a Linear Structural Equation System Involving Multiple Indicators of Unobserved Variables", University of Uppsala; Research Report 73/5.

Klovland, Jan T. (1980), "In Search of the Hidden Economy: Tax Evasion and the Demand for Currency in Norway and Sweden", Discussion Paper 18/80, Norwegian School of Economics and Business Administration, Bergen.

Kofler, Eduard and Günter Menges (1976), *Entscheidungen bei unvollständiger Information*, Springer, Berlin and Heidelberg.

Macafee, Kerrick (1980), "A Glimpse of the Hidden Economy in the National Accounts", *Economic Trends* 316, 81–87.

Pommerehne, Werner W. and Bruno S. Frey (1982), "Les modes d'évaluation de l'économie occulte", *Futuribles* 50 (Dec.), 3–32.

Smith, Adrian (1981), "The Informal Economy", *Lloyds Bank Review* 118, 45–61.

Tanzi, Vito (1980), "The Underground Economy in the United States: Estimates and Implications", *Banca Nazionale del Lavoro Quarterly Review* 135, 427–453.

Weck, Hannelore (1983), *Schattenwirtschaft: Eine Möglichkeit zur Einschränkung der öffentlichen Verwaltung. Eine ökonomische Analyse*. Finanzwissenschaftliche Schriften 22, Peter Lang Verlag, Bern.

Résumé

Les analyses qui tentent actuellement d'évaluer l'ampleur de l'économie souterraine rejettent complètement le poids croissant de l'impôt comme une cause possible de l'existence et de l'accroissement de cette économie. Il y a une exception, les évaluations d'une analyse de la demande monétaire attribuent l'augmentation du secteur souterrain à l'accroissement des impôts, ceteris paribus.

Cet article soutient que le poids fiscal n'est pas le seul facteur qui conduise les individus et les entreprises à participer activement à l'économie souterraine. Les autres facteurs déterminants peuvent être le poids de la réglementation, les sanctions légales encourues et le coût moral de travailler dans l'illégalité aussi bien que des influences structurelles. L'ampleur relative de l'économie souterraine peut être mesurée à l'aide de la méthode "des variables non observées" qui prend le taux de participation, le nombre d'heures travaillées et le taux de croissance du PNB réel comme des indices de l'économie souterraine. Les estimations comparatives des séries statistiques temporelles faites pour 17 pays de l'OCDE pour la période 1960–78 suggèrent que l'ampleur de l'économie souterraine dépend de la part de l'impôt direct dans le PNB, du poids de la réglementation (que l'on mesure par le nombre de fonctionnaires publics par rapport à l'emploi total) et du morale de payeurs d'impôt. L'analyse montre que la Suède, la Belgique, le Danemark et l'Italie ont les économies souterraines les plus importantes tandis que la Suisse et le Japon ont les plus petites.

On pourra améliorer l'estimation entreprise si l'on dispose dans le futur de meilleures données. On peut renforcer la base théorique en prenant en compte les réactions du gouvernement à l'importance de l'évolution de l'économie souterraine. Une telle extension requiert simultanément une procédure valable d'estimation de l'économie souterraine.

Measuring and Combatting Income Tax Evasion

Daniel M. Holland

A. Introduction

This paper is concerned with that portion of income tax evasion traceable to underreporting of legal income on tax returns. We do not address the underground economy, nor do we take up other sources of tax evasion, for example overstating deductions and exemptions. That form of tax evasion that we do cover is a primary source of revenue loss. In the United States, on whose experience our discussion is based, it has been estimated that in 1981, the personal income tax revenue lost because of income underreporting by those who filed tax returns was 79 percent of revenue loss due to all forms of tax evasion (measured only for the legal sector), and between 71 and 74 percent when the illegal sector is taken into account (Egger (1982)).

Until very recently, however, those interested in "measuring" tax evasion have not been able to get at the revenue loss directly but have proxied it by estimating reporting "gaps," the difference between what was reported and what could be expected to be reported.

For many years, then, students in a number of countries have been trying to get a "handle" on tax evasion by estimating the "gap" between income generated (or received) and income reported on tax returns, both for aggregate income and for particular source components thereof. Inevitably, such estimates are flawed and imprecise, which makes them suggestive rather than definitive pieces of information for the tax administrator.

Some students of the gap believe that for some countries, including the United States, their estimates are sufficiently accurate for comparisons at a point in time to be helpful to the tax administrator. Whether they are deemed helpful or not also depends to some extent on temperament and taste of the administrator. Those who insist on a high order of accuracy for their evaluation benchmarks may not find gap measures particularly useful.

Public Finance and the Quest for Efficiency. Proceedings of the 38th Congress of the International Institute of Public Finance. Copenhagen, 1982, pp. 329–348. Copyright © 1984 by Wayne State University Press, Detroit, Michigan, 48202.

Others may, and, in many cases, in fact have. Our view is that these estimates are similar to most other important features of our imperfect world. You can't live with them and you can't live without them. Gap measures have enough sources of error and uncertainty so that if you are a purist, you "cannot afford to live with them"; but since the estimates deal with an important problem, and most of us can't be purists, you "cannot afford to live without them."

In our judgment, given a consistent methodology in the underlying series from which the gap estimates are derived, there are two valid uses to which gap estimates can be put.

1. At a point in time, they permit conclusions about relative degrees of tax evasion across types of income. If *large* differences in the percentage reported are found for different sources of income they probably reflect *real* differences in tax evasion.

2. Over time the "trend" in reporting percentages can be used to evaluate the success (or lack of it) in curbing tax evasion. This second feature, we think, is particularly useful because changes in the behavior of a series over time can convey significant information even if there is considerable inaccuracy in the absolute values.[1]

Whatever their limitations, in the last ten years tax administrators have become very much more interested in income-reporting gaps, and the loss in tax revenue associated with them.

In this paper we review measures of the gap for the United States, and discuss their implications for tax administration.

B. What We Known About Legal-Source Income Tax Base Evasion at a Given Time—1976

In the United States in the last several years, much attention has been paid to under-reporting of both legal and illegal source incomes. We limit our discussion to legal source incomes.

In Table 1 we summarize two sets of estimates for the major items of legal-source income excluding capital gains for 1976.

The IRS (1979) estimates (Cols. 1,3,5,7) are primarily derived from measures developed over the years in its Taxpayer Compliance Measurement Program (TCMP), from the results of auditing the returns of individual taxpayers. The estimates labelled (BEA) Bureau of Economic Analysis, US Department of Commerce) (Park (1981)) are derived from comparing the National Income Account components of personal income estimates of what "should have been reported" with the amounts derived from tax returns. This involves numerous, frequently imprecise, adjustments of per-

Table 1

A Comparison of Reportable Income, Reported Income, and Unreported Income for Selected Categories of Legal-Source Income, as Estimated by the IRS and the BEA, Respectively, United States 1976 (Dollar Amounts in Billions)

Type of Income	Reportable		Reported		Unreported		Unreported as Percent of Reportable	
	IRS (1)	BEA (2)	IRS (3)	BEA (4)	IRS (5)	BEA (6)	IRS (7)	BEA (8)
Self-Employment	93–99	89	60	60	33–39	29	35–39	33
Farm Proprietors	—	15	—	5	—	10	—	67
Non-Farm Proprietors	—	74	—	56	—	18	—	24
Wages and Salaries	902–908	884	881	881	21–27	3	2–3	—ᵃ
Interest	54–58	76	49	51	5–9	25	9–16	33
Dividends	27–30	31	25	25	2–5	6	7–17	20
Rents and Royalties	9–12	11	6	6	3–6	5	33–50	43
Pensions and Annuities	31–33	35	27	25	4–6	10	13–18	30
Total	1,116–1,140	1,125	1,048	1,049	68–102	78	6–9	7

ᵃ 0.3 percent

Sources: Columns 1, 3, and 5 from Department of the Treasury, Internal Revenue Service, *Estimates of Income Unreported on Individual Income Tax Returns*, Publication 1104 (9-1979), Tables 1 and 2 (pp. 7 and 8).

Columns 2, 4 and 6, from estimates prepared by Thae Park, Governments Division, Bureau of Economic Analysis, U.S. Department of Commerce in connection with his work on the reconciliation of personal income with IRS adjusted gross income by type of income. An article by Mr. Park incorporating his estimates for the period 1947–78 was published in *Survey of Current Business*, November, 1981.

sonal income for items not required to be reported (e.g. subtracting from
the dividend total an estimate of those that are nontaxable because they
represent a return of capital).

In the nature of things the IRS estimates should be considered the
more appropriate for the particular purpose at hand—tax base evasion via
underreporting. But Park's estimates are extremely useful for our paper
because they permit an evaluation of the trend in reporting over time.

The IRS estimates, in other words, are to be considered the more
accurate cross-sectional picture; the BEA estimates are the only long-run
time series. Since we intend to employ both sources in our paper, it is
comforting that, for 1976, the two sets of estimates tell pretty much the
same story.

1. Nonreporting in the aggregate comes to something like $70 to $100
billion, about 6 to 10 percent of the total to be reported.

2. Both sets of estimates suggest that rents and royalties and self-
employment income have the highest nonreporting percentages. Both suggest, further, that the consequences are more severe with respect to self-
employment income, since the absolute amount of unreported income is
five to ten times more for this source than for rents and royalties.

3. In both sets of estimates, wages and salaries show by far the smallest
under-reporting percentage—reflecting quite likely the prevalence of withholding on this source rather than any differential honesty of its recipients.

4. The two sets of estimates seem to disagree rather strongly on the
degree to which nonreporting characterizes dividends, interest, and pensions and annuities. But both put these sources of income in the middle of
their respective arrays of nonreporting percentages.

To the tax administrator interested in improving income tax reporting
both estimates for 1976 give the same signals.

1. Go after the income from self-employment and interest income if it
is the *absolute* amount of under-reporting you want to remedy.

2. Go after these two categories and other sources of property income,
if it is *degree* of under-reporting that you want to improve.

3. Significantly different degrees of under-reporting appear to be associated with different administrative mechanisms that tax authorities could
employ.

a) Wages and Salaries, almost all of which are subject to tax withholding, show by far the highest degree of reporting.
b) Dividends and Interest, to a lesser extent, for which information
returns are sent by payers to IRS with a copy sent also to recipients, show a "middling" degree of nonreporting.

c) Self-Employment Income, Rents and Royalties, and Pensions and Annuities, for which there is neither withholding nor information returns, show the highest degree of nonreporting.

The implications for tax administrators seem obvious.

C. Trends in Tax Evasion Over Thirty Years—1948–78

What has happened to income tax base evasion over time? Have the tax authorities been able to bring evasion under control, or has evasion become a more severe problem over the years?

On *a priori* grounds there are reasons to "predict" that tax evasion as we have measured it would decrease over time, and there are also reasons to expect quite the opposite.

Arguing for expecting a decreasing degree of tax evasion over time are the following:

1. Considerable improvement in the last 20 years in record-keeping, particularly the introduction of form 1099 information returns.
2. Enhanced capability of the IRS because of the development of computers over the same period, with their capabilities for rapid, cheap, and efficient record scanning and matching.
3. Development of more sophisticated statistical methodologies by IRS for taxpayer audit.
4. Tax avoidance and tax evasion are related. The greater the opportunities for tax avoidance, the more moderate the pressure for tax evasion. Over the last 20 years or so in the United States, tax avoidance opportunities—viz. "tax expenditures" and "tax shelters"—have burgeoned. Other things equal, this should mean lower tax evasion.

Suggesting that the degree of tax evasion would increase over time are a growing disenchantment with the income tax, reflecting:

1. the increased complexity of the code;
2. specific incidents of starkly disparate tax liabilities—the 200 non-taxpaying millionaires, President Nixon's tax return, etc, and the widely-publicized growth of the "Underground Economy";
3. rising marginal effective rates of tax due to "bracket creep" resulting from the brisk inflation of the last decade;
4. similarly attributable to inflation, the taxation as (nominal) capital gains of what were capital losses in real terms.[2]

Suggestive of the weight of these factors is the upward drift of the Federal Income Tax in the "least fair" sweepstakes. Over the last decade, the Federal Income Tax, traditionally the Tax Professor's "best" tax, has emerged, in the taxpaying public's view, as the "worst" tax.

A growing proportion of answers to the question "Which Do You Think Is the Worst Tax—That Is, the Least Fair" by a set of respondents representative of the American population as a whole in a survey conducted annually over the last ten years named the Federal Income Tax from a set of five choices: Federal Income Tax, State Income Tax, State Sales Tax, Local Property Tax, Don't Know. And in the four most recent surveys, 1979–82, the Federal Income Tax was voted the "least fair" (Advisory Committee on Intergovernmental Relations (1982), p. 4).

Since we can identify *a priori* factors that should increase under-reporting, on the one hand, and factors that should decrease it on the other hand, what happened over time with respect to tax evasion remains a question of fact.

In Table 2 we present the record of under-reporting over more than 30 years.

1. The first column of Table 2 gives the Adjusted Gross Income Gap of taxable individuals as a percent of their total Adjusted Gross Income from 1947 through 1978. It is a seemingly impressive performance. The nonreporting percentage was cut by almost half over the most recent 30-year period. Whereas in 1947 estimated nonreported AGI was about 13.3 percent of AGI to be reported on taxable returns, by 1978 the nonreported amount came to only 7 percent of the total. Seven percent shortfall for a self-assessed income tax in a world of imperfect record-keeping and fallible human beings appears to be a noteworthy achievement.

2. Before we crow too loudly about it, consider another number. Again, from Park's data, we computed the nonreporting gap for all legal-source incomes *but* wages and salaries. In 1948 it was 32 percent; and 30 years later in 1978 it was 31 percent. Between these years as the last column of Table 2 confirms, the degree of nonreporting declined and then increased back to its earlier level.

Virtually all the substantial improvement in tax base reporting percentages over the period, particularly in the last decade, can be attributed to improvements in reporting of wages and salaries. For the other sources of income, taken together, the percentage of income not reported was as high at the end of the period as in 1948. This is discouraging news, since it indicates a sharpened differential in taxpayer experience. Wage and salary recipients were brought increasingly toward full reporting; the recipients of the other sources of income, in the aggregate, however, maintained a record of a high degree of non-reporting.

This is not a comforting picture. Despite enhanced efforts and substantially improved technologies and methodologies for detecting evasion currently, the degree of under-reporting for the aggregate of business income, dividends, rents and royalties, interest and pensions and annuities, is as great or greater than it was 30 years ago.

3. The trend analysis confirms and reinforces the conclusions about tax base evasion that have been made from the cross-sectional data.

a) As evidenced by the nonreporting percentages for Wages and Salaries, withholding has been associated both with the *lowest* degree of under-reporting and a dramatic *decline* in under-reporting over time.

b) With respect to information returns; there appears to have been a real improvement in reporting for dividends in the early years of the use of Form 1099, but a backsliding since the middle sixties. For interest, a less immediate response to the introduction of information returns is observed, but the decline in the nonreporting percentage has been greater over time. However, nonreporting remains high—in 1978, the most recent year of Park's data, it was 16 percent for dividends and 37 percent for personal interest income. Parenthetically, over a good portion of the period when information returns (Form 1099) were employed for dividends and interest, many payers apparently did not file them, and there was little attempt by the IRS to match those that were filed with the personal income tax records of recipients. In recent years practice has improved with respect to both these matters, but this improvement does not seem to be reflected in the nonreporting percentages.

c) With respect to those sources of income to which neither withholding nor information returns applied:

i. for rental income a nonreporting percentage of 50 or over was characteristic for the whole period.

ii. Reporting improved substantially for pensions and annuities.

iii. Under-reporting has always been high for proprietors' income. Reporting, however, improved in the first half of the period and retrogressed in the latter half.

D. Components of the Reporting Gap

Tax administrators may have a number of objectives. One implicitly identified in our discussion of the degree of underreporting by source of income would be to "equalize" the degree of underreporting among the various sources. Another might be to minimize the total amount not reported.

Table 2

Reporting Gap for Adjusted Gross Income
and Components Thereof, 1947–78

(Percent)

Year	Total Adjusted Gross Income	Wages & Salaries	Pensions & Annuities	Farm Proprietors' Income	Nonfarm Proprietors' Income	Dividend Income	Rental Income	Interest Income	All Legal Source Income Except Wages & Salaries
1947	13.3	3.5	55.3	74.1	8.9	24.9	54.9	48.6	35.5
1948	12.4	4.2	48.9	69.6	9.1	22.3	52.7	47.2	32.1
1949	12.7	4.9	34.2	69.4	14.2	21.5	44.1	45.1	32.4
1950	11.6	3.8	41.0	64.2	17.6	24.4	43.9	47.8	31.3
1951	11.7	3.9	43.7	66.7	18.0	23.1	46.0	49.4	33.0
1952	11.0	3.3	42.7	64.8	19.5	24.7	47.1	49.0	33.9
1953	10.9	3.2	43.9	62.9	21.2	26.6	47.0	53.0	35.1
1954	10.1	3.3	39.9	59.0	18.5	10.3	49.3	62.1	31.4
1955	9.6	3.2	44.1	52.2	19.7	10.8	48.9	63.8	29.9
1956	9.4	3.7	48.8	51.6	15.1	8.7	44.9	64.4	27.6
1957	9.0	2.9	45.6	47.9	18.9	6.5	47.1	65.0	29.2
1958	10.1	3.5	45.0	51.9	19.7	7.9	49.4	64.4	30.9
1959	9.2	2.7	48.4	57.9	18.5	8.5	51.2	61.5	28.6
1960	9.4	3.0	49.3	60.6	17.8	11.7	45.6	59.8	30.8
1961	8.5	2.4	48.7	54.3	18.4	10.1	45.3	53.8	28.6
1962	8.4	2.7	44.5	51.6	15.9	11.4	41.8	52.8	27.7

1963	8.0	2.2	42.9	58.4	15.8	11.5	46.3	46.4	27.5
1964	8.6	2.6	43.1	60.5	16.1	15.5	51.1	47.6	28.1
1965	8.2	2.0	43.0	53.1	15.1	16.8	56.1	48.5	28.3
1966	8.7	3.0	40.1	56.3	15.7	11.5	49.8	46.0	27.3
1967	7.6	2.1	40.7	50.2	15.1	13.0	51.2	44.3	25.8
1968	7.6	2.4	36.2	56.6	13.2	14.2	51.2	43.1	25.1
1969	7.5	1.9	36.9	60.2	15.7	12.6	54.1	41.8	27.4
1970	7.9	1.9	38.9	65.5	17.3	10.9	55.5	43.6	30.7
1971	7.8	1.8	38.9	71.1	18.0	13.8	54.5	40.9	30.1
1972	7.4	1.2	38.4	63.7	19.0	14.0	57.0	38.3	29.8
1973	8.2	1.5	35.5	62.6	19.4	13.3	51.5	39.5	31.3
1974	7.5	.2	32.0	71.0	22.0	12.5	52.1	37.8	32.7
1975	7.0	.7	29.8	67.5	23.1	11.1	49.7	35.5	30.4
1976	6.9	.3	29.8	69.4	24.7	19.7	43.9	33.7	30.4
1977	7.4	.8	27.2	89.4	24.6	15.7	57.7	35.5	30.9
1978	7.4	.6	28.6	74.6	23.3	16.1	56.0	35.9	31.5

Source: Thae S. Park, "Relationship Between Personal Income and Adjusted Gross Income, 1947–78," *Survey of Current Business*, November, 1981, pp. 24–28.

How importantly each source of income contributes to the Adjusted Gross Income gap depends both on the underreporting percentages that characterize the various sources, and each source's weight in Adjusted Gross Income. Wages and Salaries have the lowest degree of underreporting, but could, nonetheless, contribute importantly to the Adjusted Gross Income Gap because this income source generally accounts for 70 percent of AGI. Rental income about half of which is not reported is a very small fraction of total income, and, therefore, might not contribute importantly to the AGI gap.

In Table 3 we provide Park's estimates of the percentage that selected sources of income contributed to the total Adjusted Gross Income Gap. The time series trace out a dramatic transformation over the more than thirty-year period.

In 1948 about 75 percent of the total Adjusted Gross Income gap was due to Proprietors' Income and Wages and Salaries. Interest and Pensions and Annuities together accounted for less than 10 percent. Over time the share of Proprietor's Income (Farm and Nonfarm) declined from close to 50 percent to just under 25 percent in 1968, and then rose to over 30 percent in the years that followed. The decline reflects the growing share of total Proprietors' Income accounted for by Nonfarm Proprietors' Income which characteristically has higher reporting percentages than Farm Proprietors' Income. But the rise since 1968, reflects a rising degree of nonreporting of Nonfarm Proprietors' Income. Wages and Salaries accounted for about 25 percent of the total AGI gap up until the middle 60s. In the last 15 years Wages and Salaries have come to comprise less and less of the AGI gap; currently they represent a small fraction of nonreported income—about 7–8 percent.

Despite an improvement in reporting percentage, Personal Interest Income has come to constitute an increasing fraction of the total AGI gap. Indeed currently it vies with Proprietors' Income for first place. This reflects the relatively rapid growth in interest receipts due to greater reliance on debt financing and rising nominal interest rates that reflect expected inflation.

Pensions and Annuities, too, make up an increasing fraction of the Adjusted Gross Income gap, despite an improvement in this share's reporting percentage, because Pensions and Annuities have grown rapidly, and comprise a growing share of AGI.

It is noteworthy that although Pensions and Annuities were estimated by Park to be $46 billion (on a BEA basis) and Wages and Salaries $1,097 billion (on a BEA basis), the former accounted for more than twice as much of the AGI gap as the latter. Pensioners appear to be under-reporting a greater amount of pension income than the wages and salaries not reported by those currently working.

Table 3 points up the rapidly changing dynamics among the income source contributors to the reporting gap since 1966. In that year, Interest, Proprietors' Income and Wages and Salaries, contributed equi-proportionally to the total reporting gap—each of these three sources accounted for about 25 percent of the total.

Over the next dozen years, however, the Wages and Salaries share declined substantially to about 7–8 percent, which Proprietors' Income and Personal Interest Income contributed a rising share of nonreporting—on the order of 30–35 percent each.

E. Tax Revenue Lost Due to Income Under-reporting

From the under-reporting evidence we concluded that tax base evasion was not a self-correcting problem. Where withholding applied, as with wages and salaries, reporting has improved over time; but for the other sources of income taken in the aggregate for which there are no provisions for withholding of tax liability, reporting did not improve over the long pull.

We also concluded that the most flagrant degree of tax base evasion characterized Business Income with Interest a close second. And it was implied that in a sense, on net balance, the IRS was "holding its own," since improvements in the degree of wage and salary reporting compensated for deterioration in other sources.

But under-reporting is a proxy for the "bottom line" variable—tax revenue loss due to under-reporting. Estimates of tax revenue lost because of income under-reporting (Table 4) point toward a less comforting conclusion. From 1973 to date (1981), tax revenue "lost" because of under-reporting by filers as a fraction of total tax accruals grew substantially. While, in the aggregate, income reporting appeared to stabilize, or even improve somewhat over the years, an increasing proportion of income tax revenue has been foregone because of income under-reporting.

The recent U.S. Treasury tax revenues gap estimates permit us to judge how good a proxy income under-reporting is for tax revenue loss due to under-reporting. In Table 5, for 1976, we compare selected legal source incomes, the percentage that each source comprised of aggregate under-reporting of these sources and the percentage each source represented of the aggregate revenue loss due to under-reporting.

The differences between the latter and the former reflect more than marginal rates. The Treasury tax revenue loss estimates are based on evidence available from data derived from auditing and taxpayer compliance measurement programs of the Internal Revenue Service. The presumption

Table 3

Distribution of Adjusted Gross Income Reporting Gap,
by Type of Income, 1947–78
(Percent)

Year	Total AGI Gap	Wages and Salaries	Pensions and Annuities	Farm Proprietors' Income	Nonfarm Proprietors' Income	Personal Dividend Income	Rental Income of Persons	Personal Interest Income
1947	100.0	18.3	1.2	46.0	8.4	6.2	12.0	7.9
1948	100.0	23.8	1.2	39.1	8.9	6.1	12.5	8.3
1949	100.0	27.7	1.0	33.1	13.0	6.1	10.3	8.8
1950	100.0	23.2	1.3	27.9	18.0	8.4	10.9	10.3
1951	100.0	24.5	1.4	29.3	17.1	6.7	10.8	10.1
1952	100.0	22.6	1.6	27.1	19.1	7.2	11.7	10.6
1953	100.0	22.4	1.9	24.1	20.5	7.5	11.3	12.2
1954	100.0	25.0	2.1	20.5	19.4	3.2	12.6	17.3
1955	100.0	25.3	2.6	15.6	22.1	3.6	11.7	19.1
1956	100.0	30.3	3.2	15.9	16.7	2.9	10.3	20.6
1957	100.0	24.4	3.4	12.8	21.9	2.3	11.0	24.2
1958	100.0	26.5	3.4	14.8	19.9	2.4	10.5	22.6
1959	100.0	22.3	4.4	14.2	20.4	2.8	11.4	24.4
1960	100.0	24.8	4.8	15.3	17.8	3.9	9.0	24.5
1961	100.0	21.4	5.7	15.1	20.3	3.7	9.3	24.6
1962	100.0	25.0	5.8	13.3	17.3	4.3	8.0	26.3

1963	100.0	21.7	6.3	14.4	17.6	4.6	9.3	26.0
1964	100.0	23.2	6.3	13.0	16.6	5.9	9.4	25.7
1965	100.0	18.3	7.1	11.9	16.2	6.9	10.6	29.1
1966	100.0	26.2	6.7	13.3	15.4	4.1	7.9	26.5
1967	100.0	21.8	8.4	9.6	16.6	5.1	8.9	29.7
1968	100.0	24.5	7.5	10.8	14.0	5.6	8.5	29.1
1969	100.0	19.9	8.2	12.9	15.8	4.6	8.5	30.1
1970	100.0	18.8	9.3	11.9	15.8	3.6	8.1	32.7
1971	100.0	17.9	10.4	11.5	16.5	4.4	8.0	31.3
1972	100.0	12.2	11.6	14.4	17.8	4.6	9.5	29.9
1973	100.0	14.1	9.8	19.5	15.6	3.9	7.7	29.4
1974	100.0	2.3	10.7	21.0	18.9	4.1	8.7	34.3
1975	100.0	7.2	12.4	13.5	20.7	3.8	7.8	34.7
1976	100.0	3.6	13.3	13.0	23.3	7.7	6.3	32.9
1977	100.0	8.3	11.8	10.2	22.1	5.5	8.4	33.7
1978	100.0	6.8	12.7	13.3	19.8	5.6	7.5	34.3

Source: Thae S. Park, "Relationship Between Personal Income and Adjusted Gross Income, 1947–78," *Survey of Current Business*, November, 1981, p. 28.

Table 4

Tax Revenue Foregone because of Under-Reported Income of Filers as a
Percent of Total Personal Income Tax Liability—Selected Years, 1973–81[a]

Year	(1) Total Personal Tax and Nontax Accruals	(2) Tax Liability on Under-Reported Income	(2) as a Percent of (1)
	(In $ billions)		
1973	114.7	20.5	17.9%
1976	147.3	30.6	20.8
1979	231.4	49.0	21.2
1981	296.2	66.1	22.3

Source: Column (1)—*Economic Report of the President*, February, 1982, p. 321.
Column (2)—Attachment II to Statement of Roscoe L. Egger, Jr., Commissioner of Internal
Revenue, Before the Subcommittee on Oversight of the Internal Revenue Service, Committee
on Finance, United States Senate, March 22, 1982.

[a]The Table covers estimates for revenue lost because of under-reporting of the following
sources: Wages (including tips), Dividends, Interest, Business Income (Nonfarm and Farm),
Pensions and Rents and Royalties.

is that the IRS under-reporting estimates are more accurate than those
obtained by subtracting tax return totals from National Income estimates of
the same items.

The reporting gap estimates, developed by Thae Park that we have
used in this paper would suggest that Proprietors' Income and Interest are
the main areas requiring attention. The revenue loss gap as estimated by
the Treasury points even more strongly to Proprietors' Income but much
less so to Interest. It is impossible to say how much of this difference is due
to different marginal rates applicable to recipients of these sources of income or to different estimates of the under-reporting gap.

F. The Choices Before Us

In principle, three mechanisms are available to combat evasion.

1. More information can be supplied the revenue authorities, and taxpayers can be more fully informed to that effect. They can also be
   exhorted to be more thorough in their reporting.
2. Penalties can be made more severe, and/or likelihood of punishment
   can be increased.
3. The scope for taxpayer initiative to evade can be contained by
   witholding of income tax.

Table 5

Comparison of Relative Importance of Reporting Gap by
Source of Income Measured Alternatively with Respect to
Amount of Income Not Reported or Additional Tax
Liability Due Because of Under-Reporting,
for Filers—1976

Source of Income	Percent of Income Gap	Percent of Tax Liability Gap
Wages (Including Tips)	3.6	10.3
Dividends	7.7	7.4
Interest	32.9	6.4
Nonfarm Business Income	23.3	57.1
Farm Business Income	13.0	8.4
Pensions & Annuities	13.3	5.4
Rents & Royalties	6.3	4.9
Total	100.0	100.0

Sources: Amount of Income: Thae S. Park, "Relationship Between Personal Income and Adjusted Gross Income, 1947–78," *Survey of Current Business*, November, 1981, Table 7, p. 28.
Tax Liability: Attachment 11 to Statement of Roscoe L. Egger, Jr., Commissioner of Internal Revenue Service, Committee on Finance, United States Senate, March 22, 1982.

G. Improved Reporting

In 1959, motivated by a study of the under-reporting gap for 1956 (the methodology was similar to that Park employed in deriving his estimates), the United States Treasury instituted a program to increase voluntary reporting of dividends and interest by taxpayers. Information returns were required to be filed by all payors of dividends of $10 or more and interest of $600 or more. And the Treasury noted that a broadened and accelerated program of matching these information returns with the returns of individual taxpayers was actively in progress. Moreover an ambitious education campaign—direct mailings to payors and recipients of dividends and interest, and announcements in the media—was mounted.

In October 1960, Dana Latham, Commissioner of Internal Revenue, reported, on the basis of preliminary evidence that the program had been "amazingly successful." Treasury audits of an admittedly limited sample of 1,801 cases indicated a decline of 50 percent in the number of persons failing to report dividends, and a decrease of 45 percent in the amount of unreported dividend income. But later and more thorough evidence led Mortimer Caplin who succeeded Latham as Commissioner of IRS to conclude that there had been no material change in the degree of dividend reporting between 1958 and 1959; those whose reporting improved were balanced by others whose reporting deteriorated.[3]

Caplin's conjecture is supported by the data in this paper. Dividend reporting didn't improve in 1959 as against 1958 and it deteriorated substantially over the years that followed.

With respect to interest income, however, Park's data suggest a real improvement in reporting coincident with the information-education campaign.[4] But the stability of the reporting percentage over the most recent four years suggests that the improvement in interest reporting has levelled off.

Information returns may not have effectively improved reporting of dividends on tax returns back in 1959 because even though the Treasury announced its intention to undertake a broadened and accelerated program of matching the information returns of payments with recipients' income tax returns, it did not do so. Over the years, however, the capability of matching improved substantially, and the percentage of information returns actively matched increased sharply, running at 35, 43, 47, 50, and 74 percent, for 1974 through 1978 respectively.[5] But once again, from the data in the Table we see no increase in reporting percentage for dividends.

In short, the record of the past is mixed and not particularly encouraging with respect to the effectiveness of information returns, exhortation, or education in improving reporting compliance.

H. Stronger Sanctions

That a greater expected penalty due to either a higher penalty rate or likelihood of detection, or to some combination of both would lower tax evasion is unarguable, but by how much is another question.

The experience in the United States is not encouraging. Nor is this surprising when we realize that detecting and punishing tax evasion is a complex process with a number of decision points. Reka Hoff, drawing on her experience with the Internal Revenue Service has delineated this process and analyzed it carefully and with insight (Hoff (1982)).

Hoff "models" the decision process of the evading taxpayer.

    a) To report all taxable income or not. If all is not reported and taxpayer is not detected, he is clearly better off. If he is detected he can then decide

    b) whether to pay or contest the tax and penalty assessed on him.

    c) If he chooses to protest, he could get an administrative settlement with IRS for a lower amount.

d) If he cannot get an administrative settlement at a lower amount, he can choose between paying tax and penalty or litigating.

e) If he chooses to go to the courts he could either win his case, and the issue would be closed with no deficiency, or he would have to pay later what he was asked to pay earlier, or he does not win his case but the case is closed, after the passage of time, "on the ground that the account is uncollectible."[6]

Obviously, the self-interested nonreporter will tend to spin out this skein of events as long as possible.

It is on the basis of an analysis of over 300 cases of prosecution for underreporting that Hoff concludes that extension of withholding at the source is the most effective way of combatting evasion.

"A system of voluntary self-assessment reinforced by administrative audit activity is subject to abuse by any taxpayer who is not risk-averse. The existence of civil penalties has even less deterrent effect than does the probability of detection. It follows that mandatory withholding of tax at source, in some amount, on those income sources frequently under-reported is the most effective antidote to civil evasion by under-reporting on a false return" (Hoff (1982), pp. 449–450).

I. Conclusion

While tax evasion has been an important problem and documentable for at least 30 years, and, quite likely, going back as far as the income tax itself, only recently has it become a matter of serious public concern.

Spurred on by the increasing revenue loss in recent years (see above) a number of measures designed to curb evasion were incorporated in the Tax Equity and Fiscal Responsibility Act of 1982 (TEFRA), approved by Congress August 19, 1982.

TEFRA's provisions include:

Withholding

1. Ten percent of all interest and dividend payments will be withheld by the payor. And there are stiff penalties for failure to comply.

2. Withholding at 10 percent by the payor on pension distributions. Payee may elect no withholding by filing an exemption certificate.

Increased Information and Reporting

1. Expanded information reporting for interest.

2. Abolished Bearer Bonds which, not registered to individuals, facilitated nonreporting of interest.

3. Required brokers to report to IRS and to customers gross proceeds of customers' transactions (capital gains, not included in our paper's discussion of income source under-reporting have no counterpart in National Income Accounting, so we had no time series for the capital gains reporting gap. But Treasury estimates suggest substantial under-reporting of and revenue loss from capital gains.)

4. Expanded information return requirements for payments to independent contractors and direct sellers, by requiring the payor to file an information return to IRS on all such payment of $600 or more, and to send a statement to the payee. (Prior law already had such a requirement for all persons engaged in trade or business who made payments of $600 or more of salaries, wages, commissions or other forms of compensation for services.)

5. Reporting by payor to IRS and payee of State and Local Income Tax refunds.

6. Reporting of pension, insurance, and annuity payments to IRS and payees.

7. More thorough reporting of taxes and imputation of 8 percent of gross receipts as tips if reported tips fall below this amount.

TEFRA, clearly, marks a meaningful step forward in the attack on tax evasion. Yet withholding, the preferred weapon, has been applied only to a few sources of income that do not account for a major portion of tax evasion. For Proprietors' Income and Capital Gains, which are major sources of evasion, expanded reporting has been chosen. Whether this mechanism will be able to make a serious dent in under-reporting remains to be seen.

Addendum

After the paper was completed, Congress, in a backward step, repealed general withholding on dividends and interest, substituting the sanction of "back-up" withholding on those who failed to furnish identification information to payors.

Notes

1. For a somewhat contrary view see O'Higgins (1981a), who concluded that aggregate measures that permitted a "confident" conclusion about either the current state or trend in tax

evasion in the United Kingdom were not feasible. However in a second paper that reviews additional evidence, O'Higgins while noting "that any conclusion is a matter of faith rather than hard facts" believes that "although no one set of data provides a conclusive figure, the effect of all the data taken together make it difficult to believe in a figure of less than 5 percent." (O'Higgins (1981b), p. 378).

2. For 1973 estimates put nominal capital gains on corporate stock sold at $4.6 billion in the aggregate, but, when adjusted for price changes between date of purchase and date of sale, at −$900 million (i.e. a capital loss) on a real basis. See Feldstein and Slemrod (1978), p. 109.

3. For a detailed account of this incident see Holland (1962), pp. 91–96.

4. Later the information return reporting requirement for interest was amended to cover payments of $10 or more, which would tend to improve reporting still further.

5. It is not clear that the 74 percent for 1978 was actually accomplished.

6. See Hoff (1982), p. 445 from whom this description of the process is taken.

References

Advisory Commission on Intergovernmental Relations (1982), *Changing Attitudes on Governments and Taxes*. Washington, D.C.

Egger, R.L. (1982), Statement of Commissioner of Internal Revenue Service. Committee on Finance, United States Senate, March 22, Attachment 11.

Feldstein, M. and Slemrod, J. (1978), "Inflation and the Excess Taxation of Capital Gains on Corporate Stock", *National Tax Journal*, Volume XXXI, No. 2, pp. 107–118.

Hoff, R.P. (1982), "Tax Withholding at Source Would Reduce Underreporting of Income on False Returns," *Tax Notes*, Volume XIV, No. 8, pp. 443–450.

Holland, D. (1962), *Dividends Under the Income Tax*, Princeton University Press.

Internal Revenue Service (IRS) (1979), *Estimates of Income Unreported on Individual Income Tax Returns*, Publication 1104 (9–1979).

O'Higgins, M. (1981a), "Aggregate Measures of Tax Evasion: An Assessment—I,", *British Tax Review*, No. 5.

O'Higgins, M. (1981b), "Tax Evasion and the Self-Employed: An Examination of the Evidence—II," *British Tax Review*, No. 6.

Park, T.S. (1981), "Relationship Between Personal Income and Adjusted Gross Income, 1947–78," *Survey of Current Business*, Volume 61, November 11, pp. 24–28.

Résumé

Cet article étudie quel est le degré d'évasion de l'impôt sur le revenu et l'efficacité des méthodes susceptibles de la réduire.

S'appuyant uniquement sur les données américaines avec la sous-estimation du revenu imposable, cet article analyse à la fois les séries statistiques inter-temporelles et inter-catégorielles qui montrent l'importance des divers revenus légalement sous-évalués et la proportion de sous-évaluation enregistrée par chaque catégorie de revenus.

In 1976, de 6 à 10% environ de ce qui aurait dû figurer au titre du Revenu Brut Ajusté (RBA—approximation américaine de l'impôt sur le revenu pour le revenu global) ne figurait pas au chapitre des recettes fiscales.

Mais ce résultat était la combinaison d'un très faible taux de sous-évaluation (pas plus de 2 à 3%) pour les salaires et traitements pour lesquels l'impôt est retenu à la source, à un pourcentage de sous-évaluation 3 à 5 fois plus élevé pour les dividendes et intérêts pour lesquels les informations sont envoyées aux Services Fiscaux par les contribuables, et à une sous-évaluation allant de 13 à 50% pour les autres catégories de revenus.

L'analyse de données annuelles sur une période de 30 ans montre une baisse sensible du pourcentage de sous-évaluation des (RBA) entre 1947 et 1978 qui s'explique principalement par une amélioration importante de la véracité des déclarations relatives aux salaires et traitements.

Dans le même temps, des améliorations et des régressions étaient observées dans les sous-évaluations des autres sources de revenus, ce qui fait que globalement les revenus autres que les salaires et les traitements sont globalement sous-évalués dans la même proportion en 1978 qu'en 1947.

L'expérience confirme que la retenue à la source est le moyen le plus efficace pour empêcher l'évasion fiscale. Une brève analyse de deux autres méthodes un flux accru de renseignements sur les paiements des revenus et détection et poursuite pour non-déclaration—renforce cette conclusion.

Efficiency Implications of Revenue Limitation Measures

Werner Z. Hirsch

1. Introduction

The revenue limitation movement in the United States is widely thought to have originated in 1978 with the passage of Proposition 13 in California. This movement has been fed by a broadly based, rapidly spreading taxpayers revolt. Proposition 13 rolled back property tax assessments to their 1975 levels and restricted increases in assessments to 2% per year for as long as the property is retained by the same owner. Property taxes exceeding 1% of the property's full value are prohibited; increases in state taxes are permitted only if approved by a ⅔ majority of both houses of the state legislature; and local taxes must be approved by a ⅔ majority of a jurisdiction's voters. In the face of a multi-billion dollar State surplus, California's legislature enacted permanent bail-out legislation (Assembly Bill 8) which, for example, in fiscal 1979–80 provided local governments with $4.84 billion.

By June 1981, 29 states had enacted specific local property tax rates limits, 19 property tax levy limits, 14 overall property tax rates limits, 6 general expenditure limits, and another 6 limits on assessment increases; 5 states had general revenue limits (Advisory Commission, 1981, p. 12). Additionally 18 state governments had enacted state limits. Massachusetts and California had voted in favor of particularly severe tax limits, Arizona had in effect as many as five such limitations.

2. General Framework

Revenue limitation measures bring about significant across-the-board reductions in local property taxes and therefore change the economic and

Public Finance and the Quest for Efficiency. Proceedings of the 38th Congress of the International Institute of Public Finance. Copenhagen, 1982, pp. 349–362. Copyright © 1984 by Wayne State University Press, Detroit, Michigan, 48202.

Figure 1

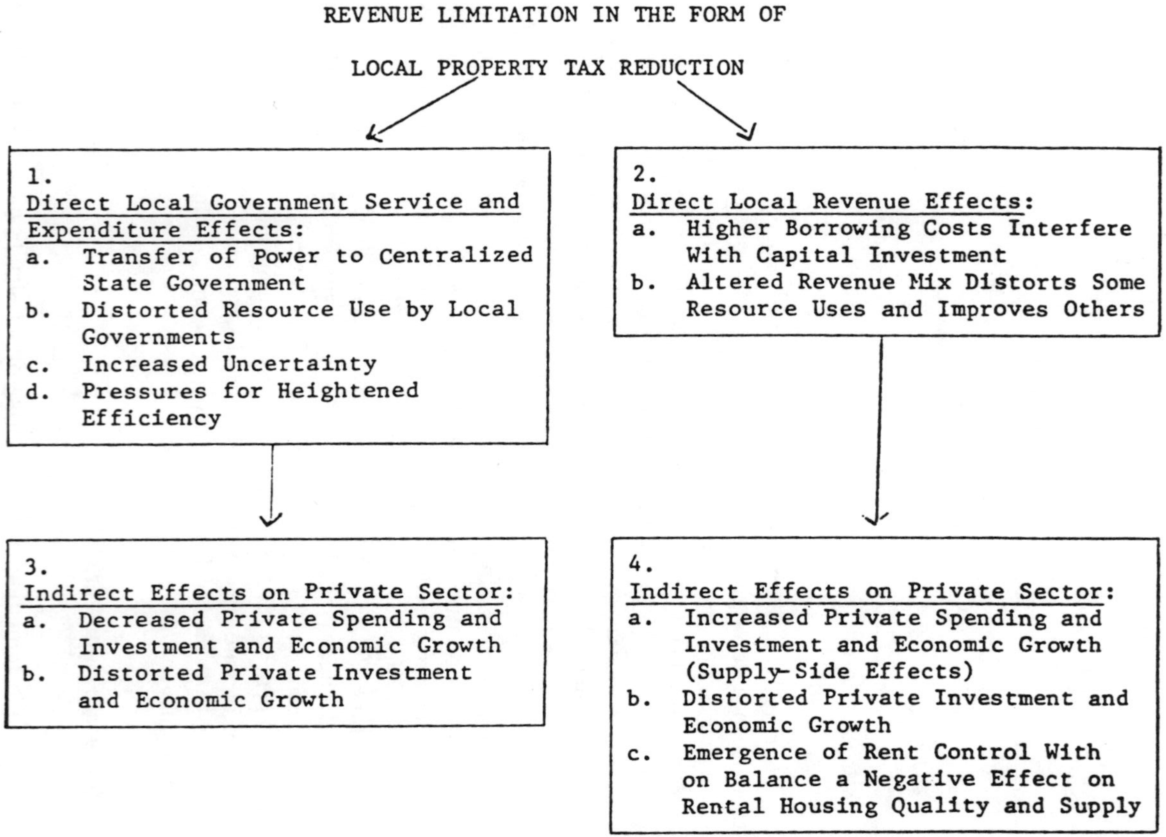

REVENUE LIMITATION IN THE FORM OF

LOCAL PROPERTY TAX REDUCTION

1.
Direct Local Government Service and
Expenditure Effects:
a. Transfer of Power to Centralized
   State Government
b. Distorted Resource Use by Local
   Governments
c. Increased Uncertainty
d. Pressures for Heightened
   Efficiency

2.
Direct Local Revenue Effects:
a. Higher Borrowing Costs Interfere
   With Capital Investment
b. Altered Revenue Mix Distorts Some
   Resource Uses and Improves Others

3.
Indirect Effects on Private Sector:
a. Decreased Private Spending and
   Investment and Economic Growth
b. Distorted Private Investment
   and Economic Growth

4.
Indirect Effects on Private Sector:
a. Increased Private Spending and
   Investment and Economic Growth
   (Supply-Side Effects)
b. Distorted Private Investment and
   Economic Growth
c. Emergence of Rent Control With
   on Balance a Negative Effect on
   Rental Housing Quality and Supply

institutional environment within which local governments make decisions. Some relate to service and expenditure and others to revenue decisions. Some are direct and others indirect or secondary. They are shown in Figure 1.

Box 1 includes four major direct local government service and expenditure effects—wholesale transfer of power from local governments to a centralized state government; major distortions in resource use by local governments, resulting in underinvestment in capital improvements, repair and maintenance as well as innovation; increased instability and unpredictability of local revenue; and an improved environment for public managers and employees to become more productive. Box 2 identifies two direct local revenue effects—heightened borrowing costs and altered revenue mix which in turn distorts resource use. As the private sector adjusts to the new local government service and expenditure environment, (as presented in Box 3), private spending and investment and therefore economic growth, can be retarded and distorted. Three likely indirect effects on the private sector that result from the new revenue environment are presented in Box 4—a supply side effect, distorted private investment and economic growth resulting from steps taken by local governments to replace property tax losses, and possibly imposition of rent control.

We will concentrate on a few of the major efficiency effects, first the mainly positive and then the mainly negative ones.

3. Financial Exigencies Tend to Heighten Local Government Efficiency

As funding becomes more difficult, the manner in which local governments produce and deliver services change. Four major approaches toward raising productivity are being tried. Measuring the performance of the labor force, aided by recent improvements in electronic and computer-based office machines, is a first step. Thus, better performance measurement enables governments to tie wages more closely to performance. Some have institutionalized monitoring and evaluation by instituting productivity bargaining, basing wage increases on agreed upon performance standards.

Secondly, managers are being induced to raise the productivity of employees by selecting and implementing more efficient production and distribution methods, and by stimulating workers to exert themselves more and thereby become more productive. To inspire their employees to exert themselves more fully, managers' performance is being tied more closely to their rewards and greater flexibility in rewards is offered. This is done by offering "Cafeteria" benefit plans to senior managers. They can take cash or such items as health insurance with built-in income protection, family dental plan, reimbursed tuition, membership dues in professional associations, paid attendance at professional conferences or seminars, sabbatical leave, etc.

Some governments have undertaken horizontal movement of managers in place of the conventional intradepartmental promotions. Moving managers horizontally has the advantage of overcoming many of the shortcomings of the old vertical movement of management personnel which tends to perpetuate a static, and often outdated, vision.

A third step seeks to provide a more competitive environment for the delivery of local government services through contracting out or privatization. Studies by E.S. Savas (1977a,b) of refuse collection found per household cost of trash collection in large cities to be 29% greater for municipal than for private collection.

A fourth step involves changes in the legal environment controlling local government employees. For example, civil service provisions are being modified by placing more emphasis on merit and less on seniority in determining promotions. Procedures are being streamlined to implement discipline so that adverse action can be taken against public employees who perform poorly by merely requiring managers to show "substantial evidence" rather than the presently commonly required "preponderance of evidence" to prove a case. Prevailing wage laws, which force jurisdictions to pay wages at least equal to those in private employment and are inflationary in some instances have been repealed.

A caveat is in order here. Quite a few decisions, made to cope with declining revenue are not primarily governed by efficiency considerations. It is often politically easier to use a meat-axe approach, i.e., cut all departments by the same percentage. This is inefficient, since various local government services have distinctly different demand elasticities. Also, layoffs are rarely selective with regard to performance; many of the least productive workers are protected by seniority rules (Ehrenberg, 1979).

4. Supply-Side Effects

Supply-side economics has been advanced in recent years with emphasis on the macroeconomic effects of tax reductions on aggregate savings, investment and labor supply as well as on tax revenues, which in turn affect the general level of economic activity (Canto et al. 1981). Supply-side economics as an application of price theory to government fiscal measures focuses on how tax rate changes affect the relative prices of leisure, consumption, non-market production and investment. Though perhaps less than an income tax reduction, a substantially lower property tax rate also ultimately raises the relative price of leisure and of current compared to future consumption, and increases the value of market work compared to work in the underground economy and of taxable investment compared to tax shelter.

Supply-side analysis can make use of the capital wedge, the divergence between return to the lender and the cost to the borrower resulting from the fact that taxes are paid to government. If taxes are high, a substantial reduction can increase the amount of capital demanded and the amount of capital supplied. This occurs because of the size of the wedge. The increase in the use of capital leads to output and employment growth. Figure 2 illustrates the capital wedge which comes about because taxes paid to government increase capital cost to entrepreneurs beyond what they actually pay for capital. Only in the extreme case at E, i.e., in the absence of taxes, will price paid for capital and price received for it be equal. As taxes on capital income increase, the cost of capital rises, while the return to those who provide capital declines, and vice versa. The tax increase, therefore, causes a decline in capital demanded as well as supplied. Consequently, the size of the wedge in Figure 2 increases up to Y_2 indicating a growing divergence between the cost of capital and yield to those who provide capital (D_c is the demand function for capital and S_c the supply function for capital). At Q_1 capital spending, capital cost is Y_2, whereas those who provide capital receive only Y_1. As taxes decline, we move towards E and Q_2, and a smaller wedge and greater capital spending. This analysis can be applied to a state-wide property tax reduction by using the "new view" of the incidence of property tax, though it assumes a nationwide uniform property tax (Mieszkowski, 1972). According to the "new view" the incidence of a uniform property tax is borne at least partly by all owners of capital instead of the consumers or just the owners of land. The burden cannot be passed entirely onto consumers because their mobility allows them to move out of the jurisdiction to escape increased prices. The burden cannot be passed entirely onto landowners because the supply of developed land is not a fixed factor.

Since the property tax is a tax on land and capital, the after-tax rate of return on capital in the state will increase if property taxes are reduced. Capital will shift into the jurisdiction. With the supply of capital not being perfectly elastic, this decrease in the supply of capital outside California will result in an upward adjustment in the rate of return to all owners of capital. The capital wedge is decreased due to the increase in the after-tax demand for capital. This decrease will not be as dramatic as the decrease caused by a capital income tax reduction of equal relative magnitude. We have only a statewide, and not nationwide, proprty tax. Still, the implications of the reduction in the capital wedge are the same: an increase in the total stock of capital, an increase in the remuneration to labor, and an increase in productivity.

Figure 2

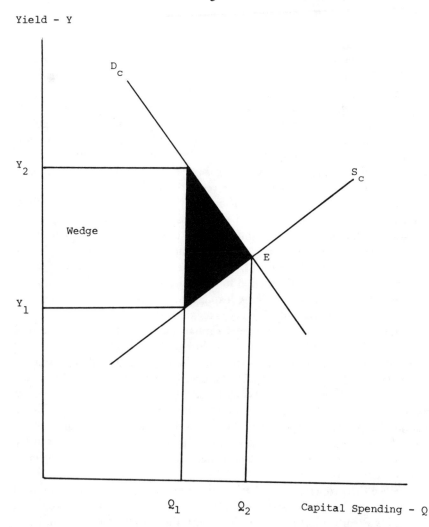

So far the supply-side effects on the federal level are unknown, and most economists expect them to be rather small. Even less evidence has been produced on the local or state level, and one must suspect that the employment and growth effects will also be quite small, particularly since California's $7.0 billion local property tax reduction was accompanied by an increase in federal income tax obligations of at least $2.5 billion. This is the result of property taxes being deductible from federal income taxes while user fees levied in place of property taxes are not.

5. Improved Government Resource Use by Altered Revenue Mix

Since local revenue limitation measures have rolled back property taxes, the relative importance of the latter has declined while that of sales taxes, subventions from higher levels of government and various fees has increased. This tendency has become even more pronounced where state governments increased their subventions which are predominantly financed by income and sales taxes. When property taxes vary from community to community, as they did for example in California prior to Proposition 13, local communities have a strong incentive to practice exclusionary zoning which can result in inefficient resource use (Hirsch, 1977). These tendencies are reduced once a uniform statewide property tax is imposed.

Furthermore in the face of a reduction in the relative importance of property taxes, those governments which provide people-related services tend to become more efficient. This condition holds for school districts and for county governments which in many states provide mainly health and welfare services. Municipal governments and special districts that provide flood control or street repair and street cleaning, i.e., those who mainly engage in property related services, will tend to lose some efficiency.

6. Transfer of Power to Centralized State Government

Even if state subventions to local governments do not increase after property taxes have been slashed, the relative share of state funds in support of local budgets increases. But in most states, major increases in state subventions have occurred. For example, following the passage of Proposition 13, state annual aid to local governments increased by about $5 billion in real terms, and with it power and control has shifted away from local governments to the state. The result has been a general decline in home rule and local control, and greater intervention by a centralized state government. Citizens, special interest business groups and labor unions are increasingly negotiating with the state legislature and governor, rather than with local officials. The latter have fewer and fewer resources with which to respond to pleas.

The efficiency implications of increased control over local governmental services by state government which lead to their homogenization are, by and large, negative. It can be demonstrated with the aid of an Edgeworth Box that, in the absence of economies of scale due to centralization and of spillover effects between localities, decentralized provision of a publicly provided good is more efficient than centralized provision. Since this has been done elsewhere, it will not be repeated here (Hirsch, 1981).

7. Distorted Resource Use By Local Government

Tight local budgets can lead to underinvestment in capital improvements, repair, maintenance and innovation as well as overinvestment in
state and federally funded programs.

Underinvestment in Capital Improvements

When budgets are slashed by revenue limitation measures, politicians
prefer to defer capital investment, repair and maintenance and innovative
programs rather than cut operating funds for the present delivery of services. This strategy minimizes the political damage to elected officials who
worry about re-election. This tendency is reinforced by heightened borrowing costs in the wake of revenue limitation measures. Public facilities are
usually considered a limited collateral at best, and investors in bonds tend
to emphasize the security of payment. Tax limitation measures have reduced the ability of governments to make debt service payments and to
some extent, increased the probability of default. Therefore, municipal
debt is more risky than before and requires higher interest payments.

With the property tax rate ceiling inflexible under Proposition 13, the
legally provided security of full faith and credit cannot be attached to new
bonds. Proposition 13 also changed the legal security behind tax allocation
bonds, in that the incremental property tax assessment from which the debt
previously was repaid will not be as large as before. Moreover, tax collection and control functions have been shifted from the tax-allocation districts
to the larger county level of government. Ann R. Thomas (1981, p. 110), in
examining this new legal arrangement, concludes, "The effect is to limit
severely, if not to eliminate, this form of financing future urban redevelop-
ment projects."

Revenue bonds that are secured in part by funds from the operating
budget of the issuing government tend to become riskier when revenue
from the project declines in a limitation era. This is especially important for
lease-purchase bonds that are totally dependent on operating funds via lease
contract payments. While the legal security of the bonds has not changed,
ability of local governments to provide debt service has been reduced. For
some local governments, selling bonds has virtually become impossible.
Since debt service is not exempt from the limitations imposed by Proposition 13 (except that approved by voters prior to July 1, 1978), local governments are severely limited in their access to credit markets. This fact is
especially damaging since increased productivity in local government often

requires investment in equipment, computers and more efficient physical facilities.

Underinvestment in Repair, Maintenance and Innovation

Many local governments are deferring repair and maintenance. Yet, as upkeep of buildings, roads, bridges, sewer systems, and busses is underfinanced year after year, large losses are likely to occur. These losses, in both monetary and human terms, are compounded by the fact that the eventual cost of restoring these facilities tends to be substantially higher than the savings from deferred maintenance. Preventive maintenance is less costly over the long run than corrective maintenance. Possible losses can result from public buildings and bridges collapsing, and accidents due to washed out roads, and inadequate mechanical maintenance of trucks, buses, and other equipment used by the public sector.

An optimal maintenance policy must take into account not only monetary costs of repair and maintenance, but also the benefits of preventing the human losses described above. The decision maker's problem is to maximize the net benefit stream, B(t), through choice of the optimal stream of maintenance expenditure, m(t) (Margolis, 1977). The choice of m(t) will affect both costs and the rate at which benefits depreciate, δ (m(t)).

The net benefit at time t is

$$B(t) = b(t)e^{-\delta t} - m(t) \, e^{-it}$$

where $\delta = \delta(m(t))$, i is the discount rate, and b(t) is benefits at t. The decision maker's problem is to maximize the stream of these net benefits over time.

The effect of incurring maintenance costs is to both shift the net benefit stream down by the discounted expenditure and to "flatten out" the stream by reducing the depreciation rate. Under increasing cost conditions, maintenance costs in each period should be increased until the increase in benefits due to slower depreciation is balanced by the increase in repair costs. Such a pattern of expenditure should constitute an optimum annual policy. If because of political considerations, these expenditures are curtailed, the optimum will not be reached. The net benefit path would shift up by the amount of cost savings, but the increase in the depreciation rate would more than offset this gain. The result would be a net social loss.

We have some tentative empirical information on budgetary changes—for example, capital spending on libraries, as a percent of all spending declined in Los Angeles County from 11.1 percent in 1978 to 0.9 percent in

1980 (Menchik, 1982, p. 39). In relation to research and innovation, the Los Angeles County Attorney reduced his staff in the Planning and Research Division by more than 50%, while all planning, research, and innovation activities of California's criminal justice system suffered (Walker, 1980).

Overinvestment in State and Federally Funded Programs

When local revenues decline, officials tend to protect federally and state subsidized programs at the expense of locally funded programs, which are cut most severely. The result is distorted local government resource use. In a program funded 75% by federal and state funds, for example, a cut that saves only 25% in local revenue would nevertheless have the consequence of reducing the program by a ratio of 4:1. This reduction of $4.00 of total program resulting from $1.00 of local fund reduction, must be compared to a $1.00 loss per dollar of local funding cut.

This hypothesis is borne out in New York City where budget-cutting in 1975 and 1976 led to major cuts primarily in locally funded services not eligible for federal or state funds, e.g., police, fire and sanitation (Temporary Commission, 1976). Likewise, passage of Proposition 13 resulted in local governments proposing greater retrenchment in locally supported basic services than in social-service programs that receive high federal and state funding (Comptroller General, 1979).

Further distortions and inefficiencies can result from local governments tending to use different standards of monitoring and of diligence in cost cutting, in relation to locally versus non-locally funded programs. The functional disjuncture between spending and raising revenue relative to heavily subsidized local operations, weakens local incentive and determination to be cost-effective.

8. Impeding and Distorting Economic Growth

Since under most revenue limitation measures, local governments' property taxes cannot exceed a specific, relatively low rate of market value, new land uses can cost governments more in services than will be covered by prospective tax receipts. Moreover, since governments have great difficulty in floating bond issues to fund an infrastructure, construction permits tend to be denied, though construction is actually efficient.

To illustrate, assume there exists in a locality a cost function for public services:

$$C = C(Q,n)$$

where Q is units of public services per household and n is number of households. Derivatives of the function with respect to both arguments are assumed to be positive. Any decision on land use must take into account the condition that costs of services provided must be balanced by tax revenues, that is:

$$rA = C(Q,n)$$

where r is the property tax rate and A is aggregate value of assessed real property. The following condition must be satisfied by any new construction in the community:

$$(\frac{\delta A}{\delta n}) = C_n(Q,n)$$

In words, tax revenues from an additional building must balance the additional costs. Now, let the tax rate be halved. In order to preserve the equality, it is necessary that the increment to assessed property value be raised, or else that Q be cut back (this assumes, of course, that the second cross partial derivative of C is positive). While it is likely that such a cut in the tax rate will lead to a one-time cut in services offered, it is less likely that each time a new construction permit is issued, Q will be cut. Rather, permits will only be issued to those with very high incremental value relative to expenditures. Consequently, many building permits will be denied for uses which would previously have been granted, including some that are highly efficient. Growth may be further retarded, because some firms facing a location decisions will not tolerate service cuts. Their decision against locating in the jurisdictions will tend to redistribute the geographic demand for public services.

In those instances in which construction permits are granted, frequently onerous terms are imposed on the developer. When burdens on developers in the form of construction fees, in lieu fees, exactions or inclusionary zoning provisions exceed costs placed on the community by the development, and have a chilling effect on new construction and retard economic growth, inefficiencies result.

There also exist distortions. Where such new taxing devices are not used, the relative decline in property taxes associated with revenue limitation will tend to increase investment in real property as compared to capital. Likewise, as a result of reassessment features exemplified by Proposition 13, repair of existing facilities will be more advantageous than constructing new ones.

This reassessment feature has also an effect on oil, gas, coal and other mineral resources exploitation. These resources, with crude oil the shining example, have substantially increased in price since 1975. Yet, they qualify for a 1975 base year evaluation plus 2% per year. Thus, the property tax payments on these mineral lands are relatively small compared to what they would be if assessments were in terms of present values. One result is a delay in exploitation of these resources.

The opposite result can occur in relation to investments in orchards and vineyards, which cost relatively little and the cost per unit of property improvement is low. While the economic productivity of orchards and vineyards increases with the passage of time, the initial low value is used as the evaluation base. Specifically, since assessed valuation is assessed upon fair market value at the time of planting, plus 2% a year compounded, compared to other investments orchards and vineyards are grossly under-taxed which in turn can result in overinvestment.

9. Some Concluding Thoughts

In the absence of careful empirical studies for the short time during which limitation measures have been in effect, I have engaged in some limited deductions and qualitative evaluation, with the following tentative conclusions:

Of the various efficiency effects of revenue limitation measures, three on balance are likely to be positive. Shrinking funding levels, or at least growth rates, have had a salubrious, disciplining effect on public managers and their employees. As a result a remarkable increase has occurred in the willingness of government officials to consider methods that can substantially increase efficiency. These tendencies are mitigated by a lack of funds and by archaic civil service rules that often leave the less productive workers on the public payroll. Secondly, there is so far little evidence of a positive supply-side effect of the tax cuts although they occurred in a period of prosperity. If heightened investment and economic growth will make their appearance somewhat later, I expect them to be rather small. Thirdly, the revenue mix change that has resulted from a decline in the importance of the local property tax is likely to have had on balance a small positive efficiency effect.

A number of other effects are strongly negative. By shifting much decision making power from local governments to the state, great centralization of power has occurred and with it homogenization of services and service levels. The result has been a significant efficiency loss. A similar result has most likely occurred because of major distortions in the use of resources by local governments. The distortions have been in the form of underinvestment in capital improvements, repair and maintenance and innovative activities on the one hand and overinvestment in State and Federally funded compared to locally funded programs. Also, private sector investment and economic growth have been retarded and distorted, in part as a consequence of local governments justifiable reluctance to issue building permits or only after attaching most onerous terms. Moreover, the changed property tax provisions have distorted major investment decisions as well as decisions about the exploitation of mineral resources.

In summary, although not all the evidence is in, it appears that the revenue limitation movement must be justified on other than efficiency grounds.

References

Advisory Commission on Intergovernmental Relations, (December 1981), *Significant Features of the Fiscal Federalism, 1980–81 Edition*, M-132, Washington, D.C.

Canto, Victor A., Douglas H. Joines and Arthur B. Laffer, (1981), "Tax Rates, Factor Employment and Market Production", *The Supply-Side Effects of Economic Policy*, St. Louis: Federal Reserve Bank of St. Louis, pp. 3–33.

Comptroller General of the United States (1979), *Proposition 13–How California Governments Coped with a $6 Billion Revenue Loss*, GGD-79-88, Washington, D.C.: General Accounting Office.

Ehrenberg, Ronald G. (1979), "The Effect of Tax Limitation Legislation on Public Sector Labor Markets: A Comment", *National Tax Journal*, 32, Supplement, pp. 261–265.

Hirsch, Werner Z. (1977), "The Efficiency of Restrictive Land Use Instruments", *Land Economics*, 53, pp. 145–156.

Hirsch, Werner Z. (1981), "The Post-Proposition 13 Environment in California and Its Consequences for Education", *Public Choice*, 36, pp. 415–423.

Margolis, Stephen E. (1977), *Depreciation of Capital in Housing*, UCLA: unpublished Ph.D. dissertation.

Menchik, Mark D., et al. (1982), *How Fiscal Restraint Affects Spending and Services in Cities*, R-2644, Santa Monica, CA: RAND Corp.

Mieszkowski, Peter W. (1972), "The Property Tax: An Excise Tax or a Property Tax", *Journal of Public Economics*, 1, pp. 73–96.

Savas, E.S. (1977a), "An Empirical Study of Competition in Municipal Service Delivery", *Public Administration Review*, 37, pp. 717–724.

Savas, E.S. (1977b), "Policy Analysis for Local Government: Public Versus Private Refuse Collection", *Policy Analysis*, 3, pp. 49–74.

Temporary Commission on City Finances (TCCF) (1976), *An Historical and Comparative Analysis of Expenditures in the City of New York*, New York: TCCF.

Thomas, Ann R. (1981), "Fiscal Limitations on Municipal Debt—The Extreme Case of Proposition 13", *The Property Tax Revolt—The Case of Proposition 13*, Cambridge, MA: Ballinger.

Walker, Warren I., et al. (1980), *The Impact of Proposition 13 on Local Criminal Justice Agencies: Emerging Patterns*, N-1521-DOJ, Santa Monica, CA: RAND Corp.

Résumé

Il est presque unanimement reconnu que les gouvernements locaux sont inefficaces. L'accord est moins général quant à ce qui peut être fait pour les rendre plus efficaces. La preuve est loin d'être faite que les mesures drastiques de limitation des recettes décrétées dans les années 70 dans différents états américains aient, tout bien pesé, accru l'efficacité des gouvernements locaux.

Parmi les différents effets des mesures de limitation des recettes sur l'efficacité, trois sont susceptibles, tout bien pesé, d'avoir des résultats positifs. La réduction des capacités de financement, ou au moins de leurs taux de croissance, a eu un effet de rigueur salutaire sur les dirigeants publics et leurs employés. Il en est résulté une volonté accrue de la part des responsables locaux pour prendre en compte des méthodes qui peuvent accroître substantiellement cette efficacité. Ces tendances sont amoindries par l'insuffisance des capacités de financement en investissement et par des réglementations archaiques du statut des agents publics qui permettent souvent aux employés les moins productifs de conserver leur emploi. Deuxièmement, on a peu de preuves que les réductions d'impôt aient eu du côté de l'offre produits et services un effet positif, bien qu'elles soient intervenues au cours d'une période de prospérité. Troisièmement, le changement de composition des recettes qui a résulté d'une baisse de l'importance qu'avait l'impôt foncier local, est susceptible d'avoir eu un petit effet positif sur l'efficacité.

Un grand nombre d'autres effets sont fortement négatifs. En transférant une grande partie du pouvoir de décision des gouvernements locaux à l'Etat, une grande centralisation du pouvoir s'est produite entraînant une homogénéization des services et de leurs niveaux. Il en est résulté une importante perte d'efficacité. Une résultat identique s'est très certainement produit par suite de distorsions majeures dans l'utilisation des ressources par les gouvernements locaux.

Ces distorsions ont pris la forme de sous-investissement dans les domaines de l'entretien et de l'amélioration du capital investi d'une part, et dans des investissements de programmes financés par les Etats ou le gouvernement fédéral par rapport à des programmes financés localement. De plus, l'investissement du secteur privé et la croissance économique ont été retardés et déformés par suite, en partie, de la répugnance justifiée des responsables locaux à délivrer des permis de construire ou uniquement en attachant des conditions très onéreuses. De plus, les changements des conditions de l'impôt foncier et immobilier ont déformé les décisions majeures d'investissement ainsi que les décisions concernant l'exploitation des ressources minérales. Enfin il est vraisemblable qu'en Californie, le contrôle des loyers a suivi le conflit apparu entre les propriétaires et les locataires qui n'ont pas bénéficié de la réduction des impôts fonciers et immobiliers. En conséquence, la rentabilité des investissements immobiliers se détériore et l'offre locative diminue.

Anciens Dirigeants/Former Officers

Anciens Présidents/Former Presidents

Edgar Allix, France	1937
William Rappard, Suisse/Switzerland	1938–1940
Max Léo Gérard, Belgique/ Belgium	1948–1950
Carl S. Shoup, Etats-Unis/USA	1950–1953
Ugo Papi, Italie/Italy	1953–1956
Fritz Neumark, République Fédérale d'Allemagne/Federal Republic of Germany	1956–1959
Maurice Masoin, Belgique/Belgium	1959–1962
Bernard Schendstok, Pays-Bas/Netherlands	1962–1965
Alan T. Peacock, Royaume-Uni/United Kingdom	1965–1968
François Trevoux, France	1968–1971
Otto Gadó, Hongrie/Hungary	1971–1975
Jack Wiseman, Royaume-Uni/United Kingdom	1975–1978
Horst Claus Recktenwald, République Féderale d'Allemagne/Federal Republic of Germany	1978–1981

Anciens Vice-Présidents/Former Vice-Presidents
Lord Beveridge, Royaume-Uni/United Kingdom
D. Diachenko, URSS/USSR
J.-C. Dischamps, France
Francesco Forte, Italie/Italy
C. Lowell Harriss, Etats-Unis/USA
Lady Ursula K. Hicks, Royaume-Uni/United Kingdom
P. Jacomet, France
Fritz Neumark, République Fédérale d'Allemagne/Federal Republic of Germany
Ugo Papi, Italie/Italy
H. de Peyster, France
Günter Schmölders, République Fédérale d'Allemagne/Federal Republic of Germany
E. Seligman, Etats-Unis/USA
Carl S. Shoup, Etats-Unis/USA
E. da Silva, Portugal
Stepan Sitaryan, URSS/USSR
Lord Stamp, Royaume-Uni/United Kingdom
Conte Volpi, Italie/Italy
Jack Wiseman, Royaume-Uni/United Kingdom

Anciens Secrétaires/Former Secretaries-General

André Piatier, France	1937–1948
Maurice Masoin, Belgique/Belgium	1948–1959
Paul Senf, République Fédérale d'Allemagne/Federal Republic of Germany	1959–1974

Présidents Honoraires et Membres Hononaires
Honorary Presidents and Honorary Members

Présidents Honoraires/Honorary Presidents
Francesco Forte, Italie/Italy
Otto Gadó, Hongrie/Hungary
Lady Ursula K. Hicks, Royaume-Uni/United Kingdom
Richard A. Musgrave, Etats-Unis/USA
Fritz Neumark, République Fédérale d'Allemagne/Federal Republic of Germany
Ugo Papi, Italie/Italy
Alan T. Peacock, Royaume-Uni/United Kingdom
Horst Claus Recktenwald, République Fédérale d'Allemagne/Federal Republic of Germany
Paul Senf, République Fédérale d'Allemagne/Federal Republic of Germany
Carl S. Shoup, Etats-Unis/USA
François Trevoux, France
Jack Wiseman, Royaume-Uni/United Kingdom

Membres Honoraires/Honorary Members
C. Lowell Harriss, Etats-Unis/USA
Motokazu Kimura, Japon/Japan
Paul Schütz, République Fédérale d'Allemagne/Federal Republic of Germany
Stepan Sitaryan, URSS/USSR